Making
the Most of Shade

How to Plan, Plant, and Grow a Fabulous Garden
That Lightens Up the Shadows

LARRY HODGSON

RODALE

The information in this book has been carefully researched, and all efforts have been made to ensure accuracy. Rodale Inc. assumes no responsibility for any injuries suffered or for damages or losses incurred during the use of or as a result of following this information. It is important to study all directions carefully before taking any action based on the information and advice presented in this book. When using any commercial product, always read and follow label directions. Where trade names are used, no discrimination is intended and no endorsement by Rodale Inc. is implied.

Printed in the United States of America

Rodale Inc. makes every effort to use acid-free ∞ recycled ♲ paper.

Book design by Christina Gaugler
Illustrations by Elayne Sears
Photography credits on page 393

Library of Congress Cataloging-in-Publication Data

Hodgson, Larry.
    Making the most of shade : how to plan, plant, and grow a fabulous garden that lightens up the shadows / Larry Hodgson.
       p.   cm.
    Includes bibliographical references and index.
    ISBN-13 978-1-57954-966-4 hardcover
    ISBN-10 1-57954-966-7 hardcover
    ISBN-13 978-1-57954-967-1 paperback
    ISBN-10 1-57954-967-5 paperback
    1. Gardening in the shade.   2. Shade-tolerant plants.   I. Title.
SB434.7.H64   2005
635.9'543—dc22   2004030186

Distributed to the trade by Holtzbrinck Publishers

2 4 6 8 10 9 7 5 3   hardcover
4 6 8 10 9 7 5 3   paperback

To all the wonderful trees that have graced every garden I have ever had the pleasure to work in and who taught me, after much head shaking and denial, that by accepting shade as a friend and not an enemy, I could accomplish wonderful things.

Donated by

The Hanover
Garden Club
2006

CONTENTS

ACKNOWLEDGMENTS

Contrary to popular belief, authors don't deserve full credit for their books. They are helped along the way by a host of people in many, many ways. This particular book was several years in the making, from the day the idea was first submitted to the day the last word was written, so putting it together took a special amount of perseverance.

For that reason, I would especially like to thank the team at Rodale Gardening Books for making the publishing of this book possible, and especially editor Christine Bucks for her tenacity and gentle but constant pressure, without which I would almost certainly never have finished writing it. Also to be thanked are the designers whose beautiful shade garden designs gave much to Chapter 5: Pam Baggett, Stephanie Cohen, Sarah Heffner, Ann Lovejoy, and Pam Ruch.

On the home front, I was able to count on my assistant, Susanne Roy, and *her* assistant, Annie Lebel, to keep the office running while my mind was elsewhere, while my poor wife, Marie, yet again put most golf widows to shame during the many months where I literally worked days, nights, *and* weekends to bring this together.

A LETTER FROM LARRY

Dear Reader,

Chances are, if you've picked up this book, shade has a major influence on your garden. And you're not alone: Most gardeners have at least a few shady spots to deal with and some have nothing but. It's easy to explain why: Yards simply tend to become shadier as they mature.

I can't recall ever having gardened without shade being a factor. I've gardened, among other spots, on a north-facing balcony, a narrow strip of land between two apartment blocks, halfway down a wooded ravine . . . and all around my current home, which was so shaded on three sides by huge spruce trees that you could scarcely tell what time of day it was. And I've usually had great success with the plants I tried. Of course, I'm an expert at picking out the word "shade" while thumbing rapidly through a nursery catalog. When plant labels have the usual white circle for sun, half-black and half-white circle for partial shade, and black circle for shade, I can spot the latter a good 20 feet away!

I can't remember ever complaining about shade myself. (Those ever-present tree roots are another story entirely!) Rather than complain, I've learned to enjoy it. It's always cool in the shade, so you don't have to worry about getting up early to beat the heat when you have a garden project to work on. There are fewer weeds in the shade, and even when they appear they grow much more slowly, so gardening in the shade is about as weed-free as gardening can ever be, especially if you're a mulcher like I am. Plants also need less watering in the shade and considerably less fussy maintenance. They tend to have fewer problems with insects and disease, so you don't find yourself having to treat for those. All in all, shade gardening requires a lot less effort than gardening in sun. Shade gardening is—to quote my son who's just himself starting to appreciate the advantages of shade—very "Zen."

A SHADE GUIDE FOR THE LAID-BACK GARDENER

This book has been designed for people like myself, who like to garden—in fact, who are even passionate about the subject—but don't necessarily want to spend their entire lives bent in half pulling weeds. You'll find it full of helpful hints in coping with the daily problems without requiring too much effort on your part. I'm not given to pinching and pruning and staking myself, so I suggest ways around them. And it's designed to be a book for gardeners of all levels. All the basics are there for the beginners, yet there are plenty of interesting, easy, rarely published techniques that even gardeners who are more experienced will enjoy knowing.

The first part of the book covers the basics and, more than anything else, how to deal with shade. You'll learn about the different types of shade and how to tackle them; how to lighten shade and how to increase it; how to cope with invasive, domineering tree roots; how to keep invasive shade plants within bounds; how to ensure your shade garden gets the moisture it needs; and many other things.

There is also a chapter on designing a shade garden. There are quite a number of differences in design between a shade garden and a sun garden: some subtle, others much more flagrant. So the book covers not only how to grow great plants in the shade, but also how to assemble them to create the best effect, with a special emphasis on texture and foliage color, two of the most intrinsic aspects of designing a shady retreat.

The lion's share of the book is, however, given over to plants themselves. In the part on plant portraits, you'll discover more than 200 descriptions of both well-known and unusual garden plants that grow well in shade. This section is divided by plant type, from perennials to ferns, plus a few categories you might not have considered, such as annuals, climbing plants, and even grasses (and indeed, reputation being sun-loving to the contrary, there are shade-tolerant grasses). Each plant has its own "Plant Profile," an at-a-glance summary of its characteristics and needs (which is great when you're in a hurry and want just the facts). There's also a more detailed description that explains what the plant looks like and how it behaves, plus recommended cultivars as well as descriptions of other plants in the same genus that are also of interest. Special features that show up regularly are "Smart Substitutes," plants that may not be related to the one described in the portrait but play a similar role, and "Kissing Cousins," other plants in related genera you might like to discover once you've had a happy experience with the main plant.

Please note that the recommendations made in this section are based on both personal experience and comments I've gleaned from other gardeners. This section differs from many books where all plants seem to get glowing reviews as if they were all equal: They aren't. Some plants *are* better than others either in shady or partially shady gardens or elsewhere, and I'll tell you so. And I do not hesitate to point out a plant's flaws. In fact, there are even plants described that I don't highly recommend under normal circumstances, but maybe your circumstances are not normal, so they still get a fair description (but always a bit of a warning).

Enjoy reading this section, and have fun gardening with the shade plants you choose. A final point that I'd like to make very clear: You *can* have a beautiful garden in the shade. In a world where garden centers are dominated by sun-loving plants, it might take a bit more time and effort to put together a good blend of plants for your shady conditions, but you will be able to do so. And to that end, here is one secret to finish off with—a rather fractured and reworked version of an old Chinese proverb, but still relevant a few thousand years after it was first uttered:

> "To be a successful gardener, all you have to do is to find out which plant grows well and plant lots of it."

And remember, you read it here first!

Larry Hodgson

PART I

Creating a Showcase of Shade

I s shade a constant problem in your landscape? Do you find yourself dealing with wimpy foliage, absent flowers, slug damage beyond belief, and lots and lots of bare soil? Well, it needn't be that way. In fact, if you apply the proper techniques and use the right plants, your shade garden can become your showcase garden—a garden that not only looks attractive in all seasons but also is easy for you to maintain.

Success with shade gardening is more a question of attitude than anything else. Don't moan over what you *can't* grow, learn to rejoice over what you *can* grow. You'll discover there are hundreds of beautiful plants that ask for nothing more than a shady nook in which to thrive. You'll also find that plants growing in shade need less watering, less fertilizer, and less overall care than plants grown in sun. Plus, they put up with abuse and neglect better than those plants from the sunny side of the yard. So hook up your hammock and learn to relax. With proper planning and just a little bit of effort, you can lie back for most of the season and let your shade garden nearly take care of itself.

Morning and afternoon sunlight comes from low angles and can provide plenty of direct sun, even to plants growing under tall, leafy trees.

Chapter 1

Shade Is What You Make of It

When it begins to dawn on you that your garden might be on the shady side, don't panic. Shade is not nearly as bad a condition as some people would have you believe. You *can* garden in the shade—it's actually fairly easy to do. It's even easier, in many ways, than gardening in the sun. In fact, there is nothing involved in shade gardening that the average gardener, even the rankest beginner, can't deal with.

DEFINING SHADE

I'm always stymied when someone asks to me to define shade. "Well, shade is shade," I feel tempted to say, then I quickly attempt to come up with something more scientific-sounding, an answer that would hopefully include numbers of hours of sunlight per day, or some mention of foot-candles or lumens. I know that's what people want to hear, but I have personally never stood in a garden with a stopwatch keeping track of just when there was sun and just when there wasn't. Nor have I actually used a light meter to check how much light was available in any specific part of the garden. (And I seriously doubt if anyone ever has.)

What is or is not shade is very empirical. It isn't based on scientific studies but on hands-on experience. Unfortunately, it can take years to get enough hands-on experience to really know what will and will not grow in your garden—and you can kill hundreds of plants before you get it figured out. In this book I'll try to help you get to know what possibilities your less-than-full-sun garden offers—without killing too much of anything.

Shade Is Everchanging

If shade is so hard to define, it's because it's always changing. Very few gardens are in shade all of the time—that just doesn't happen outdoors. Some light is always filtering through or reflecting in at all times of the day. I have yet, in all my years of gardening, to find a single spot where you need a flashlight to see your way around in daytime. So shade is not "an absence of light." A windowless basement during a power failure—now *that's* an absence of light. You literally can see nothing. No shade garden ever comes that close to being that dark. Instead, shade is muted light. And depth of shade is a question of just how muted the light is.

Actually measuring light as a definition of shade is impossible. When do you take the measurement? At noon only? That wouldn't take into account gardens that get direct sunlight early or late in the day, not just at midday. Do you take readings several times a day and average them? Should you measure it only on a sunny day? What about climates that are cloudy most of the time? And what about seasons? Should you take measurements in spring, summer, and fall and average them as well? My feeling about actually measuring shade—either in terms of hours of sunlight per day or foot-candles/lumens of light intensity—is that it is simply a waste of time. You'd learn much more actually growing plants and seeing how they react than by taking measurements of any kind.

The only true measure of shade is the good old-fashioned empirical one—you find out by trial and error. It's your gardening experience that determines a spot to be shady, partially shady, or sunny.

If the garden receives direct sun most of the day (and you can't measure "most" in terms of hours, as it will vary according to season), it is obviously in sun. It needn't be in full, blazing sun all day, from sunup to sundown—that almost never occurs unless you garden on a treeless, buildingless, fenceless, short-grass prairie where absolutely nothing blocks the sun. In most gardening situations, plants always get some shade, even if only from taller neighboring perennials or annuals. If, on the other hand, the garden gets no direct sun at all, only indirect light filtered through leaves above or reflected from nearby objects, that is full shade. Everything else—where there is some direct sun but also lots of time without sun—is partial shade.

I learned years ago the best way to determine how shady any garden spot is: to guesstimate the degree of shade using my own logic. Does it seem shady, partially shady, or sunny to me? Then I try growing full-sun plants, partial-shade plants, and shade plants where I think they'll thrive, and I see how close I come to being right. Most plant labels conveniently show a pictogram—an at-a-glance indicator of a plant's preferences. Usually, it's a sun (an empty circle) for full-sun plants; a half-sun (a half-black, half-white circle or a circle half-hidden by a cloud) for partial-shade plants; or shade (a black circle or cloud) for a shade-tolerant plant. I reclassify areas based not on what I think of the light or shade, but what the plants think: Anywhere full-sun plants thrive is full sun, no matter how shady the spot looks to me. Anywhere full-sun plants don't thrive but where partial-shade plants do is partial shade, and where partial-shade plants don't thrive but shade plants do, well, that would be shade, wouldn't it?

Rather than waste money testing shade using more expensive roses, shrubs, or perennials, though, I use cheap, bargain-

A simple test will tell whether you have sun or shade: Plant a petunia. If it grows and blooms well, there's enough light to consider the spot full sun. It if does fairly well, the spot is partial shade. No blooms at all? That's shade!

basement annuals. My favorite is the petunia. It prefers sun but will tolerate partial shade; it will *not* tolerate shade. I plant a few here and there and see how they do. Where they bloom abundantly throughout summer, I know I have sun, even if the spot appeared partially shady to me at first. Where they grow and bloom at least modestly but without the vigor that I know a petunia can have, I know I have partial shade. And where they don't bloom and grow only weakly or even die, I know I have shade.

I know some authors like to offer a range of degrees of shade: typically, full shade (also called deep shade), medium shade, light shade, filtered sunlight, and full sun, but that becomes confusing. Where is the line between light shade and partial shade? Between medium shade and full shade? Those terms are almost impossible to define. I feel all gardeners really need are three definitions of light needs: full shade, partial shade, and full sun. You can usually guesstimate all three just by looking, but a test run of petunias doesn't hurt for more definition. Then all you need to know is which plants tolerate what conditions, and you're off to the races. That's where those sun, partial shade, and shade symbols on the plant label come in handy.

Many plants, of course, tolerate more than one type of light intensity; they may, for example, have both a full sun and a partial shade symbol. That means they can tolerate both but are more likely to thrive in full sun. Likewise, a plant with both a partial shade icon and a full shade icon will do fine in both full shade and in partial shade,

but will still likely do best in partial shade. Few plants actually "like" full shade—almost any plant would prefer some sun. Those plants we call shade plants will *tolerate* shade.

DIFFERENT KINDS OF SHADE

If you're in too much of a hurry to try the petunia test and you're too new at gardening to guess the degree of shade just by looking, it can be worthwhile just thinking about how light works its way into a garden. Sunlight reaches garden plants either directly (with no obstacles) or indirectly (from the sides, through reflection, or by piercing here and there through overhanging foliage).

Much of the direct sun that does reach shady gardens comes in the morning or the evening. Because the sun is lower in the sky at that time, it isn't blocked out by overhanging vegetation. Therefore, gardens planted under a single tree—although they may be fully shaded at midday when the sun is high in the sky—actually get many hours of direct sun. There's no reason to think of them as shade gardens. In a forested situation, though, with many trees spread over a large area, no matter how low the sun is on the horizon there may be foliage blocking its path. In deep forests, not only midday sun but also early morning and late afternoon sun are often filtered through considerable foliage. Such sites are likely to be in true shade.

During the middle of the day, sunlight comes from on high and first strikes the

Much of the sun that reaches shady gardens comes in morning or evening, filtering through surrounding trees and shrubs.

foliage of the trees above. Depending on how dense the foliage is and how low the branches are, very little direct sun may work its way through, in which case the garden will be in shade. But if the foliage is open and well spaced—and if branches are mostly well up near the tops of the trees, not near eye level—much light will still work its way through. This creates the dappled effect of spots of light on the forest floor—spots that usually move not only as the sun moves across the sky but as the foliage dances in the wind. This dappled sunlight may be the equivalent of shade, partial shade, or even full sun, depending on how much sun works its way through. This is one of the hardest situations to judge with the naked eye. It's very worth planting a few petunias to see just what the conditions are.

Even in dense forest, broad-leaved trees with low branches and conifers with an abundance of dark green needles can't block all the light. Some light from the side and above filters through even the thickest foliage; otherwise, it would be too dark to see anything at all. Most of this light comes from reflection: Even the most efficient leaf can't absorb all the sunlight that strikes it, so light bounces off the leaves, trunks, branches, and other foliage and ends up lighting the forest floor. Spots that receive only reflected light *will* be in shade—you don't even have to do a petunia test because you'll easily be able to see these spots. However, these spots still receive enough light for the most shade-tolerant plants to grow, so you can garden there.

So much spring sun can work its way through bare deciduous trees that you can grow spring ephemerals, like these glories-of-the-snow (*Chionodoxa* spp.).

The Effects of Spring Sunlight and Summer Shade

Conifers and a few broad-leaved trees like live oak (*Quercus virginiana*), American holly (*Ilex opaca*), and southern magnolia (*Magnolia grandiflora*) hold onto their leaves all year. Forested areas largely composed of such evergreens will be shady year-round, and plants that live there have

WHEN GARDENERS COMPLAIN ABOUT too much shade, what they are often (in fact, usually) complaining about is too much root competition. It's not that their gardens aren't getting enough light—with the right choice of plants, they can have spectacular success in even the shadiest spots—but that the roots of nearby trees are sucking the life out of the garden. Many plants can cope with shade, but far fewer can put up with omnipresent tree roots that steal every drop of rain and hog all the minerals. Invasive tree roots are a serious setback to any gardener's plans, and they may considerably affect how well the garden grows much more than shade alone will do. We'll look at this prickly situation in the chapters "Gardening in Shade," beginning on page 37, and "Problem Solving," beginning on page 71.

to deal with shade all year long. Other forested areas involve deciduous trees. They may create dense shade during summer months, but they let in full sun (or nearly so) from late fall until the trees leaf out again late the following spring. Sure, their trunks and branches filter the sun's rays somewhat, but they don't absorb as much of that light as they reflect it. As the sun moves across the sky throughout the year, its rays ensure that abundant sunlight is available (but only seasonally). This is often called seasonal shade, but I prefer to think of it in a more positive light: not as seasonal shade, but as spring sunlight.

Not all plants can take advantage of spring sunlight—many plants are dormant at the same time as the trees above are. Two types of plants can and do take advantage of seasonal sun: low-growing evergreen perennials, and spring ephemerals.

Ground-hugging evergreen plants, like Japanese pachysandra (*Pachysandra terminalis*), periwinkles (*Vinca* spp.), and various ivies (*Hedera* spp.), are very adept at absorbing light during the off-season. They will thrive in shade during summer months, accepting even the weakest reflected rays, because in early spring they already absorbed much of the light they need. They often form the basis of the shade garden, at least in the shadiest spots.

Spring ephemerals are those plants that sprout early in spring, spread their leaves fully to absorb as much light as they can, bloom—and then beat a retreat underground, going dormant when the trees above leaf out. Others come up and bloom just as early but hang onto their leaves throughout summer, but they don't grow any more. They're often called spring bulbs (but not all of them are bulbous, so spring ephemeral is a more appropriate term). This group includes not only such popular imported plants as narcissus and squills (*Scilla* spp.), but also many native species, like bellworts (*Uvularia* spp.) and trout lilies (*Erythronium* spp.). They are also staples of the shade garden. As a result, many shade gardens bloom most heavily during spring months.

Man-Made Shady Structures

So far we've looked only at how taller plants, such as trees, create shade, but inanimate objects also cut off the sun. In towns and cities, much of the shade that is cast comes from buildings, walls, fences, and other structures. In a sense, inanimate objects cast a denser shade than most trees do, as no light filters through. They often reflect a lot of light, though. In fact, they often reflect nearly all of it—so you needn't give up hope of growing anything in their shade. Plus, the sun does move around them, usually offering some sun part of the day during summer months.

The greatest effect of man-made structures on plant growth is felt on the north side of buildings (in the Northern Hemisphere, that is; in the Southern Hemisphere, the effect is felt on the south side). Both west and east sides will get several hours per day of full sun if there are no other obstacles; the south side, obviously, will receive the sun's rays all day. Conveniently, where the sun is the weakest (in the North), the summer sun not only shines for the greatest number of hours a day, but it also travels the greatest distance. It rises not in the East but in the Northeast; it sets not in the West (at least not in summer) but in the Northwest. So northern gardens may get relatively weak sun, but they receive it over a longer period of time and it reaches even the plants on the shady northern side of objects, so shade plants on the north side of buildings do receive enough sun to grow well.

You can have a beautiful garden even in the dense shade of a city courtyard.

Country and suburban gardeners often have to deal with shade from man-made structures only on the north side of their own home or behind their own fence. In the city, shade may be omnipresent. Two- or three-story buildings all around may ensure there is constant shade without the slightest direct ray of sun. Skyscrapers can cast shade blocks away from their base, especially in early-morning and late-evening hours. This "building shade" is most noticeable at upper latitudes, where the sun is never high in the sky, but less so in the South, where the sun is nearly directly above at noon, letting its rays beam down. Fortunately, buildings reflect a lot of light, so it can still be fairly bright (if not full sunlight) even on the north side of tall buildings—certainly enough for shade-tolerant plants. Usually even partial-shade plants will grow well there. The "petunia test" is worth trying where building shade is a problem—it's very hard to judge the depth of this type of shade using just the naked eye.

Of course, man-made structures are not the only source of non-foliage shade. If your garden is on the north side of a tall hill or mountain, it will get less sunlight than on the south side. Again, this kind of shade will be mostly felt at upper latitudes, where the sun is fairly low in the sky even at noon, as that is where hills cast the most shadow. Spots that receive no direct sunlight at all still support plentiful plant growth, but the plants that grow there will likely have to fall in the shade-tolerant category, especially if there are also overhanging trees.

Large inanimate objects and tree shade can combine to create very dense shade. For-

Once you stop looking at shade as being a tragedy, you can start looking at ways to turn it to your advantage.

tunately, there are few places so dark in nature nothing will grow, but you may find your choice in plants quite limited in such spots.

THE ADVANTAGES OF SHADE

I know of many "shade-stricken" gardeners who probably can't think of a single advantage of shade. Once you stop bemoaning the woes of a situation where you can't grow hybrid tea roses and learn to accept that shade may not necessarily always be your enemy, you'll have to admit that there are many advantages to shade from a gardener's point of view.

- Foliage doesn't burn in shade as it can in full sun.
- Flower colors are more intense when the sun doesn't beat down on them.
- Flowers often last considerably longer in shade than in sun.
- Plants need less watering in shade because evaporation is reduced. They'll often come through drought situations in flying colors, while sun-grown plants burn to a crisp. When they do wilt during the day, they often recover on their own at night.
- Plants need less fertilizer in shade because they grow more slowly.
- Weeds are considerably less of a problem in shade than in sun—most "weed" species are full-sun plants.
- Shade plants need less routine maintenance, such as deadheading.
- In woodland settings, dead leaves provide excellent winter protection against cold, and plants that are just barely hardy will often thrive.
- A wide range of interesting plants will grow in the shade.
- Certain garden styles look best in shady settings, such as Oriental gardens.

ARE YOU A TYPE A GARDENER OR A TYPE B GARDENER?

HOW MUCH YOU APPRECIATE the advantages of shade gardening partly depends on your personality.

Type B personalities are ideally suited to shade gardening's reduced workload and relaxed pace. Plants growing in shade simply don't need a great deal of maintenance, and that suits them fine. Plus, a shady nook is just the right spot for a hammock, which is where many Type Bs feel they really ought to be spending most of their leisure time.

Type A personalities find shade gardening more frustrating. Plants don't grow fast enough, bloom enough, or need enough daily care. They often complain "there is nothing to do" in shade gardens, as plants there have the annoying habit of taking care of themselves.

If you're a Type B, therefore, you might want to consider *increasing* the shade on your property. If you're a Type A, consider cutting down a few trees to let in more light—or concentrating your gardens in the sunniest parts of your lot.

- Most insects are more active in sun, so there are fewer problems with insect damage in shady spots.

THE INCONVENIENCES OF SHADE

Of course, there are inconveniences to shade gardening as well. Fortunately, most are very minor and easy to compensate for. Still, as a beginning shade gardener, you should be aware that gardening in the shade will impact the way you garden. Here are some points to keep in mind.

- You won't have as many plants to choose from. Most "shade plants" will grow in a sunny spot, but few "sun plants" will grow in a shady one. Fortunately, as you'll see in Part II of this book, literally hundreds of plants will grow in the shade.
- Flowering plants rarely bloom as abundantly in shade as in sun, so you'll likely find it convenient to concentrate more on form, texture, and foliage color in the shadiest spots rather than on flowers alone.
- Plants grow far more slowly in shade and can take years to fill in. It may be necessary to plant more densely if you want good looks quickly, and that means more plants and therefore greater expense. On the positive side, though, most shade plants are permanent, making up for their slow growth by their very long life.
- Shady gardens often suffer from severe root competition and can remain

stunted (see page 44 for suggestions for coping with it).
- IFOs (identifiable falling objects) from overhanging trees (leaves, needles, fruits, berries, cones, bird droppings, etc.) can mean that shade plants are rarely pristine, a source of frustration for some gardeners. A quick spray of water quickly fixes the problem, though.
- Slugs and snails can wreak havoc in shade gardens if you don't take measures to prevent them.
- You can't grow a perfect lawn in the shade, although you can in partial shade. However, shade-tolerant groundcovers make great lawn replacements and need much less maintenance than turfgrass.
- Disease problems may increase under shady situations because foliage remains moist longer after a rainfall, and diseases tend to develop on moist leaves. Planting disease-resistant plants is an easy solution to this problem.
- Darker colors are less noticeable in shade, so it may be necessary to stick to paler-colored flowers and foliage.

SHADE IN HOT CLIMATES

Your attitude toward shade will likely vary depending on your local climate. Southern gardeners, for example, are far more appreciative of shade than northern ones. Their main problem in gardening in the South is keeping plants growing in the burning sun, searing heat, and, at least on the East Coast, unbearable humidity. So many plants burn

Gardeners in hot, humid climates are much more appreciative
of shade than those in cool, northern ones.

or wilt in full sun that shade is almost always seen as beneficial. The sun in the South is so intense that most "full sun" plants don't actually need direct sunlight all day (as they may in the North) but will do better in partial shade. The same plants that are considered good subjects for partial shade in the North will do fine in full shade in the South. If you live in the South, you'll likely find the chapter "Making Shade," beginning on page 17, particularly interesting, as it discusses ways of making your garden even shadier.

SHADE IN COLD CLIMATES

Northern gardeners are far more likely to view shade as a problem. There is less sun available to start with in colder northern climates, and even though the days are longer, the sun is also at a greater angle and therefore considerably weaker. That means the number of plants that can adapt to shade is greatly reduced: Even light shade will considerably limit plant choice and the quantity of bloom. Plus, shade gardens take longer to get going in spring, trimming a few weeks off an already short season. In some cold areas, though, summers can be hot, so shade will be appreciated for its cooling effect. Where winters are cold and summers are also cool, shade—especially deep shade—may lose a lot of its attraction. In cool summer areas, you might want to limb up a few trees (or even remove some trees entirely) to let in more light and create at least a "light shade" situation.

If you're looking for a quiet corner in which to relax, nothing beats shade.

Chapter 2

Making Shade

If you think you already have plenty of shade, you can skip right past this chapter. If you want to create more shade, you undoubtedly will find the following pages very useful.

The idea of purposely adding more shade to a garden might seem like an odd one to some gardeners. After all, isn't shade undesirable? While that may have been the old attitude, modern gardeners are learning more and more to appreciate shade and its benefits. A comfortable place to garden and relax and a peaceful haven in an otherwise frenetic world—those are all attributes of the shade garden, not the sunny garden. And if you're looking for a way to reduce garden maintenance, the last thing you want to add to a yard is more sun-guzzling lawn! A shady nook with a few trees and shrubs and a base of groundcover is just about the lowest-maintenance garden possible. The work involved can literally be counted in minutes per year rather than hours per week!

ADDING SHADE TREES

The first thing most gardeners consider when they want to add more shade is planting trees. The very name "shade tree" says it all: They are trees purposely planted to create shade.

Adding trees to any landscape is often seen as the finishing touch, but landscape planners tend to see trees and large shrubs not as final details but as the actual "bones" of the garden—the structure around which it will be based. A large home, especially, can look as if it had been dropped from the sky by extraterrestrials when it sits on a bare lawn or is surrounded only by low flowerbeds or a knee-high hedge. Some height is needed to integrate it into its surroundings, and the most logical and least expensive way of adding height is by planting trees. Even on smaller lots with limited yard space, trees are essential—although the choice of trees will likely be radically different, and there will probably be fewer of them.

Studies show again and again that trees add financial value to your home, something you may want to consider if intend to sell your home some day. You can spend $10,000 renovating the bathroom and barely recuperate the cost when you sell, yet planting a $50 dollar tree can add 10, 20, 50—or more!—times that amount to the value of your home.

There was a time when a shade tree meant a huge, spreading 50-foot silver maple (*Acer saccharinum*) or European

When planting a shade tree, consider one whose roots won't impact your gardening style at a later date.

beech (*Fagus sylvatica*), but times have changed. Smaller lots mean that there is rarely enough room for a 50-foot monster in suburbia—or, if there is, there may be room for only one. Instead, smaller trees have come into the fore. Crabapples (*Malus* spp.) and saucer magnolias (*Magnolia* × *soulangeana*) are considered fine shade trees even though they rarely reach more than 25 feet in height. The important thing about a shade tree is that you should be able set a lawn chair under it to enjoy the shade. Narrow, columnar trees, like upright English oak (*Quercus robur* f. *fastigiata*), don't cast much usable shade: You'll have to put your lawn chair on wheels and chase after the shade as it moves over the lawn. For good shade, look for trees with spreading or arching branches or a rounded top. You'll find that some of the smaller ones will need "limbing up" (having their lower branches removed) as they grow to make good shade trees, or the only way you'll get under them is by crawling!

SHADING WITH SHRUBS

Shrubs can create shade, and they have added benefits: They grow and fill in faster than trees, yet their roots are not so aggressive as to choke out lower plants. Also, their shade is not dense enough to create problems, largely because sunlight reaches both around and over them to ensure some sun to the plants they protect.

Thornless honeylocust (*Gleditsia triacanthos* f. *inermis*) is an example of a tree that creates only very light shade and has a root system that causes few problems to plants grown at its base.

20 TOP SHADE TREES

IN ADDITION TO THE USUAL CONSID-ERATIONS that come into play when looking into planting a tree, such as hardiness, season of interest, and pest and disease resistance, consider how any potential shade tree will impact your garden. Notably, will it cast shade so dense you'll have trouble finding anything that will grow under it? Even more important, is it one of those trees with aggressive roots so dense and so shallow that they'll tend to choke out all other vegetation? Many gardeners find themselves stuck with a tree that was planted years ago but was just not a good choice for people who like to garden. They put up with it simply because removing it would be too costly, and waiting for a replacement to grow would be too time-consuming. If you're adding a tree yourself, you can avoid those problems by carefully choosing trees that provide moderate shade and that have less aggressive root systems.

The trees included in the following table are generally judged "gardener-friendly." Height and spread are averages for mature trees; this will vary somewhat according to climate and growing conditions.

SPECIES	COMMON NAME
Acer palmatum	Japanese maple
Aesculus × *carnea*	Red horse chestnut
Carya ovata	Shagbark hickory
Cercidiphyllum japonicum	Katsura tree
Chionanthus virginicus	Fringetree
Cladrastis lutea	Yellowwood
Franklinia alatamaha	Franklinia
Gleditsia triacanthos f. *inermis*	Thornless honeylocust
Koelreuteria paniculata	Golden-rain tree

HEIGHT	SPREAD	ZONES	HABIT	NOTES
15–25 feet (4.5–7.5 m)	15–25 feet (4.5–7.5 m)	6–8	Rounded, with layered branches	Many cultivars with bronze foliage or deeply cut leaves. Prefers partial shade in the South.
20–40 feet (6–12 m)	20–40 feet (6–12 m)	5–8	Pyramidal, rounded at maturity	Spectacular scarlet spring blooms. Shiny green palmate leaves. Disease-resistant.
60–80 feet (18–24 m)	50–60 feet (15–18 m)	4–8	Rounded when young, more up-right at maturity	Deep-rooted, tall tree with striking shaggy bark. Compound leaves are bright yellow in fall. Edible nuts.
60 feet (18 m)	60 feet (18 m)	4–9	Pyramidal, be-coming broad-spreading	Heart-shaped leaves with beautiful fall color. Shallow roots, but not ag-gressive.
12–20 feet (3.5–6 m)	12–20 feet (3.5–6 m)	4–9	Rounded, open	Spectacular fleecy white flowers in spring. Black berries attract birds. Sun or partial shade.
30–35 feet (9–10.5 m)	40–55 feet (12–17 m)	4–8	Upright vase	Pinnate leaves that let in filtered sun. Wisteria-like white flowers in spring. Good fall color. Attractive bark.
10–30 feet (3–9 m)	10–15 feet (3–4.5 m)	5–8	Open, airy	Camellia-like white flowers in mid- to late summer. Attractive fall color. Single or multistem.
30–70 feet (9–21 m)	30–70 feet (9–21 m)	4–9	Spreading, open crown	Fine pinnate leaves create only very light shade. Several superior selec-tions, some with more compact growth for smaller yards.
30–40 feet (9–12 m)	30–40 feet (9–12 m)	5–9	Round to spreading	Upright sprays of yellow flowers in summer, attractive papery capsules follow.

(continued)

SPECIES	COMMON NAME	HEIGHT	SPREAD	ZONES
Lagerstroemia Hybrids	Hybrid crape myrtles	15–20 feet (4.5–6 m)	15–20 feet (4.5–6 m)	7–9
Magnolia × *soulangiana*	Saucer magnolia	20–30 feet (6–9 m)	20–30 feet (6–9 m)	5–9
Malus spp.	Crabapples	15–25 feet (4.5–7.5 m)	15–25 feet (4.5–7.5 m)	3–8
Nyssa sylvatica	Sour gum, tupelo	0–50 feet (9–15 m)	30 feet (9 m)	3–9
Ostrya virginiana	American hop horn-beam, ironwood	25–40 feet (7.5–12 m)	20–30 feet (6–9 m)	3–9
Oxydendrum arboreum	Sourwood	25–30 feet (7.5–9 m)	20 feet (6 m)	4–9
Pinus strobus	Eastern white pine	40–80 feet (12–24 m)	20–40 feet (6–12 m)	4–8
Quercus phellos	Willow oak	40–60 feet (12–18 m)	30–40 feet (9–12 m)	6–9
Syringa reticulata	Japanese tree lilac	30 feet (9 m)	15–25 feet (4.5–7.5 m)	3–7
Ulmus parvifolia	Lacebark elm	40–70 feet (12–21 m)	40 feet (12 m)	5–9
Zelkova serrata	Japanese zelkova	50–80 feet (15–24 m)	50–80 feet (15–24 m)	5–8

HABIT	NOTES
Variable, open to rounded	Small, often multistemmed tree with spectacular late summer bloom. Crepelike white, pink, or red flowers. Multicolored peeling bark. Look for mildew-resistant cultivars.
Broad to rounded, thick but open branches	Huge pink to white flowers in spring before leaves appear. Fuzzy buds add winter interest.
Rounded, weeping	Spectacular spring bloom. Attractive fruits in summer or fall. Look for disease-resistant varieties.
Pyramidal, becoming spreading	Brilliant fall colors. Blue berries beloved by birds. Intriguing rough-textured bark.
Conical, becoming rounded with age	Green leaves turn yellowish. Light green conelike fruits. Tolerates sun or shade.
Rounded, upright	Lustrous dark green leaves turn scarlet to purple in fall. Drooping panicles of scented white flowers in early summer. Persistent fruit.
Conical in youth, bonsailike at maturity	Long, soft, blue-green needles that let light through. Large cones. Supplies its own mulch.
Pyramidal, becoming oval	Finer-textured and smaller than most oaks. Narrow, unlobed leaves turn yellow to rusty brown in fall.
Erect, rounded	A summer-flowering tree for cold climates. Huge panicles of creamy white scented flowers. Attractive cherrylike bark. Slow to come into bloom.
Spreading, becoming rounded	Disease-resistant elm. Dark green leaves turn yellow to reddish in fall. Mottled bark ensures winter interest.
Broadly vase-shaped	Elmlike, but resistant to Dutch elm diseases. Green leaves turn yellow, orange, or red in fall. Attractively mottled bark.

TOP 9 SHADY SHRUBS

THE FOLLOWING ARE A FEW SHRUBS of sufficient size and density to create moderate shade in just a few years. Some of these make great "cutback shrubs": They can be cut to within a few inches of the ground in fall, then they sprout again in summer, growing enough to reach a good height and even to bloom that same year. The advantage for your garden plants is that cutback shrubs allow full sun penetration in spring—when the sun's rays are weak and plants need all the light they can gather—then they protect low-growing, sunlight-sensitive plants with their shade in summer, when the sun becomes too intense. Height and spread are averages for mature shrubs; this will vary somewhat according to climate and to growing conditions.

SPECIES	COMMON NAME
Acer tataricum subsp. *ginnala*	Amur maple
Buddleia davidii	Butterfly bush
Callistemon citrinus	Crimson bottlebrush
Cornus alternifolia	Pagoda dogwood
Cotinus coggygria	Smoke bush, smoke tree
Hydrangea macrophylla	Bigleaf hydrangea
Loropetalum chinense	Chinese fringe flower
Sambucus nigra	European elder
Viburnum plicatum f. *tomentosum*	Doublefile viburnum

HEIGHT	SPREAD	ZONES	HABIT	NOTES
15–18 feet (4.5–5.5 m)	15–18 feet (4.5–5.5 m)	3–8	Relatively rounded, can be shaped by pruning	Perfumed reddish flowers in early spring. Often bears bright red seeds. Spectacular fall colors.
4–10 feet (1.2–4 m)	3–6 feet (1–2 m)	5–9	Relatively rounded, arching to pendulous during bloom	Long spikes of highly scented flowers in shades of white, purple, and pink that attract butterflies.
10–20 feet (3–6 m)	10–20 feet (3–6 m)	9–11	Rounded to arching, open habit	Tall, fast-growing shrub with narrow evergreen leaves and bottlebrush flowers over a long season.
15–25 feet (4.5–7.5 m)	15–35 feet (4.5–10.5 m)	3–7	Tiered, pagodalike	White flowers, bluish black berries that attract birds. Both shade-producing and shade-tolerant.
10–15 feet (3–4.5 m)	10–15 feet (3–4.5 m)	5–9	Rounded to spreading	Oval leaves with a whitish blush. Attractive feathery fruiting panicles. Comes in green and purple foliage varieties. Good cutback shrub.
4–6 feet (1.2–2 m)	4–6 feet (1.2–2 m)	6–9	Rounded	Summer-long balls of blue (in acid soils) to pink (in alkaline soils) over dark green foliage. Some clones bloom on both old and new wood.
6–10 feet (2–3 m)	6–10 feet (2–3 m)	7–9	Irregularly rounded	Evergreen shrub bearing scented yellowish to pink flowers with strap-like petals. Leaves green or purplish.
5–20 feet (1.5–6 m)	5–20 feet (1.5–6 m)	4–9	Arching	Large shrub best used as a cutback shrub. Dome-shaped white flower clusters, edible black berries. Various foliage colors from yellow to deep purple to variegated.
8–10 feet (2.5–3 m)	9–12 (2.7–3.5 m)	5–8	Rounded to broadly rounded	Horizontal branches bearing long-lasting flattened clusters of creamy white flowers. Red fruit turning black. Reddish purple fall color.

FAST AND EASY SHADE

Growing your own shade by planting trees and shrubs is wonderful but takes time. If you just can't wait, you can also build your own shade structure. This usually costs considerably more than planting trees and tall shrubs, but it does produce fast results.

Although you can use a durable wood such as cedar for the frame of the structure and attach lattice or fencing as screening, there is practically an unlimited number of possible materials to use for both structures and coverings (including metal, plastic, fiberglass, and resin). You can design the structure to let in a little light or a lot, depending on your needs. And you can add climbing plants (see the opposite page) to provide further seasonal shade as needed.

Fences and trellises. These comparatively inexpensive structures can provide localized shade for plants to their north. The shading effect of fences may be limited

A quick fix: An arbor or pergola covered with a fast-growing vine will provide almost instant shade.

by municipal height regulations (6 feet is a common maximum), so check with your town's planning department before proceeding. Trellises tacked onto walls provide little shade, of course, but you can stand them upright to provide interest in the landscape or link them together for more impact.

Arbors and pergolas. An arbor is usually a rather modest lattice structure, often covering a path or walkway, sometimes incorporating a bench, with an open or lattice roof. It was originally designed as a support for climbing plants, but it is now often used as an ornamental structure in its own right. It becomes a pergola when it is taller and more elaborate, with parallel colonnades supporting an open roof of girders and rafters. Both supply fairly good shade from the start, depending on the density of the rafters and lattice, and can provide deep shade when they are covered with climbing plants.

Gazebos, lanais, and shadehouses. More elaborate shading structures can incorporate a raised or patio floor and an open or closed roof and are often used for relaxation or entertaining.

The original gazebo was often a six-sided outbuilding designed for gazing out over the garden in poor weather, but it has evolved to encompass a wide range of garden pavilions. Some have screen or latticework sides used for climbing plants, and they often contain a host of potted plants summering outdoors.

Lanais are like vast screened-in porches and may house a swimming pool and container gardens. They're very popular in hot climates where indoor living without air conditioning is next to impossible, and they become a sort of indoor-outdoor living room. Modern ones often feature shade cloth and trellising to support climbing plants.

A true shadehouse is generally a greenhouselike structure, but it's covered in shade cloth and is designed to cover an outdoor garden space. The shade cloth filters the sun and heat while it lets rain in. It can incorporate cooling mist systems and automated watering, creating what is essentially an artificial backyard jungle—and it will even protect plants from light frost in winter. It is popular in hot, humid climates and may cover much of the yard.

VINES MAKE QUICK SHADE

Once you have a garden structure with some sort of trellising or latticework, it's simple to turn it into a truly shady nook just by growing climbing plants over it. Many permanent, long-lived climbers, like climbing hydrangea (*Hydrangea anomala* subsp. *petiolaris*) and kiwi vines (*Actindia* spp.), however, take a while to get going, putting out bushy growth the first few years and only then truly beginning to climb. But if you want fast shade, the climbers on page 28 can do the job very quickly, covering the entire structure in one single season. Many of these plants are annuals (or tender perennials usually grown as annuals) and will have to be replaced each year, so why not combine the two? Plant the slow-growing perennial vines and let them take their time inching up, but also plant annual vines that will provide color and interest—and shade!—from the very beginning.

Remember that climbing plants need some means of support. Some will cling to just about any structure through aerial roots or adhesive disks. Others have twining stems or tendrils that wrap around structures. The latter are often unable to climb up thick posts or even latticework on their own. For these, run garden twine or netting over the structure, and they'll climb with ease. Still other climbing plants are weavers and will easily work their way in and out of latticework or netting. Finally, there are the ramblers, like climbing roses. They climb simply by leaning on objects and sending their shoots up through the branches of host trees. They are unlikely to climb on their own and have to be attached to their support with twine or twist-ties.

GIANT ANNUALS: A QUICK FIX

So many modern annuals are tiny little edging plants that we forget they weren't always that way. Many were, in fact, huge and very fast-growing plants, ideal for providing quick shade while waiting for slower-growing trees and shrubs to perform their duty as shade providers. Tall-growing annuals can literally save the lives of sun-intolerant plants that are suddenly exposed to the sun's harsh rays when a tree falls and leaves them exposed. Just sow them each spring, generally directly outdoors, until the taller woody plants gain some height.

WHY WAIT FOR SHADE? All the plants described here are fast-growing climbers, many of them annuals (although others are quick-off-the-mark perennials) that will cover a fence, arbor, or pergola the very first year and provide cooling shade in just a few weeks. Many can be grown from seed started indoors in late winter for even faster results (start them in peat pots; many climbers dislike having their roots disturbed when planted out).

SPECIES	COMMON NAME
Cardiospermum halicacabum	Balloon vine, heartseed
Fallopia aubertii, syn. Polygonum aubertii	Silver lace vine
Humulus lupulus 'Aureus'	Golden hops
Ipomoea spp.	Morning glories
Lablab purpureus, syn. Dolichos lablab	Hyacinth bean
Lathyrus latifolius	Perennial sweet pea
L. odoratus	Sweet pea
Mandevilla splendens	Mandevilla, dipladenia

HEIGHT	CLIMBING METHOD	ZONES	TYPE	NOTES
8–10 feet (2.5–3 m)	Tendrils	—	Tender perennial (Zones 9–11) grown as an annual	Fast-growing, weak-stemmed vine producing insignificant white flowers followed by papery green puffs containing black seeds bearing a distinct white heart. Easy from seed.
30–40 feet (9–12 m)	Twining	5–10	Hardy woody perennial	Fast-growing vine bearing masses of tiny white flowers. May die to the ground in Zone 5, but will still bloom the following summer.
35 feet (10.5 m) or more	Twining	3–8	Hardy perennial	Vigorous, fast-growing vine with chartreuse leaves. Ideal for lighting up a dark spot.
7–25 feet (2–7.5 m)	Twining	—	Tender perennial (Zones 9–11) grown as an annual	Many species and selections, most with heart-shaped leaves and large funnel-shaped flowers in a wide range of colors. Fast and easy from seed.
10–15 feet (3–4.5 m)	Twining	—	Tender perennial (Zones 9–11) grown as an annual	Whole plant has purplish tinge. Pealike pink flowers, flat purple pods. Pods are eaten like beans. Fast and easy from seed.
10 feet (3 m)	Tendrils	5–9	Hardy perennial	Winged stems bear clusters of scentless sweet pea flowers in white, rose-pink, or red. Blooms from midsummer to fall. Can be invasive.
4–6 feet (1.2–2 m)	Tendrils	—	Annual	Often scented pea-shaped flowers in several colors. Does best in cool summer climates. Easy from seed.
15 feet (4.5 m)	Twining	10–11	Tropical	Best grown as a houseplant to be placed outside in summer. Thick, waxy leaves. Trumpet-shaped flowers in pink or white.

(continued)

15 Vines for Fast Shade—*Continued*

SPECIES	COMMON NAME	HEIGHT	CLIMBING METHOD	ZONES
Parthenocissus quinquefolia	Virginia creeper	40 feet (12 m) or more	Adhesive disks	3–11
Passiflora spp.	Passionflowers	20–30 feet (6–9 m)	Tendrils	8–11
Phaseolus coccineus	Scarlet runner bean	15 feet (4.5 m)	Twining	—
Thunbergia alata	Black-eyed Susan vine	8–10 feet (2.5–3 m)	Twining	—
Tropaeolum majus	Nasturtium	6–10 feet (2–3 m)	Twining leafstalk	—
Vitis vinifera	Grape	50 feet (15 m) or more	Tendrils	6–9
Wisteria floribunda	Japanese wisteria	30 feet (9 m) or more	Twining	4–9

TYPE	NOTES
Hardy climbing shrub	Fast-growing, will climb almost anything. Shiny green leaves made of five leaflets turn scarlet in fall. Bluish black berries attract birds. Can be invasive.
Tropical to somewhat hardy climber	Many species, all with exotic and very complex flowers said to represent the passion of Christ. Many different colors, including reds, blues, and whites. Bring indoors in winter in most climates.
Tender perennial (Zones 10–11) grown as an annual	Fast-growing vine with edible flowers and beans. Flower colors include white, pink, red, and bi-colors. Fast and easy from seed.
Tender perennial (Zones 10–11) grown as an annual	Small heart-shaped leaves. Yellow to orange (sometimes white) flowers, usually with a dark heart. Fast from seed.
Annual climber	Shield-shaped leaves, sometimes variegated. Brightly colored scented flowers. Leaves, flowers, and seedpods edible. Does best in poor soil.
Hardy climbing shrub	Maplelike green leaves. Clusters of edible purple, red, or green grapes. Very fast-growing and vigorous. Hardier selections are available.
Hardy climbing shrub	Fast-growing and vigorous. Dripping clusters of violet to white flowers in spring, but only on mature plants. Needs solid support, as it becomes very heavy.

12 ANNUALS FOR SHADE

ANNUALS JUST DON'T COME MUCH bigger than those listed here. All are sturdy, upright plants that can be used for fast shade in flowerbeds and borders. Or try them for instant summer hedging! The very nature of annuals is to give a nonstop show very rapidly and, even from direct sowing in the garden, most will reach their full height in only 6 to 8 weeks. For faster growth, you can also start some of them indoors—but not too much in advance because these plants are *fast*. At most, they need a 4- to 6-week head start, no more.

Plants may be available in nurseries and garden centers, but seed packs are even more widely available, making this "shade solution" not only fast but very inexpensive. Then save the seed from this year's plantings for free shade next year.

SPECIES	COMMON NAME
Amaranthus caudatus	Love-lies-bleeding
Centaurea americana	Basket flower
Cleome hassleriana	Cleome, spider flower
Datura metel	Angel's trumpet
Helianthus annuus	Sunflower
Impatiens glandulifera	Himalayan balsam
Nicandra physalodes	Shoo-fly plant
Nicotiana sylvestris	Flowering tobacco

HEIGHT	SPREAD	EXPOSURE	SOIL	NOTES
3–5 feet (90–150 cm)	18–30 inches (45–75 cm)	Sun to partial shade	Well-drained	Long strings of purplish red to green flowers drip from dense green foliage. Excellent for fresh and dried cut flowers.
4–5 feet (120–150 cm)	30 inches (75 cm)	Sun	Poor to average	Huge pink or white flowers; tolerates some drought.
4–5 feet (120–150 cm)	1–2 feet (30–60 cm)	Sun to partial shade	Rich, well-drained	Hand-shaped leaves and clustered pink, white, rose, or violet flowers. Self-sows. Watch out for hidden spines!
3–5 feet (90–150 cm)	18–48 inches (45–120 cm)	Sun	Rich, well-drained	Branching and shrublike, with large leaves and huge trumpet-shaped flowers in white, yellow, lilac, or purple. All parts are poisonous.
10 inches– 15 feet (25–450 cm)	1–3 feet (30–90 cm)	Sun	Average, well-drained	Huge daisylike flowers with yellow, rouge, white, or bicolor rays. Single or double blooms. Some varieties branch abundantly. Birds love seeds!
3–8 feet (10–250 cm)	1–4 feet (30–120 cm)	Sun to partial shade	Average, well-drained	Orchidlike flowers in pink to purple. Thick, succulent stems. Can be invasive.
3–4 feet (90–120 cm)	2–4 feet (60–120 cm)	Sun to partial shade	Humus-rich, well-drained	Branching, shrublike plant with green to purplish stems and pale violet flowers. Oddly shaped inflated calyx. May self-sow.
3–6 feet (90–180 cm)	2 feet (60 cm)	Sun to partial shade	Evenly moist, well-drained	Broad-leaved, upright plant with trumpet-shaped white flowers that are fully open and fragrant only at night. Easy to grow. Self-sows.

(continued)

12 Annuals for Shade—*Continued*

SPECIES	COMMON NAME	HEIGHT	SPREAD	EXPOSURE
N. tabacum	Tobacco	3–10 feet (90–300 cm)	2 feet (60 cm)	Sun
Persicaria orientale, syn. *Polygonum orientale*	Kiss-me-over-the-garden-gate	3–10 feet (90–210 cm)	2–4 feet (60–120 cm)	Sun to partial shade
Ricinus communis	Castor bean	3–15 feet (90–450 cm)	2–4 feet (60–120 cm)	Sun to partial shade
Tithonia rotundifolia	Mexican sunflower	2½–8 feet (75–240 cm)	1–3 feet (30–90 cm)	Sun

SOIL	NOTES
Average	Huge leaves, pink flowers; prefers well-drained soil.
Average, evenly moist	Tall plant with upright stems, dripping clusters of pink flowers. Self-sows readily.
Average, well–drained	Huge star-shaped leaves in green or purple. Spiky seedpods. Poisonous; keep colorful seeds away from children. Start indoors in peat pots.
Average, well-drained	Daisylike flowers in yellow, orange, or orange-red. Broad, dark green leaves. Avoid nitrogen-rich fertilizer.

Gardening in the shade actually requires less effort than gardening in the sun.

Chapter 3

Gardening in Shade

Once you've accepted the fact that your garden—or at least part of it—is in the shade and have picked out plants that are likely to thrive there (see Part II, "The Best of the Best for Shade," beginning on page 113), actually growing them is fairly straightforward, not unlike gardening in the sun. There are a few differences, though, and we'll look at them here.

BEFORE YOU BEGIN

Before discussing how to garden in the shade, let's take a good look at your current situation and proceed from there. You probably fall into one of the following scenarios.

You already have a shade garden, and it's going fairly well. Good for you! You'll want to read over this chapter, as well as the ones that follow, for pointers that will help you do an even better job. And you'll find a whole range of fascinating new plants in Part II of this book. But, as they say, "If it ain't broke, don't fix it!" Don't make any radical changes if you're already having success.

You already have a shade garden, and it is not doing so well. Oops! Well, that happens. Take a thorough look at your garden now, as you have a major decision to make: Are you going to try and save your current garden and improve it while incorporating new plants and new gardening techniques, or do you want to start again from scratch? The latter is, unfortunately, sometimes preferable. If your plants are actually smaller and weaker than when you first bought them or if the bed just looks awful, you should certainly consider that possibility. You may want to dig up and recuperate a few of the stronger plants, of course—or even all of them if they have great monetary or sentimental value. But you'll often do better just forgetting about

I HAVE SEEN THE ENEMY, AND HIS NAME IS . . .

. . . **ROOT COMPETITION.** You thought I was going to say shade, didn't you? Shade has gotten a bad rap over the years for making nearly impossible growing conditions, but the actual truth is that shade is not the problem: The roots of the very same trees that created the shade to start with are! It's very hard to grow anything well when the soil is jammed full of the roots of woody plants. Shade gets blamed for the problem because you can actually *see* there is little light, but most of the roots are out of sight—until you begin to dig. (Or when you *try* to dig.) If you find you can't even cut into the ground without stopping to slice off roots with pruning shears or a pruning saw, you know there is going to be a problem.

Aggressive tree roots creep throughout the first few inches of the soil, often well beyond the dripline of the tree itself, stealing all the minerals and getting first dibs on any rain and irrigation water as well. Worse yet, they were there first. Most shade-tolerant plants can hold their own against tree roots if they have time to settle in before they have to compete for their very survival with tree roots, but if the trees were there first and the poor plant is simply shoved into a cramped hole hacked into the roots, it's not likely to get very far.

Not all trees have shallow, invasive roots. Those described in "20 Top Shade Trees" on page 20 make good choices if you are planning to add new trees to your yard. That way you can have shade and still profit from good, rich, friable soil.

The proof that shade isn't really the cause of poor plant growth in shady spots is most obvious in areas that are shady but treeless, such as on the north side of a home. Plants might not exactly thrive right up against the wall (because it's very dry there, as we'll see in a few pages), but just a few feet out, shade-tolerant plants are probably doing just fine.

So throughout this chapter, we'll be talking a lot about root competition, which is by far the most serious problem shade gardeners have to face. I just thought you'd want to know!

the weak plants that are currently in your shade beds and starting anew in fresh soil using fresh plants you've either purchased or started yourself.

You have a shady area set aside for a new bed and want to get off on the right foot. Bravo! You've come to the right place. I'll be teaching you methods that *will* give you good results—the first time. Learning from your bad experiences is one thing, but I've always found you learn better from good ones. So before you go out and dig on your own, read on.

You don't want to put in a garden, just add a bit of interest to an existing forest. Mother Nature does a pretty good job of things, and it isn't always necessary to tear out a living, thriving forest ecosystem in order to enjoy an attractive forest garden. You'll probably just want to add a bit more color to the foreground or install a path through the woods and do a bit of landscaping around that. If so, *don't* starting digging things up—and don't run over the forest floor with a rotary tiller. You'll want to proceed mostly by "spot planting," as described on page 53.

You're "just thinking about it." That's okay. I like to do a lot of research before I undertake any major projects, too. When you're ready to act, just read this chapter over again.

Planning Your Shade Garden

In "Making It Work: Designing for Shade," beginning on page 89, you'll find lots of helpful hints on designing a shade garden,

Plants will grow right in among dense tree roots if allowed to self-sow, like these spring snowflakes (*Leucojum vernum*). Planting new plants, though, can be a problem.

as well as five sample plans you can use as is, modify, or use as inspiration for your own concepts. But it's worth looking at how gardening in the shade affects how you plan your garden.

You'll quickly discover that few plants bloom as readily or as heavily in shade as they would in brighter light. That doesn't mean your shade garden can't be perfectly lovely, just that foliage colors and textures will likely be playing a greater role than they would have in a sunnier spot. Look principally toward plants with attractive foliage. Evergreen foliage, which guarantees some color even during the off-season, is a major plus. Ornamental shade plants do

Hostas, like *Hosta* 'Frances Williams', adapt well to root competition if large specimens are planted. Young plants, though, may take years to settle in under the same conditions.

bloom (ferns are the main exception), but if your garden is largely designed around colors and foliage textures, flowers can simply become a nice seasonal touch that won't be missed when they aren't present.

Some shade gardeners come to rely on groundcovers—those creeping plants that quickly create a carpet as they spread—as the only way to go in the shade. That's fine if you have plenty of other gardening space and you're just looking for filler material for a few out-of-the-way shady spots. But if your whole yard is shady or if a shade garden is your main gardening space, you'll probably find that using only groundcovers becomes a bit boring, certainly after a while. Try to vary what you grow in the shade, mixing plants of different heights, shapes, and colors, and use groundcovers judiciously, not as the dominant feature of your garden.

It's not as easy as you'd think to develop a detailed final plan for a shade garden that you can actually stick to. Everything may look good on paper, but when it comes to actual planting, you'll likely be stymied by shallow roots or big rocks you just didn't see lurking under the surface. As you plan, it's best to provide for a bit of bare space around any tree trunks—you're not likely to be able to dig there anyway (you can cover this space with mulch). Do consider, though, putting creeping plants, like groundcovers, fairly close to a tree trunk. They'll spread over the mulch right to the tree's trunk even if they can't root there.

Consider spending a bit more money and buying larger plants for a shade garden rather than cheaper but smaller starter plants, especially if the area is deeply shaded or if you suspect there is a lot of root competition. Plants don't grow nearly as quickly in shade as in sun, and already slow-growing plants like hostas can take forever to make any progress if they're purchased as babies, leaving your garden looking half-naked for years to come. If you buy full-size specimens, though, you'll have instant results. Although large plants require large planting holes and considerably more effort at planting time, if your budget allows for them, they may still be a worthwhile investment.

Another tip to keep in mind if root competition is a concern is to consider using long-lived, low-care plants. There are some plants that can cruise along for years without needing any help whatsoever. One often sees 40-year-old specimens of hosta that have never been divided or lifted and probably were never fertilized either, and yet they look superb. On the other hand, some shade plants go downhill if they're not lifted and divided every 3 or 4 years, so they would be best used in areas where root competition is not an issue.

Proper spacing in the shade garden is important, especially if you have more shade than less. Because plants don't grow or fill out as quickly as they would in a sunnier spot, consider planting more densely. Even groundcovers, which naturally tend to spread in all directions, may not fill in as quickly as you had hoped. When it comes to planting in a very shady spot, I suggest taking two-thirds of the plant's mature diameter and using that as the proper spacing. Only in very light shade will plants reach their full size quickly (so you could use the full diameter as the recommended spacing).

Finally, as you plan your shade garden, keep an eye open for upcoming changes. Young or middle-aged trees have not yet finished growing and will cast yet more shade. Consider how much more shade your garden will be receiving, and position plants that can take either sun or shade in spots that are still in the sun but won't be for long. Older trees on the decline might have to come out within a few years, so it might not be the time to plan a major revision of the flowerbeds at their base if growing conditions will be changing drastically. And don't forget that when you choose new trees to plant, it's possible to avoid problems with root competition by planting varieties that have deep root systems—or at least less aggressive ones. And remember, while shade is not such a bad thing and can

even be a very useful gardening tool, root competition is hardly ever anything but a major annoyance for gardeners.

GETTING READY TO PLANT

Feel like doing some digging? Why not look at the possibilities first? The first thing to determine is whether you'll be adding to an already existing shade bed or starting from scratch.

When to Start a New Bed

You can start a new shade garden at any time of the year (well, except for winter, if you live in a climate where winter means freezing temperatures and solid soil). However, for your own comfort and for that of the plants, you'd do best not to think of digging a new bed in midsummer. The heat will make the work exhausting, sweaty, and frustrating, and plants themselves don't particularly like being dug up and moved about in summer. During the still-cool days of spring, when the soil has dried out somewhat (you don't want to work in the soggy soil often present at winter's end) is a good time, but gardeners are often in a mad rush to get a hundred things done at once in spring. That's one reason why fall is an even better season for starting a new shade garden. Not only is fall a cool and comfortable season in most of the country, but fall is a more relaxed season with much less to do. You can prepare the garden in fall if you prefer, then plant it in spring, but you can also prepare *and* plant it in fall. If some plants are not available in fall, plant the rest of the bed and mark where you want to put the missing plants. The vast majority of hardy plants do as well from a fall planting as from a spring one.

The other reason I personally prefer fall planting is that I can plant fall bulbs at the same time. If I plant in spring, I have to come back in fall and dig a whole new series of holes to accommodate bulbs, practically doubling my efforts. And I can't conceive of a shade garden without its share of fall bulbs! (You'll find out more about planting fall bulbs on page 53.)

Starting from Scratch: The Traditional Way

You can start a shade garden the traditional way—by digging up what's already there—if there are no or few tree roots present. If so, thoroughly soak the designated area 24 hours before you begin digging, as slightly moist soil is the easiest to work with.

Start by removing whatever was growing there before. That may be lawn, an abandoned garden, brush, or weeds. If it's sod, cut into the soil about 2 inches deep with a sharp shovel, then slide the shovel under the sod and carefully lift it off. Use good-quality sod elsewhere in your yard, such as fixing a weakened section of lawn. Otherwise, simply compost it. If there is no sod, only weeds or other undesirable plants, dig them out individually. Make sure you get the weeds' entire root systems, or they will just sprout again.

Add a good layer of compost, peat moss, well-decomposed manure, chopped leaves, or other organic matter, and mix it into the top layer of soil. About 3 to 4 inches (8 to 10 cm) is probably enough in most soils, but if your soil is mostly clay, you might want to double that. Work it in thoroughly to a depth of 8 to 12 inches (20 to 30 cm). If you can use a rotary tiller in the chosen spot, you'll find it worthwhile renting one for this task, as turning over the soil and mixing it with the new amendments can be backbreaking work when done with a shovel or garden fork.

Personally, I gave up using the traditional method of starting a flowerbed years ago. I find it too much work, too slow (it takes about a full weekend just to prepare a medium-size bed), and too traumatic for the soil's microorganisms. Worse yet, turning the soil over that way inevitably leads to great masses of weeds sprouting during the following months. This is a result of moving dormant weed seeds from under the soil and exposing them to the light, stimulating them to sprout—and of accidentally chopping up rhizomes of invasive species, thus spreading them throughout the garden. Make sure, if you do use the traditional method, you at least put down a thick layer of mulch as soon as you finish; this will bury the weed seeds again and let you get off to a reasonable start. Pull out any weeds sprouting from bits of rhizome as you see them before they begin to take over. The mulch won't stop them, but at least it will keep the soil friable and make pulling them easier.

Also keep in mind that any aggressive tree roots that are present will react to the pruning that was done as you turned over the soil by regrowing massively within a

Preparing a Flowerbed by the Traditional Method

Step 1. Remove brush, weeds, or lawn, making sure to get all roots.

Step 2. Add a layer of 3 to 4 inches (8 to 10 cm) of compost, peat moss, well-decomposed manure, chopped leaves, or other organic matter. Double that amount if the soil is heavy clay.

Step 3. With a garden fork or rotary tiller, work the organic matter into the soil to a depth of 8 to 12 inches (20 to 30 cm). You're now ready to plant!

few short weeks. They'll quickly take over the bed again, much to the detriment of the plants you just put in. So if you use the traditional planting method in an area with heavy root competition, try to put in mature plants, as they are better able to cope with competition. Small or young plants are often unable to develop well under such circumstances and die out or grow only very weakly. Even years later, they'll be only a shadow of the plants that were grown using the traditional way with full-size plants or using the fast-and-easy method.

Starting from Scratch: The Fast-and-Easy Method

If you have a lot of tree roots in the area where you want to plant your shade garden, then this is the method to use so you don't disturb tree roots any more than necessary. (Turning over the soil can seriously damage tree roots, resulting in weakened growth or even the tree's eventual death.) This is the method I prefer. It's easy to do, as there is no digging involved and no heavy rotary tiller to lug around. It takes only an hour or so to prepare and plant a medium-size garden (the traditional method takes a full weekend). And I like the fact that it resembles Mother Nature's own way of working: You never see *her* struggling with a rotary tiller. Instead, she simply deposits a new layer of organic material directly on the old layer. Of course, the fact that the resulting bed is weed-free and tree root–free are two more reasons why I prefer this method.

The whole point of this method is to leave the original soil intact. Be it rich or poor, rocky or organic, clay or sand—don't disturb it and don't try to improve it, just leave it as it is. Instead, you'll build a new bed on top of the old one. The old soil will simply become subsoil, and the quality of subsoil is of little importance. Instead, your new plants will be growing in a fresh layer of top-quality, weed-free soil. The microorganisms in what is now the subsoil will slowly move upward into the new layer of soil, as they would in nature when a new layer of fall leaves covers the ground. The natural microflora remain intact instead of being largely destroyed as they are in the traditional method.

Before you begin the fast-and-easy method, you'll need to save up newspaper (you'll see why in a minute). You'll need quite a bit of it for an average-size bed, so start putting it aside a good 2 to 3 weeks before you plan to start.

You'll also need to shop for soil. You don't want just any soil, but the very best. The soil you buy should be rich in organic matter, have a good structure, be perfectly friable, and be completely lacking in weeds. It should *not* come out of a plastic bag (living soil has to breathe), but from an open pile that has had organic matter added and been turned again and again until all weed roots and weed seeds have burned off (been decomposed). Ask your county extension agent where you can find top-quality soil locally. Have it delivered— or, if you have a pick-up or a trailer, go pick it up yourself (it's considerably cheaper that way).

The day before you begin your bed, mow the area (if it is in lawn) or use a brush cutter to chop back the vegetation if the area is covered with taller plants. You don't need to remove the resulting residue: Just leave it where it lies. It will decompose and further enrich your soil. When the soil has been delivered or you've trucked it in, you're ready to begin.

On the big day, go pick out your plants from a favorite local nursery (unless you're growing them from seeds or cuttings). Make sure you've worked on your garden plan (see page 101) so you know exactly what you need. Bring them home, place them in a shady spot, and water them thoroughly. Of course, if you're having them delivered from a mail-order nursery, order them several weeks in advance with instructions as to the date you want them. Unwrap them upon arrival and water them well.

That same day, create a temporary barrier that will keep any weeds or other undesirable plants from pushing through the new layer of soil you are about to apply. Remember that in the fast-and-easy method you don't remove the original sod, weeds, or other growth. Instead, cover the entire bed with 5 to 10 sheets of newspaper, thus creating a barrier that efficiently controls the weeds and grasses that used to live there. Blocked under the newspaper barrier, without any access to light, the weeds will die and decompose. I've always felt that turning your enemies (in this case, weeds and invasive grasses) into compost was the best revenge of all! And this method smothers even truly nasty spreading weeds,

like goutweed (*Aegopodium podagraria*), quackgrass (*Agropyron repens*), and horsetail (*Equisetum arvense*). I can't say that I feel the slightest guilt at smothering goutweed! (In case you're worried about the possibility of colored newspaper ink containing lead and contaminating the soil, newspaper ink hasn't contained lead since 1986. Unless you're given to recycling truly old newspaper, there'll be no problem with lead contamination.)

Make sure your layer of newspaper is perfectly intact, with each section thoroughly overlapping the other at the edges; otherwise, the plants below will find a way through. And if you accidentally pierce a hole in your newspaper barrier, cover it up with a few more sheets of newspaper. On windy days, soak the newspaper in water before you apply it so it won't blow away. Then cover the entire newspaper barrier with 8 inches (20 cm) of soil (or 12 inches/30 cm of soil if there are no tree roots to protect) to bring it up to the proper planting depth—and you're ready to plant!

The newspaper barrier will last 6 months to a year, then begin to decompose. That's long enough to kill the undesirable plants, which can't live without light, but not enough to kill the microorganisms from the soil below—nor will it kill underlying tree roots. They'll simply bide their time until the newspaper rots away, then happily move back up into the fresh new soil. The barrier does, however, offer your plants a bit of leeway in establishing themselves. They have about a good 6 months to a year before the tree roots

Preparing a Flowerbed by the Fast-and-Easy Method

Step 1. Cut back vegetation, then cover the area with a thick layer of newspaper.

Step 2. Cover the newspaper with 8 inches (20 cm) of top-quality weed-free soil . . .
and start planting!

SAY "NO" TO GEOTEXTILES

YOU CAN FIND MANY DIFFERENT GEOTEXTILES on the market today, often landscape fabrics or weed-control mats, all permeable rotproof cloths usually made of various plastic products, many of which are frequently recommended as root barriers (much as newspaper is recommended here). They can be placed over the soil or used to carpet planting holes to keep tree roots out permanently. They would seem to be a better choice than newspaper that disappears in about 6 months. However, tree roots eventually do make it through and invade the garden again, but this time, you now have a permanent barrier that will *not* go away. And it will prevent the roots of the plants you purchased from growing downward into the soil the way they should, whereas newspaper conveniently disappears after a few months and lets them develop fully. The only way of removing geotextiles—even 10, 40, or 100 years later—is to *dig up the entire bed and start anew*. Geotextiles may have other uses in the garden, but they have no place in flowerbeds!

start to move in, and about 18 months before they are back in mass quantities. That gives your plants a deadline to meet: They must be well established, with a healthy root system, within 18 months. If so, they'll be able to compete with the tree roots as equals. If they are poorly established, the tree roots will take over and they'll likely weaken and possibly even die. So give your plants the best of care for the first 18 months, and they'll be able to grow happily for the next 18 years!

After the newspaper is in place, add the new soil on top of it. You'll want to add only a relatively thin layer of fresh soil—adding too thick a layer could smother tree roots, as they need to breathe. Eight inches (20 cm) seems to be just about the right amount. It gives you enough soil to plant in (well, at least you can plant medium-size plants), yet it isn't deep enough to smother tree roots. If there are no roots to protect, go for a full foot (30 cm) of soil: Many of the world's best soils are made up of a mere 1 foot (30 cm) of good topsoil, so why not give your shade garden plants the very best?

PLANTING TIME

Most likely you'll want to plant your shade bed immediately after you've finished preparing the bed—and there's no reason you can't! If for whatever reason you will *not* be planting within the next few days, though, cover the bed with mulch (we'll

Before planting or even unpotting, always set the potted plants out
at their proper spacing to test the effect.

KEEP OFF THE GARDEN!

YOU'VE JUST PUT IN FRESH, FRIABLE SOIL: The last thing you want to do is to
trample it down by walking all over it as you plant! If you can work on your garden
from the sides without stepping in the garden, do so. If your garden is too wide for
that, lay down a plank and use it as a working platform—it will better distribute your
weight. Better yet, consider adding permanent stepping-stones you can work from:
flat rocks or paving stones of some sort. They might as well be permanent—if you
can't reach parts of the garden from the side now, you'll be even less likely to in the
future. And chances are you'll want to get into your garden every now and then.

talk more about that on page 57). The mulch will create a barrier from above to keep weed seeds from floating in and taking over the fresh soil, and it will keep the soil light and friable. You can always push the mulch to one side when it does come time to plant.

Out of the Pot, into the Garden

Most of the time the plants you'll be using will be growing in pots, with the main exception of bulbs. They may be plants you purchased or ones you grew from seeds or cuttings. Separate the plants according to whether they are to be permanent plants (this will likely include mostly perennials, ferns, shrubs, and any hardy grasses), spring or fall bulbs, or annuals.

The first plants to put in the ground are the permanent ones. In the long run, they'll be taking up most of the space in the garden and will need the best care. Set them on the soil, but don't remove the pots yet. Instead, place them carefully according to their recommended spacing (see page 41 for details), using a ruler to measure if needed, according to your garden plan. Remember that in most cases, plants (especially smaller ones) will look best when placed together in groups of three or more. Also, stagger your plantings rather than planting in straight lines. (You'll find more about garden design beginning on page 89.) Once you have placed all your pots on the soil, move them around and adjust them until the effect is what you want. Then you can begin planting.

For most perennials, ferns, and grasses, a simple hand trowel will be the planting tool of choice, but for larger ones you'll need a shovel. Dig a hole for each plant, about the same depth as the pot is high, and twice as wide. Place the plant, pot and all, into the hole, making sure it is deep enough, then take it out again, adding or removing soil as needed to adjust the height. Add a dusting of mycorrhizal fungi to the bottom and sides of the potting hole (see "Fungus Amongus" on page 50 for more details). Don't yank the plant out of its pot; you could damage its root system. Instead, turn the plant upside down and, slipping your fingers around the base of the plant so your palm is supporting the rootball, give a sharp rap with the heel of your hand to loosen the pot, then pull it off. If the pot

To remove a plant from its pot, turn it upside down, supporting the crown with your hand, and pull the pot off.

FUNGUS AMONGUS

MYCORRHIZAL FUNGI IS A NEW TOOL available to gardeners. These microscopic beneficial mushrooms develop underground on plant roots. Most plants live in association with these fungi in the wild, but they are often absent from home gardens because they don't tolerate rotary tilling, heavy fertilizing, and other forms of abuse we often put our soils through. But you can now purchase mycorrhizal fungi and reintroduce them into the soil. They're inexpensive (less than a penny per application), so there is no real reason *not* to use them. If your soil already contained mycorrhizal fungi, you lost only your penny. If it didn't . . . well, that single application may well pay off for the next 20 years or so!

Mycorrhizal fungi set up a symbiotic association with the plant. They attach themselves to its roots and begin to grow. They take some sugars and carbohydrates from the plant, but in return they send out their long mycelia (essentially, the equivalent of roots) into the soil around them. Much finer than the plant's own root hairs, the mycelia can reach into tight spaces where roots can't go and travel greater distances than roots do, yet do the same jobs as the root hairs: absorb water and nutrients and transfer them to the plant. Plants that live in association with mycorrhizal fungi grow faster, are less subject to disease, and look healthier than plants that don't. They are also far more drought-resistant, as the mycelia can still pick up water in soil so dry plant roots shut down.

Not all plants live in association with mycorrhizal fungi: Plants in the cabbage and spinach families (Brassicaceae and Amaranthaceae) don't, for example, and neither do carnations and their relatives (*Dianthus* spp.)—but almost all other plants do. In fact, many shade plants are particularly dependent on mycorrhizal associations. Most of the forest wildflowers of North America, for example, are strongly mycorrhizal-dependent. All you have to do is dust a pinch of fungi spore into the hole at planting. Don't mix it in—unlike fertilizer, it works best when it is in direct contact with the roots. Then cover the roots, water, and let the fungi do their thing. You can purchase mycorrhizal fungi at your local garden center, or from most mail-order catalogs offering organic products. See "Resources" on page 390 for other sources.

doesn't want to give, you may have to cut it off.

If the rootball of the plant is lightly covered with roots or shows a lot of brown soil, plant it intact. If there are a few circling roots at the base, spread them out before planting. If the entire rootball is covered with many circling roots, that means the plant is rootbound (it's been left in its pot for too long a time). If planted as is, its own roots may remain in a circle and come to strangle it over time! To prevent this, score the rootball with a sharp knife, running it from top to bottom, about ¼ inch (6 mm) deep on all four sides. This will cut the circling roots and force the plant to form new healthy roots that will radiate outward into the fresh soil.

You may also have plants growing in peat pots. They don't need to be removed: Plant them pot and all. Do cut off any part of the pot that sticks up above the ground; otherwise, it may act as a wick, absorbing water from the soil and causing the plant's root system to dry out.

Place the plant in its hole so it touches the mycorrhizal inoculum, and half-fill the space around the roots with soil. Water well, filling the hole and waiting until the water drains away (which it should do immediately if the soil is of good quality), then finish filling the hole with soil. Firm it down with your hand, and water well a second time. The "double watering" makes sure that both the lower and upper roots get their share of water.

If the plant is rootbound (surrounded by circling roots), score the rootball on four sides to encourage new root growth with a more outward habit.

When planting, it's best to water twice: first when the planting hole is only halfway full, then when it has been filled in. That way, even the lower roots get their fair share of the water.

Finally, don't forget to insert a plant label beside the plant—either one supplied by the nursery or one you've prepared yourself—so you can remember just what you planted and where. There is little more frustrating for a gardener than having a great plant you'd like to talk about, but not having the slightest idea what it is!

Planting Bareroot Plants

Not all plants come in pots. You may have received bareroot plants through the mail or have dug up or divided plants from elsewhere. (For example, if you're over-

hauling an old and not-too-successful flowerbed, you will probably have dug out a few survivors that you want to save and put back in the new bed.) These should be kept moist and in a shady spot until planting time. Cover their roots with burlap or landscape fiber, and spray them with water every day (more often if necessary) to prevent the roots from drying out. Don't leave bareroot plants out of the soil for too long, though. If you don't expect to be able to plant them for more than a week, pot them up temporarily in garden soil until you can get to them.

Planting bareroot plants is a bit more complicated than planting potted ones, as it's harder to judge just how deep to plant them. The idea is that, when you finish planting, the crown should be at the same depth as it was originally. You can easily see this, as the parts that were originally underground will be paler in color than those that were exposed to light. However, without a solid rootball beneath them, bareroot plants tend to sink down into the soil after watering. So I suggest digging a larger hole than for potted plants, about twice the depth *and* width of the roots. In the middle of the planting hole, form a cone of soil and firm it well, then place the base of the plant on this, spreading the roots all around. This cone will hold the plant at the required depth. If the cone is too short or too tall, add or remove soil from the cone and try again. Once the cone is the right height, set the plant on it, again spreading its roots out all around the cone, then sprinkle mycorrhizal inoculum directly on the roots. Add enough soil to half-

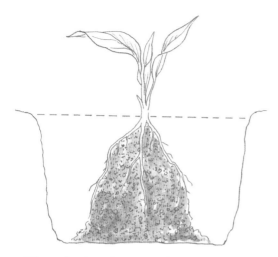

When planting a bareroot plant, create a cone of well-firmed soil and place the base of the plant on this, spreading the roots all around. This will help keep it from sinking into the soil after it is watered.

fill the planting hole, water thoroughly, then fill the hole completely with soil, tamp down, and water thoroughly a second time.

Planting Bulbs

If you're planting in fall, before you finish your shade garden with a layer of mulch, consider planting hardy bulbs. You can plant them more easily in a bed of freshly planted perennials, grasses, and ferns than you can in a bed that is established and full of plants. Simply dig a wide but shallow hole in open spaces between plants. It should be about 3 times the height of the bulb and large enough for about 7 to 10 large bulbs (or 20 or more smaller ones), spaced about 3 times their diameter. Add mycorrhizal fungi, place the bulbs in the hole with the pointed side up, half-fill the

hole with soil, water thoroughly, then fill the hole, firm the soil, and water a second time. See page 267 for more suggestions on planting bulbs.

Annuals as a "Just before Finishing" Touch

A first-year shade bed composed only of hardy, permanent plants like perennials, grasses, ferns, shrubs, and bulbs often looks disappointingly barren. After all, you've probably put in relatively small plants and left room for their future growth, but they probably won't reach their full size for 2 or 3 years—maybe more (plants fill out more slowly in shady spots than when they are grown in the sun). But that's easily fixed: Simply plant shade annuals in the empty spaces! They'll fill in the bed and provide abundant color the first year. Just plant them as suggested in "Out of the Pot, into the Garden" on page 49.

Mulch: The True Finishing Touch

Of course, the true finishing touch to any shade planting will be a nice, fairly thick layer of mulch: *No* shade garden should be without one. You'll learn more about mulch on page 57.

SPOT PLANTING

You won't always start off with a freshly prepared bed. Instead, you may add new plants to an already established bed or to a natural forest, a technique I call "spot planting." Planting under such circumstances requires special attention. For one thing, if the bed was established quite a while back or if it is a natural woodlot, it may well be full of roots from surrounding trees. This can make planting more difficult and also means the new plants will be under severe pressure from tree roots as they grow back and try to take over again. You can still grow just about any shade-tolerant plant in an established bed—if you give it half a chance to get off to a good start. The best way of doing so is to insert a barrier in the soil at the time of planting. I have two favorite barriers that I find work especially well: newspaper and plastic pots.

Spot Planting with Newspaper

This is a version of the fast-and-easy method modified for tight spaces—but it isn't quite as fast and easy in this situation.

First, dig a much larger hole than usual. It should be at least 4 times the root spread of the plant and 1½ times as deep. You may find you'll have to adjust the size, shape, and even placement of the hole according to the roots that are present in the ground. Try not to cut major roots, but don't hesitate to cut secondary ones (they'll grow back soon enough!). Your shovel will likely be of limited help in cutting roots. Cut smaller ones with pruning shears and larger ones with a pruning saw.

Remove the roots from the soil and compost them, sifting through the soil to get as many as you can (you can make a nice garden sieve by tacking ½-inch (12-mm)

mesh hardware cloth to the bottom of a small orange crate). Mix the soil you've removed with good compost (half soil to half compost), then set it to one side.

Cover the outside of the planting hole with 5 to 10 sheets of newspaper. You may have to moisten it so it will properly follow the contours of the hole. It should thoroughly cover the bottom and sides of the hole, leaving no open spaces, but it should *not* stick up above the ground, where it will act as a wick and dry out the rootball. Fold back any excess newspaper into the planting hole, or cut it off.

Using the soil you've removed, fill the bottom of the hole, then add mycorrhizal inoculant over the soil. Unpot and center the plant in the hole. Half-fill the planting hole with soil, water well, finish filling with soil, firm down, and water again. Finish up with a fresh layer of mulch.

The newspaper will keep the tree roots out for about 18 months. During that time, take extra-good care of your plant so it will be thoroughly rooted and firmly established when the roots do come back. Then it will easily be able to resist the invasion.

Spot Planting in Sunken Pots

You can put in a slightly more permanent root barrier by sinking large pots into the soil and planting inside them. You'll need a pot that's large enough so that the plant can spend its whole life inside. Nursery containers (which you probably already have a stock of if you're an inveterate gardener) are ideal, as they are both flexible yet sturdy—and essentially permanent. For

PLANTS IN POTS . . . OVER TIME

DON'T WORRY ABOUT PLANTS GROWING IN SUNKEN POTS becoming root-bound overnight. If you use a large enough pot, most noninvasive plants will never quite fill up the container with roots. And a slight restriction on root growth (roots won't be able to spread quite as far as they would if they weren't in a pot) actually encourages denser growth and better flowering. Most shade plants expand in size very slowly anyway, and many will do wonderfully in confined conditions for a decade or more.

Some plants, however, like perennials, produce numerous offsets that will truly fill the entire pot with roots over time. These are generally the same plants that would have needed division after a few years in the garden (asters, for example). You'll find it much easier removing them from the confines of a pot to divide them than digging them out of a garden full of roots for the same purpose. Just pull out the pot, divide them, refresh the soil with organic material, and repot them again. You'll easily be able to tell a plant is suffering from restrictions: Instead of increasing in size year after year or holding its own, it will begin growing less lushly. That means it's time to divide it.

most smaller perennials, a ½-gallon (2-liter) container will be sufficient. For larger perennials, a 2-gallon (7.5-liter) container is fine. Shrubs may need up to a 5-gallon (19-liter) pot. Any container used must have several large drainage holes: You don't want to turn your "sunken planting" into a water garden!

Digging a hole for a large container is no easy task. Have your pruning shears and pruning saw on hand, as you'll likely have to cut through at least secondary roots. Leave up to 2 inches (5 cm) of the lip of the pot exposed—it will be covered with mulch anyway. That will also give you something to grab onto when you want to turn or remove the pot in the future.

As with the newspaper method, sift the soil you've removed to get out all the roots, then mix with good compost (half soil to half compost). Sink the pot in the hole, then fill it with enough soil so the rootball will be at its proper depth—with the crown at its original level in the soil. Sprinkle mycorrhizal fungi over the soil in the bottom of the pot, set the unpotted plant on this, half-fill with soil, water well, fill with soil, firm down, and water again.

You can plant near a foundation but may find yourself battling constant drought. This is an ideal spot for a soaker hose.

Although container barriers are long-lasting, they won't keep out aggressive tree roots eternally: They'll eventually move in and try to take over. Give the container a one-quarter turn twice a summer (one good reason for leaving an inch or so of the pot's lip unburied). This will break off any overly adventurous roots before they do take over.

PLANTING NEAR FOUNDATIONS

Often shade comes not from tree trunks and overhanging branches, but from man-made structures like pergolas, trellises, and fences. This causes no particular problems and planting can proceed as usual. However, one "shady nook" you may want to use as a planting spot is up near the foundation on the north side of the house—and such a space does have its special needs.

First, foundations are made of cement or, for older homes, stone held together by mortar. And both cement and mortar are quite alkaline. Plants near a foundation should therefore be tolerant of conditions more alkaline that those in the rest of your landscape.

Second, home foundations radiate heat throughout the year. This may be welcome in winter (often gardeners will grow less-than-hardy plants by planting them up against the foundation so they can take advantage of extra heat), but the heat radiating from the foundation continues into summer and can cause the first 12 inches of soil along the foundation to dry out severely and repeatedly. This effect is often heightened by the rain-shadow effect of an overhanging roof. Not only is the spot naturally dry, but it receives almost no rainfall. If you must grow plants along the foundation, it would be wise to supply a soaker hose and to water them regularly. Otherwise, move your main plantings out from the wall, at least out as far as the drip line from the roof, where they'll get the same amount of rainwater as the rest of the garden.

MULCH, MULCH, AND MORE MULCH

In nature, shade plants are found mostly in forested areas. In forests, there is always a natural mulch: leaf litter. So it stands to reason that shade-tolerant plants, most of which evolved in forests, will appreciate a good mulch as much in the garden as they do in the wild. Mulch, in fact, is one of the main secrets to success in the shade garden. It's so labor-saving that if you've never mulched before, you'll hardly believe how easy it makes gardening.

Mulch is anything that covers up the top layer of the soil. The best mulches are made up of organic matter, such as chopped leaves, shredded bark, evergreen needles, composted wood residues, or whatever else is available locally (different kinds of mulch are sold in different parts of the country). And don't forget that compost can also be a mulch—but more on that in "Fertilizing" on page 61.

I use mostly chopped leaves myself: They're abundant and free. I collect leaves myself or get them from my neighbors, then run them under my lawnmower to cut them into tiny pieces that won't blow around like whole leaves do. (If you collect leaves from your neighbors, check with them to make sure they haven't sprayed pesticides on their trees.) You can also buy mulch—either bagged at outrageous prices, or in bulk at much more reasonable ones.

What do mulches do?

- They keep most weed seeds from germinating and can reduce weeding by 75 percent or more.
- They prevent the soil from becoming compacted, so roots grow better and weeds that do sprout are easier to pull out of the ground.
- They keep the soil moist and cool, reducing watering needs considerably

Fall leaves need not go into the compost pile: Instead, chop them up and use them as mulch!

and even eliminating them under many circumstances.

- They help reduce the spread of plant diseases.
- They encourage populations of beneficial insects and microorganisms that will control many pests.
- They slowly decompose and enrich the soil as they do so.
- They give a nice homogenous look to the garden.

On the negative side, organic mulches do disappear over time and need regular replacing. And certain mulches can acidify the soil excessively: If you're using pine or other evergreen needles, for example, consider adding a bit of lime every now and then unless you specifically want to grow acid-loving plants. Mulches that are still in the very early stages of decomposition, such as fresh wood chips or fresh sawdust, use up exorbitant amounts of nitrogen from the soil and can leave your plants chlorotic (yellowed). Before you apply them, always mix them with a plentiful supply of an organic fertilizer particularly rich in nitrogen, such as bloodmeal, bonemeal, cottonseed meal, or composted manure. By the second year, they'll have decomposed enough to no longer need the added nitrogen.

Many people worry about using chopped leaves from diseased trees, as they fear they may pass the disease along to other plants, but that's very unlikely. There are literally hundreds of different diseases masquerading under the names mildew,

anthracnose, black spot, and so on, and each is essentially specific to the species it affects. Mildewed leaves from a crabapple (*Malus* sp.) have nothing to do with the mildew that affects woodland phlox (*Phlox divaricata*), for example. Nor will anthracnose from dogwoods (*Cornus* spp.) affect anything but other dogwoods. So you can use chopped leaves as a mulch under any plant—except trees of the same species the leaves originally came from.

For mulch to be effective, you need quite a bit of it. Look at how deep leaf litter becomes in a healthy forest, and that will give you some idea of what you need. Normally, a functional mulch should be 3 to 4 inches (7 to 10 cm) deep when you apply it. As the mulch decomposes and becomes thinner, simply add fresh mulch to "top it up"; you don't need to remove the old mulch.

AFTER THE PLANTS ARE IN THE GROUND

Your plants are planted, watered, and mulched. What's left to do? Well, not much, that's for sure. Once a shade garden is off and running, it is more self-sustaining than just about any other kind of garden. But you may occasionally have to lend a helping hand.

Staking

Any plant can need staking, and plants grown in shade are even more likely to need a bit of support than those grown in full sun. If plants aren't getting enough sun, they tend to "stretch for the light" (etiolate), and their weak stems can't always support them. In my opinion, a plant that flops deserves to be moved or removed. I refuse to stake anything but tomato plants! You can give a plant a fighting chance and stake it the first year if it flops over, but if it starts repeating its bad habit on a regular basis, I suggest moving it to a brighter spot—and if that doesn't help, compost it. There are so many plants that *don't* require staking that it seems rather pointless to continue growing ones that do.

It is hard to stake plants gracefully: Most of the time they look better with their face in the mud than propped up with bamboo stakes or old fishing poles. Peony rings, though, are quite invisible if properly used: They look like hoops with stakes to hold them off the ground and are designed to be placed over the plant in spring before it grows too tall so the plant can grow through it. The best ones are the "grow-through" types: They have a grid across the top so individual stems get some support. The nice thing about a peony ring is that it holds the plant up at no more than mid-height, so the leaves usually cover it. Plus, it lets the plant it supports move slightly in the wind, so the effect is much more natural than standing straight upright with a bamboo stake beside it.

Place a peony ring on weak-stemmed plants early in the season. They'll grow up through it and find themselves supported very unobtrusively.

Watering

How often you need to water depends not only on your climate and the season, but also on what kinds of plants you're growing and where. In general, even with root competition stealing part of their moisture, well-established plants grown in shade need far less water than plants grown in sun. Shade plants grow more slowly and, since they don't bake under hot sun all day, lose far less water to transpiration than do other plants. Add mulch to the portrait (it cuts down considerably on water loss, both by acting as a barrier to evaporation and by keeping the soil cooler, further reducing evaporation), and watering may not even be a problem—in some climates, some years. In other climates, like the arid Southwest, there wouldn't be gardens without watering.

Recently planted beds need watering more frequently than well-established ones because new plants haven't yet developed their full root system. In fact, you should keep new plants at least slightly moist at all times so they settle in better. Where root competition is a problem, it is especially important to keep the soil around fresh plantings evenly moist, as the surrounding trees with their well-developed roots have

A soaker hose makes watering easy and inexpensive, and it requires much less water than a sprinkler.

a head start and will siphon off all the water, leaving the new plants parched.

The worst way to water is to take out the hose and water by hand—that may work for containers, whose limited soil content means they can absorb all the water they can hold in just a few minutes. But you'll rarely have the patience to stand in one place watering long enough to do much good in a flower garden. You'll need to water for a full hour if you want to efficiently moisten most flowerbeds! If you simply wander about the garden, watering here and there, you end up moistening just the surface layer. This actually hurts plants more than it helps them: It causes plants to form shallow surface roots that are highly subject to drought (deep watering, on the other hand, stimulates deep, drought-resistant roots). A sprinkler system, be it an in-ground irrigation system or simply a lawn sprinkler you move about as needed, will at least allow you to water for a reasonable length of time. Set out a rain gauge or straight-sided drinking glass to see how you're doing. One inch (2.5 cm) of water will usually water the soil to a depth of about 3 inches (8 cm). If it hasn't rained in several weeks, you may have a backlog to catch up on and may need to let the sprinkler run for 2 or even 3 hours.

I use almost exclusively soaker hoses for watering, other than for containers. They're inexpensive and get water directly to the roots of plants with the least possible evaporation. They simply seep water over their whole length with no gushing or spraying, so all the water goes to the soil—and the plant roots. Cover the soaker hose with mulch, and you reduce evaporation (and increase efficiency) even more. Just run the hose throughout the garden, in and around the plants, making sure it comes closest to the most moisture-needy specimens. Run soaker hose lines about 3 to 4 feet apart on heavy soils, up to 1 foot apart on very sandy ones. A weekly 3-hour water session is usually plenty in most gardens, but in sandy soils, where water that's not immediately absorbed by plant roots quickly drains out of their reach, you'd do better with 1-hour sessions three times a week. Unlike garden hoses, you don't need to take a soaker hose in for winter in cold climates—it holds no water and won't be subject to ice damage. Soaker hoses are inexpensive and typically guaranteed for 10 years. My soaker hose is 15 years old and has shown no sign of decay.

Watering containers is a special situation, as they tend to be packed full of plants (and therefore plant roots) and dry out very quickly. Hand-watering, either with a hose or a watering can, is very efficient: Just apply water slowly until water begins to drip from the drainage hole (for pots out of the ground; for pots in the ground, water enough to keep the soil evenly moist). In cooler, rainier climates, containers placed in shade will rarely need watering; in hot, dry ones, they should be checked daily and may even need daily watering—but at least they are unlikely to need watering twice a day, as can be the case with containers placed in full sun. A simple drip irrigation system can make watering a snap if you find watering containers is taking up too much of your time.

Fertilizing

Shade plants by nature grow more slowly than sun plants and are therefore able to get by with fewer nutrients. I personally don't fertilize shade gardens at all, at least not in the traditional way. I simply apply compost directly on top of whatever mulch I'm applying and let Mother Nature take care of distributing it—she's had millions of years of experience at working organic materials dropped on top of the soil into its depths. Rain pulls much of it down below, and all sorts of soil organisms, from big fat night crawlers to invisible microorganisms, will do their share of the work to make sure that the organic matter gets to plant roots. Add to the effect of the compost the gradual decomposition of the mulching material and the addition of plentiful compost at planting time, and you're off to the races!

If you aren't convinced your plants are getting enough nutrients through a mulch/compost combination, consider applying a relatively balanced slow-release organic fertilizer on top of the mulch. Once again, no need to work it in—that is Mother Nature's job. A single annual application, in either spring or fall, is all a shade garden will need.

Container gardens are again an exception to the rule: Because of the quantity of plants growing in very little space, they need regular and fairly heavy doses of fertilizer. Apply an all-purpose slow-release organic fertilizer in spring at the recommended rate *and* spray the plants weekly with an organic foliar fertilizer, like liquid seaweed or fish emulsion, again according to the instructions on the label.

Pinching and Pruning

Plants growing in thick shade tend to be more open and less dense than the same plants growing in brighter light. To get a plant to fill out, you can "pinch out" the growing points at the end of the branches. That means exactly what it sounds like: You pinch the growing tip between your thumb and your forefinger, cutting off the tip. You can also use scissors, pruning shears, or even nail clippers to pinch plants. When a plant is pinched, it tends to form two shoots where there was just one. And if you pinch the new stems, they also produce two new stems each, so the plant quite obviously begins to fill in.

The downside of pinching is that it can suppress flowering, and it is a lot of work. Rather than taking up pinching as a summer hobby, consider trying dwarf varieties of plants—they'll tend to branch all on their own.

Pruning is simply pinching pushed a bit further: It's usually carried out on woody plants to control their growth. As with pinching, each branch cut off usually ends up producing two new branches in the place of the original one. The pruning shear is the usual pruning tool for small branches, but a lopper or a pruning saw may be needed to remove larger ones.

When to prune depends on the type of plant. Theoretically, you can prune plants not grown for their flowers (such as boxwood) during any season, whenever they start looking untidy. Generally, though, you should prune these plants in early spring, when new growth starts, with lighter pruning or pinching through early to mid-summer if needed. It's best not to prune in later summer (from mid-August on in most climates), as this can produce tender, frost-susceptible new growth that will not necessarily have time to harden before winter. Some people prefer to prune deciduous shrubs in winter when they can better see what they're doing—and that's fine, too. Most conifers other than yews (*Taxus* spp.) are best pruned in late spring. Yews can be pruned any time from late spring to late summer.

Pruning flower shrubs is a more delicate task because pruning at the wrong season can reduce or even eliminate bloom. Shrubs that flower in spring, such as forsythias (*Forsythia* spp.) and lilacs (*Syringa* spp.), produce flower buds on the wood of the previous season, so an early pruning would eliminate their flowers. Prune them immediately after they bloom. Shrubs that flower during summer or fall, on the other hand, like peegee hydrangea (*Hydrangea paniculata* 'Grandiflora') and false spireas (*Sorbaria* spp.), produce flower buds on new spring growth, so they're best pruned in either fall or very early spring, just as new growth appears.

Of course, you can prune dead or severely damaged branches any time.

How much you can prune varies according to the plant. Most shrubs tolerate very harsh pruning: You can cut them back to 6 inches (15 cm) from the ground if you want to completely rejuvenate them.

They'll generally grow back and fill in within 2 or 3 years at the most. If your only goal is to stimulate denser growth, though, you'll probably want to prune plants only slightly—back about two or three nodes (where the leaves join the stem) from the tip. Conifers, other than yews, will not readily grow back from old wood, so prune only into the green growth.

Of course, you may also want to prune the trees above to let in more light. You'll find more about that in "Problem Solving," beginning on page 71.

Deadheading

Deadheading sounds very draconian, but it is basically the same as pinching—you just pinch or clip off flowers after they finish blooming. The idea of deadheading is that it removes the flower before it can begin to produce seed, and because producing seed requires a lot of the plant's energy, plants that are deadheaded may be better able to store up more energy for next year's flowering. Sometimes they may even rebloom the same summer.

I must admit I find deadheading a tiring and repetitive process and rarely bother with it. Instead, I just make larger flowerbeds with more plants, and the overall extra bloom that results more than compensates for my unwillingness to deadhead. I do, however, deadhead plants known to be invasive through their seedlings, such as goutweed (*Aegopodium podagraria*). My favorite deadheading tool? The electric hedge trimmer. I just let loose on the whole plant, slicing off all the flow-

Goutweed (*Aegopodium podagraria* 'Variegatum') is among many plants that will self-sow if you don't keep them deadheaded. This weedy plant is one I show no mercy: Every flowerhead is removed long before it has gone to seed!

erstalks in one quick swoop. Since most plants bear flowers that are taller than the leaves, it is easy enough to deadhead them with a hedge trimmer, a string trimmer, or even an electric knife borrowed from the kitchen rather than going from stem to stem to stem with pruning shears.

Fall Cleanup

Many gardeners feel the need to clean up their shade beds in fall, cutting back the foliage of their perennials and grasses and raking off the leaves that fall from above. But why? It doesn't help the plants in any way, and it removes the organic matter that would have decomposed on the spot to feed the plants. If you feel you must clean up, compost the material you collect and put it back in the garden at a later date. Of course that's a lot of extra work, considering Mother Nature would have done it all on her own, but it's your garden.

I do no fall cleaning whatsoever in my gardens. The fall leaves that drop on the plants give them that much extra mulch, and the dead leaves from the plants themselves have mostly decomposed by spring and are already feeding the mother plant, as nature intended it. Besides, many beneficial insects and microorganisms that I count on for pest control overwinter in plant stems and in curled-up plant leaves. I do rake leaves off paths—but only back into the nearby gardens—and that's about all. I find the less I disturb plants, the better they grow. No kidding!

Spring Cleanup

In spring, you may well want to cut back the stems of perennials and annuals that are still standing. Since these are favorite wintering spots for beneficial insects, toss them behind some evergreen foliage where they won't be noticed, but keep them in the garden. Pick up and dispose of any unwanted debris that has blown in over winter (I find my suburban garden collects dozens of plastic bags!). Most fallen leaves from the previous fall will already be well on their way to decomposing, so you don't need to remove them.

Some people like to temporarily remove the mulch from their shade gardens in spring to allow the ground to warm up, then put it back in place. Unless you have a pressing desire to see the first spring snowdrops (*Galanthus* spp.) a day or two before your neighbors, there is no need to do that. In fact, removing the mulch from a garden, even temporarily, is harmful to the beneficial soil organisms that live both in the mulch and below it. Let the old mulch remain in place until it becomes too thin to be effective, then when it gets below 2 inches (5 cm), add enough additional mulch to bring it up to 3 to 4 inches (7 to 10 cm).

Dividing Older Plants

As time goes on, most perennial herbaceous plants like perennials, ferns, grasses, and bulbs will divide at the base, producing secondary plants that will flower in their turn. At first, this division is welcome, as the clump becomes thicker, leafier, and more floriferous. However, decline eventually sets in for many plants, and they begin to bloom *less* rather than more. That's when you need to divide them. This is best done in spring or fall, either just as they begin to sprout or as they go into dormancy. (Divide spring-flowing bulbs just as their foliage goes dormant in early summer.) Using a garden fork (there is less likelihood of damaging the plant by accidentally slicing part of it off than by using a shovel), carefully push down into the soil beside the plant, then push down on the fork's handle to raise its rootball. If there are a lot of tree roots (and there often are in shade gardens), this may not work. You may well have to dig all the way around the plant with a shovel and even use pruning shears or a pruning saw to cut through the offending roots to get the plant out.

Once the clump is out of the ground, separate it into sections, each with at least one and preferably several eyes (growing points). Some species will have clearly divided into separate plants and can be simply pulled apart; others will still be joined at the base and you'll have to cut them into sections with a sharp knife. If the plant was doing well, replant it in the same space using one of the spot-planting methods suggested on page 53. If not, consider replacing it with something more appropriate, remembering that conditions in a garden change over time and some plants may no longer have their place. Pot up the extra plants and give them away as gifts, or plant them elsewhere in the garden.

There is no set time frame for when to divide any plant. Under shady conditions, many plants divide only very slowly and remain in top shape for a decade or more; others will be ready for division in only 3 or 4 years. Some never decline at all!

Reining In the Spreaders

Not all plants decline over time. Some—generally those that grow by rhizomes or stolons—spread instead, sending up new shoots further and further from the original planting. That's fine if you have the space but annoying if they wander beyond what you had planned. If this is the case, you can leave the original plant where it is, and dig out the invaders when they go too far. You can replant them elsewhere if desired.

Some plants turn out to be truly invasive and threaten to take over the garden. You'll probably have to dig them all out to stop them from spreading. In such a case, decide whether you still want the plant. If you do, replant a few clumps within a barrier, as described in "Spot Planting in Sunken Pots" on page 54. Although the purpose described for this planting technique was to keep tree roots out, it will also keep invasive plants in!

SPECIAL GARDENS

When most gardeners imagine a shade garden, they think of a forest setting with naturalized hostas and ferns, or perhaps a woodland path lined by primroses. Occasionally they consider more formal flowerbeds or English-style mixed borders under shady conditions. But there are really few limits to what can be done to beautify shade. Here are just a few examples of other garden styles you might want to try.

Container Gardens

There are plenty of shade plants that positively thrive in containers, from annuals to perennials to tender or hardy bulbs, and many are described in Part II of this book.

A container garden in the shade can truly turn a bare spot into a horticultural heaven, like this porch-top garden of annuals and much more.

Containers are handy in that they allow you to add interest and color to otherwise boring landscapes—a shady terrace or balcony, a paved driveway in deep shade, and spots where tree roots are so thick that planting is nearly impossible. Put your container garden on wheels, and you can move it into the sun to get plants blooming, then back into the shade when they are at their peak.

Container gardening can be done in just about any kind of pot or object that will hold soil, from a bird bath to a rubber boot, as long it has drainage holes or can have some drilled into it. Mix your own potting mix from 1 part peat moss, 1 part compost, 1 part perlite, and 1 part vermiculite, plus a pinch or two of lime, or use a commercial mix. *Don't* add a drainage layer of gravel or pot shards (they actually hinder drainage!). Besides, the greater the soil mass in the pot, the less you'll need to water. If you use tender perennials in your shade container garden, you can even bring it indoors for winter—where it will likely be very happy because most indoor environments are the equivalent of shade.

Container gardens look best when densely crowded with plants, so they will need more water and fertilizer than in-ground shade gardens. For more information on the subject, see "Watering" on page 59 and "Fertilizing" on page 61.

Moss Gardens

Very popular in Japan but relatively unknown elsewhere, moss gardens can be charming—and really thrive only in shade.

In fact, the deeper the shade, the less likely that weeds—always the nemesis of moss gardens—invade. Mosses are readily collected from the wild, and you probably already have mosses growing on your property (get permission before collecting them from elsewhere). You can dig up a few sections along with a bit of soil, and press them into cleared soil or between rocks. Or, toss a handful into a blender with a cup or so of buttermilk or stale beer and grind them up, then paint the mixture over the surface you want to cover with moss. Mist several times a day for the first few weeks until moss begins to grow. If the spot is naturally moist, it will pretty much take care of itself (except for weeding) after that, although it can't hurt to add a misting system on a timer for thrice-daily 15-minute misting. In a dry climate, even in dense shade, misting may be obligatory.

Rock Gardens

Rockeries are often thought of as being strictly for sun-drenched alpine plants, but a trip to any mountain will show you there are plenty of alpine plants that also thrive on the moist, shady, cool north side of the mountain. You can try creating a shade rock garden in the same way you would a regular one, by piling rocks of similar texture and shape (limestone often looks particularly nice) at the base of a slope, pouring a bit of good soil over the first layer, then putting on a another one. Build upward and backward to create the look of a natural rock outcropping. Add small plants to the spaces between the rocks with a bit of sphagnum moss to hold them in place. Most true alpines need little soil but require perfect drainage. Shady rock gardens can include true alpines as well as other dwarf plants—and mosses look fabulous on rocks!

Water Gardens

When I began gardening, I was always told you had to put a water garden in the brightest sun possible—but that was a generation ago. Modern water gardeners are learning that shade may be beneficial for water gardens, especially in preventing algae, which really only thrive in very bright light. Shade water gardens have a smaller choice of aquatic plants, although even a few waterlilies will grow in partial shade (*Nymphaea* 'Charlene Strawn', 'Chromatella', and 'Hermine' are examples), although they don't bloom as heavily. There is also a very good selection of plants that will stand even deeper shade, such as water clovers (*Marsilea* spp.), water horsetail (*Equisetum hyemale*), soft rush (*Juncus effusus*), and variegated sweet flag (*Acorus calamus* 'Variegatus'). And who says you need aquatic plants in a water garden? A quiet reflecting pond in a dark corner, a bubbling brook dancing between rocks at the bottom of a small ravine, or a small Japanese water feature, like a shishi-odoshi (also called a water hammer) made from bamboo, can all add great interest to a shady area.

The popular Zen water garden in containers for offices, with a small pump causing water to drip, gurgle, or splash over rocks and other objects, will look just as nice (and perhaps even more so) in a shady spot outdoors for summer, while they become algae-ridden if placed in sun. Do be forewarned that if algae are not a problem in shady water gardens, falling leaves are. Make sure your water garden is accessible so you can fish out the offending leaves.

Who says you can't have a water garden in the shade? Shade water gardens are beautiful and require much less maintenance than water gardens placed in full sun.

Choosing disease- and pest-resistant plants is the best way of avoiding problems.
These hostas (*Hosta* spp.), for example, are resistant to slugs and snails.

Chapter 4

Problem Solving

Good news! Shade gardens tend to be fairly problem-free, certainly much more so than a garden in full, blazing sun. But shade does have a few inconveniences you'll have to learn to live with—no garden, of course, is ever fully immune from insects and diseases.

Here are some of the problems you might run up against with your shade garden. As you read through them, you'll probably realize that most are readily solved. Once you get to *know* your shade garden and begin to understand how it works, you'll find the problems are more a question of choosing the right plants and of offering them basic routine maintenance that need not even be particularly time-consuming.

WORKING WITH DRY SHADE

Because shady conditions naturally reduce evaporation (water evaporates most quickly from sites in full sun) you'd think "dry shade" would be an oxymoron. However, several factors can combine to make your shade garden fairly dry—or even very dry. In fact, dry shade is probably the most common problem shade gardeners complain about.

Top on the list of factors leading to dry gardening conditions in shady spots is root competition. The very trees that cause shade in the first place have first dibs on the water as well and can thoroughly dry out soil, even in climates that are naturally cool and moist. Some soils, notably sandy and stony ones, though, are naturally very well-drained and tend to be dry: Water simply flows right through them. In leafy shade, there are actually two sets of plants sharing the same root space: the trees above, and the ornamental plants below. Because they both need water, you are essentially "watering for two."

The most obvious solution for dry shade is to plant drought-resistant, shade-tolerant plants, like liriopes (*Liriope* spp.) and lily of the valley (*Convallaria majalis*). Add moisture-retentive soils and amendments when planting (organic matter is inevitably moisture-retentive, so any effort to improve the soil with compost, peat moss, or similar materials will also improve its capacity to hold moisture). Mulches do a wonderful job of reducing soil evaporation and should be considered an absolute necessity under dry conditions. All efforts toward reducing moisture needs in the garden are called xeriscaping: landscaping with water conservation in mind.

Even drought-resistant plants, though, do need some water. In fact, freshly planted ones need lots of it—plants become truly drought-resistant only when they are well rooted. It's not unusual to see drought-resistant plants still struggling to survive years after they were planted because they were never given the chance to develop a good root system. So no matter what you plant, expect to do quite a bit of watering the first year! During that time, you'll need to water as needed to keep the soil evenly moist: once a week during rainless periods, possibly even more frequently. Water thoroughly, making sure that, ideally, the top foot (30 cm) of soil is thoroughly moist. Not only does deep watering ensure that the new plants get all the water they need, even at the lower level of their roots, but tree roots will not grow back as quickly or aggressively if they are well watered. It's during times of drought stress that trees develop the numerous shallow roots that are such an annoyance to gardeners. If you choose the proper plants for your growing conditions and water well at first, the watering needs of the garden should drop off considerably the following years. In most cases, watering will be needed only during periods of drought.

One way of helping keep freshly installed plants moist is to form an irrigation well. A 2- to 3-inch (4- to 8-cm) mound of soil all around the plant will create a basin

HOW DEEP ARE YOU WATERING?

YOU CAN'T TELL WHETHER YOU'RE WATERING EFFICIENTLY just by looking—the soil at the top may be perfectly moist or even soaking wet, yet the soil below can be dry as a desert. For proper growth, water should reach down at least 8 inches (20 cm); better yet a full foot (30 cm). To test if you've been watering correctly, half an hour after you feel you've done a good job watering, dig down with a trowel into a typical section of the garden and check just how deep the moisture has reached. If it isn't moist at least 8 inches (20 cm) down, try again!

Form a water well, a 2- to 3-inch (4- to 8-cm) mound of soil, around new plants. To water them, just fill up the well and the water will reach their roots—and not those of their aggressive neighbors.

power than dry mulch, and moisture stimulates the development of beneficial fungi whose mycelia (spreading underground rootlike structures) will help hold the mulch in place. Consider terracing extreme slopes—this will not only reduce erosion but ensure much better water retention. If you use a soaker hose on a slope, run it parallel to the slope rather than up and down. The hose is subject to the effect of gravity, and water will naturally seep out most heavily at the lowest point of the hose and least abundantly at the top.

Remember that if the middle and top of a slope are often very dry, its base is usually fairly moist, as the water that runs off the slope ends up there. Consider planting spreading plants at the base of the slope, where it's moist, rather than at the top or in the middle, where it's constantly dry. They'll

that can be filled with water and allowed to drain slowly. The water applied will largely go to the plant that needs it instead of spreading throughout the garden. This is a common practice when planting trees and shrubs, but it can be applied to any kind of planting. You can remove the well (just even out the soil with a rake) after the first year under most conditions, but leave it in place in spots where drought will always be a problem.

Slopes present a particular problem when it comes to moisture—water tends to flow right down them without sinking in—and the steeper the slope, the drier the soil will tend to be. Moisture-retentive soils will help considerably, as will mulching, but mulches are easily washed off steep slopes. After you apply a mulch to a slope, water thoroughly. Moist mulch has better holding

A water barrel is an age-old water-saving device: It stores up water in times of abundance so you can use it in times of drought.

crawl in every direction, even up the slope, providing green, low-maintenance cover even in an otherwise difficult spot.

Municipalities often have watering restrictions that have to be respected—and if you're using a well, you're very aware that water is a precious commodity not to be wasted—so learn to water established plants as little as possible. Again, mulching is an excellent way of reducing watering needs, and using drought-resistant plants in dry shade should be a no-brainer, but learn to find other sources of water for the garden than that coming from pipes. The old-fashioned rain barrel that catches runoff from the roof has always been a good source of water that you can use at will. Where seasonal drought is a recurring problem, consider installing a pond to retain water during periods of abundance to be used when you need it. Good gardeners are water-wise gardeners!

IRRIGATION

IN VERY DRY CLIMATES, an irrigation system of some sort may be almost a necessity. Your first thought might be to purchase a sprinkler system. Remember, though, that sprinkler systems can be very expensive to install, require considerable maintenance and adjustment, and are actually quite wasteful of water because any water sprayed into the air is likely to evaporate (at least in part) before reaching the roots of the surrounding plants. Drip irrigation is cheaper than a sprinkler system but still needs considerable upkeep. So why not consider a soaker hose as an alternative? A soaker hose is inexpensive and easy to install, once covered in mulch loses very little water to evaporation, and is essentially maintenance-free. It may not appear as high-tech as a sprinkler system and certainly works too invisibly to impress your neighbors with your technical savvy, but it does the job.

If you already have a sprinkler system, you can automate it by putting it on a timer and letting it run as needed. This takes a lot of pressure off you, as your gardens will be watered even when you're not home. Still, inspect the system monthly to make sure that no adjustments are needed (sprayers especially are prone to problems— even a slight bit of dirt in the mechanism can throw it out of whack). Consider adding a moisture detector to your system so that it will operate only when the soil is truly becoming dry. There is nothing more wasteful of water than a sprinkler system working merrily away during a rainstorm!

WORKING WITH MOIST SHADE

Because shade reduces evaporation, many shady gardens are also moist ones. Whether this is a problem depends on your point of view. The easy way out of "constant moisture" is simply to plant shade-loving plants that like things on the wet side, a group that includes ferns, hostas, chameleon plant (*Houttuynia cordata* 'Chameleon'), and many others. In fact, there are many more choices of shade plants that tolerate moisture than shade plants that tolerate dry conditions! Even truly soaking-wet conditions have plenty of takers—many bog plants such as mosses, many ferns, and creeping Jenny (*Lysimachia nummularia*) like nothing better. Dig down a bit into a permanent wet spot and you'll find yourself with a water garden that costs practically nothing and will take care of itself! This possibility is discussed in more detail in "Water Gardens" on page 68.

However, slipping on hip waders to slog around in a boggy area is the least enjoyable aspect of moist shade. Consider adding stepping-stones or an elevated walkway so you'll have easy (and dry) access to damper spots.

If you don't want abundant soil moisture, consider simply raising the flowerbeds above the surrounding area. A raised bed rising a mere foot (30 cm) above a soggy spot, filled with well-aerated topsoil, will provide ideal conditions for most shade plants—well-drained, yet with a ready source of water. Or consider planting moisture-tolerant trees or shrubs like

Many shade situations involve moist shade: areas that are moist most of the time and almost never dry out. If you see lots of moss growing in a woodland, you can assume it is moist shade.

willows (*Salix* spp.), poplars (*Populus* spp.), or red osier dogwood (*Cornus stolonifera*). They drink considerable amounts of water and can often drain a wet spot all on their own. Of course, you can also add drainage tiles to draw the water away from your garden on a more permanent basis.

DEALING WITH ROOT COMPETITION

Root competition is a never-ending situation in many shade gardens: The very trees that create shade produce roots so dense

You can grow beautiful plants even under severe root competition if you start with large plants and keep them evenly moist until they are well established.

- Get off to a good start with a larger-than-usual planting hole lined with newspaper to keep roots at bay temporarily.
- Sink pots into the ground between roots, and then plant in the pots.
- Water new plants well for the entire first summer so they can develop a good root system in their new home.
- Use creeping or spreading groundcovers and vines to cover more space—you'll dig fewer holes and have fewer plants to water during the establishment period.
- Plant full-grown plants with large rootballs—the initial digging takes more effort, but the plants start off with a good root system and are less bothered by tree roots.
- Remove secondary tree roots—but no more than one-quarter at any time. Make clean cuts with a sharp saw or pruner to allow rapid healing and minimal damage to the tree.
- Remove some main roots—but do so carefully! Keep roots intact for a distance of about 4 to 6 feet (1.2 to 1.6 m) from the trunk for medium to large trees—and plant between them.
- As a *last resort only,* consider removing the offending trees.
- Replace trees with ones that are less harmful to gardens (see "20 Top Shade Trees" on page 20).

it's hard to grow anything underneath. We looked at how to plant in an area where roots dominate on page 44, using newspaper barriers or planting in pots to keep roots out. Read on for more tips on successfully establishing and maintaining plants in and among established tree roots.

LEAF AND NEEDLE DROP

It's hard to always keep plants in perfect shape, no matter what the circumstances.

CONTAINERS TO THE RESCUE

IF ROOT COMPETITION IS MAKING YOUR GARDENING LIFE miserable (and let's be honest, some trees, like Norway maple (*Acer platanoides*) and beeches (*Fagus* spp.), produce so many roots that it is very difficult to even dig a planting hole!), why not consider putting plants in containers in places where you've been having poor results? A good, thick mulch on the ground or a vast carpeting ground-cover, keeping weeds out and tree roots happy, will make an attractive base for a container garden. Pot up the plants of your choice: shade-tolerant annuals and tender bulbs like impatiens, begonias, and caladiums; more permanent shade-tolerant perennials, like hostas and heucheras that can sit in the same pot year after year; or even sun-loving plants like gaudy cannas and brilliant-colored geraniums (*Pelargonium* spp.) that you can rotate back into the sun once they've stopped blooming, then into the shade yet again once they're back in flower.

To create a harmonious look, pick containers that have something in common: They might all be made of wood, have the same general shape, or be painted the same shade. Or use the same plant in a wide range of very different pots. "Beauty in diversity" has always been a good design theme!

Where tree roots are so thick that you can't even dig a planting hole, the easy way out is simply to cover the spot with mulch and garden in containers!

Constant needle drop under conifers means your plants will probably never look pristine. I suggest deciding that needles on hosta leaves is, in fact, quite charming. Problem solved!

Full-sun plants often suffer from leaf burn, and hail can tear leaves to shreds. In shade, sun is obviously not a problem, and leaves are usually protected from hail by overhanging foliage.

What does make shade gardens most untidy is leaves, needles, cones, and berries falling from above and accumulating on top of foliage and flowers. Birds nesting or feeding on overhanging branches also leave unsightly droppings, especially under their favorite roosts. Conifers are often the greatest annoyances on this level, as many drop their needles throughout the year. At least most deciduous trees drop their leaves all at once in fall and get it over with,

allowing you to carry out any cleaning up, if you judge it necessary, only once a year.

Heavy rain is your best friend in keeping gardens neat: It will usually carry off most debris and deposit it on the ground underneath the leaves, where it simply melts painlessly into the mulch. A blast from the hose or the leaf blower can accomplish the same thing where overhanging leaves create an umbrella effect and keep rain off. Occasionally you may need to do a bit of hand-picking to remove materials that simply won't let go.

In general, smaller-leaved plants and those with downward-pointing leaves pick up the least debris, and large-leaved plants with upward-pointing leaves or horizontal ones pick up the most. So if you're particularly sensitive to the way your garden looks and don't like a lot of litter, consider planting more species with smaller leaves.

I feel a bit of debris in a garden gives it a more natural, homey look. I've actually come to appreciate the appearance of pine needles on hosta leaves, for example. If you can develop this kind of "laissez-faire" attitude, you'll find garden maintenance *much* simpler!

LIGHTENING HEAVY SHADE

There is a limit to how deep shade can get and still give you good garden results. Really deep shade considerably limits your choice of plants, notably to only the most shade-tolerant ones. But can you lighten shade without removing its source entirely? The answer is often yes—if it comes from overhanging trees.

As trees grow in height, they produce more and more branches with more and more leaves, far more than they actually need to grow well. Over time, the lower branches, especially, become essentially superfluous. Sometimes they die, which takes any guilt out of removing them, but you can "raise the crown" of most trees over time by removing still-living branches as well.

Crown Raising

Crown raising, also called limbing up, simply means removing the lower branches of trees. How high up you can remove them depends on the conditions—you don't want to remove so many branches that the tree looks like a pogo stick, but you can usually remove branches on the lower third of the tree without any harm to the tree itself and without hurting its appearance. Very tall trees in a natural forest will actually form a canopy of dense branches above, while the more shaded branches below have very few leaves and contribute little to its growth. You can limb up such trees to just below the canopy with no damage.

When the lower limbs are small and within easy reach, you can raise the crown yourself. A hand pruner is fine for the smallest branches, up to about ¾ inch (2 cm) thick, while loppers (a long-handled pruner) will be needed for somewhat larger ones, up to about 1½ inches (4 cm) thick.

Thicker branches will require a pruning saw (there are long-reach pole saws for branches that are just beyond your immediate reach). Always wear a hard hat when

You can remove branches from the lower third of most trees without harming them in the slightest.

pruning trees, of course, and keep both feet on the ground. And a word to the wise: Any branch you can't easily reach requires the expert hand of an International Society of Arboriculture–certified arborist (tree surgeon). Avoid noncertified "arborists," landscape contractors, and others who offer to prune trees but who often know very little about the subject.

Crown Thinning

Another possibility for lightening heavy shade is crown thinning. This does *not* mean trimming all the branches to the same length (that is known as pollarding and it's considered harmful to a tree's health). Instead, a properly thinned tree will scarcely change in appearance from the original tree, only appear less dense with more sunlight shining through.

The first to go are branches that are dead, damaged, rubbing together, or with narrow, V-shaped crotches. Then, others can be removed to open up the crown and let more light shine through (a secondary benefit of this kind of pruning is that it also improves air circulation, which helps prevent disease). If you have to remove more than one-quarter of a tree's growth, crown thinning should probably be carried out over 2 or 3 years. Thinning usually takes place well above the ground and is best handled by a certified arborist.

Not all trees lend themselves to either crown raising or crown thinning, however. Many of the pyramidal conifers, like spruces (*Picea* spp.) and firs (*Abies* spp.), look best with their lower branches left intact. Few plants will grow in their dense shade, but since the branches touch the ground anyway, there is little room for vegetation at their base.

So much for lightening heavy shade under trees, but what about dense shade created by nearby buildings? Since tearing down the offending building is rarely an option, it is at least interesting to know that painting the walls white or another pale color will considerably increase the light reflected from the building—often enough to pass from deep shade to light shade. If it's your house, changing the color is up to you. It may not always be easy to get a neighbor to cooperate and paint his house white, however!

WEED TREES AND OTHER INVADERS

One of the great joys of shade gardening is the relative absence of weeds. Most of the best-known weeds (such as dandelions and crabgrass) need full sun, or at most very light shade to do well. Also, the abundant use of mulches in shade gardens prevents most common weeds from sprouting. And when they do sprout, they grow weakly and cause little damage. However, since nature is said to abhor a vacuum, it stands to reason that *something* will take their place in shady spots. And indeed, in many climates, the most common weeds in shade are small trees. Many of the tall tree species we like to use as shade trees, like beeches (*Fagus* spp.), maples (*Acer* spp.), and lindens (*Tilia* spp.), are forest trees in the wild and have, as a survival mechanism, adapted to germinating in the deepest shade. There they usually wait, in the form

Maple seedlings and other tree seedlings are often major invaders in shade gardens, sprouting even among groundcovers and deep mulches.

FOR EVERYTHING, A SEASON

PRUNING, EITHER RAISING THE CROWN OR THINNING IT, can be done at almost any time of the year but is usually best done in late winter when trees are leafless. A major exception to that rule is trees that bloom in early spring. If you want to preserve the flowers, wait until after they flower before you prune them. Pruning "in the green" (when trees are fully leaved out) is recommended for trees like birches (*Betula* spp.) and maples (*Acer* spp.) that tend to have a heavy sap flow in early spring. Early pruning could cause them to lose much of their sap, which would weaken them. Of course, you can remove dead branches during any season.

of small saplings, until a larger tree is killed by lightning or old age or falls over, and they then grow rapidly to fill in the gap. They're often referred to as "light gap species."

These small trees can be a major annoyance in the garden, blocking out sunlight as they grow and detracting from the appearance of the garden. Having evolved to sprout in the deepest leaf litter, they are among the few plants that will sprout from seed through a thick mulch. If ignored totally, they may even come to so dominate the garden that they'll crowd out the desirable plants. Tree seedlings are best handpulled when young, before their root systems have fully developed. Once established, they are very difficult to pull out and tend to resprout from the base if cut back. It may be necessary to dig out the most recalcitrant ones.

The other type of weeds that proliferate in shady spots are shade-tolerant perennial weeds that spread by rhizomes or stolons rather than by seeds. Rhizomes are underground stems that spread horizontally. Stolons (also called runners) grow above the surface of the soil, although often under mulch, and also spread horizontally, rooting and forming new plants as they go. Unfortunately, many of the "weeds" of shady gardens were actually planted originally as ornamental plants but found the conditions so much to their liking they began to take over. Goutweed, also called bishop's weed (*Aegopodium podagraria*) is probably the best known of the "weedy ornamentals," but there are dozens of others: lily-of-the-valley (*Convallaria majalis*), yellow archangel (*Lamiastrum galeobdolon*), and ground ivy, also called creeping Charlie (*Glechoma hederacea*) are just a few. In fact, most are perennial groundcovers which, by definition, have the capacity to spread and can therefore also become terrible weeds.

Many of the weeds of shady gardens are "ornamentals" that have been allowed to run wild. Here, goutweed (*Aegopodium podagraria*) is invading this yard and will soon take over entirely.

Be forewarned that the traditional methods of weeding—hoeing and cultivating—are next to useless in a shady garden. These methods are best at destroying weeds that sprout from seeds (which are nearly absent in shade), turning them under before they can develop to any degree. Turning over the soil won't stop rhizomatous or stoloniferous plants, though. On the contrary, it helps spread them—the slightest piece chopped off by the hoe, the cultivator, or worse, the rotary tiller, has the capacity to become a new plant. Most spreading weeds can be controlled only by hand-pulling the majority of the plants, then digging out the ones that refuse to budge. The best way of preventing this type of infestation is to avoid planting invasive groundcovers, or at least to keep them under control if you do plant them. Those that spread underground, like goutweed, can be planted inside pots that are sunk into the soil (see "Reining In the Spreaders" on page 65)—the pot will act as a barrier and keep the plant under control permanently. Those that spread by aboveground runners, like creeping Jenny and yellow archangel, are not so easy to restrict through barriers—they simply grow right over them. Fortunately, the latter tend to be shallow-rooted and easy to pull out by hand.

SUDDENLY SUNNY

Once you've planned and planted a shade garden and come to enjoy its slow but steady growth—and minimum care—plus the wealth of plants of different forms and colors that can grow there, it can be quite a shock when you suddenly find your garden in nearly full sun again. This usually occurs when the shade trees that were the basis of the garden fall or are cut down. If you made the decision to cut the tree, at least you have time to plant a replacement, but often the change occurs without warning—a storm knocks a tree down, or a neighbor removes it (your shade garden may well depend on shade coming from elsewhere than your property).

I've lived through the latter myself: We originally purchased our home partly because of two rows of spruce trees, one on either side of the lot, that gave our lot a feeling of privacy. I planned and planted my gardens keeping in mind the very dense shade they brought. Unfortunately, without any warning in either case, first one neighbor then the other cut the spruces down within 10 months of each other. Although the rows were near the property line, both were on *their* sides, and they had every right to do so. Suddenly, though, my shade gardens were in full blazing sun! What can do you do when this happens?

First, don't panic: Mother Nature has provided for trees toppling over (it commonly occurs in nature), and most shade plants can tolerate some sun. As I mentioned previously, some shade plants are light gap species that live modestly as understory plants for decades but really take off when they're in sun. They'll quickly grow up rapidly when exposed to more light and will help provide shade for those plants that really can't take the sun.

Also, how serious the situation is depends on your local climate. In my case, I live in the extreme North, where the summer sun is not terribly intense. Even though, in both cases, the trees were cut down in summer, none of the plants below burned. Not all plants enjoyed the change, however, and I did have to move quite a few plants to new spots. In the Deep South, the effect is much more serious, especially if it occurs in midsummer. You can count on that summer's garden burning to a crisp!

If the damage occurs during the other three seasons (fall, winter, or spring, when the sun is less intense), you at least have time to protect the more fragile plants by planting new trees (you'll need to plant fairly large ones) or, even easier, sowing tall-growing annuals (see page 32). They'll give fast cover while the replacement shade trees fill in. Or add some sort of shading structure: an arbor, a pergola, or a temporary shade house (see page 26 for other possibilities).

Fast-growing, tall annuals can provide rapid temporary protection when an "incident" suddenly shoves a shady garden into full sun.

FOR THE MOST PART, there are *fewer* pests in shady spots than in the sun. Many insects are simply less active in the shade; others, like spider mites, thrive on plants that are suffering from too much heat and too little water, so they are less prevalent. Plants don't quite get off completely, though: Slugs and snails are particularly harmful under shady conditions.

PEST NAME AND DESCRIPTION	DAMAGE	CONTROLS	LARRY'S HELPFUL HINTS
Aphids Little pear-shaped insects, often translucent green but also other colors. Generally wingless.	They pierce holes in leaves and stems and pump up the sap, which weakens plants and can cause yellowing. They may also transmit viruses.	A hard spray of water, repeated as needed, will knock them off. Or spray with insecticidal soap or light horticultural oil.	Lady beetles will make short work of aphids if you place them on infested plants.
Caterpillars There are dozens of species, usually wormlike creatures with numerous legs and smooth to fuzzy, often colorful, coats.	They eat leaves and flowers. Leafroll caterpillars roll up leaves, then live in and on the home thus created.	Bt (*Bacillius thuringiensis*) can be applied after every rain. Caterpillars eat the bacteria, then slowly die. Or handpick.	Don't forget that caterpillars are butterflies in the making. Learn to recognize the attractive species and, rather than kill them, place them on plants that are less visible.
Japanese beetles Rounded beetles with metallic green bodies and coppery wing cases. The larvae are grubs.	Adults eat holes in or skeletonize leaves and flowers, leaving almost nothing. Larvae weaken plants by eating roots.	Hand-pick and crush or drop into soapy water. Spot-treat with insecticidal soap or diatomaceous earth.	Apply milky spore disease (*Bacillus popillus*) to lawns to kill grubs and prevent their spread.

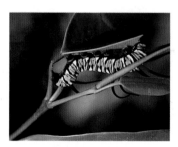

Aphids

Caterpillar

Japanese beetle

PEST NAME AND DESCRIPTION	DAMAGE	CONTROLS	LARRY'S HELPFUL HINTS
Leafminers Tiny green larvae that live within leaves. The adults are rarely noticed.	They trace pale galleries inside leaves, leaving a characteristic pattern.	Remove infested leaves. Few controls can reach them as they live inside leaves.	Leafminers are more disfiguring than truly harmful. If they are not numerous, you can ignore them.
Mammals Deer, groundhogs, gophers, rabbits, etc.	They eat foliage and flowers, often consuming the entire plant.	Apply bloodmeal: It fertilizes plants, yet scares mammals away. Rotate with other repulsives (predator urine, human hair) to keep mammals off track.	Learn which plants local pests don't eat, and plant plenty of them!
Slugs and snails The shade gardener's worst enemies! Slimy tentacled creatures: Snails have shells, slugs don't.	They eat holes in leaves and flowers and may consume young plants entirely. They leave a glistening, slimy trail.	Hand-pick at night or in rainy weather, then crush or drop into a bowl of soapy water. Bowls of beer placed on the soil draw them to their doom.	They dislike sharp surfaces: Any mulch with sharp edges (pine needles, fine wood chips, etc.) will help keep them at bay.
Spider mites Tiny spiderlike creatures with 8 legs that are nearly invisible to the naked eye, but leave spiderlike webs on foliage.	They pierce tiny holes in plant leaves and drink the sap that leaks, causing yellowing and poor growth.	Hose down infested plants or spray with insecticidal soap. Repeat treatments are needed, as spider mites are very persistent.	Most likely to be a problem during dry, hot summers. Rain washes them off leaves and lessens damage.

Leafminers (damage)

Groundhog

Snail

Spider mites (damage)

DISEASE CONTROL

IF INSECT PESTS ARE LESS OF A PROBLEM in shade gardens, diseases tend to be more common, as they develop most readily on moist leaves—and leaves in shade stay moist longer. The best control is to water from below to keep leaves dry, and to look for disease-resistant cultivars, now available for many plants.

DISEASE NAME AND SYMPTOMS	CONTROLS	LARRY'S HELPFUL HINTS
Downy mildew Leaves affected with this appear to be covered in white fuzz, especially underneath.	Give plants room to grow: This increases air circulation so leaves don't remain moist as long. Remove and destroy infested leaves.	This disease generally appears in humid, rainy weather, when days are hot and nights are cool.
Gray mold (botrytis blight) This fuzzy gray mold appears on leaves and stems. Stem bases can blacken and rot, causing stems to fall over.	Make sure plants have good drainage. Destroy infected plant material.	Gray mold usually starts on yellowing or dying foliage, but it can spread to healthy leaves, so remove weak growth when you notice it.
Leaf spot This is caused by many different bacterial diseases. Small brown to purple spots may grow in size. Leaves may yellow and drop.	Remove infested leaves. Spray with sulfur spray, treating susceptible plants weekly as a preventative.	This infestation may overwinter in seemingly healthy tissues, so if the same plant is affected year after year, remove and destroy it.

Downy mildew

Gray mold

Leaf spot

DISEASE NAME AND SYMPTOMS	CONTROLS	LARRY'S HELPFUL HINTS
Powdery mildew This is a very common problem. Leaves appear dusted with talcum powder, then turn black. It strikes when the soil is dry and the air is humid.	Spraying with light horticultural oil can help prevent the disease, as it keeps spores from germinating. Plant disease-resistant varieties. Improve air circulation.	Powdery mildew rarely does any long-term damage, as it usually occurs in late summer when plants already have enough reserves stored up for the following year.
Rots and wilts Plants seem healthy, then suddenly wilt even though the soil may still be moist. The base of the plant may turn black and smell sickly sweet. The plant eventually collapses and dies.	These are very hard to control once they appear. Try cutting out rotting tissue, then sterilizing the wound with a 10 percent bleach solution. Or take cuttings of healthy growth and plant them (destroy the rest of the plant).	They often strike without warning, leaving plants dead before you can react. Improving drainage and air circulation can help prevent them.
Rust Pale green or yellow spots appear on the upper surfaces of leaves; there are corresponding orange marks below.	Use disease-resistant cultivars. Remove infested leaves. Mulching helps keep spores from splashing up onto leaves.	If rust reoccurs year after year, destroy the infested plant and try a disease-resistant variety in a new spot.
Viruses These may cause leaf mottling, weakened growth, or even just a general lack of vigor. They're very hard to recognize.	Control insects that spread viruses, notably aphids. When pruning, sterilize tools between cuts to avoid spreading them yourself. Destroy infested plants.	Viruses tend to build up over time in plants repeatedly grown from cuttings or division. Starting plants fresh from seed gives them a chance to ward off viruses.

Powdery mildew

Wilt

Rust

Virus

Who says foliage can't be beautiful? Here's a striking example of a garden where foliage textures and colors dominate most of the year, while flowers add a bit of seasonal frosting to the cake.

Chapter 5

Making It Work: Designing for Shade

Shade gardens can be as beautiful as the sunniest landscape. Rather than blazing, put-on-your-shades-or-you'll-be-blinded color, though, they tend toward subtler shades and fascinating textures with an emphasis on attractive forms and pleasing arrangements. Beauty in simplicity, beauty in subtlety—such are the secrets of a well-designed shade garden.

FEWER FLOWERS LET FOLIAGE SHINE

Most plants need plenty of light in order to bloom well, so a shady garden is inevitably less floriferous than a sunny one. And that's a good thing, to quote a certain public personality. Or at least it can be. Sun gardeners often make such abundant use of flowers that their beds fall apart when bloom levels drop off—as they often do—in midsummer. In a garden where foliage and form dominate and where flowers are regarded as simply temporary icing on a season-long cake, bloom is nice while it lasts, but not essential. That's one of the reasons shade gardens are often more attractive over a longer period of time than full-sun gardens.

Not that there is no bloom at all in a shade garden. Judiciously chosen shade-tolerant plants *will* bloom at their proper season, but most will not flower with as much abandon as sun-loving plants.

There is some bloom in shade gardens in just about all seasons (other than the dead of winter in climates where the ground is frozen), as shade-tolerant plants have a wide variety of flowering periods. However, spring tends to be the season of greatest bloom. So many shade-tolerant plants are spring ephemerals—bulbs and perennials that take advantage of the absence of overhanging deciduous foliage to produce their own foliage and bloom while the sun penetrates, then go dormant during summer. Trilliums, trout lilies (*Erythronium* spp.), and Virginia bluebells (*Mertensia virginica*) are just a few of the many plants that can guarantee abundant bloom in even the shadiest nooks in spring. You'll learn more about them in "Bulbs for Shade," beginning on page 267.

If you doubt that a garden without flowers can be as attractive as a garden jam-packed with blooms, consider the Japanese garden. Traditionally, Japanese gardens are based on foliage color and texture, not on flowers. In fact, flowers are permitted only in spring for a brief period of rejoicing, celebrating the fragile and ephemeral beauty of the flower, and then the garden is expected to return to its usual green. The Japanese see their small, en-

SUMMER-LONG BLOOM EVEN IN SHADE

ALTHOUGH SHADE GARDENS ARE GENERALLY CONSIDERED the domain of the foliage plant, there are plants that bloom readily in light shade—and even a few that will bloom heavily all season long in deep shade. So if you do want to count on flowers, you're not at a total loss. All of these plants, however, are annuals—such as impatiens, begonias, and browallias—which means they have to be replanted each year. Annual replanting is, in a nutshell, the price you have to pay for flowers in a shady environment. These plants are suited to all sorts of shade gardens, although perhaps not to traditional Japanese ones. For more information on shade-tolerant annuals, see "Annuals for Shade," beginning on page 233.

Impatiens (*Impatiens walleriana*) is one of a select group of annuals that will bloom all summer even in full shade.

closed gardens as essentially a place for meditation and relaxation. In such a garden, flowers, with their gaudy brilliance, would distract from meditation and therefore have little place. The use of too many flowers is considered a bit vulgar by the more sophisticated Japanese gardener. So, the traditional Japanese garden relies mostly on shades of green alone in creating its beauty. If the Japanese can create a garden style renowned the world over that depends almost entirely on foliage for its beauty, there is no reason you can't have a beautiful shade garden in your landscape without nonstop bloom.

ELEMENTS OF SHADE GARDENING

Now that you understand that continuous bloom is not absolutely essential to the success of a shade garden, it's worth looking into what elements *are* essential—notably color, texture, form, and height, all working together to create yearlong interest.

Color

Try strolling through a natural forest on a summer day. What do you notice about its colors? First, green is by far the dominant color; bark and leaf litter add a few earth tones. That doesn't make the forest dull or uninteresting. Instead, the relative absence of other colors (and flowers are usually few and far between in forests in summer) allows green to really strut its stuff. From the dark green of the conifers to the tender green of new shoots to the dappled lime-

The silver variegated leaves of spotted lamium (*Lamium maculatum*, here the cultivar 'White Nancy') add color to the shade garden.

green of sun filtering through deciduous leaves, green comes in infinite shades and creates interest all on its own. In the home garden, the natural richness of forest greens can be highlighted by the blue-green of hosta leaves or the lime-green of golden Hakone grass (*Hakonechloa macra* 'All Gold') and other plants with golden foliage. And then there are variegated foliages of all sorts: leaves speckled, marbled, striped, or margined in shades of yellow, white, pink, or red. Many shade plants, like spotted lamium (*Lamium maculatum*), are overlaid with silver. So there is no need for a shade garden to lack in color even if it is dominated by foliage.

Of course, there are many colors for the shade garden other than green. Although flowers may be rarer outside of spring, they are still present and offer a wide range of colors, from the white, pink, and red stars of masterwort (*Astrantia major*) and the white and pink spires of bugbanes (*Cimicifuga* spp.) to the lavender and white bells of hostas. Of course, the addition of heavy-blooming shade-tolerant annuals and tender bulbs like impatiens and tuberous begonias (*Begonia* Tuberhybrida Hybrids) opens a whole new possibility, one where flower color can actually dominate over foliage color, just as it does in the sunny border. Even so, it is still probably best to consider the shade garden as basically the realm of the foliage plant, with flowers adding just an additional burst of color. Once you learn to use foliage as the basis for your design, you won't need to depend as heavily on flower color.

Cool Colors and Warm Colors

Green is a cool color, as are its close companions, blue-green, purple, violet, and blue. In fact, if a shady nook somehow seems cool on a hot summer's day, that's largely because of the predominance of cool colors. Cool colors give an appearance of calm and tranquility that somehow befits a shady corner. They tend to make the area look larger and farther away.

Yellows and reds, on the other hand, are warm colors. They stimulate the eye and tend to give energy to the landscape. They also make the space seem smaller and closer to the viewer. Lots of plants have golden foliage (in horticulture, "golden" tends to refer to particularly vivid shades of chartreuse or lime) that will create the appearance of patches of sunlight—doubly so if they are surrounded by dark green companions. Warm colors are so dominant you need only a few spots of them to create an effect. In general, put cool colors at the front of your bed and warm colors in the background. This will give depth to the planting.

Be aware that dark colors (deep purple or red flowers; bronze or dark green foliage) may look great in sun, but they are so somber that they appear almost invisible in

This garden brings together green-gold foliage plants that lighten up what would be a much darker landscape.

VOLUPTUOUS VARIEGATES

ONE OF THE MOST COMMON MUTATIONS that occurs in plants is variegation. An all-green plant suddenly starts producing new foliage that is marked with a contrasting color—usually white, chartreuse, or yellow, but sometimes cream, pink, or red. If this "variegated" section is removed and propagated, and if it turns out to be stable (many mutations quickly return to the original

Variegated plants, with their foliage striped or spotted with white, cream, yellow, or even pink, add bounteous color to even the shadiest corners.

form of the plant), it may produce a whole new cultivar whose leaves are often more attractive than its flowers. The genus *Hosta*, for example, is so dominated by variegated plants that many people are surprised to learn that there are all-green ones!

The best impact from variegated plants comes when they aren't used with too heavy a hand. An entire bed of various variegated plants rarely has the impact of a bed of green ones highlighted here and there by variegation. If you're a collector of variegates (and it is easy to be seduced by these spectacular plants!), consider at least separating the different varieties by green foliage so each has a chance to stand out.

Some gardeners prefer a natural look to their gardens and consider the racing stripes and spots of sunlight created by variegated plants to be garish or vulgar—I'm certainly not one of them. Call me garish or vulgar (I'm sure many people have!), but I love variegates and use them abundantly. I can't imagine a shade garden without them!

shade. There are several dark purple–leaved bugbanes, for example, including the nearly purple-black *Cimicifuga simplex* 'Hillside Black Beauty', that tolerate even the deepest shade. But you'd probably do best putting them in a sunny spot where their

oh-so-black foliage will really stand out: Their dark foliage is scarcely noticeable in a shady corner. If you do use such colors in the shade, consider surrounding them or other dark-leaved plants with lime-green or

(continued on page 96)

COLOR-CODED LEAVES

GARDENERS HAVE A LANGUAGE OF THEIR OWN when it comes to foliage colors, so here are few helpful definitions.

Background: Caladium
(*Caladium bicolor* 'Candidum')
Foreground: Variegated goutweed
(*Aegopodium podagraria* 'Variegatum')

Various bronze-foliage plants, including purple Chinese fringe flower (*Loropetalum chinense* 'Rubra') and purple feather grass (*Pennisetum setaceum* 'Purpureum')

Variegated: A leaf striped or otherwise mottled with white, yellow, cream, or chartreuse, and more rarely pink or red. The leaf may be variegated along its edge, in the center, or speckled or splotched over much of its surface. Some plants, like lungworts (*Pulmonaria saccharata* and others) with their white-speckled leaves, are naturally variegated, but most plants with variegated foliage result from mutations—part of the leaf simply lacks in chlorophyll (the green pigment that plants use to absorb sunlight), letting pigments that would normally be hidden by the dark green of the chlorophyll come to the fore. Some heavily variegated plants are less vigorous than their all-green compatriots, but many variegates seem to grow perfectly well in spite of this "infirmity."

Bronze: Purple foliage. This results when acanthocyanin, a red pigment present in small quantities in many leaves, is produced in abnormally large quantities. The mixture of red and green gives the deep purplish shade known as bronze. This large amount of red pigment does not seem to be at all harmful to plants—bronze-foliage plants grow just as vigorously as their all-green cousins.

Golden wood millet
(*Milium effusum* 'Aureum')

Bulbous oatgrass
(*Arrhenatherum elatius*)

Hosta (*Hosta* 'Halcyon')

Golden: No leaf is even close to gold in color, but gardeners use the term to refer to plants that have foliage that is entirely lime-green to chartreuse. This color results from a mutation in which chlorophyll is present in the leaf but highly diffused.

Silver: There are two kinds of silver foliage, both occurring naturally in wild plants. Some plants, like dusty millers and artemisias, are covered with white hairs that give them a silvery appearance, but this is fairly rare in shade plants. In others, like lamiums with their silver-mottled leaves, the metallic silver appearance is caused by a layer of reflective cells just under the leaf surface. This type of silver mottling is found naturally on shade-tolerant plants, and some botanists believe it helps the plants better absorb light under low-light conditions.

Blue (also called "glaucous"): This is the blue-green shade common to blue hostas. It results from leaves that are lightly covered with a waxy white substance called "bloom" (also the powdery substance found on fruits such as grapes and plums). The white powder covering the green leaf gives the overall appearance of a blue-gray, blue-green, or chalky blue coloration. Although commonly seen on hostas, bloom is actually most often seen on full-sun plants, like blue fescue (*Festuca glauca*), and is believed to act as a natural sunscreen. Why a shade plant like hosta would have glaucous leaves is unknown.

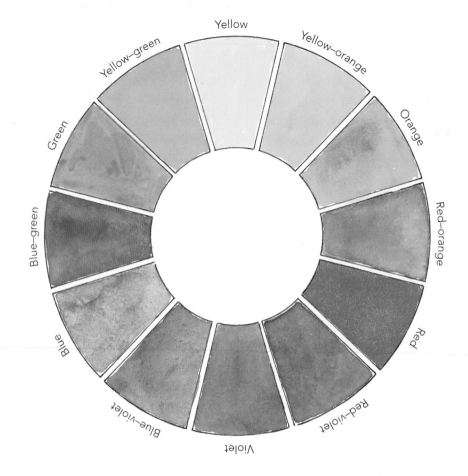

The color wheel is a handy tool for learning to combine flower colors. Consider analogous colors (colors next to each other on the color wheel) for a soothing effect, and contrasting colors (opposite each other on the color wheel) for a bit more pizzazz.

golden yellow foliage and they'll come into their own. In fact, the combination of dark green and bright yellow foliage, either in two separate plants or in plants with variegated foliage, creates some of the most vivid effects possible in a shade garden.

Combining Colors

Foliage of varying colors has a nice way of fitting together, no matter what the combination. Combining flowers with success, though, takes a little more dexterity. You may find a color wheel handy to help you make your choices. Each color on the wheel is flanked by two other colors, called *analogous* colors. When two analogous colors are used together, such as blue and violet, the effect is considered soothing and pleasing to the eye. Colors directly across from each other on the wheel, like red and green, are called *complementary* colors and, when used together, are so contrasting they really stand out, creating a feeling of excitement. For a peaceful mood or for a meditation garden, therefore, you might want to stick to analogous colors, while complementary colors are stimulating and ideal for gardens where you want to create a feeling of vibrancy and pizzazz. Add white and silver shades to tone down excessive intensity.

Of course, those are the "rules" followed by those who believe that color has to be chosen with great forethought. Many gardeners, though, have no use for color wheels and prefer to choose their own colors no matter what the theory says. I actually tend to side with the latter group. I usually just pick colors I like, without any thought to whether they might be analogous or complementary. My own theory is that, with a green background of foliage creating a general feeling of harmony in the garden, you can get away with any color combination you choose!

Planting by spots of color makes each color really hold its own: Here, various cultivars of coleus (*Solenostemon scutellarioides*) are planted in groups to produce this surprising foliage effect.

Safety in Numbers

One way to ensure that plants create a maximum amount of impact is to always plant by spots of color rather than randomly mixing plants together. A single Japanese painted fern (*Athyrium niponicum* var. *pictum*), with its silvery leaves and purplish petioles, for example, is pretty enough, but, at only about 12 inches (30 cm) high and 18 inches (45 cm) wide, it's too small to create much of a splash on its own. Five or six Japanese painted ferns placed here and there in the garden would therefore have very little impact. However, group five or six plants together in a cluster, forming a spot of color, and the fern now has enough mass to stand out in a medium-size bed. The bigger the garden, the more plants you'd need to create a decent spot of color. Of course, plant size is also a factor. A large plant like goat's beard (*Aruncus dioicus*), which reaches 4 to 6 feet (120 to 180 cm) tall and wide, is large enough to create a spot of color all on its own, and three medium-size plants can make up a spot of color for a small bed. In a container, on the other hand, even a small plant is large enough to create a spot of color that will stand out.

Self-sowing dame's rocket (*Hesperis matronalis*) brings harmony to this garden by repeating its bright pink flowers here and there along the shady garden path.

Multiply and Conquer

The next step is a simple one. Repeat the spot of color in the same bed and you get: harmony! The human eye loves repetition, so if it sees a spot of Japanese painted fern in one part of the bed and another spot of the same plant elsewhere, the eye will be very, very happy. Of course, you don't necessarily have to use exactly the same plant in repetition. If you repeat the same color but in two different plants, you'll still create a harmonious effect. For example, goat's beard (*Aruncus dioicus*) looks like a giant white astilbe, so planting a small white astilbe somewhere in the front of the garden and a goat's beard at the back elsewhere will cause the same feeling of harmony. The bigger the bed, the more often you might have to repeat a spot of color in order to bring the whole thing together.

Texture

In the shade garden more than any other, texture is of vital importance, given the decreased importance of flower color in shade. A forest made up of nothing but sugar maples, as often happens, is not nearly as interesting as a forest made up of a mixture of trees, shrubs, and perennials with leaves of different shapes and sizes. This is true even if all the plants are in similar shades of green because the difference in their textures creates interest.

There are three main textures: fine, medium, and coarse (or bold). Fine-leaved plants have small or deeply cut leaves. Most ferns are in that category. The giant, broad leaves of hostas and Siberian bugloss (*Brunnera macrophylla*) are definitely bold—and leaf sizes in between (such as those on astilbes and epimediums) are of medium texture.

The contrast between the bold foliage of the hostas and finely cut foliage of the ferns adds drama and mystery to this shady nook.

You can use texture much as you would color: For a calm, tranquil corner, mix analogous textures, like fine and medium. For a striking arrangement, combine fine and bold foliage. The classic arrangement is finely cut ferns and massive-leaved hostas. Again, plant by spots of texture to bring out the effect, then repeat to create a sense of harmony.

Form

Plant forms can be used just as color and texture are. The basic ones are vertical (plants that grow mostly upward, like many shrubs), spreading, weeping, prostrate (creeping), rounded, and irregular. On top of this, plants can be dense or open. If you throw together too many forms without any particular organization, the result can appear chaotic. Choose a limited number of forms, group by spots, then repeat the spots—and you'll find you have a garden of uncommon beauty on your hands.

Try not to overdo more unusual shapes. A weeping plant or a topiary will always be a focal point in the garden, but one (or a small grouping of the same plant) is enough. A whole series of different weeping plants will tend to confuse the eye rather than enhance the appearance of the garden.

Height

The classic arrangement in a flowerbed with a solid background (placed against a wall, a hedge, a forest, or a fence, for example) or highlighting the edge of a prop-

This superb Japanese maple (*Acer palmatum*), with its hazy, see-through foliage, adds a romantic look to this landscape, but it's such a dominant plant that repeating it would be overkill.

erty is to put the shortest plants in the front, gradually raising the height with an increasingly taller series of medium-size plants in the middle, with the whole thing culminating in a background of tall plants. In a plant island designed to be viewed from all sides, tall plants go in the middle, medium plants around them, then short plants along the border. This "short-to-tall rule" is so instinctive few gardeners even have to be told about it—they plant that way without thinking about it. But don't overdo it. In a very formal garden or a meditation garden, yes, you can repeat the short-medium-tall organization infinitely. However, if you're looking for a more natural style, break the rule every now and again, moving a tall plant to the front of the garden or letting a low-growing one push its way toward the back. You find the effect magical, and there is nothing like breaking such a cardinal rule to make you feel deliciously decadent in your gardening style!

GARDEN ART, PATHS, AND OTHER FEATURES

A garden is not built on plants alone, and all sorts of structures can find their way into one. In fact, the shade garden, with its mix of greens and typical tranquility, benefits more from garden features than a full-sun garden, where boisterous blooms can overwhelm your efforts to add structural interest. A flagstone path meandering through a flowerbed, a comfortable bench in a cozy niche, a statue half-hidden behind billows of green foliage, and a small fountain adding sound and movement are just some of the possibilities that are open to you. A visit to a garden center, a garden art store, or a gardening Web site will give you a good idea of the structures you can add.

With garden art and structures, moderation is usually the best solution. Yes, statues of Snow White and maybe one dwarf would be reasonable—but all seven plus the prince and the whole royal family would probably be overkill. In most cases, look for natural colors and textures, such as stone, wood, and concrete. Colorful garden gnomes, pink flamingos, and tire planters painted white have long been the cliché of poor taste in gardening. Use them sparingly if at all—unless you purposely intend to shock or amuse!

PLANNING FOR YEARLONG INTEREST

One advantage of a shade garden is that, with foliage taking precedence over flowers, it's easier to create yearlong in-

There's nothing like a gurgling fountain to add interest to a shady corner.

terest. Many foliage shade plants, from low-growing pachysandras to the tall evergreen conifers that created the shade in the first place, have persistent foliage and will be attractive year-round. As you plan your shade garden, remember to include a nice portion of evergreens, both broad-leaved and needled, and including not only the usual trees and shrubs but also other plants that retain their foliage all year. This is a relatively small group of plants that includes certain climbers, perennials, grasses, and ferns (as well as pachysandra and Christmas ferns). If only one-fifth of the plants hold onto their leaves year-round, you'll already have a surprisingly colorful garden in winter. Fortunately, the choice of plants with persistent leaves is surprisingly vast.

Remember, too, that colorful or unusually shaped or textured stems and trunks also add off-season interest. Papery white birches (*Betula* spp.), striped-bark maples (*Acer* spp.), gray-barked beeches (*Fagus* spp.), corkscrew hazel (*Corylus avellana* 'Contorta')—all of these and many more may lose their leaves yet still offer winter interest. Plants like peonies and many hardy geraniums (*Geranium* spp.) have

colorful fall hues that can also add interest to the shade garden, while bergenias and a few other plants have leaves that are both persistent and colorful, since they change color in fall and maintain their winter coloration until spring is back again. And an abundant planting of those spring-blooming ephemerals we call bulbs, many of which adapt perfectly to shade, will bring us full circle to the shade garden in summer once again.

5 DESIGNS FOR SHADE GARDENS

Still not sure enough of your knowledge to feel at ease designing your own shade garden? Take a good look at the plans in the following pages. Each was designed with the home gardener in mind, using plants and plantings adaptable to shady parts of the average backyard. These designs were created by professional designers for ease of care using very adaptable plants and so can be used in a wide variety of situations.

You can use the designs as is or expand or reduce the number of plants to fit the space that is available to you. Better still, use them as inspiration, borrowing certain elements for your plan, then adding your own personal touches. The important thing, I feel, is to get personally involved in your plan. When you let someone else do all the planning, it really doesn't feel like your garden, even if it is on your property. If you add your own grain of salt, the plan very much becomes your own, and you'll find you feel much more at ease with it.

With a hemlock (*Tsuga* spp.) bowing its dark green needles under a light dusting of snow while an ornamental grass still hangs on bravely against the winter cold, this waterside landscape is just as attractive in winter as during the growing season.

A VICTORIAN SHADE GARDEN

THE VICTORIANS WERE INTERESTED in exotic-looking plants (ferns and palms were all the rage!), diverse garden styles, masses of colorful annuals arranged in ribbons of color called carpet bedding, and lots of architectural elements, such as wrought-iron fencing, gazebos, and garden statuary. This cozy nook by garden designer Sarah Heffner highlights the romance of a cool Victorian retreat planted in the shade of deciduous trees or the north side of a fence. The garden includes large pedestal urns filled with variegated ivy and white garden impatiens on either side of a garden bench. The surrounding garden bed has Victorian shade favorites, beginning with spring daffodils, followed by the cool green of ferns and fragrant Solomon's seal. The foliage plants are complemented by annual white impatiens and lime-green blooms of flowering tobacco. The plan ensures constant color from spring well into fall, while the garden ornaments and yew guarantee interest even in winter months. This garden is hardy from Zones 5 to 9, and even Zone 4 in a protected spot.

PLANT LIST

1. Oakleaf hydrangea (*Hydrangea quercifolia*) (2 shrubs)
2. Soft shield fern (*Polystichum setiferum*) (9 plants)
3. Flowering tobacco (*Nicotiana sylvestris*) (10 plants)
4. 'Repandens' English yew (*Taxus baccata* 'Repandens') (3 shrubs)
5. White-flowered garden impatiens* (*Impatiens walleriana*) (16 plants)
6. Variegated English ivy (*Hedera helix* [many cultivars are available]) (4 plants)
7. Variegated fragrant Solomon's seal (*Polygonatum odoratum* 'Variegatum') (6 plants)
8. Narcissi (*Narcissus* spp. [your choice of cultivar]) (30 to 50 bulbs, depending on cultivar)

Note: Victorian gardeners didn't actually use garden impatiens (*Impatiens walleriana*) outdoors: It was considered at the time strictly a hothouse plant, although they would certainly have used them abundantly had they been available. They would have used garden balsam (*Impatiens balsamina*), though, and there are several dwarf white hybrids you could use as substitutes if you are a purist about garden history. Because their availability is more limited, you may have to grow them yourself from seed.

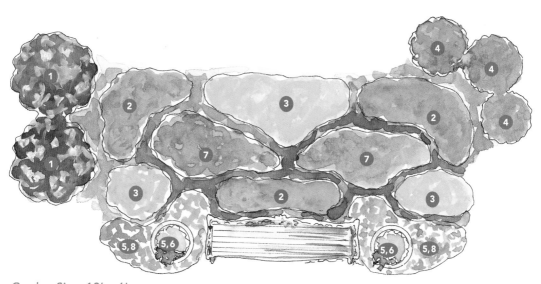

Garden Size: 12′ × 6′

Scale of Plan: ⅜″ = 1′

A JAPANESE SHADE GARDEN

A JAPANESE SHADE GARDEN typically showcases sculptural shrubs and trees, carefully partnered with architectural perennials and evergreen groundcovers. Each plant is placed to emphasize its essential character through the seasons. In warm climates broadleaved evergreens make up the background plantings, but in colder areas deciduous shrubs with handsome winter silhouettes are used. Perennials are placed in sweeps or clusters, underplanted with groundcovers that set off the color or shape of a leaf or blossom. The overall appearance is spare and subtle, so the sumptuous bursts of spring flowers and fall color come as delightful surprises.

This richly textured vignette by designer Ann Lovejoy would be happy in a woodland glade that receives morning sun and dappled afternoon shade. The Japanese hydrangea vine could clamber up a large canopy tree or be trained over two or three sturdy bamboo trellis panels used for privacy screening. Where no tree is available, a Japanese torii gate or sturdy bamboo screens could work as vine support. This little piece of Japan would adapt to Zones 7 to 10, and even 5 to 10 if the Japanese aralia is grown in a pot and overwintered indoors and if a hardier rhododendron is chosen.

PLANT LIST

1. Stewartson rhododendron (*Rhododendron stewartsoniana*) (3 shrubs)

2. 'Jane Platt' fothergilla (*Fothergilla gardenii* 'Jane Platt') (5 plants)

3. 'Wester Flisk' stinking hellebore (*Helleborus foetidus* 'Wester Flisk') (15 plants)

4. Fingerleaf rodgersia (*Rodgersia aesculifolia*) (5 plants)

5. Japanese aralia (*Fatsia japonica*) (1 plant)

6. 'Moonlight' Japanese hydrangea vine (*Schizophragma hydrangeoides* 'Moonlight') (1 plant)

7. 'Sulphureum' bicolor barrenwort (*Epimedium × versicolor* 'Sulphureum') (21 plants)

8. Perennial impatiens (*Impatiens omeiana*) (15 plants)

9. Black mondo grass (*Ophiopogon planiscapus* 'Nigrescens', syn. 'Black Dragon', 'Ebony Knight') (45 plants)

10. Autumn fern (*Dryopteris erythrosora*) (25 plants)

11. Red laceleaf maple (*Acer palmatum* 'Red Dragon', or other purple-leaf cultivar) (1 tree)

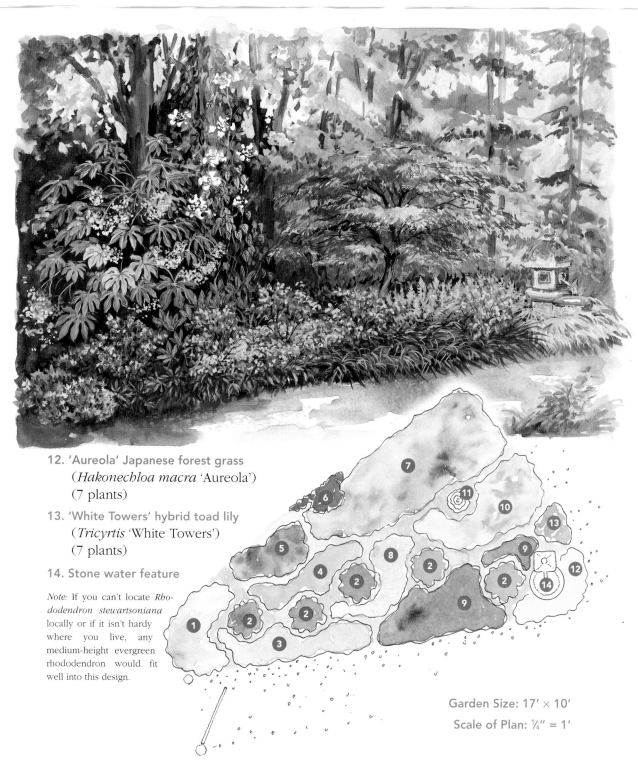

12. 'Aureola' Japanese forest grass
    (*Hakonechloa macra* 'Aureola')
    (7 plants)

13. 'White Towers' hybrid toad lily
    (*Tricyrtis* 'White Towers')
    (7 plants)

14. Stone water feature

Note: If you can't locate *Rhododendron stewartsoniana* locally or if it isn't hardy where you live, any medium-height evergreen rhododendron would fit well into this design.

Garden Size: 17' × 10'

Scale of Plan: ¼" = 1'

A NATIVE PLANT SHADE GARDEN

NATIVE PLANTS are often neglected in our landscapes, yet North America was once dominated by forests, so what better place to reintroduce them around our homes than in a shade garden? There is no lack of shade-tolerant species to choose from, and they have the advantage of having evolved over thousands of years to the climatic conditions of our continent.

This lovely shade garden was designed by Stephanie Cohen. Here, a quiet patio is surrounded on three sides by a secret garden where the occupants can feel com- pletely isolated from the rest of the world. The garden was planned around a forested setting with mature trees and moisture-re- tentive soil. It starts to glow in earliest spring as the purple leaves of 'Forest Pansy' eastern redbud unfurl, soon followed by reddish pink flowers. Plants in the under- story bloom in turn, from tall to short and tall again, providing color from spring through fall. The garden is also a wonderful combination of great foliages with con- trasting dark and golden shades. This design would adapt well to Zones 5 to 9.

PLANT LIST

1. 'Corbett' Canadian columbine (*Aquilegia canadensis* 'Corbett') (11 plants)

2. Goat's beard (*Aruncus dioicus*) (5 plants)

3. Canadian wild ginger (*Asarum canadense*) (5 plants)

4. 'Hot Lips' turtlehead (*Chelone lyonii* 'Hot Lips') (10 plants)

5. Black snakeroot, black cohosh (*Actaea racemosa*, formerly known as *Cimicifuga racemosa*) (13 plants)

6. 'Elizabeth Ann' spotted cranesbill (*Geranium maculatum* 'Elizabeth Ann') (7 plants)

7. 'Sunspot' foamy bells (× *Heucherella* 'Sunspot') (8 plants)

8. Crested iris (*Iris cristata*) (14 plants)

9. 'Ruby Slippers' cardinal flower (*Lobelia cardinalis* 'Ruby Slippers') (3 plants)

10. 'Lilac Candles' great blue lobelia (*Lobelia siphilitica* 'Lilac Candles') (7 plants)

11. Allegheny spurge (*Pachysandra procumbens*) (12 plants)

12. 'Cygnet' foamflower (*Tiarella* 'Cygnet') (11 plants)

13. 'Iron Butterfly' foamflower (*Tiarella* 'Iron Butterfly') (7 plants)

14. 'Athen's Gold' allspice (*Calycanthus floridus* 'Athen's Gold') (1 plant)

15. 'Forest Pansy' eastern redbud (*Cercis canadensis* 'Forest Pansy' (1 tree)

16. Golden American elder (*Sambucus canadensis* 'Aurea') (1 tree)

Garden Size: 14' × 11'

Scale of Plan: ¼" = 1'

AN ANNUAL SHADE GARDEN

WHY WAIT YEARS FOR YOUR SHADE GARDEN to fill in when you can have great results nearly overnight? That's what annuals promise you: quick color. The other advantage of an annual garden is that you can create one in any climate. This garden has no zone restrictions: You could just as easily create it in Zone 2 as in Zone 11.

This garden, by Pam Baggett of Singing Springs Nursery, was inspired by a pair of fuchsias (*Fuchsia* 'Angels' Earrings Cascading'), pruned into 3-foot (90-cm) standards. You might like to do the same in your annual garden: Choose a star plant that inspires you, and use it to set the color scheme for the rest of the garden. Here, the deep rose and purple flowers over the white-mottled foliage set the tone: pink for pizzazz, purple to soothe, and a good dose of white, notably from variegated foliage, added to bring in more light. The dangling bells of the fuchsia are repeated with both the smaller bells of the flowering tobacco (*Nicotiana langsdorfii*) and the much larger blooms of the variegated angel's trumpet (*Brugmansia suaveolens* 'Variegata'). The latter is the only plant not truly shadeworthy, so it may flower sparsely, but its white-and-green leaves will carry the show as a foliage plant.

PLANT LIST

1. 'Dragon Wing Pink' begonia (*Begonia* 'Dragon Wing Pink') (14 plants)
2. 'Blue Bells Improved' browallia (*Browallia* 'Blue Bells Improved') (14 plants)
3. 'Little Miss Muffet' caladium (*Caladium* 'Little Miss Muffet') (9 tubers)
4. 'Jack of Diamonds' coleus (*Solenostemon scutellaroides* 'Jack of Diamonds') (2 plants)
5. 'Accent Lavender Blue' impatiens (*Impatiens walleriana* 'Accent Lavender Blue') (18 plants)
6. 'Angels' Earrings Cascading' fuschia (*Fuchsia* 'Angels' Earrings Cascading') (2 standards)
7. 'White Queen' caladium (*Caladium* 'White Queen') (22 tubers)
8. Flowering tobacco (*Nicotiana langsdorfii*) (3 plants)
9. Variegated angel's trumpet (*Brugmansia suaveolons* 'Variegata') (2 plants)
10. 'Magenta Frills' coleus (*Solenostemon scutellaroides* 'Magenta Frills') (3 plants)
11. Persian shield (*Strobilanthes dyerianus*) (6 plants)
12. Giant taro (*Alocasia macrorhizos*) (1 plant)

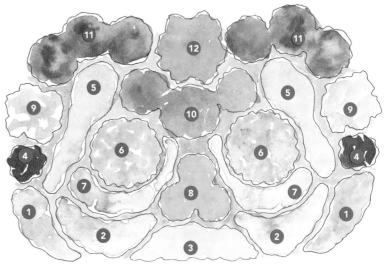

Garden Size: 16' × 10½'

Scale of Plan: ¼" = 1'

A TEXTURED SHADE GARDEN

FLOWER COLOR IS ISN'T EVERYTHING IN THE GARDEN, and that's an important lesson to learn in the shade garden, where flowers are less frequent and more fleeting than in sunny spots. This garden by designer Pam Ruch, adapted to Zones 5 to 9, takes full advantage of those spring–blooming flowers, but it mostly depends on the contrasting textures of foliage and form to make it interesting. Even in winter, the climbing hydrangea on the wall shows its exfoliating bark, and the evergreen hellebore, ferns, and wild ginger remain a presence. A river of foamflowers generates the rhythm that holds the planting together.

The show starts off with a bang very early in spring when the stinking hellebore blooms. For more interest, add early spring bulbs (not shown in the plan) among the bigleaf ligularias and the Japanese painted ferns, which emerge later in the season. Next to bloom are the foamflowers, the fragrant cloud of woodland phlox, and the Japanese roof iris. After the spring flowers fade, foliage takes over.

Graceful clumps of Japanese forest grass on each side of the bench and variegated Solomon's seal add a touch of color.

PLANT LIST

1. Variegated fragrant Solomon's seal (*Polygonatum odoratum* 'Variegatum') (6 plants)

2. Ostrich fern (*Matteuccia struthiopteris* var. *pensylvanica*) (5 plants)

3. Autumn fern (*Dryopteris erythrosora*) (5 plants)

4. 'Spring Symphony' foamflower (*Tiarella* × 'Spring Symphony') (21 plants)

5. Meadow rue (*Thalictrum rochebruneanum*) (3 plants)

6. 'Desdemona' bigleaf ligularia (*Ligularia dentata* 'Desdemona') (4 plants)

7. Japanese painted fern (*Athyrium niponicum* var. *pictum*, syn. *Athyrium niponicum* var. *metallicum*) (5 plants)

8. Stinking hellebore (*Helleborus foetidus*) (8 plants)

9. 'Aureola' Japanese forest grass (*Hakonechloa macra* 'Aureola') (6 plants)

10. European wild ginger (*Asarum europaeum*) (16 plants)

11. Japanese roof iris (*Iris tectorum*) (3 plants)

12. 'London Grove' woodland phlox (*Phlox divaricata* 'London Grove' (6 plants)

13. Climbing hydrangea (*Hydrangea anomala* subsp. *petiolaris*) (1 plant)

Garden Size: 6' × 15'

Scale of Plan: 3/8" = 1'

The Best of the Best for Shade

The plants presented here in Part II are all capable of growing and thriving in partial shade—and many will grow and thrive in shade as well. It does *not* mean they won't grow in full sun, too; many will, especially in northern gardens where the sun is never very intense (if that's the case, I've noted it in the plant's description). That means the plants described here will look good and healthy and bloom well (if blooming is something they're supposed to do—not all ornamental plants are grown for their flowers) in less than full sun.

You'll see that each plant has a description discussing its needs and its idiosyncrasies, plus plenty of tips on how to grow it. You'll also find suggestions of plants that it grows well with to help you better plan your garden. Finally, I'll give some suggestions of the better varieties for you to try, and in some cases plants that could replace the plant described—or a few other plants that are lesser known but that you might want to try.

Perennials dominate in this quiet shady corner.

Chapter 6

Perennials for Shade

Let's jump right into the thick of things: Perennials are the most popular garden plants in temperate climates these days. They are also by far the most popular plants for shade gardens. But if you think your choice of shade perennials is limited to hostas and goutweed (*Aegopodium podagraria*), think again. There are lots and lots of choices, as you'll see as you read through the following pages.

First, though, let's define what a perennial is.

The term "perennial" as used by gardeners usually refers to what botanists call "herbaceous perennials": plants that come back year after year from the same crown, but without producing woody stems. In other words, most plants that live more than 1 year but are neither shrubs nor trees. That does not mean perennials are necessarily small plants, although most are no more than medium in size—but some can reach 6 feet or more during summer. However, they can't "build on" previous seasons' growth as trees and shrubs can, and therefore they tend to reach their full size relatively quickly (usually 2 to 5 years), then remain stable in height.

Most perennials die to the ground in winter, losing both leaves and stems. A few, though, have evergreen foliage and some even have persistent stems. Evergreen perennials are especially treasured, as they add color to fall, winter, and early spring landscapes. Some turn attractive shades of burgundy or red in fall, although other evergreen perennials are much the same green in the off-season as during summer.

A PERENNIAL IS AS A PERENNIAL DOES

Of course, what is and is not a perennial also varies according to climate. Some plants (the garden impatiens, *Impatiens walleriana,* is a good example) are perennials in tropical climates but die in colder ones. In this book I've put them in with the annual plants, as that is how most gardeners think of them. And not all the plants described as perennials are cold-hardy enough for all gardens: Some will have to be grown as annuals or as potted plants if you live in very cold climates. Likewise, gardeners in hot-summer/mild-winter areas will find some "perennials," like common monkshood (*Aconitum napellus*), fail to thrive or even die out if summers are too hot or if winters are not cold enough.

Diamonds Are Forever, and So Are Some Perennials

"Perennial" does not necessarily mean eternal, either. Some perennials live only 2 or 3 years, then peter out or disappear. Columbines (*Aquilegia* spp.) are in this group. Most shade-tolerant perennials, however, are long-lived. One of the main strategies for surviving in less-than-perfect lighting is to take longer to reach full maturity than sun plants, but then to compensate by living for many more years. Most shade-tolerant perennials very much take this rule to heart and tend to be very long-lived. Certainly most will still be in your garden 15 years or more after you plant them.

Slow but Steady

If you're used to dividing your sun-loving perennials on a regular basis, you'll find you can relax with shade-tolerant perennials.

Slow-growing, long-lived: The two combine to form plants that don't tend to die out in the middle as some fast-growing sun-loving perennials do. Instead, most shade-tolerant perennials are "plant-'em-and-leave-'em" plants. They'll slowly grow to full size and need not be divided thereafter—or at least not very often. Not that they *can't* be divided, though: A 40-year-old hosta may provide dozens if not hundreds of divisions. But the point is, you didn't have to divide it over all those 40 years and, had you not needed divisions, it could have been left alone for another 40 years! You'll find most shade-tolerant perennials are in this "low-care/no-care" category.

PERENNIALS AS GROUNDCOVERS

Shade perennials can, of course, be used to create beautiful garden spaces: planting them by spots of color, with tall plants to the back and shorter ones to the front, carefully selecting them by flower or leaf color, by texture, or by shape to create a harmonious appearance. But you can also use them as groundcovers.

Groundcovers are mostly low-growing perennials (although there is no official "maximum" height for a groundcover— some can reach 4 feet/120 cm in height!) capable of creating a carpetlike effect in the garden. They're *very* popular in shady nooks, as they need little maintenance once planted and readily replace the endless lawns of suburbia that rarely thrive in shade. The goal with a groundcover perennial is to create not spots of color but vast, fairly even surfaces of the same plant. You don't usually mix groundcovers, but plant one type to cover the entire surface, or perhaps, on very large surfaces, a second one.

To Run or Not to Run?

Almost any shade perennial can be used as a groundcover; it just depends on how you plant it. Create carpets of nonrunning perennials in a large planting area by staggering their planting in a triangular pattern. Space the plants about three-quarters of their maximum diameter apart. The idea of this tight spacing, which is much closer than you would normally plant perennials, is that the plants will merge at their edges, creating a carpetlike effect. If a given hosta, for example, measures 24 inches (60 cm) in diameter when fully mature, create a carpet effect by planting several 18 inches (45 cm) apart, spaced in a staggered pattern.

Most perennials typically used as groundcovers, however, *spread.* Instead of slow-growing, stable plants that stay put, they are aggressive, almost weedy plants, with creeping stems that root as they grow or offsets sprouting either all around the mother plant or at quite a distance from it. You can space these farther apart than the width of a mature rosette would seem to indicate, as they'll produce abundant offsets to fill in any empty spaces. For example, each rosette of a common ajuga (*Ajuga reptans*), a typical spreading groundcover, covers only about 4 inches (10 cm), yet you can plant small plants (in 2¼-inch/6-cm pots) 8 inches (20 cm) apart, or larger plants (in 6-inch/15-cm pots) 1 foot (30 cm) apart.

Holding Them Back

Because spreading groundcovers can be spaced well apart, you need fewer plants to create a carpetlike effect, cutting down on your initial investment. On the down side, though, they don't know where to stop. A sturdy metal border or plastic lawn border about 8 inches (20 cm) high, inserted into the soil with about 1 inch (2.5 cm) remaining above ground is enough to stop perennials that spread by underground runners or offshoots.

Groundcovers that spread above the ground with creeping stems or aboveground stolons, like ajuga and strawberries (*Fragaria* spp.), aren't as easily stopped—they'll leap right over underground barriers. A wall of taller plantings or a ring of stones jutting well above the ground may hold them back, but often they need to be restrained by an occasional pruning. No need to get down on your hands and knees, though—a string trimmer turned on an angle will work just as well and is much faster. Or grow creeping groundcovers along a path or a lawn, where the passage of feet will crush wayward plants.

Acanthus
Bear's breeches

PLANT PROFILE

ACANTHUS
uh-KAN-thus

Bloom Color:
Pink-and-white and purple

Bloom Time:
Late spring to midsummer

Length of Bloom:
3 to 4 weeks

Height:
30 to 60 inches (75 to 150 cm)

Spread:
2 to 3 feet (60 to 90 cm)

Garden Uses:
Container planting, cut flower garden, groundcover, mass planting, mixed border, seasonal hedge, specimen plant, woodland garden; at the back of beds and borders

Light Preference:
Full sun to partial shade; tolerates deep shade

Soil Preference:
Average, well-drained soil

Best Way to Propagate:
Take root cuttings in spring or fall; sow seed in winter

USDA Plant Hardiness Zones:
Varies by species; see individual listings

Bear's breeches is a spectacular perennial, with or without bloom. The majestic appearance of the rosette of arching, deeply cut, shiny, dark green, sometimes evergreen leaves with soft spines at the tips of the lobes would be reason enough to grow this plant, but then come the stately, long-lasting spikes of curiously colored flowers. With their deep purple somewhat spiky hoods over white or pale pink blossoms, they have an almost menacing appearance that is certain to attract attention.

GROWING TIPS

Bear's breeches is fairly slow-growing. It grows best in partial shade (especially in the South, as full sun in a hot, muggy summer climate can do it in), but it puts up admirably with full sun in the North and in cool-summer areas. It will tolerate deep shade as well, but unless it gets several hours of fairly bright sun, it is unlikely to bloom. Not that lack of bloom is a major problem: The foliage is magnificent!

Bear's breeches is quite adaptable. Any garden soil that is well drained and neither extremely acid nor alkaline will do just fine. It is also very drought-tolerant, at least once established, but still does better in soils that naturally remain slightly moist during hot weather.

Bear's breeches will tolerate root competition once established. Where roots are likely to be a problem, it's best to start with a large plant with a dense root system rather than with a small plant that might find the surrounding roots overbearing.

Warning: While this plant is not naturally invasive, it can become quite the thug when disturbed. That's because it offsets only lightly if left alone, but if its roots are damaged, it can send up shoots from the slightest piece of root.

Multiply this plant by thrusting a shovel into the ground at its base in fall so as to section a few roots. When spring comes, they'll be plenty of baby plants for you to dig up and replant. Larger offsets will be in bloom within 2 or 3 years. Bear's breeches can also be grown from seed, but may then take several years to reach blooming size.

PROBLEMS AND SOLUTIONS

Fresh young leaves are susceptible to slugs and snails, so a bit of hand-picking early in the season may be necessary. Aphids are occasional problems later in the season; blast them off with a sharp spray of water.

TOP PERFORMER

Larry's Favorite: *Acanthus hungaricus,* also known as *A. balcanicus* (Balkan bear's breeches): I consider this the best species for most gardeners not only because it is hardier than the others, but also because it blooms later than most—in midsummer, which puts its flower buds out of reach of late-spring frosts. It is otherwise almost a clone of the much more readily available *A. mollis* (common bear's breeches), with similar deeply cut leaves and 12- to 18-inch (30- to 45-cm) spikes of white flowers topped off with deep purple bracts. Height: 30 to 60 inches (75 to 150 cm). Spread: 3 feet (90 cm). USDA Plant Hardiness Zones 4 to 9.

MORE RECOMMENDED BEAR'S BREECHES

Acanthus mollis (common bear's breeches): Definitely the most widely available species, but its limited hardiness and susceptibility to late-spring frosts limits its usefulness in the North. It is essentially identical to *A. hungaricus* except for somewhat less deeply cut leaves, and flowers that often have a pinkish tinge and appear earlier, toward the end of spring. Height: 30 to 60 inches (75 to 150 cm). Spread: 3 feet (90 cm). USDA Plant Hardiness Zones 7 to 9.

A. spinosus (spiny bear's breeches): This is a spinier bear's breeches, with more narrowly lobed leaves but otherwise similar to *A. mollis.* It blooms readily only in climates with hot summers, but the foliage is, of course, attractive in any climate. The wickedly prickly *A. spinosus* Spinosissimus Group is made up of selections as spiny as any thistle. All are particularly heat-resistant and ideal for the Deep South. Height: 3 to 4 feet (90 to 120 cm). Spread: 3 feet (90 cm). USDA Plant Hardiness Zones 6 to 10.

Balkan bear's breeches
(*Acanthus hungaricus*)

LARRY'S GARDEN NOTES

The deeply cut leaves that decorate Corinthian columns represent *Acanthus* leaves, most likely *A. mollis.* Legend has it that in Ancient Corinthia, bear's breeches were found growing next to some marble pillars that lay on the ground awaiting a few finishing fluorishes and that their arching form inspired the artists to carve the shape of the leaves into the column's top. Acantha, by the way, was a Greek nymph who, trying to dissuade an overly amorous Apollo, scratched his face and was turned into a plant with spiny leaves: the *Acanthus.*

Aconitum

Aconite, monkshood, wolf's bane

ACONITUM
ack-oh-NEYE-tum

Bloom Color:
Blue, pink, and white

Bloom Time:
Midsummer to late fall

Length of Bloom:
2 months

Height:
3 to 6 feet (90 to 180 cm)

Spread:
1 to 3 feet (30 to 90 cm)

Garden Uses:
Cut flower garden, meadow garden, mixed border, woodland garden

Light Preference:
Full sun to partial shade

Soil Preference:
Humus-rich, moist but well-drained soil

Best Way to Propagate:
Divide in spring or fall

USDA Plant Hardiness Zones:
1 or 2 to 7

Take a delphinium and make it easy to grow, long-lived, insect- and disease-resistant, and strong enough to stand up without staking, and you'd pretty much have an aconite. The aconite's hooded flowers, though, have the appearance of a "monk's hood," and they couldn't be more different than the wide-open flowers of the better-known delphinium. Only aconites can make any claim toward being shade-tolerant, though, so they alone deserve a spot in this book.

GROWING TIPS

Aconites can tolerate full sun as long as you keep their soil cool and moist, but even so, most gardeners (especially those in hot-summer areas) will find them easiest to grow in partial shade. They are very slow-growing plants, taking several years to reach their full potential, but are also tough and long-lived. Once they get going, they give full satisfaction!

They prefer good, humus-rich soils, but will do well enough in any well-drained but moist spot. They'll even grow very well in clay soils that so many other plants despise. Most aconites have a massive, turniplike root system and dislike being moved or divided. One thing they do not like, though, are endlessly hot summers, making aconites a poor choice for the Deep South.

Maintenance is minimal. Division is not required but can be done if you need more plants. Do it in fall, taking care to cut offsets free while not damaging the mother plant.

PROBLEMS AND SOLUTIONS

Slugs, snails, and aphids are occasional problems. Leaf diseases are possible where air circulation is poor. However, most gardeners find aconites to be trouble-free.

TOP PERFORMER

Aconitum septentrionale 'Ivorine' (ivory monkshood): This aconite is probably the most shade-tolerant. It is also the earliest to bloom (in early summer; most of the others bloom in late summer or even fall) and likewise one of the shortest.

Its long roots, with no apparent tuber at the base, are particularly easy to establish in the garden. Its habit is more mounding than other monkshoods, with much shorter, ivory-colored flower spikes. Height: 2 to 3 feet (60 to 90 cm). Spread: 1 foot (30 cm). USDA Plant Hardiness Zones 1 to 7.

MORE RECOMMENDED ACONITES

There are some 100 species of aconite, but only a few are widely available, including the following. Most have purple to blue flowers.

Aconitum 'Bressingham Spire' ('Bressingham Spire' monkshood): This newer introduction is closely related to *A. napellus* (see below) and has a similar mid- to late-summer flowering season, but its dark violet flowers are borne on sturdier, shorter stalks and never need staking. Height: 3 feet (90 cm). Spread: 1 foot (30 cm). USDA Plant Hardiness Zones 2 to 7.

A. × *cammarum* 'Bicolor' (bicolor monkshood): An old-fashioned favorite with purple-and-white flowers on open, branching stalks less upright than most monkshoods. It is in bloom from mid- to late summer. Sterile, it must be multiplied by division. This one does particularly poorly in the South. Height: 3 to 4 feet (90 to 120 cm). Spread: 2 feet (60 cm). USDA Plant Hardiness Zones 2 to 7.

A. carmichaelii (azure monkshood): A "typical" monkshood, with tall, upright stalks of large, paler blue flowers than most of its brethren. It blooms from late summer through much of fall on tall stems and may need staking. 'Arendsii' (or *A.* × *arendsii*) has darker blue flowers. Height: 4 to 6 feet (120 to 180 cm). Spread: 3 feet (90 cm). USDA Plant Hardiness Zones 2 to 7.

A. napellus (common monkshood, garden monkshood): The one often seen in older gardens, as it has been around for generations. The species has deep blue to purple flowers, but there are several cultivars with white or even pinkish or reddish flowers (the latter shades wash out readily and are best in cool-summer climates). This mid- to late-summer bloomer is one of the better choices for the South. Height: 3 to 4 feet (90 to 120 cm). Spread: 2 feet (60 cm). USDA Plant Hardiness Zones 2 to 7.

Common monkshood
(*Aconitum napellus*)

LARRY'S GARDEN NOTES

Warning: Pretty as they are, aconites are toxic. In fact, one of their common names, wolf's bane, comes from their former use as a poison used to kill vermin in Europe. The poison can be absorbed through the skin and even sap from a broken stem can cause a feeling of numbness. There is fortunately little about this plant that attracts children or pets to eat it, so poisonings are rare, but it should nevertheless be planted well back from play areas or even avoided entirely in gardens visited by the younger set. Wear gloves when handling aconites—or at least take a shower when you finish.

Actaea

Baneberry

ACTAEA
ak-TEE-uh

Bloom Color:
White

Fruit Color:
White, red, and black

Bloom Time:
Late spring

Length of Bloom:
3 to 4 weeks

Height:
2 to 3 feet (60 to 90 cm)

Spread:
2 feet (60 cm)

Garden Uses:
Groundcover, mass planting, mixed border, woodland garden; at the back of beds and borders, in wet areas

Light Preference:
Full sun to shade, depending on species

Soil Preference:
Humus-rich, moist, slightly acid soil

Best Way to Propagate:
Divide in spring or fall

USDA Plant Hardiness Zones:
2 to 7

A perennial grown for its berries? Why not? Not that baneberries aren't attractive in bloom, with their white ball-shaped flower spikes, or even just in foliage (their deeply cut leaves always remind me of astilbes). As the shiny green berries form in midsummer, though, and turn their final bright red, creamy white, or deep black before summer's end, they really do steal the show. As an added plus, the berries hang on for ages, brightening up the fall garden.

GROWING TIPS

Baneberries are shade plants *par excellence.* In their native haunts, they are found in forests, often forming nearly pure stands because the conditions are too dark for anything else. In the North where the sunlight is naturally less intense, partial shade is best and plants will even tolerate full sun. In truly hot-summer locations, keep baneberries in the deepest shade.

Ideally baneberries would grow in rich, friable, slightly acid soil that remains moist most of the time, but they will adapt to most forest conditions, especially if you mulch them well. I find they are perfectly resistant to root competition, but only once they are established. So keep watering them well, as needed, for at least 2 years until their roots have fully developed, or plant them within a root barrier where the surrounding roots won't be able to touch them for a few years. They become much more drought-resistant once they have settled in.

It's easy to multiply baneberries by dividing established plants in spring or fall, separating them into sections with at least one growing point. My advice: Plant 'em and leave 'em. Baneberries will spread on their own, albeit slowly. Buy whatever quantity of plants you need to create an interesting if sparse look, and just let them fill in on their own.

Warning: As the name "baneberry" suggests ("bane" originally meant "death"), these plants are poisonous. All parts are toxic, but the beautiful berries can be especially tempting to young children and are the main concern. It's best to avoid this plant if children regularly visit your garden—or to remove the berries when kids are present.

PROBLEMS AND SOLUTIONS

These are essentially problem-free plants, but leaf spot diseases can occur, especially when the plants are grown in hot, humid conditions not to their liking.

TOP PERFORMER

Actaea alba, also known as *A. pachypoda* (white baneberry, doll's eyes): This is the most interesting choice for the shade garden because it bears luminous white berries that really stand out in a dark place. This North American native is quite a variable plant, with berries than can be all white, cream-colored, or white with a black tip. The latter form, called "doll's eyes," is perhaps the most attractive. Making the berries stand out even more, the flowerstalks become red and fleshy as the berries mature. The late spring flowers also show up beautifully against the dark green foliage. A true winner! Height: 2 to 3 feet (60 to 90 cm). Spread: 2 feet (60 cm). USDA Plant Hardiness Zones 2 to 7.

MORE RECOMMENDED BANEBERRIES

Note: Taxonomists have recently transferred the genus *Cimicifuga* to *Actaea,* although this decision is still hotly debated. Look for *Cimicifuga* on page 146.

Actaea rubra (red baneberry): Just as attractive as white baneberry, and in fact almost indistinguishable from it until its berries start to change color, red baneberry, likewise a North American native, produces bright berries on thinner red stalks. The two make a smashing couple—try growing them side by side! In some climates they bloom concurrently; in others, red baneberry is a bit earlier. That's actually a nice effect as it extends the blooming season. Height: 2 to 3 feet (60 to 90 cm). Spread: 2 feet (60 cm). USDA Plant Hardiness Zones 2 to 9.

A. spicata (baneberry): This is the common baneberry of Europe and Western Asia. It has the typical white flowers, but berries are jet black. Height: 2 to 3 feet (60 to 90 cm). Spread: 2 feet (60 cm). USDA Plant Hardiness Zones 2 to 7.

White baneberry
(*Actaea pachypoda*)

LARRY'S GARDEN NOTES

Make sure you obtain baneberries that were nursery-grown. They are such slow-growing plants that many suppliers harvest them from the wild. As far as I know, baneberries are not threatened anywhere (they're fairly common plants throughout the temperate regions of the Northern Hemisphere), but they live in such fragile forest areas that it is hard to see how this practice cannot be harmful to the environment. Personally, I simply won't grow anything that is wild-collected, period. I'd rather pay a bit more and obtain a plant that is nursery-grown, or grow the plant myself from seed.

Aegopodium
Goutweed, bishop's weed

PLANT PROFILE

AEGOPODIUM
ee-go-POH-dee-um

Bloom Color:
 White

Bloom Time:
 Early to midsummer

Length of Bloom:
 3 to 4 weeks

Height:
 1 to 2 feet (30 to 60 cm)

Spread:
 Indefinite

Garden Uses:
 Container planting, edging,
 groundcover, mass planting,
 woodland garden

Light Preference:
 Full sun to shade

Soil Preference:
 All but the very driest,
 poorest soil

Best Way to Propagate:
 Divide at any time

USDA Plant Hardiness Zones:
 3 to 8

This is the groundcover/weed your mother warned you about! (Or she should have.) I recommend this plant only to those who have some expectation of being able to control it, for few plants are more invasive than goutweed. That said, it is a plant that can be very useful, with its deeply cut foliage usually variegated with white that will grow almost anywhere, even in the most root-infested, shadiest spots when you've failed to get anything else to grow. The dome-shaped inflorescences of tiny white flowers, looking rather like the blooms of wild carrots, are not particularly interesting, but as a foliage plant for impossible places, it is truly spectacular.

GROWING TIPS

Is there any perennial that is easier to grow? Try it in rich soils or poor, sand or clay, moist conditions or dry, full sun or deep shade—it always seems to thrive. It does do better in cooler conditions and in partial to deep shade than in hot, baking conditions and full sun, but the only real difference is that it grows a bit more slowly when heat- and sun-stressed.

You'll only ever need one single division because this plant spreads like wildfire, its underground rhizomes stretching off in all directions and managing to work their way through soil so filled with roots even the sharpest shovel won't make a dint. But neither will simple barriers stop it. I've seen it push its way through asphalt, so that gives you some idea that a simple edging of stones or brick is not going to hold goutweed back. As a barrier, sink a pot or a pail with the bottom knocked out into the soil, leaving a slight lip above, and you can stop it. In fact, it grows more densely when it is held in place by a barrier, and the result is a much more attractive plant.

Consider this plant as a groundcover only—and uniquely for places where its spreading habit is not a problem, such as in a forested area. Never let this plant loose in a flowerbed or it will take over, smothering many less-resistant perennials as it goes. It is stupendous in containers, though—try it and see!

Since you don't want goutweed to self-sow, it is best to remove the flowerheads before they go to seed.

Multiplication is a snap by division in spring or fall (even in midsummer!). The slightest piece of rhizome will produce a new plant. The variegated type does not come true from seed.

PROBLEMS AND SOLUTIONS

Leaf blight can cause brown marks during summer, especially on drought-stressed plants. Simply mow the plant back, and new blemish-free growth will quickly grow back in.

TOP PERFORMER

Think Twice: *Aegopodium podagraria* 'Variegatum' (variegated goutweed, variegated bishop's weed): This is the usual form seen in nurseries and gardens, with mid-green leaves bearing creamy white margins. It is said to be somewhat less invasive than the all-green form, but you won't notice the difference—this plant *spreads!* Complain as you will about its invasive nature, but it sure creates a beautiful effect when allowed to spread at will in deep shade. With its white-splashed leaves, it brings a touch of light to spots that really need it. It is especially beautiful when allowed to mingle with plants with extremely dark or even purple leaves: Imagine it as a carpet under purpleleaf plums, like *Prunus cerasifera* 'Newport' or *P. × cistena!* Height: 1 to 2 feet (30 to 60 cm). Spread: Indefinite. USDA Plant Hardiness Zones 2 to 8.

OTHER GOUTWEED
(NOTE: WE CAN'T REALLY USE "RECOMMENDED" HERE!)

Think Twice: *A. podagraria* (goutweed, bishop's weed): Rarely available commercially, this form of the previous plant with entirely green leaves can show up in gardens when *A. podagraria* 'Variegatum' is allowed to self-sow, as it produces green plants, not variegated ones, from seed. A true plant thug with few redeeming qualities, the best that can be said of it is that at least its dome-shaped white flowerheads show up better on the green background it creates than on the white-and-green foliage of variegated goutweed. Height: 1 to 2 feet (30 to 60 cm). Spread: Indefinite. USDA Plant Hardiness Zones 2 to 8.

Goutweed (*Aegopodium podagraria* 'Variegatum')

LARRY'S GARDEN NOTES

Goutweed is so ubiquitous and so well recognized that it probably has more common names than any other garden plant. Here are just a few: goutweed, bishop's weed, ground ash, ground elder, ashweed, herb Gerard, creeping Charlie, goatweed, snow on the mountain, and bishop's goutweed. There are probably dozens more in English alone, plus plenty in just about any language you can think of. Many of these names derive from the shape of the leaflets, said to resemble a goat's foot (*aego* is Greek for goat and *podion* for foot) or a bishop's hat. *Podagraria* also comes from Greek: *Podagra* means gout, a disease goutweed has long been used to treat.

Ajuga
Ajuga, bugleweed

AJUGA
uh-JOO-guh

Bloom Color:
Violet-blue, pink, and white

Bloom Time:
Late spring to early summer

Length of Bloom:
2 weeks or more

Height:
Varies by species; see individual listings

Spread:
Varies by species; see individual listings

Garden Uses:
Container planting, edging, groundcover, mass planting, mixed border, woodland garden; along paths, on slopes

Light Preference:
Full sun to shade

Soil Preference:
Humus-rich, well-drained, sandy soil

Best Way to Propagate:
Divide at any time

USDA Plant Hardiness Zones:
3 to 9 for most; see individual listings

If you're looking for a low-growing evergreen groundcover for both sun and shade, you've found it. Ajugas produce rosettes of somewhat spatula-shaped, shiny leaves that can be green but also purple or variegated. To add interest, at the end of spring, your almost-flat carpet of ajuga suddenly sends up numerous flowering spikes. After a few weeks of spectacular flowering, the blooms fade and the plant simply goes back to being a groundcover with attractive foliage. What's not to like?

GROWING TIPS

Just plant ajuga and let it grow—it will spread to cover as much or as little space as you want. It prefers partial shade and a moist, well-drained soil, but will still thrive in full sun as long as the soil remains relatively moist in summer. Even deep shade is fine as long as the plant gets its share of spring sun. Ajuga seems relatively unconcerned about soil quality, but it grows most thickly in soils that are both rich and well drained. Avoid low-lying spots that stay soaked; it will quickly rot away under such circumstances.

Dividing plants is the usual means of propagation. The species (and even some cultivars) come true from seed and often self-sow. If this is not what you want, consider mowing (yes, with the lawn mower!) the flowerstalks after the last flower fades but before seed is produced.

PROBLEMS AND SOLUTIONS

Poor drainage and poor air circulation, plus cold winter weather when the plants are not covered with snow, can occasionally cause major dieback. The plants do grow back, but may take a year or so. Try to ensure perfect drainage with an abundant supply of moisture, and dieback won't be a problem. Because of this, ajugas on slopes, where drainage is a given, often do better than ajugas planted on flat surfaces.

TOP PERFORMER

Ajuga reptans (common ajuga, common bugleweed): This is by far the most common species, although it is not really typical of ajugas in general because it multiplies not only slowly by short, creeping, underground rhizomes as do other ajugas, but also by longer above-ground stolons, so it spreads much more quickly than the others. It also means common ajuga can't be held back by root barriers—their aboveground stolons leap right over them. It will even creep over rocks or stumps to root on the other side. In other words, it's a bit invasive.

The species has green leaves and violet flowers, but there are now dozens of cultivars, either with green leaves and other flower colors ('Alba' has white blooms; 'Rosea' has pink ones) or, more commonly, with colorful foliage. There are numerous purple-leaf varieties, most with violet flowers, such as 'Atropurpurea' ('Purpurea'), with coppery leaves with a purple tinge, and 'Braunherz', which is even darker purple. 'Catlin's Giant' is, as the name suggests, twice as big as the others (to 12 inches/30 cm tall!) and looks like a giant 'Atropurpurea'. 'Silver Carpet' has green leaves overlaid with silver and is my favorite "silver" variety. 'Multicolor' ('Tricolor', 'Rainbow') has, as the name suggests, leaves that display three or more colors at once—purple, pink, yellow, and green are possible combinations. Height: 6 to 8 inches (15 to 20 cm). Spread: Indefinite. USDA Plant Hardiness Zones 3 to 9.

MORE RECOMMENDED AJUGAS

Ajuga genevensis (Geneva bugleweed): If common bugleweed's propensity to spread rapidly makes it a great groundcover, this species' slower increase makes it a choicer plant for edges. It has longer, hairy, coarse-toothed leaves, usually dark green, and forms a thick, weedproof mat of foliage. The upright spikes of violet-blue appear just a bit later—more early summer than late spring. The leaves are completely evergreen only where winters are mild; elsewhere they may burn in winter. 'Pink Beauty' is the usual cultivar with pink flowers. It is slightly less hardy (Zone 5) than the species. Height: 6 to 8 inches (15 to 20 cm). Spread: 8 to 10 inches (20 to 25 cm). USDA Plant Hardiness Zones 3 to 9.

Bugleweed (*Ajuga reptans*)

LARRY'S GARDEN NOTES

I like the way common bugleweed spreads in and around other plants without smothering them. It is ideal under shrubs, trees, and also even fairly short perennials, such as barrenworts and geraniums. I let *A. reptans* 'Atropurpurea' run into the lawn, where it forms small patches of purplish foliage here and there and fills in those spots where the lawn grasses weren't doing too well anyway. Too bad it isn't more resistant to foot traffic (it will tolerate some, but not nearly as much as a grass lawn), as it would make a great lawn. Imagine—it needs mowing only once a year to cut back the fading flowers!

Anemone

Anemone, windflower

PLANT PROFILE

ANEMONE

uh-NEM-oh-nee

Bloom Color:
White, pink, red, and purple

Bloom Time:
Late summer to late fall

Length of Bloom:
5 weeks or more

Height:
18 to 60 inches (45 to 150 cm)

Spread:
18 to 24 inches (45 to 60 cm)

Garden Uses:
Cut flower garden, groundcover, mass planting, mixed border, woodland garden; at the back of beds and borders

Light Preference:
Full sun to partial shade

Soil Preference:
Humus-rich, moist, well-drained soil

Best Way to Propagate:
Divide or take root cuttings in early spring

USDA Plant Hardiness Zones:
Varies by species; see individual listings

The genus *Anenome* has some truly great flowers to offer shade gardeners, notably some spectacular early-blooming bulbs, which are described on page 274. The fall-blooming anemones, described here, don't grow from tubers but are fibrous-rooted plants that come from open woodlands in Asia. They're rather like two plants in one: From spring through midsummer their beautifully textured maplelike leaves create a wonderful groundcover effect, then at the end of summer and into fall they produce tall, wispy flower stems that bear surprisingly large daisylike flowers, often in such great numbers the shade garden seems to sparkle like a thousand jewels.

GROWING TIPS

You have to coddle anemones initially as they are slow to establish. Provide moist, well-drained, rich soil and let them get a bit of extra light by thinning overhead branches or pruning back any competitors. Once they reach the stage where they're starting to spread, though—and this takes a few years—they become tough as nails, so you can just sit back and let 'em rip.

Division is the most obvious way to reproduce them, although you can also multiply them by root cuttings. They won't need any care, not even division, to bloom up a storm for decades.

Anemones prefer partial shade (deeper shade in the South) but tolerate full sun where the soil is moist. Rich, friable soils are very much to their liking, but ordinary garden soil is fine as well, especially if you cover it with a good mulch. A mulch is also very wise in the South—they don't appreciate hot summers so a good mulch, plus periodic watering, will help keep them cooler.

Warning: All parts of these plants are poisonous, so keep them out of the hands of young children.

PROBLEMS AND SOLUTIONS

Leaf diseases, most of little consequence, can occur. See "Disease Control" on page 86 for suggestions on controlling them.

TOP PERFORMER

Anemone tomentosa (grapeleaf anenome): This is probably the most widely adapted anemone, growing equally well in both cold climates and warm ones and just a bit more shade-tolerant than most, although partial shade is still better than shade. The foliage is very attractive in itself, so it makes an outstanding groundcover, but the 2- to 3-inch (5- to 8-cm) cup-shaped flowers with a yellow center are also most inviting. It forms dense clumps, spreading by occasional underground stolons that form new clumps at a distance. The grapeleaf anemone is one of the earliest-blooming fall anemones, usually starting to flower in late summer. Identity theft is a common crime among fall-flowering anemones; plants sold as *A. vitifolia* probably belong here, although there is a true *A. vitifolia* that is less commonly grown. 'Robustissima' (don't be surprised to see it labeled *A. vitifolia* 'Robustissima' or *A.* × *hybrida* 'Robustissima' as well as *A. tomentosa* 'Robustissima') is a particularly hardy clone, to Zone 3, and is therefore the fall anemone of choice in cold-winter areas. Height: 3 feet (90 cm). Spread: 20 to 32 inches (50 to 80 cm). USDA Plant Hardiness Zones 4 to 8.

MORE RECOMMENDED ANEMONES

Anemone × *hybrida*, often called *A. japonica* (Japanese anemone, hybrid anemone): As the name suggests, this is a hybrid plant of Japanese origin, resulting from crosses between *A. hupehensis* var. *japonica* and *A. vitifolia*. Nearly sterile, it only rarely produces seed and is multiplied by division or root cuttings. It is usually a fall bloomer and has a suckering habit, forming an even carpet of foliage as it spreads. Because of its large flowers (up to 4 inches/10 cm across) and generally greater height than other fall anemones, it is the species most likely to need staking. Dozens of cultivars are available with single, semi-double, or double flowers. These include 'Honorine Jobert', with single white flowers; 'Königin Charlotte' (also called 'Queen Charlotte'), a semidouble pink; 'Pamina', a shorter-growing (only 2 to 3 feet/60 to 90 cm) cultivar with double red blooms; and an early-blooming cultivar called 'Whirlwind' with semidouble white flowers. Height: 2 to 5 feet (60 to 150 cm). Spread: 18 to 24 inches (45 to 60 cm). USDA Plant Hardiness Zones 5 to 7.

Japanese anemone
(*Anemone* × *hybrida*)

LARRY'S GARDEN NOTES

Anemone is a Greek word of uncertain origin. Some claim it comes from *anemos* (wind), for many species grow in windy spots, and windflower is a common name used for most anemones. Alternately, it may be named for the Greek hunter Naamen, an alternate name for Adonis. Killed by a wild boar, his blood splattered onto the flowers of the field where he died, turning them blood red—and to this day, Greece's common anemone, *A. coronaria*, has red flowers. Of course, there is also another Greek flower with blood red blooms called *Adonis annua*, which also has claims to that story—but let's not go there!

Aquilegia
Columbine

The word "dainty" always comes to mind when I think of columbines. Their thin yet solid stems bear delicate, wedge-shaped leaves and upright or dangling flowers that dance lightly in the wind. The blooms are often bicolored, with tubular petals surrounded by a crown of sepals of a very different shade. I particularly like the kinds that have backward-projecting spurs: They're the ones hummingbirds like the best.

GROWING TIPS

How well columbines adapt to shade is variable: Most are fine in sun to partial shade, but some take much darker conditions. Curiously, the degree of shade-tolerance can vary even among plants in the same hybrid series. I suggest growing columbines from seed (a very simple process) and giving them a trial run in a fairly shaded spot. The most shade-tolerant will settle into your darkest nooks.

Good, rich garden soil is best, although sandy soil is acceptable. Heavy clay is best avoided. Columbines do best in spots that remain at least slightly moist. They prefer cooler summers and are not the best choices for the Deep South. You can, however, have success there by giving them fairly dense shade and deep mulch—or treating them as annuals.

This is one plant you *will* want to self-seed because columbines are notoriously short-lived. You'll want volunteer plants to ensure their long-term survival. Just make sure you leave a bit of soil unmulched here and there so they can sow themselves in.

PROBLEMS AND SOLUTIONS

Think Twice: Pest and disease resistance is *not* the columbine's forte. Leaf miners are essentially ubiquitous, and often the leaves that miners miss are fully consumed by caterpillars, infested by aphids, or ravaged by mildew. By midsummer, most columbines have few if any leaves left. I recommend a preemptive strike: Cut the leaves back after the plant blooms. Depending on the species, either new foliage appears immediately (and, oddly enough, fresh leaves seem fully pest- and disease-resistant!), or the plant remains dormant until the following spring, then sprouts anew.

TOP PERFORMER

Aquilegia canadensis (wild columbine, Canadian columbine): This spring-blooming plant, one of the earliest columbines, is native to much of eastern North America and is often found in dense shade in the wild. It is more resistant to pests and diseases than most columbines. The flowers have red to dark pink sepals and yellow petals. 'Corbett' is entirely yellow; 'Little Lanterns' is a dwarf form only 10 to 12 inches (25 to 30 cm) tall. Height: 2 to 3 feet (60 to 90 cm). Spread: 1 foot (30 cm). USDA Plant Hardiness Zones 2 to 8.

MORE RECOMMENDED COLUMBINES

Aquilegia caerulea (Rocky Mountain columbine): Another shade-tolerant columbine, with large, upright flowers bearing long spurs. The species has white petals and blue to purple sepals, but there are now dozens of cultivars in various shades of red, pink, white, and yellow, most of which are probably hybrids with other species: 'Crimson Star', for example, with crimson-and-white flowers. This is one of the longest-lived columbines—some plants live to be as ancient as 4 or 5 years! Height: 20 to 30 inches (50 to 75 cm). Spread: 1 foot (30 cm). USDA Plant Hardiness Zones 3 to 8.

A. × hybrida (hybrid columbine): Do you like your columbines tall or short? Spring-blooming or summer-blooming? With bicolor or unicolor flowers? You'll get all this and more with the hybrid columbine, a true mishmash of columbines of all sorts. Most popular are the long-spurred hybrids, with long, elegant projections from the back of the flowers. The short-spurred strains, closely related to the European species *A. vulgaris* and often listed under that name, also include some rather hideous doubles. The latter, like the green-and-pink 'Norah Barlow', look like a flower that is trying hard to be a dahlia but has failed miserably. Height: 9 to 30 inches (23 to 75 cm). Spread: 1 foot (30 cm). USDA Plant Hardiness Zones 3 to 9.

KISSING COUSINS

One plant I grow that always stumps even visiting plant experts is semiaquilegia (*Semiaquilegia ecalcarata*)—it is so much like a columbine, even down to the foliage and short life cycle, that it is easy to fool people, yet botanists insist it is a different genus. The only real difference I can see is that the hanging flowers have no spurs at all, not even short ones, and have wider sepals than true colmbines. For some reason, the dangling blooms always remind me of helicopters! *S. ecalcarata*, the only species with much of a distribution, has pink to reddish flowers—both petals and sepals are similar or identical in color. Grow under the same conditions as columbine, in sun to partial shade. Height: 16 inches (40 cm). Spread: 1 foot (30 cm). USDA Plant Hardiness Zones 3 to 7.

Wild columbine
(*Aquilegia canadensis*)

Aruncus
Goat's beard

Goat's beard is a big, bushy plant that looks more like a shrub than a typical perennial. Its feathery plumes of creamy white flowers at the tips of its stems are its main drawing card. Once the flowers are less dominant, the beautiful dark green fernlike leaves take over as visual appeal, maintaining interest through fall.

GROWING TIPS

Tough as nails, slow as molasses. That about sums it up. It can take a clump of goat's beard a full decade or more to reach its full height and spread, especially when it is grown in deep shade, but it looks good, if less dense, from year one. If you want instant height, try to buy mature plants rather than the young specimens usually sold.

Goat's beard will likewise put up with most growing conditions, from full sun to deep shade. Partial shade is best, though, allowing for abundant bloom (plants in deep shade flower only weakly) yet helping to protect goat's beard from its worst enemy: drought. Established plants (and remember, it can take years for a young plant to get to this stage) are drought-resistant but obviously don't enjoy the experience. It's best to grow this plant in constantly moist soil or to keep it well mulched. It will even grow beautifully in boggy conditions. Extreme heat is likewise harmful—the farther south you live, the happier the plant will be in shade. Mulching will help there, too.

Just plant it and leave it. This plant never needs dividing and thrives on neglect—moving it around or dividing it regularly slows it down. However, division of young plants is the easiest means of multiplying it: Older plants have woody roots, and you'll need an axe or a saw to divide them.

The only thing you'll probably want to do with this no-nonsense perennial is cut back the dead stems in spring, at snow melt, to leave room for those of the coming season.

PROBLEMS AND SOLUTIONS

What problems? This plant comes about as close to being trouble-free as any. Leaf spot is occasionally a problem, notably when the plant is heat- or drought-stressed, but is rarely visible enough to require treatment.

TOP PERFORMER

Aruncus dioicus, also called *A. sylvester* or *Spiraea aruncus* (goat's beard): By far the most common of the goat's beards. In fact, it is native throughout much of the Northern Hemisphere. This is the big, shrubby plant most people think of when they picture a goat's beard and produces the massive, frothy, creamy white flower spikes described above. There are several varieties and cultivars, although only 'Kneiffii', with deeply incised leaves much like a Japanese maple, is widely available. The latter is only about 3 feet (90 cm) tall and wide. It must be multiplied by division as it is not true from seed. 'Zweiweltenkind' ('Child of Two Worlds') is a purported hybrid between *A. dioicus* and Chinese goat's beard (*A. sinensis,* a rarely grown Asiatic species that may in fact be simply a variant of *A. dioicus*). It is said to have somewhat bronzy leaves and a more upright habit, but I've only just obtained a plant and can't yet comment on its performance. Height: 4 to 6 feet (1.2 to 1.8 m). Spread: 4 to 6 feet (1.2 to 1.8 m). USDA Plant Hardiness Zones 2 to 7.

MORE RECOMMENDED GOAT'S BEARDS

Aruncus aethusifolius (dwarf goat's beard): The taxonomy of goat's beards is very confused and some authors allow only two species, *A. dioicus* and this one, all other species being variants or hybrids of the two. Certainly this is the only "other" goat's beard with any distribution in nurseries. This is a much smaller species, ideal for tighter spots where its giant brother just has no space, but it is just as inherently tough. It produces dark green, deeply cut leaves that are almost lacy in appearance, as well as smaller, finer sprays of the same feathery white flowers as *A. dioicus.* Its leaves turn a very pretty yellow in fall. Height: 4 to 6 inches (12 to 15 cm). Spread: 1 to 1½ feet (30 to 45 cm). USDA Plant Hardiness Zones 4 to 7.

LARRY'S GARDEN NOTES

One of the nicest hedges I ever saw was composed not of shrubs but of goat's beards planted in a row in front of a farmhouse. The hedge was as full and as dense as any shrub could be and coiffed with beautiful feathery white blooms. When I stopped to take a picture, the owner came out and we talked a bit. It turned out the owner had unsuccessfully tried twice to grow a "traditional" hedge, once of arborvitae and the other time of lilacs, but snow shoved onto the plants from a passing snowplow kept tearing off branches, and they never filled in properly. With goat's beard, though, the entire hedge sprouts anew from underground each spring, eliminating damage from the snowplow.

Goat's beard (*Aruncus dioicus*)

Asarum

Wild ginger

PLANT PROFILE

ASARUM

uh-SAH-rum

Bloom Color:
Brown and purple

Bloom Time:
Spring

Length of Bloom:
2 weeks

Height:
4 to 9 inches (10 to 23 cm)

Spread:
Indefinite

Garden Uses:
Edging, groundcover, mass planting, rock garden, woodland garden; on slopes

Light Preference:
Partial shade to shade

Soil Preference:
Humus-rich, well-drained, evenly moist soil

Best Way to Propagate:
Divide in spring or fall

USDA Plant Hardiness Zones:
Varies by species; see individual listings

I find it curious that wild gingers remain so little known outside of collectors' gardens. With their creeping rhizomes densely covered with overlapping heart-shaped foliage, they make ideal groundcovers, creating a perfect carpet of greenery even in deep shade, yet they spread slowly enough not to be invasive. As for their flowers—well, you can't have everything. Most wild gingers have insignificant blooms that lie on the ground and are often covered by dead leaves. Slugs and beetles, it is said, are their main pollinators!

GROWING TIPS

Shade is a way of life for wild gingers. In their native haunts, the deep deciduous woodlands of the Northern Hemisphere, they rarely receive anything more than the occasional dappled ray of sun. In culture, they're the perfect choice for shade of all levels. They prefer deep, humus-rich soil, but they cope very well with root competition once established. Wild gingers tolerate drought but not constantly dry soils. In the wild, they are often located in seasonally wet soils that dry out more thoroughly during summer.

There is not much to growing wild gingers—just plant them about 9 to 12 inches (23 to 30 cm) apart, mulch them, and keep them moist for the first summer. You can then totally ignore them. No care whatsoever is required: no pruning, no deadheading, no dividing, not even any fertilizing. Should they wander too far, you can readily pull out the surplus plants. Planting them along a path is an ideal way of controlling their spread as they're intolerant of foot traffic and therefore you control their spread as you stroll along. As you step on wayward stems, the air will fill with a deliciously gingerlike scent.

Multiplication by division is a snap; large colonies will yield many plants.

PROBLEMS AND SOLUTIONS

Slugs and snails seem to relish the first tender leaves of spring but tend to leave the mature ones alone. See page 85 for suggested controls. Leaf diseases are occasional problems.

TOP PERFORMER

Asarum canadense (Canadian wild ginger): This species gets top billing for its great adaptability. It already has the widest range of any *Asarum* in nature—throughout most of Eastern North America—and is hardier than the other species yet just as heat-tolerant. As long as your local climate is considered temperate and not tropical, you can probably grow it. It is one of the few deciduous species of wild ginger. The heart-shaped leaves, about 6 inches (15 cm) in diameter and dull green with an interesting texture, die back in fall and sprout again early in spring. The jug-shaped greenish brown flowers appear at the same time, so they are sometimes visible on their leaf-litter bed before the leaves fill in entirely. This is probably the fastest-growing of all wild gingers and rapidly makes a superb groundcover. Height: 4 to 8 inches (10 to 20 cm). Spread: Indefinite. USDA Plant Hardiness Zones 3 to 8.

MORE RECOMMENDED WILD GINGERS

Asarum shuttleworthii, also called *Hexastylis shuttleworthii* (mottled wild ginger): This species from the Appalachians is perhaps the most widely available of a whole range of evergreen wild gingers with silver mottled foliage. If the leaves are stunning, though, the purplish flowers are typically insignificant, as with most wild gingers. Each colony seems to have its own leaf color, and even self-sown seedlings have their own silver pattern, so it isn't surprising that there is an increasingly wide range of cultivars, including 'Callaway', with very heavy silver marbling. It is far hardier than given credit for, thriving in my Zone 3 garden under snow, but can suffer severe winter burn when leaves are left exposed, even in Zone 4, so Zone 5 is a more appropriate category. Look for other silver-mottled wild gingers, including *A. arifolium*, *A. maculatum*, *A. splendens*, and dozens more. Once you've discovered the silver-mottled foliage of these wild gingers, you'll want them all! Height: 4 to 9 inches (10 to 23 cm). Spread: Indefinite. USDA Plant Hardiness Zones 5 to 9.

Mottled wild ginger
(*Asarum shuttleworthii*)

KISSING COUSINS

Upright wild ginger (*Saruma henryi*) is a close relative of the wild gingers but with a different growth habit. Instead of spreading horizontally via underground rhizomes, it forms clumps of upright stems. The light green leaves are slightly hairy. It is deciduous, dying to the ground in winter. Unlike its creeping relatives, this plant has very visible yellow flowers that first appear in late spring but continue sporadically throughout summer thereafter, especially in cool-summer areas. It is just as much of a "plant-it-and-leave-it" plant as *A. canadense* and its relatives. This plant is relatively new and has not yet been thoroughly tested, but I feel that the Zone 6 given by some authors is drastically underestimating its true potential. It positively thrives in my Zone 3 garden, although in a protected spot. Height: 18 to 24 inches (45 to 60 cm). Spread: 30 inches (75 cm). Approximate USDA Plant Hardiness Zones 4 to 9.

Astilbe
Astilbe, false spirea

Ask any gardener to name a shade perennial and he'll first say hosta. But his *second* choice will be astilbe! And why not? There are literally hundreds of varieties to choose from, ranging from tiny edging or rock garden plants to tall, back-of-the-border giants, with green or reddish green leaves and a huge range of flower colors. Typically astilbes have deeply cut, fernlike leaves that show up early in spring and last until frost, with feathery bouquets of tiny flowers that last for ages and which, if you leave them alone, dry on the spot, even adding winter color. Easy, varied, and beautiful—no wonder astilbes are so popular.

GROWING TIPS

First and foremost, it must be said that astilbes aren't really "shade plants" per se; they're "partial-shade plants." In true shade, they'll grow and produce great foliage but bloom only very lightly. In partial shade, you'll get both great foliage and superb bloom. They'll even do perfectly well in full sun, especially in cooler climates, as long as their roots remain moist at all times.

Constant moisture truly is the secret to their success. Astilbes will adapt to most soils, but not to dry ones. They'll quickly peter out under root competition where trees above suck the soil dry, yet thrive in root competition if moisture remains available.

Astilbes can be truly no-care if you let them. They don't need much of anything—just plant 'em and leave 'em. I never prune off the faded flowers, for example (unless I need some for dried arrangements)—they turn brown, it's true, but still add interest right into winter. By spring, both foliage and flower stems have collapsed, and new foliage quickly sprouts to cover the remains. Even division isn't technically necessary. True enough, when they become crowded they may bloom less, but they still do bloom. Just plant them in clumps of 5 to 7 or more plants so any decrease in flowering won't be noticed.

PROBLEMS AND SOLUTIONS

Drought is their main enemy, and newly planted astilbes may die if they are not kept moist. Established plants may turn brown along the edges or even go dormant for summer if allowed to dry out, but they usually survive. However, a dry astilbe is not a happy camper. Mulch them, water them, but keep them moist! Other than that, there are few problems, although Japanese beetles will eventually get to them—once they've eaten everything else. For treatments, see page 84.

TOP PERFORMER

Astilbe × *arendsii* or simply *Astilbe* Hybrids (hybrid astilbe): Taxonomists have sometimes tried to classify the numerous complex astilbe hybrids under various names such as *A.* × *hybrida, A.* × *rosea, A. japonica* Hybrids, and so on, but then can't seem to agree which cultivar belongs where. I prefer to present them under the name *A.* × *arendsii*, after the man who created most of them (see "Larry's Garden Notes"), also the name preferred by most reference books. This is a real mixed bag of plants of various heights and colors, mostly early- to mid-season bloomers. Most have green leaves, but some, especially the red-flowered ones, have bronze foliage, and leaves can be as deeply cut as lace or fairly coarse. There are well over 100 cultivars that belong here, including 'Peach Blossom' (my wife's favorite), a peachy pink early bloomer; 'Peaches and Cream', a midseason bloomer with peach-pink blossoms; 'Fanal', early with dark red flowers and bronzy foliage; and 'Weisse Gloria' ('White Gloria'), in my opinion the best white and a late bloomer. Height: 24 to 48 inches (60 to 120 cm). Spread: 24 to 30 inches (60 to 75 cm). USDA Plant Hardiness Zones 4 to 9.

MORE RECOMMENDED ASTILBES

Astilbe Simplicifolia Hybrids, also sold as *A. simplicifolia* (star astilbe): There are some 12 species of astilbe and all make great garden plants. The true star astilbe (*A. simplicifolia*) is a dwarf plant with simple, toothed leaves, I'm told, as I have never seen it nor have I seen it for sale. However, through hybridization, it has transmitted its small size to a whole series of tiny astilbes, all with deeply cut foliage. They produce loose clusters of starlike flowers, generally in late summer, and are among the smallest astilbes. 'Sprite' was the Perennial Plant Association's perennial of the year for 1994. It's a cute little thing with dark bronzy green foliage and light pink flowers. Height: 10 to 18 inches (25 to 45 cm). Spread: 2 feet (60 cm). USDA Plant Hardiness Zones 4 to 9.

Astilbe (*Astilbe* 'Peaches and Cream')

LARRY'S GARDEN NOTES

One thing that really irks me about astilbes is the multiplicity of their names. Most of the garden hybrids we grow were developed by the incredible German hybridizer George Arends (1862–1952), and he dutifully gave his plants cultivar names (generally in his own language, German). The whole point of cultivar names is to identify a plant so no confusion can occur, and they are *never* to be translated. Yet nurserymen have freely broken that international code of ethics, with the result that many of his hybrids show up on the market under two different names! Who knew that 'Bridal Veil' was really 'Brautschleier' or 'Ostrich Feather' was really 'Straussenfeder'? It's infuriating to gardeners to buy "different" plants only to find they've purchased the same plant twice.

Astrantia
Masterwort

Here's a plant that has so many advantages it should be among the most popular of garden plants, yet it remains relatively unknown to most North American gardeners. I love both its attractive deep green maplelike leaves and its curious but beautiful flowers. The blooms are actually inflorescences—tiny flowers arranged in rounded bundles and surrounded by a spiky collar of bracts (colored leaves), giving the impression of a tiny pincushion. Since each flowerstalk produces numerous pincushions over a very long period (indeed, under the best conditions, there will be sporadic bloom right through summer), the effect is quite magical.

GROWING TIPS

The masterwort is a plant of the open woods and moist meadows in its native Europe and will appreciate similar conditions in culture: sun to partial shade, fairly rich soil, and even moisture. It does not appreciate extreme heat and humidity. However, in the Deep South, where sunlight is intense anyway, try them in deep shade—and mulch to keep the roots cool.

Masterworts are fine under controlled conditions like formal borders, easily creating a mass effect. They do spread a little through underground rhizomes but can easily be held back if they go too far, and you can deadhead them to prevent self-seeding. That said, however, I prefer using them in less formal situations. Plant them on the edge of a woodland garden, for example, and let them find their own spot. They self-sow here and there, creating a natural appearance that no amount of careful planning can ever seem to recreate.

The best way of multiplying masterworts is by division, either by lifting and dividing the mother plant as the original clump becomes fuller, or simply by cutting free and removing the offsets borne by creeping underground stems. If you're striving to maintain choice cultivars, consider deadheading them to prevent the production of seed and the resulting appearance of not-quite-identical self-sown plants. If cultivar names mean nothing to you, though, just pick masterworts in an array of colors and let them self-sow with abandon, creating a rainbow of colors.

PROBLEMS AND SOLUTIONS

Slugs or snails may be a minor problem, especially on new leaves, but I've personally never had any problems with masterwort.

TOP PERFORMER

Astrantia major (great masterwort): This is the most popular species and also the most widely adaptable. It blooms abundantly for a long period in late spring through early summer, but also sporadically throughout summer where conditions are to its liking. The species normally produces greenish flowers surrounded by white bracts, themselves highlighted by green veins. 'Alba' is a good choice for shadier nooks, as its pure white flowers really stand out in a dark environment. *A. major* var. *rosea,* often sold as *A. major* 'Rosea', gives pink blooms, but the exact coloration varies from plant to plant. 'Rosensymphonie' ('Rose Symphony') is a more intense pink; 'Rubra', as the name suggests, is red. As it is often raised from seed, its color can be a bit variable. *A. major* ssp. *involucrata* is a subspecies with extra-large collars of which 'Shaggy' ('Margery Fish'), a beautifully fringed variety in white with a distinct green tip, is the most widely available selection. 'Sunningdale Variegated' is the most popular variegated clone, with pink-tinged bracts but leaves margined in yellow to white. Height: 24 to 36 inches (60 to 90 cm). Spread: 18 to 24 inches (45 to 60 cm). USDA Plant Hardiness Zones 4 to 7.

MORE RECOMMENDED MASTERWORTS

Astrantia carniolica (lesser masterwort): As the common name suggests, it's a smaller plant than greater masterwort, with narrower, more deeply cut leaves. It blooms as readily and abundantly as its bigger cousin and over just as long a season. The species has greenish white flowers that often take on a pinkish tinge as they mature, but the cultivar most offered, 'Rubra', has dark red flowers with a silvery sheen. Height: 12 to 18 inches (30 to 45 cm). Spread: 18 to 24 inches (45 to 60 cm). USDA Plant Hardiness Zones 4 to 7.

Great masterwort (*Astrantia major* ssp. *involucrata* 'Shaggy')

LARRY'S GARDEN NOTES

The botanical name *Astrantia* comes from the starlike shape of the flowers—*aster* is Latin for star. However, the derivation of the English name "masterwort" is less clear. One theory is that it also comes from *aster* and that the plant was originally called "asterwort" (wort is Old English for plant). The "m" would have been added later because the word "master" sounded more familiar to English ears than "aster." Another theory is that the plant was formerly associated with its relative, *Angelica*, also called "masterwort" in English (and justifiably so, since it is a gigantic plant that easily "masters" the plants around it).

Bergenia
Bergenia, pigsqueak

PLANT PROFILE

BERGENIA

ber-GEEN-ee-uh

Bloom Color:
  Pink, rose, red, purple, and white

Bloom Time:
  Late winter through mid- to late spring

Length of Bloom:
  3 weeks or more

Height:
  12 to 18 inches (30 to 45 cm)

Spread:
  1 to 2 feet (30 to 60 cm)

Garden Uses:
  Container planting, cut flower garden, edging, groundcover, mixed border, rock garden, wall planting, woodland garden; along paths, on slopes, in wet areas

Light Preference:
  Full sun to shade

Soil Preference:
  Moist, humus-rich, well-drained soil

Best Way to Propagate:
  Divide in spring

USDA Plant Hardiness Zones:
  3 to 9

Cabbage, anyone? Not that I mean that in a bad way, but the huge, shiny, leathery, rounded leaves of the bergenia, formed into open rosettes, do make it look a lot like a cabbage—an ornamental cabbage, of course. I suggest growing this plant essentially for its foliage and seeing flowers as a secondary effect. Not that they're not attractive, mind you; the stout flowerstalks rise up early in spring, making this one of the first perennials to bloom. Even so, it's the evergreen foliage—dark green in summer, purple-tinged to entirely bronzy purple fall through late spring—that makes this plant justly popular.

GROWING TIPS

Bergenia will grow practically everywhere: in fairly dry soils or moist, swampy ones; in nearly pure compost or pure sand; in full sun or deep shade. Indeed, it's hard to imagine a spot where it won't thrive.

Shade gardeners will find bergenia does best in areas with some sun (i.e., partial shade). It will grow but not bloom (or bloom only rarely) in shade. Also, its foliage turns more attractive colors in fall in sun or partial shade. On the other hand, if you don't care about the blooms or leaf color, deep shade is fine. Full sun is also great, although the bergenia does prefer moist soil under such circumstances and may suffer from winter damage to its foliage (there is nothing harder on evergreen leaves than the drying effect of winter sun!). Where snowfall is abundant, though, and even where the climate is downright cold, the leaves come through winter in mint condition.

Since bergenias root slowly, it's best to divide them in early spring, just after they flower, rather than in fall. That way the plant will be well established by fall and not subject to frost-heaving. For a slow-growing plant, bergenias are surprisingly easy from seed. Scatter the fine seed over the still-cold ground in spring, and solid (if small) rosettes will already be very evident by fall. These can be transferred to a more permanent space the following spring. Remember that most bergenias are hybrids and will not come true from seed.

PROBLEMS AND SOLUTIONS

Winter damage can be considerable on bergenias grown in full sun in snowless but cold climates. They do recover in spring, but they'll be happier campers if you move them to partial shade.

TOP PERFORMER

Bergenia Hybrids (hybrid bergenia): Most plants labeled *B. cordifolia* (heartleaf bergenia) actually aren't; they are hybrids with a lot of *B. cordifolia* "blood." This group of plants has the shiny, leathery, heart-shaped foliage we think of as typical for a bergenia and usually pink flowers, although there are red-, purple-, and white-flowered cultivars as well. There are dozens of cultivars, most fairly similar. For a good, solid plant with typical pink flowers and good fall/winter color, think of 'Abendglut' ('Evening Glow'). 'Baby Doll' stands out from the crowd due to its much smaller leaves, giving the plant a more "delicate" appearance. 'Silberlicht' ('Silver Light') is my favorite, with white flowers with a pink eye; the flowers age to pink. If you want white flowers that stay white, try 'Bressingham White'. If you want redder flowers (more carmine than scarlet, though), try 'Morgenröte' ('Morning Red'), which sometimes blooms twice a year, in both spring and fall. 'Tubby Andrews' has pink flowers like so many others but interestingly variegated leaves: mottled creamy yellow in summer, but pink in winter. It also tends to rebloom, albeit modestly, in fall. Height: 12 to 18 inches (30 to 45 cm). Spread: 12 to 24 inches (30 to 60 cm). USDA Plant Hardiness Zones 3 to 9.

MORE RECOMMENDED BERGENIAS

Bergenia ciliata (winter begonia, fringed bergenia): There are lots of evergreen bergenias that look a lot like *B. cordifolia* and its hybrids; *B. crassifolia, B. purpurascens,* and so on are all are interesting. But for a truly different bergenia, try *B. ciliata*. Its leaves are fuzzy, making it look like an African violet, although the upright stalks of white flowers fading to pink are a dead giveaway. It loses its leaves in fall and prefers a good, thick mulch in colder climates. Height: 12 to 15 inches (30 to 38 cm). Spread: 1 foot (30 cm). USDA Plant Hardiness Zones 4 to 9.

Heartleaf bergenia
(*Bergenia cordifolia*)

LARRY'S GARDEN NOTES

Bergenia probably has one of the greatest ranges of any perennial. I've seen it growing well in Scandanavia, above the Arctic Circle, where winters are extremely cold, yet also in Cannes, on the Cote d'Azur, where frost is rare and palm trees are more common than spruce trees. Likewise, it can be a permanent groundcover or a flowerbed component, but it also makes a superb container plant. I've even seen it dangling from a cliff face, its thick stems stretching downward a good 15 feet (5 m). In other words, no matter where you garden or under which conditions, this is one perennial you can grow without problem.

Brunnera

Brunnera, Siberian bugloss

PLANT PROFILE

BRUNNERA

BRUN-er-uh

Bloom Color:
  Blue

Bloom Time:
  Early to late spring

Length of Bloom:
  4 weeks or more

Height:
  12 to 18 inches (30 to 45 cm)

Spread:
  18 to 24 inches (45 to 60 cm)

Garden Uses:
  Cut flower garden,
  groundcover, mass planting,
  mixed border, specimen
  plant, woodland garden; in
  wet areas

Light Preference:
  Sun (spring); partial shade to
  shade (summer)

Soil Preference:
  Evenly moist, humus-rich soil

Best Way to Propagate:
  Divide in spring or fall

USDA Plant Hardiness Zones:
  3 to 7

Rarely do you see a plant change so radically in appearance in just one season. In spring, brunnera is a rounded mass of thin stems and small, medium-green leaves abundantly dotted with tiny five-petaled blue flowers just like forget-me-nots (*Myosotis* spp., page 198). After a fairly lengthy period of bloom, the flowerstalks bend down, the small leaves fade away, and brand-new leaves, this time huge, 8 inches (20 cm) across and heart-shaped, appear, forming a wide rosette more like a hosta than a forget-me-not. The result is you get two plants for the price of one: a light, airy flowering plant in spring, and a mounded hosta substitute in summer.

GROWING TIPS

Siberian bugloss likes rich, deep soil and lots of moisture. It will even grow with its roots dipping into a water garden or a gurgling brook—or in one of those spots, so common in nature, that is soaking wet for weeks in spring, then drier in summer. A good mulch and a soaker hose may be needed to keep Siberian bugloss happy in dry summer areas.

This plant seems relatively indifferent to light. Partial shade is ideal, but shade is fine as well as long as it is summer shade only (i.e., under deciduous trees). It does seem to need some full sun in spring. And Siberian bugloss is fine in full sun as well where you can keep it evenly moist.

The individual plants are not long-lived—4 or 5 years at the most. You can maintain the species itself by simply letting it self-sow, but none of the cultivars come fully true from seed. Instead, propagate them by division in fall, when the plants are nearing dormancy.

If you've purchased seed of Siberian bugloss, simply sprinkle it on the ground in late summer or fall, where it is to grow or in a nursery bed. Rake in lightly and water well. Seeds often sprout immediately. Or, they may not sprout until the following spring. To sow indoors, just sprinkle seed on top of a container of moist soil and refrigerate for a month. When exposed to heat and to light, the seed should germinate promptly.

PROBLEMS AND SOLUTIONS

Pests and diseases are infrequent, but do be prepared to water regularly to prevent drought damage (dry, brown leaves).

TOP PERFORMER

Brunnera macrophylla (Siberian bugloss): There is just one species of brunnera commonly grown—this one. It is most widely offered in its natural form, with green foliage and blue flowers.

There are also variegated forms of Siberian bugloss, some with white to cream mottling, others with silver variegation. Both types are extremely attractive and liable to set gardeners' mouths watering. They also tend to be expensive, as they are difficult to reproduce on a large scale. 'Dawson's White' ('Variegata') is irregularly margined white or cream and has typical blue flowers. It is a knockout but can be hard to grow. Keep it cool and moist and avoid intense summer sun and strong winds, as it burns readily. 'Hadspen Cream' is very similar and just as gorgeous and is said to be a tougher plant, more tolerant of both drought and sun, but still, I find it rather short-lived and hard to reproduce (root cuttings, notably, sometimes give all-green plants). 'Gordano Gold' is another variegate, with green leaves irregularly mottled golden yellow—pretty, but touchy to grow.

Much easier to maintain are the silver variegated plants. That's understandable because if white and yellow variegation result from a partial lack of chlorophyll and therefore a leaf that does not perform its full duties of light absorption, silver variegation is just a translucent overlay on the leaf. The whole leaf surface can still carry out "business as usual," leading to a plant that ought to be as sturdy as its all-green parent. First to come out was 'Langtrees' ('Aluminum Spot'), with beautiful silver spotting on a dark green leaf, but more recently 'Jack Frost' has come on the market: Its leaves are entirely iridescent silver with only green veins, giving the leaf a beautiful plushy texture. Striking! 'Silver Wings' has more green to the leaf but still plenty of silver, and also a thin white margin. I grow both of the latter plants and would be hard-pressed to recommend one over the other—they are both drop-dead gorgeous!

Siberian bugloss
(*Brunnera macrophylla* 'Langtrees')

LARRY'S GARDEN NOTES

Brunnera flowers appear a rich sky blue to the naked eye but inevitably come out a wishy-washy pale violet (sometimes even pink) when you take photos of them. This is also true of other blue flowers, like those of borage (*Borago officinalis*), forget-me-nots (*Myosotis* spp.), Italian bugloss (*Anchusa azurea*), and lungworts (*Pulmonaria* spp.), all plants that, by the way, are in the borage family (Boraginaceae) along with brunnera. It also happens with other blue flowers, like the beautiful 'Heavenly Blue' morning glory (*Ipomoea nil*). A photographer friend of mine suggested a solution: Use a pale blue filter to take pictures of blue flowers. It worked for me!

Caltha
Marsh marigold

CALTHA
KAL-thuh

Bloom Color:
Yellow and white

Bloom Time:
Mid- to late spring

Length of Bloom:
3 to 4 weeks

Height:
6 to 24 inches (15 to 60 cm)

Spread:
12 to 24 inches (30 to 60 cm)

Garden Uses:
Edging, mixed border; in wet areas

Light Preference:
Sun (spring); sun to shade (summer)

Soil Preference:
Rich, moist soil

Best Way to Propagate:
Divide after blooming or in fall

USDA Plant Hardiness Zones:
2 to 7

Not all shady spots are bone-dry: Some, on the contrary, are naturally moist or even soaking wet. Rather than drain such a spot and destroy rare natural bogs and marshes, why not enhance them by adding a bit more color? One plant to consider for this is the marsh marigold. It is a common native plant throughout much of the Northern Hemisphere to well above the Arctic Circle, but it certainly packs a lot of punch for a wildflower! This is not your frail, wispy, don't-notice-it-unless-it-is-in-bloom meadow bloomer—the brilliant yellow flowers are large, numerous, and very showy, and the leaves are also large and striking.

GROWING TIPS

Marsh marigold does not *have* to grow in a bog or marsh in order to thrive. It does just fine in any reasonably moist garden soil, even in spots that dry out considerably in midsummer. It really becomes useful, however, in those problem spots where Mother Nature seems a bit too generous with her watering can in spring. It will even thrive in spots that are under up to 9 inches (23 cm) of water at that time of year—as long as the spot becomes dry ground later in the season. It does prefer a little less moisture, though: A thin covering of water or simply boggy soil is ideal. Under very wet conditions, it will grow taller and wider—up to 2 feet (60 cm) tall and wide—than it does in drier soils, as if it were stretching upward to avoid the coming flood. In garden soils, the same plant will often remain only 6 to 15 inches (15 to 38 cm) tall and 12 inches (30 cm) wide, yet it blooms just as heavily and creates as much impact as it does when it grows as a springtime aquatic.

Marsh marigold is one of the "spring ephemerals," a category mostly dominated by bulbs, not perennials. It starts its season early, comes to full and glorious bloom while most other plants around are still dressed in their winter grays, and is fully dormant by midsummer. The secret to success in a shady spot is therefore to make sure it gets plenty of sunlight in spring, before the trees above leaf out. By the time summer rolls around, the flowering is over and although the leaves may still be around (they die back quickly in spots that become very dry but hang on for quite a while in damp spots), they seem indifferent to light—sun or shade is just fine with them as long as they've had their fill of sunlight in spring.

Remember to plant marsh marigolds with other plants that can help fill the gap when their foliage does die back. That could include marsh plants like rodgersias or ligularias in spots where soils are constantly wet, or plants more used to terra firma, like hostas and many ferns, where the soil is naturally drier in summer.

Marsh marigold is most easily propagated by division in spring or fall. If you want to divide them in fall, though, be sure to carefully mark their space.

Warning: Marsh marigold contains an irritating sap that is toxic if ingested and should be kept away from small children. Oddly enough, though, both the leaves and flower buds are used as spring vegetables in many parts of the world—once they have been cooked to destroy the toxin!

Marsh marigold (*Caltha palustris*)

PROBLEMS AND SOLUTIONS

Leaf diseases, such as powdery mildew, sometimes appear toward the end of the plant's growing cycle but do no real harm. Simply cut the leaves back if their appearance bothers you.

TOP PERFORMER

Caltha palustris (marsh marigold): The bright yellow flowers are this plant's main draw, but the dark green, kidney-shaped leaves are not unattractive, creating a dense mound that sets off the flowers perfectly. Underground, the plant is made up of a crown of fleshy roots that store of a lot of water in provision for drier conditions during summer months. The species has single yellow flowers, while 'Flore Pleno' (also called 'Multiplex' or 'Plena') produces a ring of normal "petals" (in actuality, marsh marigolds have no petals; what look like petals to our eyes are sepals) surrounding a dense mass of petaloides, making the flower look not just double but triple! *C. palustris* var. *alba* is a subspecies with white flowers and a yellow center. Both varieties are likely to be found in the water garden section.

LARRY'S GARDEN NOTES

The rich yellow buttercuplike flowers of the marsh marigold really do indicate a family relationship: It is a member of the buttercup family (Ranunculaceae). And just like a buttercup, if you hold it underneath someone's chin, its golden sheen will reflect on his skin. "Do you like butter?" is the traditional question. And the answer is always yes—unless the person tested has a heavy beard!

Cimicifuga

Bugbane, cimicifuga, snakeroot, cohosh

PLANT PROFILE

CIMICIFUGA

sih-mih-cih-FYU-guh

Bloom Color:
  White and pink

Bloom Time:
  Varies by species; see
  individual listings

Length of Bloom:
  4 to 8 weeks

Height:
  Varies by species; see
  individual listings

Spread:
  Varies by species; see
  individual listings

Garden Uses:
  Cut flower garden, specimen
  plant, woodland garden; at
  the back of beds and borders

Light Preference:
  Full sun to shade

Soil Preference:
  Humus-rich, moist soil

Best Way to Propagate:
  Divide in spring or fall

USDA Plant Hardiness Zones:
  Varies by species; see
  individual listings

These slow-growing but majestic plants can be absolutely spectacular when properly used. Their deeply cut green or purple foliage forms a dense, shrublike base upon which tall, narrow spikes of miniscule fluffy flowers rise like Roman candles. As the blooms start at the base of the flowerstalk and slowly open several at a time, the effect can last for weeks. You do have to be patient, though—most take several years to reach blooming size and a decade or more to reach their full potential.

GROWING TIPS

Bugbanes are native to woodlands throughout much of the Northern Hemisphere, forming large, dense clumps by natural division. It takes these slow-growing plants at least 3 or 4 years to reach a size where they are large enough to bloom. Although partial shade is acceptable, they'll even take full sun as long as the soil remains moist, so a good thick mulch and a soaker hose become very useful tools. Deep shade won't kill them, of course, but, as in the wild, while they may thrive there, they won't bloom.

Other than needing decent if not strong light, bugbanes are easy to grow. They dislike being babied and disturbed. Plant them, water them well the first year, then ignore them. They are relatively indifferent to soil type, even adapting to dense clay, and once established will tolerate drought as long as it is occasional. Moving them around can, however, slow or stop their progress. Likewise, dividing them can set them back years in their growth. Since they are also painfully slow from seed, the best way to obtain new plants is to buy them!

Although bugbanes grow as well in the South as in the North, down to Zone 9, that's the case only when they get sufficient winter chill. They'll produce only foliage in climates where frost is rare or fleeting. Ideally, they prefer at least a few weeks of freezing temperatures each winter.

PROBLEMS AND SOLUTIONS

With a name like bugbane, it's perhaps not surprising that these plants seem to have few enemies.

TOP PERFORMER

Cimicifuga racemosa, actually *Actaea racemosa* (black snakeroot, black cohosh): This species is native to much of Eastern North America. The "black" in its common name refers to the dark green of the foliage, one of the few ways of telling it from American bugbane or summer cohosh (*C. americana*), a smaller, later-blooming species with which it shares part of its territory. It's called "snakeroot" because native people used the roots to treat snakebite. It is the tallest of the commonly available bugbanes, with narrow spikes that seem to reach for the sky. Another reason that it is a "top performer" is that it is the earliest bloomer in the genus and therefore capable of flowering even in short-summer areas. In the South, it begins blooming as early as July but not until August further north. The flowers last for almost 2 months! Be forewarned: It has unpleasantly scented flowers. Height: 6 to 8 feet (1.8 to 2.4 m). Spread: 3 to 4 feet (90 to 120 cm). USDA Plant Hardiness Zones 3 to 7.

MORE RECOMMENDED BUGBANES

Cimicifuga simplex, actually *Actaea simplex* (Kamchatka bugbane): This is a very varied species, not in the least because a lot of cultivars of unknown or doubtful origin have been lumped together under this name. It is generally a smaller species than *C. racemosa* and a much later bloomer. In fact, some cultivars, like the popular 'White Pearl' (actually, to confuse things further, it would appear this one is being moved to the species *C. matsumerae,* a.k.a. *Actaea matsumerae*), often don't have time to bloom in short-season climates! In general, *C. simplex* has short, sometimes arching flower spikes that are odorless or fragrant. Among the early-blooming cultivars are 'Pritchard's Giant', a tall (to 5 feet/1.5 m) cultivar with deliciously scented flowers, plus the whole range of Kamchatka bugbanes with purple foliage. This includes the old favorite, Atropurpurea Group, once sold as 'Atropurpurea'. Height: 3 to 5 feet (90 to 150 cm). Spread: 2 to 3 feet (60 to 90 cm). USDA Plant Hardiness Zones 4 to 7.

Black snakeroot
(*Cimicifuga racemosa*)

LARRY'S GARDEN NOTES

Cimicifuga is from the Latin *cimez* (bug) and *fugere* (to repel)—and the name bugbane, too, has the same meaning of driving away bugs. Until recent times, the leaves of *C. foetida* (stinking bugbane, a European species) have traditionally been crushed and added to pillows and bed linens in the hopes of driving away bedbugs away. Most bugbanes are not as foul-smelling as stinking bugbane, but the flowers of the popular black cohosh (*C. racemosa*) are not something you'd want to slip into a bouquet and offer your sweetheart!

Convallaria
Lily-of-the-valley

PLANT PROFILE

CONVALLARIA

con-val-AIR-ee-uh

Bloom Color:
  White and pink

Bloom Time:
  Mid- to late spring

Length of Bloom:
  2 to 3 weeks

Height:
  6 to 12 inches (15 to 30 cm)

Spread:
  Indefinite

Garden Uses:
  Container planting, cut flower garden, edging, groundcover, mass planting, rock garden, seasonal hedge, wall planting, woodland garden; along paths, on slopes, in wet areas

Light Preference:
  Full sun to shade

Soil Preference:
  Rich, moist, well-drained soil

Best Way to Propagate:
  Divide in spring or fall

USDA Plant Hardiness Zones:
  1 to 8

Who doesn't recognize this plant? It has a long tradition of use in gardens and has been planted just about everywhere—so much so that this plant, originally of Eurasian origin, is now found as a garden escapee on six continents (it's waiting for the ice cap to melt to attack Antarctica). Its renown belies the fact that it is, individually, very small and insignificant: one stalk, two or three oval leaves, an arching stem with half a dozen tiny bell-shaped flowers, and that's all. A single plant creates no impact whatsoever. However, it will stand out if planted two or three to a pot; in mass plantings, it makes a superb groundcover.

GROWING TIPS

You can grow lily-of-the-valley nearly everywhere, from full sun to deep shade and in just about any kind of soil. But an unhappy lily-of-the-valley is not a pretty sight. Oh, it will be green enough first thing in spring and will probably bloom, but for foliage that remains lush and green all summer without drying at the edges or yellowing, dry conditions or extreme heat just won't do. Try planting it in partial to deep shade in a rich soil that remains evenly moist. It can even be soaking wet in spring!

So much for great foliage, but what about great bloom? Well, the above suggestions hold (rich, moist soil, cool conditions, etc.)—except for the deep shade bit. It will produce green leaves in shade, but not too many flowers. Try for partial shade and you'll have a happy plant.

Where it is not happy, you might want to restrict it to the cut flower garden, where its bedraggled midseason appearance won't be so annoying. Just harvest the flowers for mini-bouquets and ignore the plant's sullen summer demeanor. In fact, you can simply mow it down when it starts to turn yellow: out of sight, out of mind! In cool, moist, partial shade, however, it makes a stupendous, dense, green-all-summer groundcover with the added bonuses of fragrant spring blooms and brilliant red berries. And the foliage even turns bright yellow in fall (unless it already turned brown and yellow in the heat of summer). The moral of this story is: Treat lily-of-the-valley well, and it will reward you generously.

Be forewarned, though, that a happy lily-of-the-valley is an invasive lily-of-the-valley, and it is well nigh impossible to eradicate once it is has been set loose. In hot, dry conditions, it just sort of clumps up and doesn't go very far. In cool, moist, partial shade, though, it will make a valiant effort to take over the entire garden—plus the lawn, veggie patch, and anything else with a modicum of soil. It has even been known to punch holes in asphalt, so bye-bye driveway! Lily-of-the-valley should therefore be planted only within some kind of root barrier that can stop its progress. Fortunately, you only have to worry about its spreading rhizomes; rarely does it self-seed.

To multiply lily-of-the-valley, just lift and separate. You'll discover mature patches are a mass of long, creeping rhizomes, with a bud (pip) at the tip of each. Each rhizome with its pip will produce a new plant. Theoretically, division is best carried out in early spring or fall. In fact, though, you can do almost anything to a lily-of-the-valley at any time of the year and it will be back in bloom the following season.

Think Twice: The beautiful red berries of lily-of-the-valley are poisonous and can cause a nasty stomachache. It is perhaps wise to remove them when young children are present.

PROBLEMS AND SOLUTIONS

Leaf spot can occur in late summer but is rarely visible enough to be worth treating.

TOP PERFORMER

Convallaria majalis (lily-of-the-valley): This is the only species with any commercial distribution worth mentioning and is by far the nicest one anyway. It usually has plain green leaves and white flowers, but specialized nurseries offer more unusual types, all as easy to grow as the species. Variety *rosea* has pale pink flowers, for example, while there are several variegated cultivars, notably 'Striata' (also sold as 'Aureovariegata', 'Lineata', and 'Variegata') with cream- to yellow-striped leaves. It needs a fair amount of sun for the color to come through. 'Fortin's Giant' is a big guy, with larger white flowers on a much bigger plant, to 15 inches (38 cm) tall. And 'Plena' has double white flowers that last and last. There are other cultivars, but they can be hard to locate.

Lily-of-the-valley
(*Convallaria majalis*)

KISSING COUSINS

Canada mayflower (*Maianthemum canadense*), also called wild lily-of-the-valley, can be seen as the North American version of the essentially Eurasia lily-of-the-valley. The leaves are so similar to lily-of-the-valley that they are hard to tell apart when the plant is not in bloom, but the dense spikes of tiny white flowers, highly scented, are star-shaped and look nothing like the upside-down urns of true lily-of-the-valley. The berries are a much paler red. This is a great groundcover for partial to deep shade. Height: 3 to 8 inches (8 to 20 cm). Spread: Indefinite. USDA Plant Hardiness Zones 1 to 7.

Cornus
Bunchberry, dwarf cornel

PLANT PROFILE

CORNUS
KOR-nus

Bloom Color:
Greenish white to white

Bloom Time:
Midspring to early summer

Length of Bloom:
4 to 8 weeks

Height:
3 to 9 inches (8 to 23 cm)

Spread:
Indefinite

Garden Uses:
Edging, groundcover, mass planting, rock garden, woodland garden; along paths, on slopes; attracts birds and mammals

Light Preference:
Full sun to shade

Soil Preference:
Humus-rich, acid, evenly moist soil

Best Way to Propagate:
Divide in spring or fall

USDA Plant Hardiness Zones:
1 to 6

A green carpet of bunchberry is a joy to behold. And it is just as beautiful when the plants are covered with clusters of bright red berries as when the flowers, huge by comparison to the size of the plant, are in bloom for a long period in spring and early summer. In fact, it's a very pretty plant even without flowers or berries: The leaves are shiny and dark green, forming an absolutely perfect carpet. Where it can be grown well, this is absolutely one of the best groundcovers—but let's be honest, it is not always the easiest plant to establish.

GROWING TIPS

Bunchberry does best when you comprehend its needs. It is essentially a plant of the northern woods. Studies show it fails to thrive when soil temperatures reach above 65°F (18°C). That may seem impossibly cool, but remember that in a shady location with plenty of mulch and where the soil is kept constantly moist, the ground may well remain cool, even on 100°F (38°C) days. So mulch, moisten, keep it out of direct sun, and you'll have a good chance at success!

For best growth, supply a humus-rich soil, preferably acidic (add chopped oak leaves or apply a conifer-needle mulch), and use a soaker hose to maintain even humidity. Partial shade gives the best results, but bunchberry will grow and flower abundantly even in the deep shade of conifers. It will also grow in full sun in cooler climates.

Bunchberries bloom readily enough, even in the deepest shade, but the dense clusters of fruit that so beautifully adorn wild colonies of bunchberry are often frustratingly absent in culture. Why? For one, the plant is essentially self-sterile: It will produce little or no fruit unless pollinated by a different clone. Make sure you start off with plants from at least two different sources. Second, bunchberries growing in deep shade are less likely to produce fruit. So partial shade—or even, where summers are cool, fairly intense sun—are best if you want more than just flowers.

Propagation of this plant can be complicated. It produces woody underground rhizomes that spread exponentially in all directions but may not actually root for several years. So when you dig up what appears to be a healthy, well-established plant, it may still be without any roots at all, entirely depending on its mother plant—whose life-giving rhizome you just severed! It's therefore best to move clumps, soil and all, not individual plants: You're more likely to have a few rooted sections in the mix. (And actually, the easiest way to reproduce this plant is by buying new nursery-grown ones that are well-rooted in pots!)

PROBLEMS AND SOLUTIONS

As long as bunchberry is kept cool and moist, it has few pest enemies—unless you consider the grouses, pheasants, wild turkeys, thrushes, vireos, chipmunks, and other fruit-eating animals that are attracted to the berries in late fall and winter.

TOP PERFORMER

Cornus canadensis (bunchberry): Most *Cornus* are shrubs and are collectively known as dogwoods. Only a handful of species could be considered perennials—and of these, only bunchberry is of any major interest for gardeners. It's a very simple plant bearing a single whorl of four to six dark green, deeply veined leaves on a short stem topped off by a single surprisingly large flower in mid-spring. Each "bloom" is actually a complete inflorescence: The true flowers are the rounded greenish mass in the center, while the "petals"—usually four, but sometimes five or six, are colored leaves called bracts. They are greenish white at first, fading to pure white. The ensemble looks precisely like the inflorescence of the bunchberry's much larger cousin, the flowering dogwood (*Cornus florida*). Because bracts are colored leaves, they tend to remain in good shape longer than most petals would, which explains the plant's long flowering season. By the time the bracts *do* dry up, the dark green berries (if there are any that year) are already starting to appear. They turn bright red in fall and last for months, usually until birds or animals find them. The leaves turn beautiful shades of red or burgundy in fall before dropping off. In mild climates, they may persist until spring.

Bunchberry (*Cornus canadensis*)

LARRY'S GARDEN NOTES

Bright red berries invite tasting, but you'll probably be disappointed with bunchberry. Not that they're tart or poisonous, just rather insipid. That doesn't stop young children from consuming them where bunchberries grow wild. And in traditional New England Christmas cake, bunchberries were added for a bit of extra color. Native peoples have long used them, both fresh and as an ingredient of pemmican, a mixture of dried meat, fat, and berries, prepared during times of plenty for use when traveling or during periods of famine. Unless you're going through a period of famine yourself, though, let the birds eat them.

Darmera
Umbrella plant

PLANT PROFILE

DARMERA
DAR-mer-uh

Bloom Color:
  Pink and white

Bloom Time:
  Late spring to early summer

Length of Bloom:
  3 to 4 weeks

Height:
  2 to 6 feet (60 to 180 cm)

Spread:
  4 to 6 feet (120 to 180 cm)

Garden Uses:
  Seasonal hedge, specimen
  plant, woodland garden; in
  wet areas, at the back of beds
  and borders

Light Preference:
  Full sun to partial shade

Soil Preference:
  Humus-rich, damp to wet,
  acid soil

Best Way to Propagate:
  Dig out sections of
  underground stems
  (rhizomes) in spring

USDA Plant Hardiness Zones:
  4 to 9

You're out in the back 40 and are caught in a sudden shower without your raincoat. What do you do? Well, you cut off a leaf from your umbrella plant, of course! Umbrella plant is mostly grown for its large, rounded leaves borne on sturdy stalks, but the tall stalks of pink to white flowers, rising out of the bare ground like flowering periscopes, are nothing less than spectacular. In fact, you'll find visitors doing a double-take. All in all, a curious, exotic, and very garden-worthy plant.

GROWING TIPS

In its natural habitat, the mountains of the western United States, the umbrella plant grows in dense colonies on stream banks. In culture, too, it loves moist or even wet soil: It's a great subject for the background of a water feature or for naturalizing along rivers or lakes, where its dense root system will do a wonderful job as a soil stabilizer.

In spite of this love of wet places, though, boggy conditions are not a necessity. I have my umbrella plant growing in a regular flowerbed in partial shade where it gets no special care and it positively thrives. Of course, I always mulch. The advantage of growing umbrella plants under regular-but-moist garden conditions rather than soggy soil is that their growth is much more restrained and they don't tend to become invasive. The downside is that the leaves are smaller and the plants don't necessarily attain their full height—only 3 to 4 feet instead of up to 6 feet (180 cm).

In most gardens, partial shade is the best choice. Full sun is perfectly fine, but only if you can keep the soil moist at all times. Even with its roots practically soaking in water, the leaves of plants grown in full sun can still wilt at midday in intense heat and look awful. Partial shade will bring the temperature down and keep the plant looking good all day long.

Think twice: The root system of this plant is proportionate to its gigantic stature: Thick rhizomes that form a dense, impenetrable mass. In ordinary garden soils, it simply forms a thick clump and causes no harm, but it can be very invasive if planted in boggy soils. Always plant it within a root barrier of some sort, and make sure the barrier is sturdy.

Propagating a plant with such a dense root system is quite something. Probably dynamiting it would work well, although I have yet to test this; you could just pick up resulting chunks of rhizome and plant them. Instead, I've found it fairly simple to chop a rhizome (with its growing point) free with an axe in spring. If you can manage to dig out the entire root system, try sawing it into sections.

Of course, you can always grow the umbrella plant from seed. Since it is rarely available commercially, it's best to harvest it from your own plants when it matures in early summer. Sow in a damp spot in spring or fall and it should germinate within a few weeks.

PROBLEMS AND SOLUTIONS

I've heard that slugs and snails can do damage, but I have yet to see any in eastern North America. Maybe slugs in their native western North America have stronger mouthparts, but the eastern ones don't seem to be able to put a dint in this plant's thick leaves. There are few other pests.

TOP PERFORMER

Darmera peltata, also called *Peltiphyllum peltatum* (umbrella plant). There is only one species in this genus, potentially a monster of a plant. It begins its growing season by producing a bristly reddish flowerstalk devoid of any foliage that rises sky-ward from an underground or partly covered creeping stem (rhizome). The stalk can reach up 3 to 6 feet (90 to 180 cm) tall and bears a dense cluster of pink (sometimes white) flowers re-sembling bergenia flowers. Foliage starts to appear as the flow-ering progresses: rounded leaves up to 2 feet (60 cm) across with deeply cut edges and up to 6 feet (180 cm) tall. I find leaves are smaller when the plant is grown in regular garden soil rather than in bog conditions: about 12 to 18 inches (30 to 45 cm) in diameter and rarely much more than 4 feet (120 cm) in height. The leafstalk is attached to the middle of the leaf, giving the leaf the umbrellalike appearance that is its trade-mark. The leaves turn a beautiful coppery red in fall before dying back. There is a dwarf form, 'Nana', that reaches only 12 to 18 inches (30 to 45 cm) tall and is ideal for smaller gardens, but it can be hard to locate.

Umbrella plant (*Darmera peltata*)

KISSING COUSINS

For even bigger and bolder leaves than the umbrella plant, think of shieldleaf (*Astilboides tabularis*, also called *Rodgersia tabularis*). Its rounded leaves have a similar umbrella shape but are larger, up to 3 feet (90 cm) in diameter— very striking! They are otherwise quite different, with more deeply cut edges, a softly fuzzy texture, and a lesser height—rarely much more than 3 feet (90 cm) high. The spectacular white blooms, which appear *after* the leaves have formed, are taller, about 5 feet (1.5 m) tall and very feathery, like a giant astilbe. It needs similar growing conditions to *Darmera* but won't take waterlogged soils. Height: 3 to 5 feet (90 to 150 cm). Spread: 2 to 4 feet (60 to 120 cm). USDA Plant Hardiness Zones 4 to 9.

Dicentra
Bleeding heart

Bleeding hearts have been a flower garden staple since your great-grandparents were kids—and for good reason. They are easy to grow, bloom readily even under less-than-perfect conditions, have attractive foliage, and the flowers are just so original—they really do look like miniature hearts! And then there is attractive, deeply cut fernlike foliage. There are two main types: tall ones and dwarf ones, and each has its special needs.

GROWING TIPS

Both types of bleeding heart adapt to a wide range of conditions but are at their best in cool air and moist soil. They will thrive in full sun and tolerate drought, but usually that pushes them into summer dormancy, which is rather a shame when you realize that many of them will bloom off and on all summer where conditions are more to their liking. So partial shade, regular watering, and a good mulch are the name of the game. Some will thrive even in deep shade, although they won't bloom as heavily.

Common bleeding heart (*D. spectabilis*) is a slow-growing, clump-forming plant that prefers to be planted and left alone. It takes 3 to 4 years to start to approach its full size, and if you divide it you'll set it right back to stage one. Stem cuttings taken in early summer sometimes root, and it can be grown from fresh seed, but both techniques result in young plants that take years to bloom. This is definitely one plant I prefer to buy than to multiply myself.

There are several species of dwarf bleeding hearts that are faster-growing and easier to reproduce. A small plant will form a fair-size clump after 3 or 4 years and can be divided to form more plants.

PROBLEMS AND SOLUTIONS

Problems? What problems? For the most part, these plants are tough as nails!

TOP PERFORMER

Dicentra hybrids (hybrid dwarf bleeding heart): Many, many moons ago, East met West, and the gardening world hasn't been the same since. Crosses between fringed bleeding heart

(*D. eximia*) from eastern North America and Western bleeding heart (*D. formosa*) from the other side of the continent proved to be ideal plants for partial shade or even shade. I felt it was best to lump all three (*D. eximia, D. formosa,* and their hybrids) together here. All three types (the two species and the resulting crosses) produce dense mounds of deeply cut leaves topped off with thick clusters of heart-shaped flowers in pink, red, or white.

The leaves can be apple green, mid-green, or distinctly bluish. Where partial shade, moisture, and cool growing conditions can be maintained, hybrid dwarf bleeding hearts will bloom from spring right through into fall, although most heavily in spring. Where heat and drought affect them, they will stop blooming in summer, sometimes blooming again in fall when cooler conditions return. Under severe drought conditions they can even go summer-dormant.

There are dozens of cultivars, including 'King of Hearts', with pink flowers and distinctly blue foliage; and 'Langtrees', with white flowers tinted coral. Height: 8 to 18 inches (20 to 45 cm). Spread: 12 to 18 inches (30 to 45 cm). USDA Plant Hardiness Zones 3 to 9.

Golden common bleeding heart (*Dicentra spectabilis* 'Gold Heart')

MORE RECOMMENDED BLEEDING HEARTS

Larry's Favorite: *Dicentra spectabilis* (common bleeding heart): You'll often see this bleeding heart still thriving around old homesteads where they were planted generations ago without ever having been divided. The plants are truly beautiful, with tall, ferny foliage, much less deeply cut than that of the dwarf hybrids, and arching stems bearing dangling hearts. Pink is the usual color, but 'Alba' has pure white flowers. This species generally goes into summer dormancy, so learn to plant other perennials with some summer attractiveness, like ferns and hostas, next to them to fill in when the leaves fade. 'Gold Heart', a super new cultivar with golden foliage and pink flowers, will brighten up a shady spot better than almost any perennial I have ever seen. Height: 18 to 36 inches (45 to 90 cm). Spread: 2 to 4 feet (60 to 120 cm). USDA Plant Hardiness Zones 2 to 8.

KISSING COUSINS

There are also several tuberous species of bleeding heart that really should be in chapter 8, "Bulbs for Shade," but in a spirit of keeping families united, it seems logical to mention them here. The most striking is Dutchman's breeches (*D. cucullaria*), whose gray-green leaves give rise to arching stems of particularly charming flowers, looking like puffy white doubloons dangling upside down from a clothesline. It is a true spring ephemeral, sprouting and blooming early in spring, then going summer-dormant. Height: 6 to 14 inches (15 to 36 cm). Spread: 6 to 8 inches (15 to 20 cm). USDA Plant Hardiness Zones 3 to 7.

Digitalis
Foxglove

PLANT PROFILE

DIGITALIS
dij-uh-TAL-is

Bloom Color:
Yellow, cream, pink, purple, and red

Bloom Time:
Varies by species; see individual listings

Length of Bloom:
3 to 4 weeks

Height:
2 to 5 feet (60 to 150 cm)

Spread:
1 to 2 feet (30 to 60 cm)

Garden Uses:
Background, cut flower garden, mass planting, meadow garden, mixed border, woodland garden; at the back of beds and borders; attracts hummingbirds

Light Preference:
Full sun to partial shade

Soil Preference:
Humus-rich, moist, well-drained soil

Best Way to Propagate:
Divide or sow seed in spring or fall

USDA Plant Hardiness Zones:
Varies by species; see individual listings

What would a cottage-style garden be without the skyrocketing spires of foxglove blooms? Rising from a ground-hugging rosette of beautifully textured leaves, the sturdy stems produce downward-pointing tubular flowers, often spotted with darker colors, that open bit by bit, starting from the base of the stem, then working their way upward, prolonging the flowering season. Hummingbirds have learned to adore them.

GROWING TIPS

Foxgloves naturally grow on the wood's edge, thus in partial shade, and they look best in such situations. They'll also do fine in more intense shade under deep-rooted deciduous trees as long as they get plenty of sun before spring leaf-out. Sun is also fine—as long as you can ensure even moisture throughout summer—although when they self-sow, they *do* tend to migrate toward shadier quarters.

Most foxgloves are perennials and will come back in the same spot year after year, but remember to leave some space for the devastatingly charming common foxglove (*Digitalis purpurea*). It is a biennial and therefore needs patches of un-mulched soil where it can self-sow. It will form only a rosette of leaves the first year, then a flowerspike followed by seed the next, and then it dies and starts all over.

You can often get common floxglove to bloom a second time, albeit on a shorter plant, by cutting back the original flow-erstalk to just above the rosette before the last blooms have faded. If you cut the second stalk back, it will often produce secondary rosettes that overwinter for yet another season, so this is one biennial you can "perennialize." The perennial species too often rebloom if their spikes are cut back, usually in early fall, although the new flowerstalk is usually consider-ably shorter than the original.

Division is the usual way of multiplying perennial foxgloves, although most also grow readily from seed, whether sown in containers, directly in the garden, or allowed to self-sow. Theo-retically you can reproduce common foxglove *only* from seed, but, as mentioned, if you keep cutting back its flowerspikes be-

fore it finishes blooming, you can encourage it to produce offsets that can be lifted and replanted.

Warning: All parts of foxglove are poisonous—in fact extremely poisonous. Keep them out of reach of children and
pets. Some people may suffer contact dermatitis just from handling them.

PROBLEMS AND SOLUTIONS

Slugs like foxglove leaves, so keep them under control. Also,
after blooming, the hitherto attractive foliage tends to go
downhill. As a biennial, common foxglove naturally goes into
decline after flowering and the leaves begin to look ratty.

TOP PERFORMER

Digitalis purpurea (common foxglove): Although not a true
perennial, this biennial does self-sow readily and becomes such
a permanent presence that many gardeners come to think of it
as a perennial. It is by far the most popular foxglove in the
garden. Originally purple in color with darker spots, there are
now strains in all shades of white, pink, lavender, peach, and
cream, with or without spotting. You'll find dwarf forms as well as
the usual tall ones and even a (in my opinion) rather sickly variegate that comes somewhat true from seed. By deadheading,
you can extend the already long blooming season from late
spring/early summer until early fall. Staking may be needed for
some of the taller types. Height: 4 to 7 feet (1.2 to 2 m) for stan-
dard forms; as little as 2½ feet (75 cm) for dwarf varieties. Spread:
1 to 2 feet (30 to 60 cm). USDA Plant Hardiness Zones 4 to 8.

MORE RECOMMENDED FOXGLOVES

D. grandiflora, also called *D. ambigua* or *D. orientalis* (yellow
foxglove): This is probably the best of the perennial species
under most circumstances because of its tough-as-nails disposition. Just plant it and ignore it! The pendant flowers are usually in paler shades of yellow with brown spotting, and the
ground-hugging rosettes of narrow fuzzy leaves are quite attractive even when the plant is not in bloom. Flowers occur in
early to midsummer; sometimes it will rebloom in fall if deadheaded. Height: 24 to 40 inches (60 to 100 cm). Spread: 12 to
18 inches (30 to 45 cm). USDA Plant Hardiness Zones 3 to 8.

Common foxglove
(*Digitalis purpurea*)

LARRY'S GARDEN NOTES

Have you ever wanted to attract
fairies to your garden? Try
growing foxgloves! The "little
people" are said to live in and
around them. In fact, the "fox" in
foxglove has nothing to do with
foxes, but rather with "folk," as in
"wee folk." They're often depicted
wearing foxglove flowers as hats
or robes, and the poisonous nature of the plant is not unrelated
to its fairy connections: Poisonous
plants were considered mysterious
and often linked to the realm of
the wee people. As for the "glove"
in foxglove, it comes from the
shape of the flowers, said to resemble the fingers of a glove with
the tips cut off.

Doronicum
Leopard's bane

In early spring, when most perennials are just struggling to wake up from their long winter's rest, leopard's banes rapidly spring to life and fill the garden with their gorgeous sunny daisies. With their starlike appearance and narrow rays, they make a perfect foil for the heavier flowers of tulips and narcissi that bloom at the same season. Or plant them just inside an open woodland, where their sunny disposition brightens the landscape while waiting for leaves to fill in. After the flowers fade, the dark green kidney-shaped leaves are intriguing and different, sure to attract the attention of visiting gardeners.

GROWING TIPS

That leopard's banes come up so early in spring tells you that they aren't afraid of cold weather. In fact, the cooler the spring, the longer the flowers last. They don't like hot summers: Where summers are hot, they may even go summer-dormant, so plan your plantings with enough heat-resistant neighbors, like hostas and ferns, to fill in the open spaces they leave when planted in full blazing sun. In cooler, shadier spots the leaves will more likely last through summer. A spot that is quite moist although not waterlogged will also help keep them cool and happy.

So much for temperate climates. Leopard's banes simply aren't good choices for hot climates: They seem to need cold or at least cool winters and fairly cool summers. Consider them one of the rare advantages of having to deal with cold winters!

Partial shade is ideal for leopard's banes, especially spots under or near deciduous trees that get full spring sun, then dappled shade for the rest of summer.

A single clump of leopard's bane will eventually give rise to others; the plant spreads via underground runners. Not to worry, though—they aren't weedy. Move any extras to new flowerbeds, or give them as gifts to gardening friends. Older clumps age quite quickly, so if you notice them blooming less over time, consider dividing them. This can be as often as every 3 or 4 years. The best time for dividing or moving leopard's banes is in later summer or early fall.

PROBLEMS AND SOLUTIONS

Leopard's banes are not to subject to pest problems. If powdery mildew strikes, remove the damaged leaves.

TOP PERFORMER

Doronicum orientale, syn. *D. caucasicum* (Caucasian leopard's bane): It forms a dense groundhugging rosette of large, frost-resistant, kidney- to heart-shaped leaves, attractively fringed along the edges. There are also smaller leaves on the flowerstalk itself. The solitary daisy-shaped flowers are made up of a golden yellow disk of fertile flowers surrounded by a ring of numerous pure yellow, narrow, sterile ray flowers: the typical pattern of daisies everywhere! It tends to go summer-dormant where summers are hot. 'Magnificum', with larger flowers on a taller plant (2 to 2½ feet/60 to 75 cm), is by far the most common variety, although the dwarf 'Little Leo', with fairly large flowers on a plant only 12 to 18 inches (30 to 45 cm) high, is a very close second. It blooms fairly early in spring, at the same time as the midseason tulips it looks so delicious with. Height: 1 to 2 feet (30 to 60 cm). Spread: 1 foot (30 cm). USDA Plant Hardiness Zones 3 to 7.

MORE RECOMMENDED LEOPARD'S BANES

Doronicum Hybrids (hybrid leopard's banes): The Caucasian leopard's bane has been widely hybridized with lesser-known species, resulting in a range of hybrids that are, for the most part, fairly similar in appearance and habit to the species itself (often a bit later-blooming, although only by a few days). In most cases, the only way you can tell it is an interspecific hybrid is because the label says only *Doronicum* and not *Doronicum orientale.* Often the hybrid forms are a bit less likely to die back in summer heat than Caucasian leopard's bane. 'Finesse' is by far the best-known cultivar these days, with much narrower ray petals than most, giving the yellow blooms a delicately fringed appearance. All leopard's banes make excellent cut flowers, but this one is particularly choice: It reaches 15 to 20 inches (38 to 50 cm) tall. Height: 12 to 24 inches (30 to 60 cm). Spread: 12 to 18 inches (30 to 45 cm). USDA Plant Hardiness Zones 3 to 7.

Caucasian leopard's bane
(*Doronicum orientale*)

LARRY'S GARDEN NOTES

The name leopard's bane would seem to suggest you could plant beds of *Doronicum* around your property and keep leopards out— and certainly I have seen no leopards digging in my flowerbeds since I began planting them. However, I have heard no reports from African gardeners, wiser to the ways of leopards than North Americans, that they've had any success with *Doronicum* barriers— and no wonder! The name leopard's bane was actually given to this plant by accident when it was mistakenly believed to be the source of a poison once applied to arrows used to hunt leopards. It is now known that leopard's banes are not poisonous, neither to leopards nor to people, but the common name has stuck over the generations.

Epimedium

Epimedium, barrenwort, bishop's hat

Justice can't possibly be done to the varied and beautiful genus *Epimedium* in only a few short paragraphs. There are so many species with such varied appearances—and new ones are being discovered nearly every year! Although easy to grow (in fact, rock solid!), epimediums have yet to catch on with gardeners in a big way, so if you grow them, you're a pioneer! In general, they are mounded or slightly running plants with striking compound foliage that is either evergreen or deciduous, depending on the species and the climate. Although mostly grown as foliage plants, the spring blooms are devastatingly dainty, like dangling mini-columbines, although they are sometimes partly hidden by the foliage.

GROWING TIPS

Given their druthers, epimediums would grow in moist, rich soil in partial shade. However, they'll also put up with full sun as long as they aren't allowed to dry out too deeply; they'll also grow beautifully, albeit much more slowly, in full shade as well. They'll even do quite well with fairly heavy root competition as long as you keep them well moistened until they are completely established. For plants mostly native to cool woodlands, they do surprisingly well in warmer climates, but they really do appreciate a thick mulch to keep at least their roots cool.

The deciduous varieties usually have the most showy flowers, but only because the foliage of the evergreen ones often hides the blooms. In my climate, the weight of the snow flattens out the evergreen leaves, allowing the flowers to rise well above them; in other areas, mow the plant to within 1 inch (2.5 cm) of the ground in early spring to let the flowers through.

To obtain more plants, divide epimediums in fall or early spring. Many species can thrive for decades without division, although the clumps do get slowly wider. Although most epimediums form this sort of slowly expanding mound, there are a few that produce underground runners and thus spread more quickly, although not to the point of invasiveness. All make great accent and edging plants, but they are truly outstanding as groundcovers. Given their slow rate of growth, plant them quite closely together, about 10 inches (25 cm) apart to create a carpet effect more rapidly.

PROBLEMS AND SOLUTIONS

Epimediums are surprisingly insect- and disease-free. Even deer and rabbits avoid them! Winter-weary leaves may show signs of spotting or browning but can simply be cut off if their appearance offends.

TOP PERFORMER

Epimedium × rubrum (red barrenwort): This plant might just be the best groundcover ever! The compound leaves are usually evergreen even in my Zone 3 climate (under snow cover, that is), lime-green heavily overlaid with red in spring, beautifully reddish-tinged in fall, then mid-green in summer. In cool summer areas like mine, they retain some of their red marbling throughout summer as well. I mustn't forget the mid- to late-spring flowers: Small but numerous, they have curving red sepals and creamy white petals. Height: 8 to 12 inches (20 to 30 cm). Spread: 1 foot (30 cm). USDA Plant Hardiness Zones 4 to 8.

MORE RECOMMENDED EPIMEDIUMS

Epimedium grandiflorum, also called *E. macranthum* (longspur barrenwort): This species is renowned for its extra-large mid- to late-spring flowers, up to 2 inches (5 cm) across. The species comes in a wide array of whites, pinks, and lavenders. This is a deciduous species in most climates, with coppery brown spring leaflets with prickly margins that turn green in summer, then purplish red in fall. 'Lilafee' ('Lilac Fairy'), with magenta flowers, is the most popular of dozens of cultivars; 'Rose Queen' is a nice deep pink. I don't think I need to describe the color of 'White Queen'! Height: 8 to 15 inches (20 to 38 cm). Spread: 15 to18 inches (38 to 45 cm). USDA Plant Hardiness Zones 4 to 8.

E. × perralchicum 'Fröhnleiten' ('Fröhnleiten' barrenwort): Very popular. It has evergreen foliage: green in summer, but bronze in both spring and winter. The large, bright yellow flowers lack the spurs so typical of many other epimediums. Height: 14 to 16 inches (35 to 40 cm). Spread: 20 to 24 inches (50 to 60 cm). USDA Plant Hardiness Zones 5 to 8.

Red barrenwort
(*Epimedium × rubrum*)

SMART SUBSTITUTES

In spots that are too shady for even epimediums, galax (*Galax urceolata*, syn. *G. apetala*) really stands out. It forms a similar deep, even carpet of evergreen, shiny leaves, but the leathery leaves are kidney- or heart-shaped and the flowers—wand-shaped spikes of small but densely packed pure white blooms in spring—are likewise very different. This eastern North American native will thrive in shade so deep that almost nothing else will grow. The leaves are popular in floral arrangements—but don't start harvesting them until the plant is mature, which can take 3 or 4 years. Height: 12 to 18 inches (30 to 45 cm). Spread: 12 inches (30 cm). USDA Plant Hardiness Zones 5 to 8.

Filipendula
Meadowsweet

PLANT PROFILE

FILIPENDULA

fil-uh-PEN-dew-luh

Bloom Color:
White, pink, and red

Bloom Time:
Summer

Length of Bloom:
3 weeks or more

Height:
Varies by species; see individual listings

Spread:
Varies by species; see individual listings

Garden Uses:
Cut flower garden, mass planting, meadow garden, mixed border, seasonal hedge, specimen plant; in wet areas

Light Preference:
Full sun to partial shade

Soil Preference:
Moist to well-drained, preferably neutral to alkaline soil

Best Way to Propagate:
Divide in spring or fall

USDA Plant Hardiness Zones:
3 to 8

"Tough as nails" well describes meadowsweets: They are long-lived, sturdy perennials, often shrublike in appearance. They're very close to shrubs in many ways, with a distinctly woody base. Not so long ago, as a matter of fact, they were included in the genus *Spiraea* (spireas), which is well known for its shrubs. The pinnate or hand-shaped leaves have deeply imbedded veins, giving meadowsweets an attractive "rough" texture. The flowers are extremely tiny, with minuscule petals but comparatively long stamens.

GROWING TIPS

Meadowsweets positively thrive in partial shade, such as on the edge of a woodland. In the wild they are often found on the edges of swamps and indeed prefer moist conditions at all times, especially when they are grown in full sun. Established plants will put up with occasional drought but will not likely thrive in spots that regularly remain dry for long periods.

These are pretty much "plant-'em-and-leave-'em" perennials. They don't need staking, deadheading, or any other kind of fussy care. About the only thing you may want to do is to cut back the previous year's flowerstalks in fall or spring.

Meadowsweets slowly increase in diameter over many years and will one day get to the point where it is time to consider dividing them. This is not an easy task, as the root system is quite woody and hard to dig out: You may need an axe or a saw to separate them. Once the chopping is finished, though, they recuperate readily from transplanting shock.

PROBLEMS AND SOLUTIONS

Meadowsweets often seem to breeze through periods of drought unscathed, but then their leaves go white with powdery mildew. Keep them moist and there will be no problem.

TOP PERFORMER

Filipendula ulmaria 'Aurea' (golden meadowsweet, golden queen-of-the-meadow): This is the gold-leaf form of the species and absolutely the best meadowsweet for the shade garden. The chartreuse-yellow saw-toothed leaves literally glow in the dark! The fuzzy white, deliciously scented blooms, however, don't show up particularly well on this cultivar, but then who cares? This one is truly grown for its foliage. Since flowers are of little importance, you can plant this in deeper shade than other meadowsweets; if it doesn't bloom or blooms only lightly, you won't be missing much. Set this plant off against the dark foliage of forest shrubs and just watch your shady nook come to life! Of course, the species itself (*F. ulmaria*), with dark green leaves, is also very nice—as is the even more popular cultivar 'Flore Pleno', with longer-lasting double white flowers. 'Variegata' ('Aureovariegata') has dark green leaves with a yellow splotch in the center and single white flowers. Height: 30 to 72 inches (75 to 180 cm). Spread: 36 inches (90 cm). USDA Plant Hardiness Zones 3 to 7.

Golden meadowsweet
(*Filipendula ulmaria* 'Aurea')

MORE RECOMMENDED MEADOWSWEETS

Filipendula multijuga (dwarf meadowsweet): This is a brand-new one to me that I've only just started testing. It has palm-shaped leaves and fluffy pink astilbe-like flowers on a very dwarf plant. It seems to like its soil truly damp and would be best used at the bottom of a slope or on the border of a water garden. A great groundcover for a moist, semi-shady to sunny spot! 'Fuji Haze' has variegated foliage speckled creamy yellow in spring, but the leaves often green up in summer. Height: 8 to 10 inches (20 to 25 cm). Spread: 12 to 15 inches (30 to 38 cm). USDA Plant Hardiness Zones: Not fully tested, but certainly a safe bet in Zones 5 to 8.

F. rubra (queen-of-the-prairie): This Eastern native is a real monster, with huge fluffy flowerheads of peachy pink blooms borne on sturdy stems over dark green leaves. It makes a fantastic background plant—and what an accent for the partially shady border! More popular than the species itself is 'Venusta' (also sold as 'Magnifica'), with huge clusters of deep rose flowers. Height: 6 to 8 feet (1.8 to 2.4 m). Spread: 3 to 4 feet (1 to 1.2 m). USDA Plant Hardiness Zones 3 to 8.

LARRY'S GARDEN NOTES

Like many plants now considered ornamentals, meadowsweets have a long history of use as medicinal plants. In fact, it was from *Filipendula ulmaria* that ASA (acetylsalicylic acid) was first derived back in 1835 by a French chemist. However, the chemical sat unnoticed for more than 60 years until 1897, when a German scientist working for Bayer, Felix Hoffman, discovered the product's usefulness and found out how to synthesize it. Thus aspirin was borne, from "a" as in acetylsalicylic acid and "spir" from *Spiraea ulmaria*, as *Filipendula ulmaria* was known at the time.

Fragaria
Strawberry

Strawberries have attractive evergreen trifoliate leaves and pretty flowers looking rather like single roses—so why not try moving strawberries from the vegetable patch to a more decorative setting? There are, in fact, several varieties of strawberries that are grown more for their ornamental qualities than their gustative ones. Most are used as low-growing groundcovers, taking advantage of their natural tendency to spread, but they also look spectacular tumbling from containers or cascading down over walls.

GROWING TIPS

Strawberries sometimes wander into truly shady corners and root there, but in fact they prefer partial shade to sun. Most well-drained soils are fine, although they do best in richer soils that remain slightly moist at all times.

Individual plants are often short-lived, dying out after 2 or 3 years, but each crown produces a number of wirelike creeping stolons, each bearing a baby plant at its tip, often at quite some distance from the mother plant. These root in their turn so it matters little if the original crown dies, as its offspring will carry on. This means of spreading makes them interesting for use as groundcovers, as they often fill in empty spots all on their own. If not, you only have to direct a stolon to the right spot and plunk a stone down on it to hold the plantlet in place while it roots. It also means strawberries wander terribly, and keeping them under control may take a bit of effort: Try surrounding a strawberry patch with such dense plantings of taller plants that their stolons can't find their way through.

Although strawberry leaves are evergreen in most climates, it's best to cut them back in early spring to leave room for new growth and to clean up older leaves as they start to become frayed or spotted. This can be done quickly and easily with a lawn mower or a string trimmer.

Multiplication is a snap. Simply dig up and move rooted plantlets to a new planting bed as needed. Most ornamental strawberries are hybrids, however, and don't come true from seed.

Note: Taxonomists have more than a few doubts about the

validity of the genus *Fragaria*, and most now agree that strawberries really belong in the genus *Potentilla*.

PROBLEMS AND SOLUTIONS

Leaf diseases can be a problem and are best prevented by cutting off and destroying the old leaves in spring and removing dead or dying plants as you notice them. Avoid crown rot by making sure the plants are well drained.

TOP PERFORMER

Fragaria Hybrids, actually *Potentilla* × *rosea* (pink strawberry, strawberry cinquefoil): When you know that all wild strawberries have white flowers, it can be a bit of a shock to discover pink-blooming ones—and even a few that are nearly red! The secret is that these plants are not pure strawberries but crosses between a strawberry and bog cinquefoil (*Potentilla palustris*), a more upright plant with red flowers. The resulting plants look just like strawberries, except for their pink to deep rose blooms. Most even produce edible strawberries, although they are not produced too prolifically. Blooms, on the other hand, are abundant, especially in late spring and early summer, although they do appear sporadically throughout summer and into fall. 'Frel' ('Pink Panda') has mid-pink flowers, 'Lipstick' has deeper pink flowers, 'Shades of Pink' has flowers that range from near white to deep rose, while 'Samba' ('Red Ruby') is pretty much the color the name suggests. Height: 6 inches (15 cm). Spread: Indefinite. USDA Plant Hardiness Zones 2 to 8.

MORE RECOMMENDED STRAWBERRIES

Fragaria vesca, actually *Potentilla vesca* (alpine strawberry): This is the plant known as *fraise des bois* in better restaurants. In the ornamental garden, it is grown mostly for its numerous white flowers produced over a long season, from late spring through fall, and for its sweet but tiny red berries. 'Yellow Wonder' has attractive yellow berries that the birds don't seem to notice. The most popular ornamental variety is, however, 'Variegata'. It is a poor bloomer and even poorer fruit producer, but it has leaves attractively variegated white. Height: 6 to 10 inches (15 to 25 cm). Spread: Indefinite. USDA Plant Hardiness Zones 4 to 8.

Pink panda strawberry
(*Fragaria* Hybrid 'Frel')

LARRY'S GARDEN NOTES

Strawberries can be wildlife magnets, especially species that fruit prolifically. Birds and mammals really enjoy their berries and will often come back day after day looking for more, as ornamental strawberries tend to produce their berries a few at a time over several months. For best results, let the plants spread at will in a secluded part of the yard where the visiting animals won't sense too much of a human presence—and keep your pets indoors or tied up so they won't scare the visitors off.

Galium

Sweet woodruff, bedstraw

If you're looking for a carpeting groundcover that can thrive under the harsh combination of severe root competition and fairly deep shade, sweet woodruff is an excellent choice. Thanks to its shallow root system, it can settle in right over tree roots, spreading horizontally just under a layer of mulch. It produces numerous pure white flowers in spring, enough to make you think the wood has been hit by a late snowfall, and its delightfully whorled foliage maintains the display throughout summer and into fall. In moderate climates, it is evergreen; elsewhere it remains green until late fall but sprouts very early the next spring, so its winter absence is not too noticeable.

GROWING TIPS

All sweet woodruff really needs is evenly moist soil and some protection from burning sun to thrive. Any type of soil seems to suit it, from acid to alkaline and rich to poor, but it won't do well in areas where the soil becomes bone-dry in summer. Consider mulching it well in spots you think might be too dry: It will push right through mulch, and the mulch will keep its roots cooler and moister. In cooler climates, it seems equally at home in sun or even fairly deep shade; in hotter areas, though, it doesn't seem to adapt as well to either sun or deep shade, so partial shade is best.

If you can find a neighbor with a supply of sweet woodruff, there should be no need to buy it. Just dig up a shovelful, wash off the roots to see what you are doing when dividing, and then divide the clumps (often into 40 or more plants!). Even if you buy a pot of it, you can usually divide it immediately and get several plants—enough to get your groundcover going. All each division needs is a short bit of rhizome and a few roots. Division can take place in spring or fall, and even in midsummer. You can even root cuttings from fresh spring growth if you prefer.

Sweet woodruff is so easy to grow that containing it will likely be your main concern. Like many creeping groundcovers, it knows no limits and will form a wave of greenery that will sweep over the landscape if you let it. Now, it's true that it is a small plant not given to choking its neighbors but just filling in any open spaces it encounters, but still, you may not want to see it set up shop just anywhere. If so, install planting barriers when you plant it (even commercial lawn border will do)— it creeps underground, so leaving a 1-inch (2.5-cm) lip aboveground will limit it quite nicely.

As a low-growing carpeting plant, sweet woodruff looks great with ferns, goat's-beard, and other woodlanders. I especially like to combine it with spring bulbs: Even the small ones like Siberian squill are tall enough to rise above its still-short spring growth; then as the bulb leaves fade, they are hidden by the woodruff carpet. Or try liberating it in a forested area whose undergrowth seems a bit colorless, and its spring green foliage will soon add a lot of pizzazz to the effect.

Sweet woodruff (*Galium odoratum*)

PROBLEMS AND SOLUTIONS

Pest and disease problems are rare.

TOP PERFORMER

Galium odoratum, syn. *Asperula odorata* (sweet woodruff, bedstraw): There are almost 400 species of *Galium,* but most are not particularly attractive, and in fact many are pernicious weeds. Sweet woodruff is the only species that seems to have any true ornamental use. The small white flowers are very lightly perfumed and a delight to see and smell, of course, but the name *odoratum* comes not from the flowers but the foliage, which is even more delightfully scented when crushed. In fact, the plant is also called bedstraw because the dried leaves and stems were once added to pillows and mattresses so they could give off their pleasant strawlike scent as people slept. It was also used as a strewing herb on dirt floors to chase away foul odors. The Germans use sweet woodruff (they call it "Waldmeister" or master of the woods) in preparing a popular drink, Maiwein (May wine). You can buy Maiwein in liquor stores, but you can also make your own by steeping chopped-up spring stems and leaves in white wine.

KISSING COUSINS

Sweet woodruff has an absolutely charming cousin in annual woodruff (*Asperula orientalis*). This is a slightly taller plant with similar but longer whorled leaves topped off with clusters of tubular blue flowers throughout summer and sometimes right through fall. It is as shade-tolerant as its cousin but will also grow in sun, self-sowing lightly (but not to the point of weediness) where it is happy. It's an easy annual to grow (just sow it directly *in situ*) but rather hard to obtain. For reasons unknown, it is rarely seen in garden centers and nurseries, it's easy enough to find in catalogs and through the Internet. Height: 8 to 12 inches (20 to 30 cm). Spread: 3 to 4 inches (8 to 10 cm).

Geranium
Hardy geranium, cranesbill

PLANT PROFILE

GERANIUM

juh-RAIN-ee-um

Bloom Color:
Blue, purple, magenta, pink, red, and white

Bloom Time:
Varies by species; see individual listings

Length of Bloom:
Varies by species; see individual listings

Height:
Varies by species; see individual listings

Spread:
Varies by species; see individual listings

Garden Uses:
Container planting, edging, groundcover, mass planting, mixed border, rock garden, woodland garden

Light Preference:
Full sun to shade

Soil Preference:
Humus-rich, evenly moist, well-drained soil

Best Way to Propagate:
Divide or take stem cuttings in spring

USDA Plant Hardiness Zones:
Varies by species; see individual listings

Many of the over 250 species of *Geranium* are ideal for shade. The hardy geraniums have starlike, five-petaled flowers in a wide range of colors and deeply cut, maplelike foliage that often turns brilliant colors in fall. There are dozens of species, ranging from low border types to tall background varieties. Most bloom in late spring, but some are repeat-bloomers and will continue to flower through much of summer.

GROWING TIPS

Hardy geraniums are very adaptable plants and will grow under a wide range of conditions, but most do tend to prefer evenly moist soil. The shade-tolerant varieties described here can take full sun in the North but prefer partial shade in the South. Some are very shade-tolerant and not at all bothered by deep shade.

Division is the most popular means of propagation, and indeed some hardy geraniums are so prolific there is plenty of material to work with.

PROBLEMS AND SOLUTIONS

Slugs can damage young leaves but are rarely a serious problem. Rust can be a problem on some species, and mildew may affect the foliage at the end of the season.

TOP PERFORMER

Geranium macrorrhizum (bigroot geranium, scented geranium): This geranium can be a thug because it spreads so rapidly. In a shady, root-infested corner where little else does well, though, bigroot geranium is more likely to be friend than a foe. It is a truly tough geranium, growing equally well in both hot- and cool-summer areas, in full sun (in the North at least) and deep shade. True, it blooms for only a relatively short period in spring, but the large, deeply cut leaves, evergreen in warmer climates or where snow cover is good, are attractive all summer and have excellent fall color. The leaves are scented when crushed—the "oil of geranium" used in perfumery is derived from this plant. The species has magenta flowers, but there are several cultivars in shades ranging from white to pink to near red, such as 'Ing-wersen's Variety (violet-pink) and 'Album' (white with a light pink tinge). 'Variegatum' has leaves irregularly mottled cream and lilac-pink flowers. Height: 15 to 18 inches (38 to 45 cm). Spread: Indefinite. USDA Plant Hardiness Zones 3 to 9.

MORE RECOMMENDED HARDY GERANIUMS

Geranium × *oxonianum* (Oxford geranium): This natural hybrid is a tough, spreading geranium along the lines of bigroot geranium, but it blooms for nearly 2 months in the South and almost continuously in cool-summer areas. The flowers are small but numerous, usually in shades of pink with darker veins. As with most geraniums, there are dozens of cultivars, among which 'A. T. Johnson' (rose-pink) and 'Claridge Druce' (purple-pink with dark veining) are the most widely available. This species is best in full sun to partial shade; it blooms poorly in true shade. Height: 2 feet (60 cm). Spread: Indefinite. USDA Plant Hardiness Zones 4 to 9.

G. phaeum (mourning widow): This hardy geranium has unusually colored nodding flowers that are deep purple, indeed almost black. The dark color is responsible for the common name—it does seem to be wearing widow's weeds (mourning clothes). Or, try one of the numerous cultivars available in other shades, such as 'Album', which is white and sometimes faintly flushed pink; or 'Lily Lovell', with dark mauve flowers and lighter green leaves. Height: 18 to 24 inches (45 to 60 cm). Spread: 18 inches (45 cm). USDA Plant Hardiness Zones 3 to 9.

G. sanguineum (bloody cranesbill): This is a very common hardy geranium of very modest size with an attractive mounding habit that can be used as a groundcover or an edging plant. It prefers some sunlight, so it's better in partial shade. The flowers are small but numerous and appear from mid-spring through early summer, sometimes right through summer for some cultivars, such as the classic *G. sanguineum* var. *striatum* (*G. sanguineum* 'Lancastriense' or 'Prostratum'), almost never without a few light pink flowers with darker veins. There are dozens of cultivars. Height: 9 to 12 inches (23 to 30 cm). Spread: 12 inches (30 cm). USDA Plant Hardiness Zones 3 to 9.

Bloody cranesbill (*Geranium sanguineum* var. *striatum*)

LARRY'S GARDEN NOTES

Confusion reigns when it comes to geraniums, as there are two very different plants masquerading under the same name: hardy geraniums, of the genus *Geranium*, and the pelargoniums or "garden geraniums" (genus *Pelargonium*). True geraniums (*Geranium* spp.) are, for the most part, hardy plants (although some are of subtropical origin) and usually grow from a central crown or have creeping rhizomes. Pelargoniums, which include that ever-popular "annual," the zonal geranium (*P.* × *hortorum*), as well as the ivy geranium (*P. peltatum*), usually have thicker, sometimes almost woody stems and are not hardy in most climates. Instead they're grown as annuals or brought indoors in winter. Both do share a similar seed capsule: long and pointed, like a stork or crane's bill. In fact, both botanical names refer to the beaklike appearance of the capsule: *Geranos* means crane and *pelargos* means stork.

Gillenia
Bowman's root

PLANT PROFILE

GILLENIA

jil-LEE-nee-uh

Bloom Color:
  White and pinkish white

Bloom Time:
  Late spring to early summer

Length of Bloom:
  3 to 4 weeks

Height:
  2 to 4 feet (60 to 120 cm)

Spread:
  3 feet (90 cm)

Garden Uses:
  Mass planting, mixed border,
  woodland garden

Light Preference:
  Full sun to shade

Soil Preference:
  Rich, moist, well-drained soil

Best Way to Propagate:
  Divide in spring or fall

USDA Plant Hardiness Zones:
  4 to 8

This pretty, underused perennial always strikes me as being halfway between a shrub and a perennial. It has the woody root system of a shrub and even fairly woody branches. Even the leaves are set on the reddish stems in a rather shrublike pattern. But when it is in bloom, the dainty, dancing butterfly flowers on their thin stems are very much those of a perennial. Even after the flowers have dropped off the red sepals remain, extending the "blooming period" well into fall. Oddly enough, this North American native perennial is far more popular in European gardens than in its native home. Perhaps this description will help change that!

GROWING TIPS

If bowman's root is fairly unknown, it's not because it is hard to grow. Native to open woodlands, it does best in fairly good light but with at least some protection from the heat of the sun. I have a colony growing on the east side of my home where they get only the very earliest morning sun and are in deep, sunless shade for the rest of the day, yet they absolutely thrive. Humus-rich soils ranging from slightly alkaline to fairly acid are best, but it seems to adapt well to most soil conditions. Good, even soil humidity is a must during the establishment phase, but it eventually becomes quite drought-resistant. Mulching is still wise to help keep the soil cool and moist—even if the plant tolerates drought, that doesn't mean it prefers it!

Once your plant is established, you'll discover that it actually spreads quite readily—not to the point of being truly weedy, but you'd do best not to plant it in a tight spot. If you're worried about it becoming too aggressive, grow within a root barrier (see page 54). I suggest naturalizing it in an open woodland where it can spread at will. Under such circumstances, its casual spreading habit slowly leads to the development of a sizeable and attractive colony. The offsets, which pop up here and there from underground runners, are the ideal sources of multiplication material—simply dig them up and move them!

Cut back the flowerstalks in spring. It's just as well to leave them standing during winter, as the seed-heads are not unattractive and often remain in place until spring.

PROBLEMS AND SOLUTIONS

There are no particular insect problems. Rust is a potential threat, but it doesn't appear frequently in garden plantings.

TOP PERFORMER

Gillenia trifoliata, syn. *Porteranthus trifoliatus* (bowman's root, Indian physic): This is a very attractive shrubby perennial with, as the name suggests, trifoliate leaves. The leaves are borne on very short stems and are pointed and finely toothed along the edges. They sometimes have a reddish green tinge to them, a shade that carries over from the branching mahogany-red stems, and turn bright red in fall. The star-shaped flowers have long, often twisting petals and are produced in great numbers on established plants. They are usually white, although pinkish varieties are said to be available. If you can't find this plant in your local garden center, try an herb specialist. There is a very dwarf cultivar, 'Pixie', only 6 inches (15 cm) high in bloom, that has become available in the last few years, although its commercial availability is still very limited. It makes a wonder groundcover. Height: 2 to 4 feet (60 to 120 cm). Spread: 3 feet (90 cm). USDA Plant Hardiness Zones 4 to 8.

MORE RECOMMENDED BOWMAN'S ROOTS

Gillenia stipulata, syn. *Porteranthus stipulatus* (American ipecac): This species is so similar to the previous one in general appearance that the two would be hard to tell apart, except it has five leaflets instead of three. (In fact, the two extra leaflets aren't true leaves, but "stipules.") It is likewise native to eastern North America but is more abundant in the South. Correspondingly it does better in humid, hot summers than bowman's root. It has a long use as a medicinal plant, as the common name suggests. Height: 2 to 4 feet (60 to 120 cm). Spread: 3 feet (90 cm). USDA Plant Hardiness Zones 5 to 9.

Bowman's root (*Gillenia trifoliata*)

LARRY'S GARDEN NOTES

Bowman's root gets its name from its long, underground rhizomes, straight as a bowstring. Native peoples used to harvest the rhizomes and remove the bark to be ground up for medicinal purposes. It's not clear, however, that the rhizome was ever used as a bowstring: Stripped of its bark, it may simply have had the appearance of bowstring.

Helleborus

Hellebore

PLANT PROFILE

HELLEBORUS

hell-uh-BOR-us

Bloom Color:
White, green, pink, purple, red, and yellow

Bloom Time:
Late winter to midspring

Length of Bloom:
8 to 12 weeks or more

Height:
8 to 24 inches (20 to 60 cm)

Spread:
10 to 18 inches (25 to 45 cm)

Garden Uses:
Edging, groundcover, mass planting, mixed border, rock garden, woodland garden; along paths

Light Preference:
Partial shade to shade

Soil Preference:
Humus-rich, moist, well-drained soil

Best Way to Propagate:
Divide in spring or sow fresh seed when ripe

USDA Plant Hardiness Zones:
4 to 9

Hellebores are among the earliest of all spring-flowering perennials and certainly the longest-lasting. Their cup-shaped, semi-hanging flowers can be in bloom as early as December in truly mild climates, but more likely February, March, or April. They were long the preserve of plant collectors because they were so expensive and slow growing, but they've come a long way down in price now, and full-size plants are often quite affordable.

GROWING TIPS

Immature plants are slow to establish and can take a decade before they become truly productive. They'll start new colonies by self-sowing, but only after yet another decade. If you want fast results, go for a large pot with a well-established plant.

Best results are obtained in rich, humusy soil that is always slightly moist and in partial shade or seasonal sun, such as under deciduous trees. They will tolerate drought once they're established, but not wet feet. Full sun is fine in cooler climates but should be avoided in warm ones.

The best advice I can give about hellebores is to plant them, mulch them, and ignore them. They don't like being disturbed and really don't need your help. Dividing or moving them sets them back, and they can take years to recover. If you want more, wait until they self-sow, which they will do eventually. Young seedlings transplant quite well, so move them where you want them.

If you want to obtain an exact clone of the original, you can divide hellebores. You'll likely see little bloom for 2 or 3 years, but for choice varieties, the wait is well worth it.

Warning: Hellebores are poisonous in all their parts, especially the roots, and some people even break out into a rash by simply getting sap on their skin. Wear gloves if you're subject to skin irritation.

PROBLEMS AND SOLUTIONS

Like many other slow-growing perennials, hellebores are little troubled by insects and diseases, and most herbivores avoid them.

TOP PERFORMER

Helleborus × *hybridus* (hybrid hellebore): Hellebore labeling is terribly confused, and most plants labeled *H. orientalis* or *H. niger* are actually of hybrid origin. That's fine, as the hybrids tend to be easier to grow than the species, adapting readily to average garden conditions. They tend to most closely resemble Lenten rose (*H. orientalis*) in their general habit of growth: dark green deeply cut leaves, with usually several cup-shaped flowers per stem. The leaves, as with most hellebores, are evergreen and attractive throughout the year. The blooms of hybrid types can be white through purple and any shade in between, with pendant flowers or nearly upright ones, single or double. They usually bloom in very late winter or early spring. Height: 16 to 24 inches (40 to 60 cm). Spread: 12 to 18 inches (30 to 45 cm). USDA Plant Hardiness Zones 4 to 9.

MORE RECOMMENDED HELLEBORES

Helleborus foetidus (stinking hellebore): With a name like that, you'd expect quite a stink, but in fact the odor is scarcely noticeable outdoors: Cool spring temperatures tend to put a cap on it. This is not a good choice for a bouquet in a warm room, though—you'll definitely notice it then! This is very different from the average hellebore with its upright stems (the more common hellebores are stemless), numerous but small green flowers, and fast rate of growth. In fact, stinking hellebore reaches full size in just 2 to 3 years. It isn't as long-lived as the other hellebores, but it self-sows with much greater abandon. It blooms in late winter or early spring. Height: 18 to 24 inches (45 to 60 cm). Spread: 18 inches (45 cm). USDA Plant Hardiness Zones 4 to 9.

H. niger (Christmas rose): True, this is a particularly persnickety hellebore, given to disappearing without a trace if conditions aren't to its liking. But it *is* the first perennial to bloom each year, and if there is any chance a hellebore will bloom at Christmas, this is the one that will do it. The blooms are white to whitish green, sometimes with a pink tinge, gradually turning green to pink over the long flowering season. Height: 12 to 18 inches (30 to 45 cm). Spread: 12 inches (30 cm). USDA Plant Hardiness Zones 3 to 9.

Christmas rose (*Helleborus niger* 'Potter's Wheel')

LARRY'S GARDEN NOTES

A plant with a name like Christmas rose *must* have a legend to go along with it—and there are actually many of them. Here's just one.

At the first Christmas, a young peasant girl was upset because she had nothing to offer the baby Jesus. She began to cry, and an angel appeared before her, sweeping away the snow to reveal a beautiful white flower that she offered to the Christ child. So ever after, the Christmas rose has bloomed at Christmastime in the hopes of yet again being offered to Jesus.

Hepatica
Hepatica

Until you've seen a hepatica in full bloom, you might wonder what the fuss is all about. After all, the five or more petaled flowers aren't particularly large and they certainly don't last long. Of course, the foliage is nice enough, but there are other plants with pretty leaves. Then you actually see a clump of hepaticas—or better yet, a woodland full of them. A tiny plant, true enough, but so abundantly covered in bloom. In the cold of early spring, when little if anything else is in bloom, their brilliant colors literally jump out at you. And so you find yourself hooked on hepaticas, like so many other passionate gardeners!

GROWING TIPS

Hepaticas are plants of deep deciduous forests. They don't need a lot of sunshine during summer months but do appreciate good light in spring when the leaves are off the trees. They gather yet more solar energy when tree leaves drop off again in fall, as hepaticas keep their leaves until the following spring.

You'll usually find wild hepaticas in alkaline or neutral soils, often in leaf litter over heavy and claylike soil, yet they seem surprisingly adaptable. I have a thriving, self-sowing colony in compost-enriched peat all around my rhododendrons! Hepaticas like moist springs but are tolerant of summer drought.

Hepaticas are slow to establish and don't appreciate disturbance. When you divide them, do so carefully, and water them well for the entire first summer. When they're established, they'll let you know: They'll bloom their heads off, and soon self-sown seedlings start to appear. You could collect the seed and sow them yourself, but they do such a good job of sowing themselves that it's practically a wasted effort. Instead, wait a year or so until the seedlings have three to five leaves, then move them carefully to their new home. Most come true to type from seed unless there are other clones in the neighborhood, in which case you'll find some interesting mixes.

PROBLEMS AND SOLUTIONS

Snails and slugs are a problem in spring but don't bother mature leaves. Leaf disease is possible; remove infected foliage.

TOP PERFORMER

Hepatica acutiloba (sharp-lobed hepatica): This is one of the two eastern North American species (the other is *H. americana*) that actually share the same habitat and often grow together in the wild. They are, in fact, so similar in appearance when in bloom that only their foliage gives them away: The three-lobed leaves of *H. acutiloba* have pointed tips; those of *H. americana* have rounded ones. Sometimes plants don't clearly belong to one species or the other and are probably hybrids. Certainly their flowers look the same, though: five rounded "petals" (actually sepals, as hepaticas have no true petals) with yellow stamens in the center. The usual color is lavender-blue, but purple, pink, and white forms are available. After the flowers fade (and they scarcely last a week), the leaves take over. Their leathery texture and capacity to survive right up until the first snows and beyond mean hepaticas make great groundcovers. By spring the old leaves are looking pretty battered, but new ones appear with the flowers so the plant looks great all summer again. Height: 3 to 9 inches (8 to 23 cm). Spread: 6 inches (15 cm). USDA Plant Hardiness Zones 3 to 9.

MORE RECOMMENDED HEPATICAS

Hepatica americana (round-lobed hepatica): The common name says it all: It looks just like sharp-lobed hepatica except for the rounded leaf lobes. Same color range, same care, same effect. Height: 3 to 8 inches (8 to 20 cm). Spread: 6 inches (15 cm). USDA Plant Hardiness Zones 3 to 9.

H. nobilis (European hepatica): With leaves between *H. americana* and *H. acutiloba*—that is, neither pointed nor truly rounded—you'd think it was a cross between the two. Actually, though, *H. nobilis* comes from an entirely different region; it's native to much of Eurasia. Some taxonomists suggest there is, in fact, but one circumpolar species of hepatica that has a few regional variations; it makes sense to me! Height: 3 to 8 inches (8 to 20 cm). Spread: 6 inches (15 cm). USDA Plant Hardiness Zones 3 to 9.

Sharp-lobed hepatica
(*Hepatica acutiloba*)

LARRY'S GARDEN NOTES

According to the *Doctrine of Signatures*, very popular in sixteenth-century Europe, God made all plants for man's use and left a sign to indicate what it was for. Obviously, therefore, hepatica, with its liver-shaped leaves, was to be used to treat liver ailments. In fact, the genus name is derived from the Greek *hepar*, for liver, while "liverwort" is a common name for the genus in Europe. Although the *Doctrine of Signatures* is now considered the wildest of fiction, there are still numerous home remedies for liver problems that involve using dried hepatica leaves or roots.

Heuchera

Heuchera, alumroot, coral bells

PLANT PROFILE

HEUCHERA

HUE-ker-uh

Bloom Color:
Pink, red, white, purple, and greenish white

Bloom Time:
Late spring to early summer

Length of Bloom:
3 to 4 weeks

Height:
12 to 36 inches (30 to 90 cm)

Spread:
12 to 18 inches (30 to 45 cm)

Garden Uses:
Container planting, edging, groundcover, mass planting, mixed border, rock garden, specimen plant, woodland garden; attracts hummingbirds

Light Preference:
Full sun to shade

Soil Preference:
Average, moist, well-drained soil

Best Way to Propagate:
Divide in spring or fall

USDA Plant Hardiness Zones:
4 to 9

Heucheras used to have attractive but rather ordinary foliage forming a mound that set off narrow upright stalks of white, pink, or red flowers—and it was the flowers that counted! Then the varieties with colorful foliage appeared, and suddenly blooms didn't even matter. Purples, silvers, oranges, yellows—only the foliage counted. Indeed, within a 10-year period, heucheras have gone from pretty but little-known flowering plants to staple garden foliage plants that rival hostas in popularity!

GROWING TIPS

Heucheras are very adaptable plants, putting up with most kinds of soil except those that are waterlogged. In the wild, they are plants of the deciduous forest, so deep to partial shade is just perfect. They do like their spring sun, though, and won't grow as well under conifers. They'll also put up with full sun in the North and in cooler climates. The foliage types seem to grow equally well in cool as in warm climates.

Heucheras age badly—their crowns begin to rise up above the soil, leaving them exposed to the elements, and then they suddenly die. You can chop these off and hope new sprouts will appear, or dig them up, divide them, and replant them so the crown is level with the ground around it.

Modern cultivars are complex hybrids and don't even come close to coming true from seed. Commercially the plants are produced by tissue culture, but division is the way to go in the home garden.

Maintenance may also require cutting back damaged foliage in spring. Heucheras are "partially evergreen": In colder climates, leaves can suffer various degrees of damage and will look much better if you remove damaged leaves in spring to make room for new leaves. Cut off flowerstalks after they bloom unless you want them to self-sow.

PROBLEMS AND SOLUTIONS

Heucheras rarely suffer from serious pests or diseases. If caterpillars show up (and it does happen), hand-pick or spray with BT (*Bacillus thuringiensis*).

TOP PERFORMER

Heuchera Hybrids (heuchera): I have given up even trying to categorize all those heucheras with attractive foliage according to species. I consider them all mixed hybrids, identifiable only by cultivar name. There was a time when affinities were more evident: *H. micrantha* var. *diversifolia* 'Palace Purple', with deep purple leaves and insignificant flowers, is the granddaddy of all the heucheras with colorful leaves and could be placed within the species *H. micrantha.* But today's cultivars are definitively a mixed bag. I almost feel there is no point in presenting them, as dozens of new ones appear on the market every year, pushing dozens of old ones to one side. However, here are a few I feel might have lasting qualities. 'Pewter Veil' has silvery gray leaves with purple tones and gray veins; 'Chocolate Ruffles' has large ruffled leaves of chocolate brown; 'Plum Pudding' has smaller ones of deep purple, and the list goes on. Then there are the golds and ambers, colors that really stand out in dark corners: 'Amber Waves' with amber-gold wrinkled foliage; 'Lime Rickey' with bright chartreuse; 'Marmalade' with orange foliage and red highlights. Height: 12 to 36 inches (30 to 90 cm). Spread: 12 to 18 inches (30 to 45 cm). USDA Plant Hardiness Zones 4 to 9.

Heuchera
(*Heuchera* 'Amethyst Mist')

MORE RECOMMENDED HEUCHERAS

Heuchera sanguinea (coral bells): These are the "other" heucheras, the ones with smaller green to gray-green leaves, grown mostly for their flowers. I suggest calling them "coral bells" (for their bell-shaped flowers) to help distinguish them from the foliage crowd, almost universally called heucheras. Admittedly, a lot of hybridizing has been going on, and many coral bells are not pure *H. sanguinea* (the name *H.* × *brizoides* is often used for hybrids of mixed origin), but all share the narrow upright flowerstalks and tiny but attractive white, pink, coral, or red flowers that are their claim to fame. Partial shade is best and full sun is tolerated, especially in the North or if the plants are well mulched. Height: 12 to 36 inches (30 to 90 cm). Spread: 12 to 18 inches (30 to 45 cm). USDA Plant Hardiness Zones 4 to 9.

KISSING COUSINS

One can scarcely mention *Heuchera* without mentioning foamy bells (× *Heucherella*), a hybrid between *Heuchera* and *Tiarella*, but they are described with the latter on page 218. Another heuchera cousin that deserves a plug is the piggyback plant (*Tolmiea menziesii*). Its evergreen hirsute apple green leaves make a great groundcover and have the curious habit of producing baby plantlets at their base. These weigh the leaf down until it touches the ground, then the babies root and produce their own plants, making a self-sufficient groundcover that spreads all on its own. There's a gold-mottled cultivar called 'Taff's Gold' ('Variegata') that is widely available. Height: 12 to 24 inches (30 to 60 cm). Spread: Indefinite. USDA Plant Hardiness Zones 4 to 10.

Hosta

Hosta, plantain lily, funkia

Hostas are mounded perennials with broad, often variegated leaves and upright stalks of bell-shaped flowers usually in shades of lavender and white. They are ubiquitous shade plants—it's hard to image a shade garden without them. And for good reason: Hostas are attractive, simple to grow, long-lived, and really do put up with shade.

GROWING TIPS

Hostas are the consummate shade plants. In no hurry to grow, they just take advantage of what little light there is to slowly reach their full size, then they stay there, forever. You never need to divide them or replant them: Just ignore them.

Hostas will adapt to most soils, rich or poor, but prefer humus-rich, moist, well-drained soils. Established plants put up with drought, but they do like a bit of moisture at all times. Partial shade to shade is perfect, but many will take full sun in the North as long as you can keep their roots cool.

Hostas are most easily multiplied by division, either early in spring just as the new sprouts appear, or in fall. Theoretically you could divide hostas yearly and get lots of new plants, but then they'd never have time to mature. Practically, division is reserved for old, well-established plants with lots of extra sprouts.

PROBLEMS AND SOLUTIONS

You'll likely take back anything nice I've written about hostas if yours are attacked by snails and especially slugs. I suggest just avoiding the issue. Plant slug-resistant hostas, period. In most climates, under most conditions, that's all you need to do. Where slugs are especially numerous, mulch with pine needles; slugs hate them. Deer are another story and one not so easy to solve; see page 85 for suggestions.

TOP PERFORMER

Hosta Hybrids (hosta): There are dozens of species of *Hosta,* but the vast majority of hostas offered these days are hybrids. There are literally hundreds of varieties, including mini-hostas for container gardens and giant hostas that can swallow up an entire flowerbed with their foliage; hostas with narrow, broad, and heart-shaped leaves; with green, golden, blue, and variegated foliage; and even a few with large, scented flowers (most hostas have relatively insignificant flowers, and some people cut them off feeling they distract from the beauty of the foliage). One suggestion: Buy only pest-resistant hostas. With so many no-care hostas available, why would you want to start off with a plant that requires heavy maintenance?

Here are just a few suggestions, all of them slug-resistant.

'Fragrant Bouquet': One of the rare hostas grown as much for its flowers as its foliage. The huge white trumpet flowers are highly scented and produced in midsummer. The deeply ribbed leaves are pale green with a variable yellow-to-cream margin. Height (flowerstalk): 36 inches (90 cm). Height (foliage): 18 inches (45 cm). Spread: 26 inches (65 cm). USDA Plant Hardiness Zones 3 to 9.

'Great Expectations': A slow-growing hosta with beautifully heart-shaped leaves, blue-green with a large yellow central blotch. Flowers are white or very pale lavender. Height (flowerstalk): 33 inches (85 cm). Height (foliage): 22 inches (55 cm). Spread: 33 inches (85 cm). USDA Plant Hardiness Zones 3 to 9.

'Halcyon': A distinctly ribbed hosta with powder blue leaves in spring that turn dark green as summer advances. Scented pale lavender flowers in midsummer. Height (flowerstalk): 26 inches (65 cm). Height (foliage): 21 inches (53 cm). Spread: 38 inches (97 cm). USDA Plant Hardiness Zones 3 to 9.

'Patriot': 'Patriot' produces dark green leaves with a broad cream margin that becomes pure white over time. The midsummer flowers are lavender. Height (flowerstalk): 30 inches (75 cm). Height (foliage): 15 inches (38 cm). Spread: 30 inches (75 cm). USDA Plant Hardiness Zones 3 to 9.

'Sum and Substance': One of the most rewarded hostas ever, a true giant with enormous, thick, slug-resistant golden yellow leaves. It's very slow growing, though, so leave lots of room. It produces pale lavender flowers in late summer. Height (flowerstalk): 6 feet (1.8 m). Height (foliage): 3 feet (90 cm). Spread: 5 to 9 feet (1.5 to 2.7 m). USDA Plant Hardiness Zones 3 to 9.

Hosta (*Hosta* 'Halcyon')

LARRY'S GARDEN NOTES

Hostas are nearly perfect shade plants, but they are slow to come up in spring. In fact, beginning gardeners often panic when everything else seems to be up and growing while the hostas are still dormant. Don't worry, though, they *will* be back. But all that empty space in the meantime! That's where spring bulbs come in. I like to surround my hostas with an abundance of early spring bulbs: Siberian squill (*Scilla siberica*), snowdrops (*Galanthus* spp.), wood anemone (*Anemone nemorosa*), grape hyacinths (*Muscari* spp.), and so on. They're up and blooming first thing in spring, taking advantage of the abundant light filtering through the barren trees above, then just as they start to lose their charm the hostas sprout, and their spreading leaves cover up the soon-to-be bare spots. It's a perfect marriage between two stalwart and permanent groups of plants!

Houttuynia
Fishwort

PLANT PROFILE

HOUTTUYNIA
hoo-TYE-nee-uh

Bloom Color:
White

Bloom Time:
Late spring to early summer

Length of Bloom:
3 to 4 weeks

Height:
12 to 15 inches (30 to 38 cm)

Spread:
Indefinite

Garden Uses:
Container planting, edging, groundcover, water garden, woodland garden; in wet areas

Light Preference:
Full sun to partial shade

Soil Preference:
Humus-rich, moist to wet soil

Best Way to Propagate:
Divide in spring or take cuttings of new growth

USDA Plant Hardiness Zones:
4 to 8

Fishwort is a spreading deciduous plant with short but upright stems bearing heart-shaped leaves, often with a purplish tint, and very attractive and curious white flowers that always remind me of bloodroot blooms. In fact, the "flower" is an inflorescence: The elevated spike is made up of dozens of yellow flowers surrounded at their base by immaculate white petallike bracts. When crushed, the leaves give off a strong scent—and not always a pleasant one (this plant isn't called "fishwort" for nothing). However, different clones do have different scents and some are quite pleasant and lemony. Be forewarned: This plant makes a great groundcover, but also a very invasive one. Don't plant it just anywhere!

GROWING TIPS

Although I've often seen this plant recommended as an all-purpose groundcover, my experience is that it will not do at all well in ordinary garden soil. It is a semi-aquatic plant in the wild and will only really succeed in soils that stay moist. In fact, you can grow it with its roots constantly standing in water. Where the soil dries out, it will grow weakly or even slowly die away. Partial shade suits it best as the soil is less likely to dry out, but full sun is fine in aquatic conditions. It will wander into and even thrive in deeper shade but won't bloom there.

The creeping rhizomes of this plant are terribly invasive. That's not necessarily a bad thing for a groundcover, mind you, but something you should be aware of. It is best grown within an impenetrable barrier and not "let loose" in a moist flowerbed where it can spread beyond control. For that wet spot you simply don't know what to do with, this is the plant to choose! It also makes a nice choice for container water gardens.

Maintenance is fairly basic: Just keep it moist and let it grow! Some people like to mow it down in spring to clean up the dead growth from the previous year, but this isn't absolutely necessary. New spring growth provides quick cover for the previous year's leaves. Mowing can also help thicken up patchy growth. In areas of borderline hardiness, consider covering the planting with evergreen boughs for winter.

Like most naturally invasive plants, fishwort is certainly easy enough to multiply. Any rooted piece will readily start a new plant, and a shovelful will often yield dozens of divisions, enough to cover considerable ground. You can also take stem cuttings when they harden off a bit (late spring or early summer). For fast cover, plant starter plants about 8 to 10 inches (20 to 25 cm) apart.

PROBLEMS AND SOLUTIONS

Slugs and aphids are occasional problems; see page 85 for suggested controls.

TOP PERFORMER

Houttuynia cordata 'Chameleon', syn. 'Variegata' (chameleon plant): This horticultural selection, with green leaves abundantly variegated red, pink, and yellow, is far more popular than the species itself (although I must admit I find it a bit garish, especially when grown in full sun). The colors are less intense in medium shade. It blooms only sporadically, unlike the species. I'm not quite sure why a plant this colorful would bear the name "chameleon," which I think would better suit a plant that blends into its surroundings rather than stands out. This plant is said to be less invasive than the species but is still quite aggressive. Height: 12 to 15 inches (30 to 38 cm). Spread: Indefinite. USDA Plant Hardiness Zones 4 to 8.

MORE RECOMMENDED FISHWORTS

Houttuynia cordata (fishwort): The species is rarely grown as an ornamental, unfortunately, as I find it has many advantages over 'Chameleon'. It has a denser growth habit and a not unattractive reddish tinge to the foliage. It blooms quite abundantly, and the flowers are very showy. Also, there are several clones, not named though, with different scents: You can find both lemon-scented and coriander-scented cultivars, as well as others with a fishy odor. I suggest looking for this plant in Asian markets; it is a popular condiment, added notably to salads for flavoring. Look too for the double-flowered form, *Houttuynia cordata* 'Plena' (syn. 'Flore Plena')—it's absolutely charming. Height: 12 to 15 inches (30 to 38 cm). Spread: Indefinite. USDA Plant Hardiness Zones 4 to 8.

Chameleon plant
(*Houttuynia cordata* 'Chameleon')

SMART SUBSTITUTES

Groundcovers that can stand soaking-wet conditions are not legion. In fact, I can only think of one other: The flamingo plant (*Oenanthe javanica* 'Flamingo') is a perennial with deeply cut leaves beautifully colored pink, white, and light green that just loves wet conditions and will grow with its roots entirely underwater if necessary. It will also do fine in ordinary garden soil as long as it is kept at least slightly moist at all times. Like most groundcovers, where it is happy it is also quite invasive, so plant it within a barrier of some sort to keep it under control. The dome of white flowers in late summer adds a bit of spice to the display, but it is worth growing for its leaves alone. Height: 8 to 16 inches (20 to 40 cm). Spread: Indefinite. USDA Plant Hardiness Zones 5 to 11.

Iris

Iris

PLANT PROFILE

IRIS
EYE-ris

Bloom Color:
Varies by species; see individual listings

Bloom Time:
Varies by species; see individual listings

Length of Bloom:
2 weeks

Height:
Varies by species; see individual listings

Spread:
Varies by species; see individual listings

Garden Uses:
Dried flower, edging, groundcover, mass planting, mixed border, rock garden, woodland garden

Light Preference:
Full sun to shade

Soil Preference:
Humus-rich, well-drained soil

Best Way to Propagate:
Divide in early fall

USDA Plant Hardiness Zones:
Varies by species; see individual listings

The vast majority of irises love sun, and the more sun the better. However, in a genus of over 300 species, there are bound to be a few exceptions—and that's the case with the irises described here. The crested iris is a ground-hugging, carpet-forming iris with surprisingly large flowers in pale blue with a bright yellow or orange patch: a striking combination that really shows up well in darker spots. The stinking iris lives up to its name only if you crush its flowers—and you won't want to. This taller plant is especially renowned for its colorful seeds, revealed to the world when the pods split open in fall. Both are relatively little-known irises well worth discovering. And most gardeners would agree you can never have too many irises!

GROWING TIPS

Shade-tolerant irises like rich, well-drained soil that never dries out to any great degree. Mulching is very much to their liking, as it keeps the soil not only moister but also cooler. They like morning sun all year and appreciate a spot where lots of sun filters through leafless trees in spring, but they prefer the coolness of a shady to partially shady nook in the afternoon throughout summer.

Both irises described here can remain in the same spot for many years but can be divided if you need more plants. Late summer or early fall is the best time to divide them—that way they have enough time to root well and be ready to bloom the following season. They can also be grown from seed, sown fresh when the capsules mature in later summer or fall.

PROBLEMS AND SOLUTIONS

Slugs and snails can be a problem early in the season; see page 85 for suggestions on controlling them. Mulching helps prevent leaf diseases. Iris borer, which is a problem with bearded irises, is not much of a problem with these two varieties.

TOP PERFORMER

Iris cristata (crested iris): As the common name suggests, this iris has a distinct crest on its flowers, but not the fuzzy beard so well known to many iris growers. It produces a profusion of rhizomes at or just below the soil surface. The short deciduous leaves form a dense, spreading carpet; this is one of the rare irises that can be used as a groundcover. The blooms appear in mid- to late spring while the leaves are still short. (They nearly double in height after flowering.) Although the species with its pale blue flowers is still best known, there are now several cultivars, including 'Alba', with white flowers, and 'Powder Blue Giant', which is larger than the others both in leaf and flower size. All are conspicuously marked with yellow to orange crests surrounded by a white blotch and usually also darker markings. Divisions of a single rhizome placed about 6 inches (15 cm) apart will form an impenetrable, weed-free groundcover within 2 years. Height: 3 to 10 inches (8 to 20 cm). Spread: Indefinite. USDA Plant Hardiness Zones 3 to 9.

MORE RECOMMENDED IRISES

Iris foetidissima (stinking iris, stinking gladwyn): With a name like *foetidissima,* which means "the stinkiest," you'd expect a rather undesirable plant. The scent is, however, released only when you crush the flowers, and why would you want to do that? This is a very different iris than the crested iris, with a totally different growing habit, forming dense clumps of narrow, upright, evergreen leaves. The midsummer flowers are dull shades of purple, even gray, and not very seductive. Fortunately, the flowers give way to seed capsules that split open in late summer to reveal striking brilliant scarlet seeds—the plant's main drawing card. The seeds remain on the plant all winter unless birds or animals find them, and they look quite spectacular on a dull winter's day when there is nothing in bloom. This is a plant of limited hardiness, and the leaves often burn during winter. If so, no harm comes of cutting them back in spring. There are several cultivars, including ones with yellow flowers like 'Citrina' and 'Lutea', both of which are actually more attractive in bloom than the species. 'Fructo-alba' is grown for its white seeds. I do find 'Variegata' interesting, with its leaves that are striped creamy white or yellow: They really stand out in a shady garden and, of course, since the leaves are evergreen, the plant is attractive in all seasons. Height: 18 to 24 inches (45 to 60 cm). Spread: 18 inches (45 cm). USDA Plant Hardiness Zones 6 to 9.

Crested iris (*Iris cristata*)

KISSING COUSINS

The Japanese roof iris (*Iris tectorum*) is another shade-tolerant iris that is closely related to the crested iris, although larger in size. It gets both its common and its botanical names (*tectorum* means "of rooftops") from the curious habit the Japanese had of growing this plant on their thatched roofs. This was done because space was at a premium, yet the plant provided such a vital resource every family needed some. You see, the root, ground into flour, was used by Japanese women to powder their faces—and still is in kabuki theater! The flowers are lilac-blue with white crests and purple spotting and appear in summer. 'Variegata', with white-striped leaves, is particularly attractive. Height: 12 to 18 inches (30 to 45 cm). Spread: 18 inches (45 cm). USDA Plant Hardiness Zones 4 to 9.

Kirengeshoma

Kirengeshoma, yellow waxbells

Green batwings: That's what I'd call kirengeshoma if I were the one choosing a common name. And I mean that in the nicest way! The green, velvety, opposite leaves, vaguely maple-shaped with attractively toothed margins, are sessile (without petioles), at least at the top of the plant, and seem to join at the base in a batwing pattern. This is the kind of plant you'd grow for its leaves alone—and leaves are all you get from spring to late summer; then the plant is topped off with a series of pale yellow bell-shaped flowers with a waxy appearance, from whence the "yellow waxbells" you sometimes hear. This is a big, shrublike perennial and looks best when it is allowed to cover quite a bit of ground. Set it loose on the edge of a forest where it can spread slowly to its heart's content, and you'll be *really* impressed with the results!

GROWING TIPS

Think of kirengeshoma as a plant of the open deciduous woodlands and you won't go wrong. It loves the leaf litter, spring sun, and dappled summer light of such sites, and you'll find it is an absolutely permanent plant under such circumstances. In a more typical flowerbed, consider a site with morning sun and afternoon shade. Remember it looks best when it is allowed to spread (which it does, although ever so slowly), so do give it space for future expansion. It prefers humus-rich soil at least a bit on the acid side, although I've seen it growing in plain old "dirt" and it was doing fine. It does not appreciate drying out, though, so a good mulch and regular watering may be needed.

Remember this plant is very slow-growing, yet this is one plant that needs a bit of volume to look its best. For (fairly) fast results, plant five or more plants about 3 feet (90 cm) apart. A single plant can take 4 or 5 years to fill out and start looking impressive, and nearly 10 years to form a really nice clump.

Considering how long it takes this plant to start to really shine and that the less you divide it, the better it looks, you'll probably find it more advantageous to buy new plants rather than to divide your own plant yourself.

Kirengeshoma stems are solid—in fact, nearly woody—and don't need staking. In spring, just cut them back to the ground to leave room for those of the coming year.

PROBLEMS AND SOLUTIONS

Perhaps it's because this plant is fairly new to the garden world and its native pests haven't yet followed it, but kirengeshoma has so far seemed pretty much pest-free. Certainly deer don't seem to like it! Whiteflies may show up but can be dispatched with insecticidal soap.

TOP PERFORMER

Kirengeshoma koreana (Korean kirengeshoma, Korean waxbells): Sorry to direct you to the rarer of the two species, but I do feel that that if you have the choice between common kirengeshoma and Korean kirengeshoma, the latter is the better garden plant. Of course, the two are very similar, so if you can't find the Korean version don't hesitate to try the other. It's just that Korean kirengeshoma has more rigidly upright flowerstalks and the flowers are a shade less nodding, so the impact when the plant is blooming is greater. It is also a taller and somewhat hardier plant than the common version. At full maturity, this plant has a distinctly shrublike appearance. If you think of it as a shrub rather than a perennial, you'll have better luck properly placing it in the landscape. In fact, try it as a hedge: spectacular! Height: 5 to 7 feet (1.5 to 2.1 m). Spread: 2 to 4 feet (60 to 120 cm). USDA Plant Hardiness Zones 3 to 9.

MORE RECOMMENDED KIRENGESHOMAS

Kirengeshoma palmata (common kirengeshoma, yellow waxbells): This is the most widely available of the kirengeshomas. Other than for its drooping rather than upright flowerheads, its purplish stems (those of *K. koreana* tend to be greener), and its lesser stature, the two are so similar you can use them interchangeably in your garden. Of course, where you don't have a lot of vertical space, the distinctly shorter *K. palmata* will be the best choice. Height: 3 to 4 feet (90 to 120 cm). Spread: 2 to 4 feet (60 to 120 cm). USDA Plant Hardiness Zones 4 to 9.

Korean kirengeshoma
(*Kirengeshoma koreana*)

LARRY'S GARDEN NOTES

Could kirengeshomas be used as a deer barrier? A friend of mine in upstate New York noticed that part of her arborvitae hedge, with a large clump of kirengeshoma growing right up against it, was intact while all the rest was eaten. She asked friends who were growing kirengeshomas, and all affirmed not only that deer won't eat kirengeshoma, but they seem to shy away from it. I can't test this one out personally (tragically for me, there are no deer in my garden, and my neighbors are reluctant to let me introduce them), but planting deer barriers of kirengeshoma might be worth a try!

Lamium
Lamium, dead nettle

PLANT PROFILE

LAMIUM

LAY-mee-um

Bloom Color:
Varies by species; see individual listings

Bloom Time:
Late spring to early summer

Length of Bloom:
4 weeks or more

Height:
Varies by species; see individual listings

Spread:
Varies by species; see individual listings

Garden Uses:
Container planting, edging, groundcover, mass planting, mixed border, rock garden, wall planting, woodland garden; along paths, on slopes, in wet areas

Light Preference:
Full sun to shade

Soil Preference:
Average, well-drained soil

Best Way to Propagate:
Take stem cuttings at any time

USDA Plant Hardiness Zones:
3 to 9

Lamiums are truly choice groundcovers for shady parts of the garden: They're fast-growing, create complete cover, and look just as good in deep shade as in filtered light or even sun. Most also have attractive silvery foliage that is semi-evergreen and lights up dark nooks, plus all have beautiful, abundant flowers. What more could you ask? Well, perhaps a little discipline! They are a bit too aggressive for the formal flowerbed.

GROWING TIPS

Few perennials are easier to grow than lamiums. Any soil will do, although they do prefer a bit of moisture at all times. Plus they thrive in most light conditions. In the South, though, they can burn in full sun, so partial shade or shade is better.

Lamiums spread by creeping stems that then root and form other plants. Some species and cultivars have short runners and are fairly easy to control. Yet others have long creeping stems that root at every node and can quickly take over your entire yard (or at least the shady spots). The latter species are best naturalized in spots where you don't mind them spreading.

In the South, especially, lamiums tend to slip into the mid-summer doldrums and look open and ratty. Mow them into submission and they'll sprout again almost overnight.

Due to their invasive nature, rooting here and there throughout the garden, lamiums provide ample material for division. But why bother going through the effort of digging them out when stem cuttings root in less than a week?

PROBLEMS AND SOLUTIONS

Southern gardeners often find their plantings decimated by leaf diseases or crown rot. Mow the plants nearly to the ground and they'll usually bounce right back. Slugs and snails may eat a few leaves, but lamiums quickly outpace them.

TOP PERFORMER

Lamium maculatum (spotted lamium): This lamium is easier to control than some of the others. The original species had green leaves with a small splotch of silver in the center, but many modern cultivars essentially have silver leaves with only a thin green margin. They can positively dazzle the eye in a deep, dark corner! Flowers range in color from white to pink to pinkish purple and appear in spring and sometimes sporadically into summer and fall. There are dozens of cultivars, including 'Silbergroschen', sold as 'Beacon Silver' or 'Silver Dollar', with silver leaves edged green and pinkish purple flowers. 'White Nancy' and 'Pink Pewter' are similar in leaf color, but have, respectively, white and pink flowers. 'Orchid Frost' is yet another silver-leaved cultivar, but with orchid pink flowers, and is more disease-resistant than the others and an ideal choice for the South where leaf problems are common. 'Aureum' has chartreuse-yellow leaves with a silver blotch and light pink flowers but can be hard to establish: It needs some sun to thrive, yet will burn if it gets too much. Better for adding a bit of "gold" to the garden is 'Delham' ('Golden Anniversary') with tricolor leaves: yellow, green, and silver. Its flowers are lavender. Height: 6 to 12 inches (15 to 30 cm). Spread: Indefinite. USDA Plant Hardiness Zones 3 to 9.

MORE RECOMMENDED LAMIUMS

L. galeobdolon, syn. *Lamiastrum galeobdolon, Galeobdolon luteum* (yellow archangel, golden dead nettle): A very popular groundcover with silver-marbled leaves and yellow flowers. 'Florentinum', also called 'Variegatum', with silver and green leaves, runs like the dickens in all directions, rooting as it goes, and can cover an entire flowerbed in just one summer. It's great for adding quick color to a forested area and spectacular hanging from a flower box like a silver waterfall, but never plant it in a formal setting. 'Hermann's Pride', on the other hand, is probably the least aggressive of the lamiums: It forms an upward-directed clump of silver-patterned green leaves and produces few if any stolons. Truly a charmer and the only lamium I recommend for formal beds. Height: 9 to 15 inches (23 to 38 cm). Spread: Indefinite (45 cm for 'Hermann's Pride'). USDA Plant Hardiness Zones 3 to 9.

LARRY'S GARDEN NOTES

No need to panic over the "nettle" in dead nettle. None of the lamiums sting in any way. They get their common name "dead nettle" from the fact they look superficially like nettles (*Urtica dioica*) because of their leaf shape and general habit, especially after the flowers drop, leaving bristly-looking seed capsules like the stinging hairs of the true nettles. However, lamiums are "dead" nettles, in the sense of unarmed, and the seed capsules don't sting you. Lamiums and nettles are not even closely related: Lamiums are in the mint family; nettles have a family all of their own.

Spotted lamium (*Lamium maculatum* 'Silbergroschen')

Ligularia
Ligularia, groundsel, golden-rays

PLANT PROFILE

LIGULARIA

lig-you-LAIR-ee-uh

Bloom Color:
Yellow

Bloom Time:
Summer

Length of Bloom:
3 to 4 weeks

Height:
Varies by species; see
individual listings

Spread:
2 to 4 feet (60 to 120 cm)

Garden Uses:
Cut flower garden,
groundcover, mass planting,
meadow garden, mixed
border, seasonal hedge,
specimen plant, woodland
garden; at the back of beds
and borders, in wet areas

Light Preference:
Full sun to shade

Soil Preference:
Rich, moist to wet, cool soil

Best Way to Propagate:
Divide in spring

USDA Plant Hardiness Zones:
Varies by species; see
individual listings

It's not so much that ligularias like shade as they hate heat and drought—and it is more likely to be cool and moist in the shade than in the sun. So if they attract you (and with their great foliage and stupendous bloom, why wouldn't they?), you're likely going to have to find them at least a semishady spot. These are big, bold, beautiful plants, with attractive foliage and brilliantly colored flowers: They aren't good choices for modest, self-effacing landscapes. They seem to yell, "Look at me!" Indeed, visitors will notice them. Cars driving past your home at 70 miles per hour will notice them—they're that kind of plant.

GROWING TIPS

In nature, ligularias are mostly denizens of moist forests and marshes, often in areas with very cool summers, so the more your yard is like a cool, shady swamp, the happier they will be. They actually adapt well to most types of soil, from rich to poor, but dryness just isn't their thing. Add full sun and heat and you have some very unhappy plants! Typically they look splendid early in the morning when the air is cool and the leaves are well hydrated. In the afternoon, when the sun beats down, both flowers and foliage wilt like lettuce in a car window. This is caused by excessive transpiration: Under the heat of the burning sun, the plant simply loses moisture faster through its huge leaves and abundant flowers than it can pump back in through its roots. Concerned gardeners often rush out and water, but to no avail: Soak the roots all you want, the plant still loses water faster than it can absorb it. Rather than having floppy ligularias growing in the sun, move them to partial shade (even deep shade in the South) and they'll perform perfectly.

Obviously, these plants are going to be particularly happy campers in boggy areas, around water gardens, and underneath leaky faucets. In cool-summer areas, they do perfectly fine under average garden conditions as well. They're long-lived plants that need little care and seldom need division, although they can be a tad invasive over time in spots that really suit them. Do divide them if you need more plants—most cultivated ligularias are of hybrid origin and will not come completely true from seed.

PROBLEMS AND SOLUTIONS

Slugs and snails are a major problem: They can turn the tender young leaves of ligularias into Swiss cheese! See page 85 for suggestions on how to control them, at least in spring. Once the leaves have hardened off, they're no longer in danger.

TOP PERFORMER

Ligularia przewalskii (Shavalski's ligularia): Drop-dead gorgeous leaves—deep green, palmately cut, dark (almost black) petioles—start off the season, but just wait until you see the flowers! Tall, narrow spikes of spidery, golden yellow blooms. Magnificent! Equally impressive is narrow-spiked ligularia (*L. stenocephala*) and its popular cultivar 'The Rocket': same colors, but with equally beautiful heart-shaped leaves. Either or both will truly brighten up a cool, moist, semishady spot for decades to come. Height: 4 to 6 feet (1.2 to 1.8 m). Spread: 4 to 6 feet (1.2 to 1.8 m). USDA Plant Hardiness Zones 4 to 9.

MORE RECOMMENDED LIGULARIAS

Ligularia dentata (bigleaf ligularia): The dinner plate–size, round to kidney-shape dark green leaves, with a shiny, almost leathery texture, are beautiful enough—then come the tall stems of yellow-orange daisies. Quite impressive, especially when the clumps fill in, as they do after a few years. There are several dark-leaved cultivars, including 'Britt-Marie Crawford', whose shiny purple leaves are so dark they appear almost black. For these to show off well in shade, though, you'll need some golden-leaved foliage in the background, like the giant hosta 'Sum and Substance' or a bright patch of golden meadowsweet (*Filipendula ulmaria* 'Aurea'). The species itself, with green leaves, can stand on its own. Height: 3 to 4 feet (90 to 120 cm). Spread: 2 to 4 feet (60 to 120 cm). USDA Plant Hardiness Zones 4 to 9.

Shavalski's ligularia
(*Ligularia przewalskii*)

KISSING COUSINS

The leopard plant (*Farfugium japonicum* 'Aureomaculatum', also sold as *F. tussilaginea* 'Aureomaculatum') is still sold under the name *Ligularia tussilaginea* 'Aureomaculatum.' It is smaller than most ligularias, with beautiful shiny leaves curiously spotted with bright yellow dots, and makes a wonderful groundcover where it is hardy. The flowers are light yellow daisies. There is a beautiful white-and-green variegated version ('Argentea') and a totally weird ruffled form looking for all the world like thick, green rumpled paper ('Crispata'), plus a few other choice plants. Height: 1 to 2 feet (30 to 60 cm). Spread: 18 to 24 inches (45 to 60 cm). USDA Plant Hardiness Zones 7 to 10.

P.S. If you can't grow it outdoors in your climate, the leopard plant makes a great houseplant!

Liriope
Liriope, lilyturf

Who says you can't have a decent lawn in the shade? You may not be able to grow a *grass* lawn, but you can have lilyturf. The narrow evergreen leaves make a dense lawn and could easily be mistaken for extradark lawn grass—until the plant begins to flower. Then spikes of purplish (sometimes white) blooms, like miniature lily-of-the-valley flowers, appear, often partly hidden among the foliage, followed by dark black berries: a totally intriguing and surprising touch. Of course, lawns are only part of the story—this is a superb container plant, an interesting rock garden plant, and makes a great edger. But it's not resistant to foot traffic, so no football: It's not *that* kind of lawn.

GROWING TIPS

Liriope makes a great groundcover for almost any growing condition, even for deep shade. Avoid alkaline soils, but just about any other soil type, from rich to poor, is fine. It does like good drainage and will need regular watering for the first year so it can settle in. Once established, it is very drought-resistant.

If you're using liriope as a lawn substitute, remember it is a slow-growing plant that won't fill in as quickly as a grass lawn; plant it quite densely for a faster result. All you need is a bitsy clump of two or three fleshy-rooted plants spaced every 4 inches or so for dense cover within 2 years.

Maintenance is truly minimal. Established plants need watering only during periods of extreme drought, and an annual mowing in late winter or early spring, to about 1 inch (2.5 cm) high, will remove the previous year's flowerstalks and yellowing older leaves. Of course, if you're not using lawn edging, you may also have to dig wayward plants out of the lawn occasionally—all forms of lilyturf do tend to wander.

PROBLEMS AND SOLUTIONS

Slugs and snails sometimes cause minor damage, but liriope is so dense it usually hides any gnawed-on leaves all on its own. Leaf diseases can occur but are easily obliterated by mowing.

Variegated lilyturf
(*Liriope muscari* 'Variegata')

TOP PERFORMER

Liriope muscari (big blue lilyturf): This is the traditional liriope and pretty much ubiquitous in the Southeast: In fact, I suspect it is the most common perennial of all south of the Mason-Dixon line. It has grasslike leaves with a leathery texture and somewhat rounded tips. The late-summer to fall spikes of lavender flowers (white on some cultivars) are held well above the foliage on young plants, although often partially hidden on older ones, especially cultivars with taller leaves. The blooms give rise to berries that are green at first, then nearly black. This plant naturally forms dense clumps but does spread by offsets as well. There are dozens of cultivars of liriope. 'Big Blue', with lavender-blue flowers, is probably the most common—a sort of hand-me-down plant that most people in the South generously share with their neighbors. It is also hardier than most others, sometimes thriving in Zone 5. 'Variegata' is the most popular of the colored-leaf varieties: Its leaves are striped with yellow, although second-year leaves often fade to all-green. 'Monroe White' ('Alba') is the most popular white-flowered cultivar but is a true plant of the South, rarely hardy beyond Zone 8. There are dozens of other liriopes from among which to choose. Height: 8 to 18 inches (20 to 45 cm). Spread: 12 inches (30 cm). USDA Plant Hardiness Zones 6 to 10.

MORE RECOMMENDED LIRIOPES

Liriope spicata (creeping lilyturf): This species is very similar to big blue lilyturf, but with narrower evergreen leaves that distinctly yellow in winter, plus narrower spikes of pale lavender or white flowers. The blue-black berries are similar. There are two principal reasons for using this species over the other. First, it has a distinctly more spreading habit, thus filling in much more quickly than "big blue." Also, it is hardier and helps extend the range of lilyturf into the North. The best known cultivar is 'Gin-ryu', sold as 'Silver Dragon', with white-striped leaves. It is, however, less hardy than the species (Zone 6). Height: 8 to 12 inches (20 to 30 cm). Spread: 12 inches (30 cm). USDA Plant Hardiness Zones 5 to 10.

KISSING COUSINS

Mondo grasses (*Ophiopogon* spp.) are mini-versions of liriope. They form dense clumps, with new clumps appearing a certain distance from the original via underground stolons. They are evergreen north of Zone 7 but may die back in winter elsewhere. Mondo grass (*O. japonicus*) is about 8 to 12 inches (20 to 30 cm) tall with light lilac flowers and blue berries. Dwarf mondo grass (*O. japonicus* 'Compactus') is only 2 inches (5 cm) high and a real charmer! Even more popular is black mondo grass (*O. planiscapus* 'Nigrescens', syn. 'Black Dragon', 'Ebony Knight'), 5 to 7 inches (13 to 18 cm) tall, with leaves so dark purple they appear black. Nice! The flowers are light lilac and followed by black berries. Although black mondo grass is said to be hardy only from Zone 6 to 10, as is *O. japonicus*, it has been thriving in my Zone 3 garden under abundant snow cover for over a decade.

Lobelia
Perennial lobelia

Many gardeners think of lobelias as being cute little annuals used in edging and flowerboxes, but that is bedding lobelia (*Lobelia erinus*). There are in fact over 350 species of lobelia spread all over the world, and a few are hardy perennials. One of those is among the most extraordinary garden perennials of all: cardinal flower (*Lobelia cardinalis*). This plant has such brilliant red flowers that it literally stops traffic—and it is considered by many to be the best hummingbird flower of all. Try it and see!

GROWING TIPS

In the wild, cardinal flower is usually found in moist forest clearings or along the borders of lakes and ponds. In the garden, it prefers similar conditions: moist, even wet soil and partial shade. It will, however, also adapt to full sun and drier soils, but not to truly dry soil—there must be some moisture available at all times. Great blue lobelia is somewhat more drought-tolerant, but again, you'll find it does better where there is always a bit of moisture available. Both plants will therefore greatly appreciate a good, thick mulch, especially if you plant them in full sun.

In "ordinary" garden soils, cardinal flower tends to be short-lived, dying out after a few years. To keep it going, divide it regularly. It will be much longer-lived in swampy conditions and in fact spreads slowly (but without ever becoming invasive) under such conditions. Where it is happy, it will also self-sow quite abundantly.

PROBLEMS AND SOLUTIONS

Rust is an occasional problem, especially on great blue lobelia. Destroy the infested plants and start new ones from seed, planting them elsewhere in the garden. If you see nursery plants that already have symptoms of rust (see page 87 for details on symptoms), *don't* buy them—you can't control this disease once it is present. Slugs and snails can be a problem early in spring, nibbling on tender young leaves (see page 85 for slug and snail solutions).

TOP PERFORMER

Lobelia cardinalis (cardinal flower): This is the lobelia everyone wants. Probably the most stunning of all North American wildflowers, it is now grown around the world as a cultivated ornamental. It has plain green, lance-shaped leaves that form a rosette in spring, then a tall stem (usually just one per rosette) starts to rise up and soon transforms into a spike of brilliant cardinal red flowers, tubular at the base, but opening into two narrow upper lobes and three broader lower ones, the typical shape of lobelia flowers. (The plant gets its name from the red robes of Roman Catholic cardinals, not from the bird, by the way.) It has the reputation of being short-lived in the garden, which can be true under average garden conditions, but it is quite permanent in truly damp soils. There are a number of cultivars with white or pink flowers, but I wouldn't consider growing anything but a red cardinal flower— it just doesn't seem right! Please note that unscrupulous nurseries often sell *L.* × *speciosa* hybrids, especially those with purple foliage, as being *L. cardinalis,* but this is a very different plant and not nearly as hardy as the true cardinal flower. Height: 2 to 4 feet (60 to 120 cm). Spread: 1 foot (30 cm). USDA Plant Hardiness Zones 2 to 9.

MORE RECOMMENDED PERENNIAL LOBELIAS

Lobelia siphilitica (great blue lobelia): This beautiful plant with the unfortunate botanical name (don't worry, it doesn't cause syphilis, it was once used to treat it!) looks a lot like cardinal flower, but with deep blue flowers. It is somewhat more drought-tolerant than cardinal flower but still much prefers moist or soggy soil at all times. The species itself is most often grown, but you will find plants with white flowers ('Alba') or pink ones ('Rosea'). For more color variety, try *L.* × *gerardii* (Gerard's lobelia), a cross between *L. siphilitica* and *L. cardinalis,* which offers flowers in various shades of pink, red, white, and purple. Height: 2 to 3 feet (60 to 90 cm). Spread: 1 foot (30 cm). USDA Plant Hardiness Zones 3 to 8.

Cardinal flower (*Lobelia cardinalis*)

LARRY'S GARDEN NOTES

Taxonomists had a mystery on their hands. They discovered a spreading aquatic lobelia that seemed to be completely asexual, never producing a bloom. What was it? The mystery was solved when a pond where the plant was being studied dried up. The aquatic suddenly started producing entirely different leaves, then a tall, upright stem, then the unmistakable red flowers of *Lobelia cardinalis*. The mystery plant was simply the aquatic form of cardinal flower! It turns out cardinal flower can live for decades as an aquatic plant, spreading through offsets but never blooming.

Mertensia
Bluebells

PLANT PROFILE

MERTENSIA
mer-TEN-see-uh

Bloom Color:
Lavender-blue

Bloom Time:
Early to midspring

Length of Bloom:
2 to 3 weeks

Height:
Varies by species; see
individual listings

Spread:
Varies by species; see
individual listings

Garden Uses:
Rock garden, wildflower
meadow

Light Preference:
Partial shade to shade

Soil Preference:
Humus-rich, moist soil

Best Way to Propagate:
Sow seed in summer or divide
in spring

USDA Plant Hardiness Zones:
3 to 9

Here's a plant that is particularly shade-tolerant—because it avoids the shade! Virginia bluebells (the only commonly offered species) sprouts early in spring, rapidly producing its smooth blue-green leaves, then its upright stalks of pendulous flowers, before the trees leaf out. The buds are distinctly pink but do a radical change as they begin to open, turning into trumpet-shaped flowers that are lavender-blue. Then suddenly, the leaves begin to fill in above, the blooms fade, the leaves turn yellow, and it is all over once again for Virginia bluebells until the following spring.

GROWING TIPS

Plant Virginia bluebells in humusy soil where it is cool and at least somewhat moist at all times. Unlike many other plants that are summer-dormant and don't seem to mind that the soil turns bone-dry or baking hot while they are asleep, bluebells insist on cool conditions and at least moderate moisture at all times.

Talking about cool shade, in climates that are truly cool in summer, the leaves may not go dormant. Under most garden conditions, though, it's best to consider that this plant will have entirely disappeared by midsummer. I like to let it peek out above low-growing plants with attractive foliage, like wild gingers (*Asarum* spp.), smaller ferns, common periwinkle (*Vinca minor*), or any number of other shade-tolerant groundcovers. That way, the leaves can simply fade away and the groundcover provides summer interest.

The best way to obtain new Virginia bluebells is to let them spread on their own. (Don't worry about the plant being invasive—it spreads slowly and the blue-green leaves are easily seen, so it if does overstep its limits, it is easy enough to yank out.) Division, usually done just as the plants go dormant, is possible, but it is easy to damage the rhizomes as you plant them. I've had best luck digging out clumps of several stems rather than trying to free individual rhizomes.

PROBLEMS AND SOLUTIONS

Plants are short-lived in hot, dry climates, but rarely suffer anything more than a few nibbles from slugs or snails in the cool, moist, shady conditions they prefer.

TOP PERFORMER

Mertensia virginica, syn. *M. pulmonarioides* (Virginia bluebells): There are some 50 species of *Mertensia,* many with undeniable ornamental properties, but just try to find them! Only Virginia bluebells are at all commonly offered. Even then, you may have to search a bit. Look for a nursery that specializes in native plants or shade perennials, though, and you'll find it with no difficulty. The nodding flowers appear in one-sided clusters of 5 to 20 flowers. The species is by far the most popular form, although one hears rumors of white ('Alba') and pink ('Rosea') flowers. I've never seen 'Rosea' and have seen 'Alba' only once—and that was in a botanical garden! Height: 18 to 24 inches (45 to 60 cm). Spread: 12 inches (30 cm). USDA Plant Hardiness Zones 3 to 9.

MORE RECOMMENDED BLUEBELLS

Mertensia sibirica (Siberian bluebells): This is essentially the Asian version of Virginia bluebells, with similar blue-green leaves (although more distinctly heart-shaped and definitely bluer) and the same pendant clusters of lavender-blue trumpets that some people still insist are sky blue. However, this is (in my opinion) a far superior garden plant, notably because the foliage lasts right through summer. I find it easier to divide successfully and just as easy to grow from seed. The only mystery is why this plant is not more often cultivated. I suspect it will be soon—it is truly a charmer! It starts blooming a few days after Virginia bluebells, so the two could be combined to create a longer blooming period. It seems just as dependent on cool, moist growing conditions, so is not likely to catch on in the South except in cooler mountain areas. Height: 12 to 24 inches (30 to 60 cm). Spread: 12 inches (30 cm). USDA Plant Hardiness Zones 3 to 9.

Virginia bluebells
(*Mertensia virginica*)

LARRY'S GARDEN NOTES

Always use a modifier with the name "bluebells" or no one will know what you're talking about—any plant with blue or violet-blue bell-shaped flowers is likely to be called bluebells somewhere in the world. In eastern North America, where Virginia bluebells grow wild, everyone assumes that bluebells are *Mertensia virginica*. In England, though, bluebells are clearly *Hyacinthoides non-scripta* (English bluebells), while on the continent, everyone knows that bluebells are *Hyacinthoides hispanica* (Spanish bluebells). Both of these two are bulbs (they're described on page 296) and in no way related to Virginia bluebells. And the Scots just *know* that true bluebells are *Campanula rotundifolia*, a mounding rock garden plant we call bluebells of Scotland that is not related to either of the other bluebells. And that's just a start! Perhaps using the botanical name is the only way out of this horticultural Tower of Babel.

Mitchella

Partridgeberry, twinberry, running box

Could this be the perfect groundcover for cool shade? Partridgeberry is a creeping plant native to eastern North America that forms an ever-expanding low carpet of attractive evergreen foliage that accepts foot traffic, has great flowers and even better fruits—and both flowers and fruit are often present at the same time. Its tiny egg- to heart-shaped leaves, dark shiny green with beautiful white veins, create a perfect carpet, and they are the plant's drawing card—although the berries that form in late summer and are often still present the following spring are a definite plus.

GROWING TIPS

In the wild, partridgeberry is usually found growing in shade on sandy, acid, well-drained soils, often under conifers, although mostly under more open trees, like larches and hemlocks, than in the truly dense shade of spruces or firs. It will adapt well to most soil types, as long as there is a certain amount of acidity. It is not a good choice for neutral or alkaline conditions. It does best in moist soils but will learn to tolerate drought. For this to happen, keep it well-moistened for the first 2 years until it is well established, and from there on in spring until after blooming.

Full sun is a definite no-no in the South, but it does fine there in the North where the soil is moist, acid, and cool. "Cool" is the key word: Although this plant is often seen as a plant of the northern woods, it thrives well into Zone 9 in mountainous areas and indeed is native right along the eastern seaboard into Mexico. The result is that it does not require cold winters to thrive but will not tolerate hot summers. In the South, consider planting it near a stream or other cooling water feature.

Partridgeberry spreads slowly but surely, and some pruning will eventually be necessary in a more formal situation. Naturalized in a forest area, though, you can simply let it grow and spread as it pleases. I like to let it wander through paths, as it will take considerable foot traffic or tumble off walls. Due to its low height, it makes an ideal living mulch for shrubs and even taller perennials: It *surrounds* them without *suffocating* them. Ferns, hostas, bergenias, and others are good partners.

Multiplication could be from seed—if you're very patient. Seed needs at least one cold treatment and often two or more before it even begins to germinate, and the young plants are rather slow-growing at first. Since its creeping stems root wherever they touch the ground, it is far easier to simply cut free already-rooted stem segments and move them wherever you want them. You can also air-layer the plant where it doesn't root on its own by pinning the stems to the ground at a leaf axil.

PROBLEMS AND SOLUTIONS

This is real no-brainer: Not even slugs or snails bother it. Possibly you might consider the birds and mammals that come to harvest the berries to be pests, but most people, on the contrary, are charmed by their presence.

Partridgeberry (*Mitchella repens*)

TOP PERFORMER

Mitchella repens (partridgeberry, twinberry, running box): There are many other common names for this perennial, ubiquitous in cool, forested areas throughout its natural territory. The name partridgeberry is most evocative, perhaps, because the bright red berries truly do attract partridges (ruffed grouse), but also wild turkeys, chipmunks, and even deer. Animals and birds tend to wait until spring to harvest the fruit, so partridgeberries provide a good source of food early in the season when few other fruits are present. People can eat the berries too, but most find the taste rather bland. The name twinberry comes from the curious fact that the pleasantly scented flowers are always produced two by two, yet each pair produces only one berry. Even more curious, the two blooms are not identical: both are white (rarely tinted pink) and generally funnel-shaped, but one will always have long, fuzzy stamens and a short pistil, the other a long pistil and short stamens. As for running box, well, the leaves, other than for their white veins, are very like those of boxwoods—and the plant certainly runs!

Generally the species is sold, but *M. repens* f. *leucocarpa*, with white fruit, is seen in botanical collections and may be available in a few specialist nurseries.

SMART SUBSTITUTE

A similar plant with similar needs, although with larger leaves, is common wintergreen (*Gaultheria procumbens*), an evergreen sub-shrub with lustrous dark green leaves and tiny pinkish white spring flowers that look like upside-down urns. The berries are large, bright red, and, as with partridgeberry (*Mitchella repens*), produced in fall but persist over winter. Wintergreen gives off a delightfully minty scent when crushed (it will tolerate light foot traffic) and indeed was for a long time the principal ingredient of wintergreen extract, used in making wintergreen gum. The berries are edible and indeed quite tasty. Height: 3 to 5 inches (8 to 12 cm). Spread: Indefinite. USDA Plant Hardiness Zones 3 to 7.

Myosotis
Forget-me-not

MYOSOTIS

my-uh-SOH-tiss

Bloom Color:
 Blue, pink, and white

Bloom Time:
 Varies by species; see
 individual listings

Length of Bloom:
 Varies by species; see
 individual listings

Height:
 6 to 8 inches (15 to 20 cm)

Spread:
 6 to 8 inches (15 to 20 cm)

Garden Use:
 Edging, groundcover, mass
 planting, mixed border, rock
 garden, woodland garden; on
 slopes, in wet areas

Light Preference:
 Full sun to partial shade

Soil Preference:
 Humus-rich, moist to wet soil

Best Way to Propagate:
 Varies by species; see
 individual listings

USDA Plant Hardiness Zones:
 Varies by species; see
 individual listings

Who doesn't recognize at a glance the abundant but tiny blue flowers of the forget-me-not? They're among the few old-fashioned garden flowers that have never truly gone out of style. Part of its popularity undoubtedly comes from the flower color: They are generally a true sky blue, one of the rarest colors of all in the plant kingdom, with a white or yellow eye. The other reason for their ubiquity is probably simply that, once you have them, they are hard to get rid of. Be it by creeping stolons or self-seeding, forget-me-nots do manage to ensure a place for themselves in the garden.

GROWING TIPS

Among the over 50 species of *Myosotis*, most prefer partial shade (full sun is fine in the North) and humus-rich, moist soil. They tend to be fast-growing but short-lived plants. Many indeed are biennials or even annuals, although they give the appearance of being perennials because they self-sow so efficiently.

The truly perennial species of forget-me-nots can be propagated by division; the biennials or annuals by seed. You rarely need to concern yourself with multiplying them, though: They do a good enough job on their own. Just dig up a clump and move it where you want it. I find the blue- and white-flowered forms most vigorous, but pink forget-me-nots tend to die out over time. Plantings have to be "reinfused" with fresh pink genes occasionally.

Forget-me-nots are considered a bit invasive. Not truly weedy, mind you, but they are best in informal plantings where their vagabond habits are more acceptable. They're also very nice naturalized in open forest areas.

PROBLEMS AND SOLUTIONS

Mildew, gray mold, and other leaf diseases commonly appear after the plants have bloomed and are best controlled by mowing the infected foliage down. The plant will at least put up fresh foliage, if not always flowers, for the rest of the season. See page 85 for ideas on controlling slugs and snails.

TOP PERFORMER

Myosotis scorpioides, syn. *M. palustris* (water forget-me-not): This is the least invasive and the longest blooming of the common forget-me-nots. A true perennial, it doesn't self-seed much but instead has creeping stems that root as they grow. It is essentially a semi-aquatic plant, preferring to have its feet wet all at times. It does fine as well in damper spots of a flowerbed, but not in dry soil. The cultivar 'Sempervirens', with the typical blue flowers of the species, continues blooming right through summer and into fall when grown in cool, moist conditions. Other cultivars include 'Sapphire', with flowers of a particularly intense blue; 'Pinkie' (a pink form); and 'Snowflakes' (a white one). Height: 6 to 8 inches (15 to 20 cm). Spread: 6 to 8 inches (15 to 20 cm). USDA Plant Hardiness Zones 3 to 9.

MORE RECOMMENDED FORGET-ME-NOTS

Myosotis sylvatica (garden forget-me-not): This is the common forget-me-not of both fields and woodlands. Although originally from Europe, it is thoroughly established in the New World as a garden escapee. The flowers are normally sky blue, but most naturalized plantings also include white-flowered plants, and sometimes pink ones. This plant is just barely a perennial, germinating one year and generally dying after blooming the next, which would make it a biennial. Some plants do live to bloom a second year. The popular Victoria Series includes dense, clump-forming plants with particularly intense colors: 'Victoria Blue', 'Victoria Rose', and Victoria White', but there are dozens of other cultivars and series. Alpine forget-me-not (*M. alpestris*) is very similar. Height: 6 to 12 inches (15 to 20 cm). Spread: 6 to 8 inches (15 to 20 cm). USDA Plant Hardiness Zones 3 to 9.

LARRY'S GARDEN NOTES

What description of the forget-me-not would be complete without recounting the legend about how the plant got its name? A young man went to the water's edge to gather the beautiful blue flowers that grew there for his betrothed. Unfortunately, he fell into the water and was carried away by the swiftly moving current. With his last breath, he raised the flowers into the air and cried, "Forget me not!" This legend is widespread, as witness the common names "Vergissmein-nicht" in German, "Nomeolvides" in Spanish . . . and the list goes on and on.

Forget-me-not
(*Myosotis semperflorens*)

Pachysandra

Pachysandra, spurge

PLANT PROFILE

PACHYSANDRA

pak-ih-SAN-druh

Bloom Color:
  White

Bloom Time:
  Spring

Length of Bloom:
  1 to 2 weeks

Height:
  6 to 12 inches (15 to 30 cm)

Spread:
  Indefinite

Garden Uses:
  Edging, groundcover, mass planting, rock garden, wall planting, woodland garden; along paths, on slopes, in wet areas

Light Preference:
  Partial shade to shade

Soil Preference:
  Rich, moist soil

Best Way to Propagate:
  Divide at any time

USDA Plant Hardiness Zones:
  Varies by species; see individual listings

If pachysandras produced only individual stems, no one would think of growing them: The leaves are of only moderate interest and the flowers are a disappointment. But it doesn't; it forms carpets—dense, green, ground-hugging carpets that spread indefinitely—creating a perfect underpinning for trees, shrubs, and taller perennials, a dark green nongrass lawn for places where true lawns would never wander. And so pachysandra has come to represent the pinnacle in groundcovers for shady conditions: no mowing, no weeding, no fussy care … gardening life just doesn't come any easier.

GROWING TIPS

Pachysandra's capacity to grow in impossible places is almost legendary. It grows perfectly well in the deepest imaginable shade and shrugs off root competition as if it weren't there, forming a spreading carpet that gets wider and wider over time until it has filled up all the available space. You may have to put it in its place occasionally, as it doesn't know the word "stop." A barrier inserted in the ground will stop its progress quite neatly.

It will grow in almost any soil, and established plants will tolerate moderate drought. It puts up with sun in the North but yellows badly in sun elsewhere, so should be restricted to spots with at least with some protection from sun at the hotter hours of the day.

You can easily multiply pachysandra by digging out rooted sections and moving them, a technique that can be applied whenever you feel like it, even in the heat of summer (you probably won't feel like it when the ground is frozen solid, though!). Stem cuttings are another possibility for multiplication.

PROBLEMS AND SOLUTIONS

In most cases, pachysandra marches on, blissfully unresponsive to insects or disease. In areas where summers are hot and muggy, leaf blights can be a problem. Thin out dense plantings to help control them—or grow something else.

TOP PERFORMER

Pachysandra terminalis (Japanese pachysandra, Japanese spurge): It has dark green, slightly toothed evergreen leaves on short upright stems. The plant produces dense, short spikes of white flowers in spring, but they are of little ornamental impact. Plant it on 6- to 10-inch (15- to 20-cm) centers for complete coverage in a year or two. Several cultivars exist, including 'Green Carpet', only 6 to 8 inches (15 to 20 cm) tall with darker green leaves, and the delightful 'Green Sheen', with dark green leaves that are so smooth they seem to shine. It is said to be more heat-tolerant than the species. 'Variegata' is a great choice if you want a bit of color, as the leaves have white margins. It is a bit slower-growing than the species. 'Silveredge' seems identical to 'Variegata'. Height: 8 to 12 inches (20 to 30 cm). Spread: Indefinite. USDA Plant Hardiness Zones 4 to 9.

MORE RECOMMENDED PACHYSANDRAS

Pachysandra procumbens (Allegheny pachysandra, Allegheny spurge): This is the American version of pachysandra, a much prettier plant actually, but not as good a groundcover, as it tends to form clumps rather than spread. The leaves are not necessarily evergreen, suffering considerably during harsh winters, especially in the North. They are larger and often mottled brown in spring, plus they take on a reddish tinge in fall. The shorter flower spikes are interesting—if you look at them at ground level. They are white with a pinkish tinge. They bloom very early in the season, practically at snowmelt. With snow protection, you can grow this plant at least to Zone 3 (where mine are thriving). Height: 8 to 12 inches (20 to 30 cm). Spread: 6 to 12 inches (15 to 30 cm). USDA Plant Hardiness Zones 5 to 9.

Japanese pachysandra
(*Pachysandra terminalis*)

LARRY'S GARDEN NOTES

Spurge is usually the common name for plants in the genus *Euphorbia* and traces its origin back to the old French world *espurger*, meaning to purge. Indeed, euphorbias are renowned for their purgative properties . . . violently purgative, that is. They are actually considered far too toxic for human consumption and few euphorbias are used medicinally anymore. But how did pachysandra, which is in no way related to euphorbias, the true spurges, come to bear the name spurge? Early settlers saw native peoples in the Allegheny mountains using *Pachysandra procumbens* as a purgative and gave the plant the common name Allegheny spurge.

Polygonatum
Solomon's seal

PLANT PROFILE

POLYGONATUM

poe-lig-oh-NAY-tum

Bloom Color:
Whitish and white tipped with green

Bloom Time:
Spring to early summer

Length of Bloom:
2 to 3 weeks

Height:
Varies by species; see individual listings

Spread:
1 to 2 feet (30 to 60 cm)

Garden Uses:
Container planting, cut flower garden, edging, groundcover, mass planting, mixed border, rock garden, woodland garden; at the back of beds and borders, in wet areas

Light Preference:
Partial shade to shade

Soil Preference:
Average, moist to slightly dry soil

Best Way to Propagate:
Divide in spring or fall

USDA Plant Hardiness Zones:
3 to 9

This old-fashioned flower looks just as lovely today as it did in Great-grandma's garden. The gracefully arching stems with alternating smooth, broadly lance-shaped leaves are charming all on their own, helped out, though, by creamy white flowers tipped in green dangling from the leaf axils in spring, then long-lasting blue-black berries in summer. In fall, the whole plant turns a beautiful golden yellow. All in all, it's a pretty, elegant, yet not flashy plant, perhaps best described as a "subtle beauty."

GROWING TIPS

Over 50 different species are native to shady areas throughout the Northern Hemisphere, and all seem equally at home in shade and partial shade. They burn in the sun in most climates, but will put up with it in northern gardens where the sun is never very intense.

Cool shade is best: This is not a happy plant in great heat! Where summers are hot and humid, a mulch may be wise. Solomon's seal will tolerate just about any soil, but prefers moist soil and will even put up with soggy conditions in spring. By summertime, when its growth has slowed, established plants will put up with drought.

Solomon's seal is very slow-growing, so place several plants about 8 to 12 inches (20 to 30 cm) apart for a faster result. Well-established plants do fill out and provide plenty of material for division. Be forewarned that it can become a bit invasive over time!

PROBLEMS AND SOLUTIONS

Slugs and snails are an occasional problem. Much more worrisome is the lily beetle, a bright orange bug that can literally devour all the plant's foliage. Regular treatments with neem oil can keep them at bay.

TOP PERFORMER

Polygonatum odoratum (fragrant Solomon's seal): Confusion reigns supreme in the world of Solomon's seals, and you can rarely be entirely sure the plant you buy is exactly what it says on the label. That's understandable because of most of the species look a lot alike. Fragrant Solomon's seal, notably, is frequently confused with common Solomon's seal (see below), but with somewhat shorter leaves (6 inches/15 cm). As the name suggests, fragrant Solomon's seal has particularly perfumed flowers. They are tubular and dangling, creamy white with green tips, and appear in pairs or alone from spring to early summer. 'Variegatum', with medium green leaves outlined in white, is a choice cultivar. Height: 18 to 24 inches (45 to 60 cm). Spread: 1 to 2 feet (30 to 60 cm). USDA Plant Hardiness Zones 3 to 9.

MORE RECOMMENDED SOLOMON'S SEALS

Polygonatum biflorum (small Solomon's seal, great Solomon's seal, giant Solomon's seal): This is the most common North American species east of the Mississipi. It was originally considered three different species: small Solomon's seal (*P. biflorum*), only about 1 to 2 feet (30 to 60 cm) tall; great Solomon's seal (*P. commutatum*), from 3 to 5 feet (90 to 150 cm); and giant Solomon's seal, from 5 to 7 feet (1.5 to 2 m). When you buy this plant, ask how big it becomes or you could be in for a surprise! Height: 1 to 7 feet (30 to 200 cm). Spread: 2 feet (60 cm). USDA Plant Hardiness Zones 3 to 9.

P. × hybridum (common Solomon's seal): A hybrid of *P. odoratum* and *P. multiflorum.* For a description, just reread that of *P. odoratum:* The two are very similar. *P.* × *hybridum* 'Striatum' (often confused with *P. odorarum* 'Variegatum') is the most popular form, with leaves both edged and striped white. Height: 18 to 24 inches (45 to 60 cm). Spread: 1 to 2 feet (30 to 60 cm). USDA Plant Hardiness Zones 3 to 9.

Variegated Solomon's seal (*Polygonatum odoratum* 'Variegatum')

KISSING COUSINS

The genus *Disporum* (fairy bells) is very closely related to *Polygonatum.* The most obvious difference is the pendulous flowers that are more open and produced at the tips of the stems rather than at the leaf axils, plus the berries are usually red instead of bluish black. Several species are offered, but the most common is undoubtedly Japanese fairy bell (*D. sessile*), with sessile leaves (the leaves that join the stem directly, with no petiole), and especially its shorter, variegated cultivar 'Variegatum', with leaves charmingly striped white. It reaches only 9 to 15 inches (23 to 38 cm) high, compared to the species' 1 to 2 feet (30 to 60 cm). Japanese fairy bells are just as happy in shade and evenly most soil as Solomon's seals. Spread: 1 to 2 feet (30 to 60 cm). USDA Plant Hardiness Zones 4 to 9.

Primula
Primrose

PRIMULA

PRIM-you-luh

Bloom Color:
Most colors

Bloom Time:
Varies by species; see individual listings

Length of Bloom:
3 to 4 weeks

Height:
Varies by species; see individual listings

Spread:
Varies by species; see individual listings

Garden Uses:
Container planting, edging, groundcover, mass planting, mixed border, rock garden, wall planting, woodland garden; along paths, on slopes, in wet areas

Light Preference:
Partial shade (full sun in cool climates)

Soil Preference:
Humus-rich, moist, well-drained soil

Best Way to Propagate:
Divide in summer after flowering

USDA Plant Hardiness Zones:
Varies by species; see individual listings

Primroses are such a staple of the spring garden it's hard to imagine one without them. They often bloom so early there is still snow on the ground, but there are other primroses that bloom throughout spring into early summer—so you can keep a primrose bed going for 3 months or more, depending on the local climate. There are so many species (over 425, plus thousands of cultivars) that the hard thing about primroses is choosing which ones you want to grow. For the most part, they form ground-hugging rosettes of tongue-shaped foliage plus dense clusters of five-petaled flowers either directly in the center of the rosette or on elevated stalks of varying heights. All the colors of the rainbow are available—and then some.

GROWING TIPS

The key secrets to healthy, happy primroses are moisture and protection from the hot sun. In the wild, they often grow underneath deep-rooted deciduous trees, where they receive full sun in spring but deep shade during the summer. In culture, you can grow them the same way—or anywhere with good morning sun but not too much afternoon heat. In cool-summer areas, they even thrive in full sun; elsewhere, partial shade is best. All primroses like their soil moist and cool, but how moist depends on the species.

Keeping the soil cool is also important, so apply a good mulch and water regularly to increase transpiration which, in turn, lowers both soil and air temperatures. In hot-summer areas, they'll often be happiest around fountains or water gardens.

In most climates primroses are permanent garden subjects, but in the Deep South, where winters aren't cold enough for them to bloom and summers are too to hot for them to survive, they are often treated as winter-blooming annuals.

Primroses often look like something the dog dragged home in summer: wilted, floppy leaves lying in a heap on the ground. In hot-summer areas, many will even go summer-dormant. Always consider ways of hiding them during summer, such as interplanting them with late-to-leaf-out hostas or putting them in an out-of-the-way spot you take visitors to only in spring. In cool-summer areas, you may also want to bring visitors to see them in fall, as many rebloom—although more lightly—then.

Multiply your primroses by dividing them after they finish blooming.

PROBLEMS AND SOLUTIONS

Watch out for spider mites in hot, dry climates. Spraying with water may be all you need to control them.

TOP PERFORMER

Primula × polyantha (polyantha primrose): The Brits call these, their favorites, "polyanthus." Originally crosses between the yellow cowslip primrose (*P. vulgaris*) and the English primose (*P. veris*), lots of other primrose chromosomes now float around the *P. × polyantha* gene pool, including *P. juliae* and *P. elatior,* to the point that their exact background is impossible to unravel. Experts subdivide them into all sorts of subcategories, but for the average gardener there are essentially two groups: those that are stemless, bearing flowers directly from the center of the rosette, and those that have short but upright flower stems. Both types produce single or double flowers in all shades of yellow, red, pink, purple, blue, white, and other shades, plus bicolors, with or without a contrasting eye. The wrinkled, lettuce-like leaves can be green or tinted red. This plant is commonly offered as a potted plant for spring bloom but does not make a good houseplant. Instead, plant it outdoors as soon as the weather permits. Plants bloom fairly early in spring, and sometimes lightly in fall. Height: 6 to 12 inches (15 to 30 cm). Spread: 8 to 9 inches (20 to 23 cm). USDA Plant Hardiness Zones 3 to 9.

MORE RECOMMENDED PRIMROSES

Primula denticulata (drumstick primrose): This one is on everyone's list of "primroses I can't possibly live without." The plant produces a low rosette of spoon-shaped leaves and, very early in spring, one or more upright thick stalks, each bearing a rounded ball of lilac, pink, or white flowers. This is one of the "swamp" primroses: keep 'em wet, keep 'em happy! Height: 8 to 12 inches (20 to 30 cm). Spread: 8 to 10 inches (20 to 25 cm). USDA Plant Hardiness Zones 3 to 9.

Polyantha primrose
(*Primula × polyantha*)

LARRY'S GARDEN NOTES

When you see primroses in the garden, you know spring has arrived: After all, their name means "first flower." The English name comes to us, via Old French, from the Latin *prima rosa* or first rose. At the time, "rose" had a larger sense than it does today and simply meant "flower." In Spanish, the connection between springtime and primroses is even more obvious: They call them "primaveras"—and *primavera* also means spring. So when you plant primroses in your garden, you're essentially planting springtime!

Prunella
Self-heal, heal-all

Some plants just don't get no respect (to paraphrase a popular comedian), and that's certainly the case with self-heal. That this easy-to-grow, long-blooming groundcover is not available in most nurseries practically speaks of prejudice. Everyone grows its close relative, spotted lamium (*Lamium maculatum*), so why doesn't self-heal get a chance? With its dense foliage, it looks good even out of bloom and the blooms are spectacular: Colorful two-lipped flowers poke out from among a dense spike of bracts at the tip of each stem. It's a plant that fills in nicely and makes a nice, even carpet in almost no time. What's not to like?

GROWING TIPS

Self-heal will grow almost anywhere: in sun or shade, rich soil or poor, moist or very dry, and both acid and alkaline soils seem perfect. But that's where it *can* grow. It actually prefers sun or partial shade in the North and partial shade or shade in the South, in a rich soil kept evenly moist. It is fairly drought-tolerant, at least once it's well established.

Since self-heal is offered as a groundcover, one should expect it to cover ground. It is not surprising then to hear it spreads quite readily by short rhizomes, rapidly creating a thick, semi-evergreen carpet (it may lose its leaves in winter in the North). So far, so good. It can also spread much more widely if you let it go to seed, as into your flowerbeds, lawn, walks, and vegetable garden. I suggest simply mowing the plant down (yes, with the lawn mower!) after it blooms. If you cut off the faded flowers, it will not be able to produce seed, and therefore its wayward seeds will not be a problem.

Preventing self-heal from spreading beyond its allotted space via stolons, which is its alternative method of getting around, is much simpler. As with most other groundcover plants, simply make sure it is surrounded by taller plants with a solid constitution, such as shrubs, ferns, and hostas. Please note that root barriers, like a pail with the bottom cut out sunk into the garden, are not effective with this plant, as its stolons run above ground and will simply climb over the barrier. If a few plants extend beyond their bounds (and that can happen!), just pull them out soon after you see them, rather then a few years later.

Propagation is possible by stem cuttings, but typically gardeners simply divide the plant. After all, it produces abundant offsets—and what are offsets if not prerooted cuttings? Just dig out a few offsets and plant them. Most ornamental self-heals are hybrids and will not come 100 percent true from seed, so growing from seed is seldom worthwhile. Another good reason to mow the plant back when it stops blooming so it won't go to seed!

PROBLEMS AND SOLUTIONS

Leaf spot, powdery mildew, and various other leaf diseases sometimes occur after flowering has ceased. If so, cut the plant back harshly, removing the troubled leaves. Inevitably the new growth that now appears will be disease-free. Slugs and snails can be a minor nuisance to new leaves in spring, but the plant usually recovers once its growth gets truly underway.

TOP PERFORMER

Prunella grandiflora (large-flowered self-heal): This is the only species of self-heal that is at all available. Hailing from Europe, it forms a thick clump of upright, almost woody stems, with oval or pointed, heavily veined, deep green leaves with scalloped margins. At flowering time, compact spikes of bracts appear at the tip of each stem and begin producing, a few at a time, attractive tubular two-lipped flowers in a striking shade of purple. There is a range of other colors, from white to pink to red, plus all possible shades of purple. Particularly popular are the plants of the Loveliness Series, including 'Loveliness' itself, with lavender flowers, as well as 'White Loveliness', 'Purple Loveliness', and 'Pink Loveliness'. 'Rotkäppchen' ('Little Red Riding Hood') is a beautiful dwarf variety not seen nearly enough in gardens: It has crimson-red flowers and reaches only 6 inches (15 cm) high. Height: 6 to 12 inches (15 to 30 cm). Spread: 12 inches (30 cm). USDA Plant Hardiness Zones 4 to 9.

Large-flowered self-heal (*Prunella grandiflora* 'Pink Loveliness')

SMART SUBSTITUTE

Another purplish creeper for shady nooks is woodland phlox (*Phlox divaricata*). It produces creeping stems with upright spikes of scented bluish purple flowers from mid-spring to early summer, and there are several cultivars, including 'London Grove', with bluer flowers; 'Dirigo Ice', with pale blue flowers; and 'Fuller's White' (white, of course!). Height: 8 to 15 inches (20 to 38 cm). Spread: Indefinite. USDA Plant Hardiness Zones 3 to 9.

Pulmonaria

Lungwort, pulmonaria, Bethlehem sage

PLANT PROFILE

PULMONARIA

puhl-muhn-AIR-ee-uh

Bloom Color:
Blue, pink, purple, and white

Bloom Time:
Early to late spring

Length of Bloom:
3 to 4 weeks

Height:
10 to 18 inches (25 to 45 cm)

Spread:
1 to 2 feet (30 to 60 cm)

Garden Uses:
Edging, groundcover, mass planting, mixed border, rock garden, woodland garden; in wet areas

Light Preference:
Full sun to shade

Soil Preference:
Humus-rich, evenly moist soil

Best Way to Propagate:
Divide in fall or after flowering

USDA Plant Hardiness Zones:
Varies by species; see individual listings

The lungwort tribe has undergone an explosion in introductions of new species and in intensive hybridizing, the likes of which are rarely seen in the horticultural world (*Heuchera* has gone through the same process). From a solid but rather dull perennial, a whole range of new plants has been created: some with blue flowers, others with pink, white, red, peach, or purple ones, and foliage that now ranges from plain green to so heavily covered in silver there is literally no green to be seen. All this, and shade tolerance too? Give the plant a cigar!

GROWING TIPS

Lungworts are certainly easy enough to grow. For starters, just about any well-drained soil will do, be it rich or poor, damp or fairly dry, acid or slightly alkaline—although if you supply humus-rich soil and even moisture, your lungworts will love you for it. Don't leave them soaking in water, though, or they *will* rot away. Same story for light: Anything goes, from full sun to deep shade; partial shade is ideal. As with so many plants, the farther north the garden, the more sun the plant tolerates; the farther south, the more it appreciates shade.

Lungworts form rosettes, then more as the plants expand, which they do without ever being truly invasive. They don't need to be divided every 3 or 4 years like some perennials, although in areas where summer heat is a problem, it can be wise to split them up every 5 or 6 years, as overcrowding under such conditions can lead to rot.

Division is a snap and can be carried out at any time, but preferably just after blooming or in fall. Lungworts can also be raised from seed, although cultivars won't come true to type. Start seed indoors in late winter or outdoors in early spring, barely covering the seed.

PROBLEMS AND SOLUTIONS

Slug damage is usually minor, but mildew can be a serious problem on some cultivars. The best control is to plant resistant varieties; the second best, remove diseased foliage.

TOP PERFORMER

Pulmonaria Hybrids (hybrid lungwort): Most of the new pulmonarias are crosses between two or more species. They include hybrids between *P. officinalis, P. saccharata, P. vallarsae,* and others, and most have pink buds opening to blue flowers and very silvery foliage—not just the silver-spotted green foliage of older cultivars. Among the innumerable cultivars are such plants as 'Spilled Milk' (highly silver mottled foliage on a dark green background, bright blue flowers) and 'Excalibur' (silver leaves with green margins, rosy pink buds opening to blue flowers). I find both very resistant to mildew. Height: 10 to 18 inches (25 to 45 cm). Spread: 12 to 24 inches (30 to 60 cm). USDA Plant Hardiness Zones 3 to 8.

MORE RECOMMENDED LUNGWORTS

Pulmonaria longifolia (longleaf lungwort): As the name suggests, this species has narrower leaves than most of the other lungworts. The leaves are dark green with silver spots, and the flowers are more purple than blue, unlike many other lungworts. It tends to be more heat-resistant than many of the other species and is therefore a good choice for southern gardens. One outstanding variety is *P. longifolia* ssp. *cevennensis,* with long leaves (up to 2 feet/60 cm long) and very heavily spotted silver and dark violet-blue flowers. It has shown no signs of mildew in my garden. Height: 9 to 18 inches (23 to 45 cm). Spread: 24 to 40 inches (60 to 100 cm). USDA Plant Hardiness Zones 3 to 9.

P. rubra (red lungwort): Truly the "odd plant out" with its coral-red flowers in a group more renowned for its blue blooms. The velvety leaves are almost sans petiole and fairly broad. They tend not to be spotted, but are a most unusual color for a lungwort: medium green. 'Redstart' is a compact form with dark red flowers; 'David Ward' has the coral-red flowers of the species, but its leaves are heavily variegated white. Both species seem very mildew-resistant. Height: 12 to 24 inches (30 to 60 cm). Spread: 24 to 40 inches (60 to 100 cm). USDA Plant Hardiness Zones 4 to 9.

Red lungwort
(*Pulmonaria rubra* 'David Ward')

LARRY'S GARDEN NOTES

According to the *Doctrine of Signatures,* which principally held sway in the sixteenth and seventeenth centuries (but is still kept alive by herbalists throughout the world), lungworts, with their mottled leaves looking like a diseased lung, must necessarily have been put on this planet by God for use in treating lung diseases. So millions of lungworts were ground up and used to treat lung problems and other bronchial difficulties— and still are in some parts of the world. Personally, I grow them just as ornamentals. Call me old-fashioned, but if I have lung problems, I see a doctor.

Rodgersia

Rodgersia

RODGERSIA

row-JER-zee-uh

Bloom Color:
White, pink, and red

Bloom Time:
Varies by species; see
individual listings

Length of Bloom:
3 to 4 weeks

Height:
Varies by species; see
individual listings

Spread:
Varies by species; see
individual listings

Garden Uses:
Cut flower garden, mass
planting, meadow garden,
mixed border, specimen
plant, wall planting,
woodland garden; at the back
of beds and borders, in wet
areas

Light Preference:
Full sun to partial shade

Soil Preference:
Humus-rich, moist to wet soil

Best Way to Propagate:
Divide in spring

USDA Plant Hardiness Zones:
Varies by species; see
individual listings

Bold foliage is the very soul of the rodgersia. Yes, the flowers are spectacular, rather like tall, fuzzy clusters of astilbe blossoms, but oh, what leaves! They are huge, beautifully textured, deeply cut, reddish at opening—a landscape planner's dream come true. Already in early spring, before the leaves have fully unfurled, they are intriguing and mysterious, rising clawlike from thick, creeping rhizomes. Then they open and give the bed such an exotic look you'll have visitors convinced they've been magically moved to some mist-filled rainforest.

GROWING TIPS

The ideal situation for a rodgersia is in a swamp or marsh: They like their soil moist at all times and are not put off by poor drainage. Besides, their huge, deeply veined leaves look good with water near them: Try growing them on the border of a water garden and you'll see. Rodgersias also adapt well to ordinary garden conditions, at least to places where you can ensure a certain amount of soil moisture even in midsummer (hint: mulching will help keep the roots moist). Leave the mulch on in winter for added protection from the cold, at least where winters are harsh. Try to avoid windy spots: Strong winds can damage the leaves.

Where the soil moisture suits them, rodgersias are not too difficult about light. Full sun is fine in cool-summer areas, but partial shade is best elsewhere. They'll also do fine in the shade of tall trees where some direct sunlight filters through.

Truly happy, well-established rodgersias can have rhizomes the thickness of a man's arm that you'll need an ax to chop through. Cutting them up to move them sends them back into adolescence—they take several years to settle down and fill in. So the best means of multiplication is often to buy new plants.

PROBLEMS AND SOLUTIONS

Most insects and diseases take one look at rodgersia and flee.

TOP PERFORMER

Rodgersia podophylla (bronzeleaf rodgersia): Clearly my favorite: I can't imagine more dramatic foliage! The huge palmate leaves are made up of five jagged segments with three to five lobes. They are bronze-colored in spring, then shiny dark green in summer, turning reddish bronze again in fall. Oops, almost forgot to mention the upright, arching stalks of yellowish white astilbelike flowers in early to late summer. There are a few cultivars, like 'Rotlaub', with redder leaves in spring and fall and flowers more distinctly white. Height: 3 to 5 feet (90 to 150 cm). Spread: 2 to 4 feet (60 to 120 cm). USDA Plant Hardiness Zones 4 to 9.

MORE RECOMMENDED RODGERSIAS

Rodgersia aesculifolia (fingerleaf rodgersia): Rodgersias are already large plants, but this one is the biggest of all. The leaves are arranged like fingers (the Latin epithet suggests they are like the leaves of a horsechestnut) on the tip of the petiole, forming a "hand" 10 inches (25 cm) or more in diameter. There can be five to seven leaflets per leaf. It is readily distinguished from the others by thick, woolly, reddish brown hair that covers the leafstalks, the flower stems, and the leaf veins. It is the latest of the rodgersias to bloom, in late summer and early fall, producing airy plumes of white flowers. Height: 4 to 6 feet (120 to 180 cm). Spread: 3 to 4 feet (90 to 120 cm). USDA Plant Hardiness Zones 4 to 9.

R. pinnata (featherleaf rodgersia): This species has foliage with a wonderfully crinkled texture that is probably its best trait, although the bronzy spring coloration is not to be sneezed at either. I don't find the leaves at all featherlike, though, but understand the allusion: The five to nine leaflets are arranged on either side of the midrib one leaflet at a time, like a feather—but surely no feather was ever so broadly textured! The flowers range from white to pink to nearly red and appear in early to midsummer. 'Superba', with deep bronze spring leaves and white flowers, is widely available, as is 'Elegans', with rose-pink flowers. Height: 3 to 4 feet (90 to 120 cm). Spread: 2 to 4 feet (60 to 120 cm). USDA Plant Hardiness Zones 4 to 9.

Featherleaf rodgersia
(*Rodgersia pinnata* 'Superba')

SMART SUBSTITUTES

Even bigger than a rodgersia and just as impressive is the Japanese butterbur (*Petasites japonicus*). I hesitated even mentioning it in this book because it is so invasive, yet I concede that it does have its usefulness. Certainly the huge heart-shaped leaves (those of the giant form, *P. japonicus* var. *giganteus*, can measure 4 to 5 feet/1.2 to 1.5 m across on 6-foot/1.8-m stems) create an impact like no other. Never release this plant in a flowerbed, though, or it will entirely take it over—its underground rhizomes know no limits and can run 4 to 5 feet (1.2 to 1.5 m) in a single year, leaving you with no garden. I suggest planting it in a tub sunk into the garden, and keeping it wet (it wilts terribly but does not die in dry soils). The curious pale yellow flowers appear in spring while the leaves are still dormant, on a separate stem, and look for all the world like an entirely different plant. Height: 4 to 6 feet (1.2 to 1.8 m). Spread: Indefinite. USDA Plant Hardiness Zones 4 to 9.

Smilacina
False Solomon's seal, Solomon's plume

PLANT PROFILE

SMILACINA

smy-lass-EE-nuh

Bloom Color:
White

Bloom Time:
Spring

Length of Bloom:
2 to 3 weeks

Height:
Varies by species; see
individual listings

Spread:
1 to 2 feet (30 to 60 cm)

Garden Uses:
Mass planting, mixed border,
specimen plant, woodland
garden; in wet areas; attracts
fruit-eating birds

Light Preference:
Partial shade to shade

Soil Preference:
Humus-rich, moist to wet,
acid soil

Best Way to Propagate:
Divide in fall or very early
spring

USDA Plant Hardiness Zones:
3 to 8

I first saw this native North American wildflower used in an ornamental garden during a trip to Europe! Like the Solomon's seal it clearly resembles, it produces upright, arching stems of oval, alternate, shiny leaves, and it may indeed be mistaken for Solomon's seal before it comes into bloom. In flower, though, it is completely different: Each stem produces a large pyramidal terminal cluster of fluffy white to creamy white flowers, and afterward, large numbers of bright red berries.

GROWING TIPS

This is a typical plant of the North American forest, found, in one form or another, throughout the continent, from Alaska to Mexico. As a forest-dweller, it is of course quite habituated to low light: It does best in shade to partial shade and may burn in full sun, especially in the South. In the wild it tends to grow mainly in deep leaf litter on moist, very acid soils. In the garden, it adapts well to most soil types except truly alkaline soils— even poor, stony, or clay soils. It is a very unhappy camper in hot-summer areas, though, even more so where the heat is combined with drought. Keep it moist, mulched, and out of the full southern sun if you want to keep it happy.

Plant false Solomon's seal, keep it well mulched and well watered for the first two summers, then just ignore it: It is slow to establish and dividing it arbitrarily just because it has been in the ground for X number of years doesn't make for an attractive plant. It is among those plants that only slowly increase in size over many years, as the clump gradually expands in diameter, but that doesn't seem to decline through overcrowding.

Multiplication is by division of mature plants, best done very early in spring when the plant is just awakening from dormancy, or, even better, in fall. Be careful of harvesting this plant from the wild or of buying wild-harvested plants. False Solomon's seal is already considered threatened in some American states and, even where it is not (and it is still very abundant in many areas), it *is* very slow at reproducing, and that could put it at the mercy of unscrupulous collectors should it suddenly gain the popularity it deserves.

False Solomon's seal
(*Smilacina racemosa*)

PROBLEMS AND SOLUTIONS

Slugs and snails relish the new growth, but the plant quickly outgrows the "tender-leaf" stage. By mid-summer, the leaves have hardened off and slugs then ignore them.

TOP PERFORMER

Smilacina racemosa, syn. *Maianthemum racemosum* (false Solomon's seal, Solomon's plume): This is by far the most commonly cultivated species and also probably the most attractive *Smilacina*. It produces the upright, arching stems, dark green shiny leaves, and fluffy pyramidal clusters of fragrant white flowers described above. After the blooms fall, they are replaced by small bright red berries. They are numerous but generally don't last long, as they are a favorite food of birds and small mammals. There are a couple of natural varieties, such as *S. racemosa* var. *amplexicaulis* (Western false Solomon's seal, Western Solomon's plume), but they are not widely available. Height: 2 to 3 feet (60 to 90 cm). Spread: 1 to 2 feet (30 to 60 cm). USDA Plant Hardiness Zones 3 to 9.

MORE RECOMMENDED
FALSE SOLOMON'S SEALS

Smilacina stellata (starry Solomon's seal, starry Solomon's plume, star-flowered false lily-of-the-valley): This a somewhat smaller plant, likewise found throughout much of North America and often found growing side by side with its cousin, false Solomon's seal. As the names suggest, it is most easily distinguished from the other species by its star-shaped white flowers borne in a more open cluster. The foliage tends to more closely resemble that of a lily-of-the-valley, hence one of its common names. The flowers give way to small berries that change from green to red to black by summer's end, and they may persist through fall if they are not consumed by wild birds and animals. This plant is much more expansive than false Solomon's seal and in fact has spreading rhizomes that will certainly wander if allowed to do so. It likewise blooms in spring. Height: 8 to 24 inches (20 to 60 cm). Spread: 12 to 24 inches (30 to 60 cm). USDA Plant Hardiness Zones 3 to 9.

KISSING COUSINS

Indian poke or American white hellebore (*Veratrum viride*) is a *Smilacina* relative that is a common denizen of North American forests where its large, very pleated, light green leaves rising from the ground are a sure sign of spring! Their curious and attractive appearance also outweighs the plant's blooms, which, though abundant and borne in dense terminal panicles, are too small and too greenish to attract much attention. After all, they bloom in summer when the forest is in full leaf: green flowers on a green background? It's no more exciting in the garden than it sounds on paper. Partial shade to shade is best: This plant burns in full sun. Division is the usual means of multiplication—growing from seed is a long and fastidious process. Be forewarned that this plant is toxic in all its parts. Height: 2 to 6 feet (60 to 180 cm). Spread: 1 to 2 feet (30 to 60 cm). USDA Plant Hardiness Zones 3 to 9.

Spigelia

Spigelia, Indian pink, Maryland pinkroot

PLANT PROFILE

SPIGELIA

spy-GEEL-ee-uh

Bloom Color:
Red and yellow

Bloom Time:
Late spring to early summer

Length of Bloom:
4 to 6 weeks

Height:
1 to 2 feet (30 to 60 cm)

Spread:
2 feet (60 cm)

Garden Uses:
Mass planting, mixed border, rock garden, specimen plant, woodland garden; attracts hummingbirds

Light Preference:
Full sun to shade

Soil Preference:
Fertile, well-drained soil

Best Way to Propagate:
Divide in spring or plant seed

USDA Plant Hardiness Zones:
4 to 9

It's hard to believe that a plant with such an exotic appearance is actually a native North American wildflower—and a forest-dwelling one at that. The smooth, stalkless, dark green leaves on upright stems look tropical from the start, but when the flowers appear—upright tubular red blooms that burst open into yellow stars at the tip—the illusion is complete. This *can't* be a plant of the temperate woods, but surely some exotic fuchsia! If its exotic appearance and beautiful blooms were not enough, this plant attracts hummingbirds like a pro!

GROWING TIPS

The ideal situation for spigelia is partial shade. It tends to grow in the wild in open forest or at the forest's edge. It tolerates deeper shade in the South where the sun is more intense and will take full sun in the North as long as you keep its roots moist, but you'll likely find it easiest to grow when you give it partial shade in any climate.

Soilwise, it's quite an adaptable plant. In the wild, it most commonly grows in leaf litter on limestone soil. However, in culture it has shown itself adaptable to at least moderately acid soils. Lots of organic material helps simulate its natural conditions, so add lots of compost at planting time and mulch abundantly. It does not appreciate drying out.

It's a pretty enough plant, but for maximum impact it looks best in groups. Try planting it in patches of five plants or more if you really want to wow people and to create enough of a nectar source for hummingbirds to feel it is worth being part of their daily visitation schedule.

Multiplication is a bit of a challenge. The abundance of stems seems to indicate it would grow well from cuttings, but most gardeners report little luck with them. It grows in dense clumps and is not given to producing offsets, so division seems unlikely. However, established clumps can be carefully divided in early spring, although they rarely yield more than the original plant and one or two sections. That leaves seed, which fortunately germinates readily—but just try to harvest it! It goes from "too green to harvest" to "oops, I missed it" almost overnight. Put a bag over the maturing seed capsule if you want to make sure you don't miss it, or simply let it self-seed. By leaving a few unmulched spots in its immediate neighborhood, you'll usually find yourself the proud possessor of a handful or so of young spigelias the following spring that you can replant as required. If you sow the seed yourself, do so without too much delay; it germinates best when sown fresh.

PROBLEMS AND SOLUTIONS

I've never heard of anyone who's had problems with spigelia, although one British publication, disguised (through a title change and the addition of a few hardiness zones) as something solidly all-American, suggests powdery mildew and leaf spot are possible. If they do show up, see page 86 for suggestions on controlling them.

TOP PERFORMER

Spigelia marilandica (spigelia, Indian pink, pinkroot): This is the only species with any kind of national distribution and it remains a relatively obscure, although increasingly popular, plant. Only the species, with red tubular flowers opening to yellow stars at the tip, is available. As time goes on and its popularity increases, which it will surely do, horticultural varieties selected for different colors, more abundant bloom, and other such features will undoubtedly appear on the market. For the moment, though, you're likely to find this plant only through wildflower nurseries or mail order. Height: 1 to 2 feet (30 to 60 cm). Spread: 2 feet (60 cm). USDA Plant Hardiness Zones 3 to 10.

MORE RECOMMENDED SPIGELIAS

Spigelia gentianoides (purpleflower pinkroot, gentian pinkroot): Only truly dedicated plant hunters will be likely to find this rare plant from Alabama and Florida. In spite of the common name, the upright flowers are actually closer to pink than to purple, at least to my eye. The tubular blooms "open" into five upright petals. Height: 1 foot (30 cm). Spread: 1 foot (30 cm). USDA Plant Hardiness Zones 7 to 10.

Spigelia (*Spigelia marilandica*)

SMART SUBSTITUTE

Better known than spigelia are the curiously named "turtleheads" (*Chelone* spp.). You really have to squint to see anything turtlelike in the puffy flowers. This plant is a tough, sturdy, upright perennial for shade to part shade in wet to not-too-dry soils. The dark green leaves are attractive, but the fall flowers, in white or pink, are even better. There are three main species: pink turtlehead (*Chelone lyonii*), rose turtlehead (*C. obliqua*), and white turtlehead (*C. glabra*). They reach from 1 to 3 feet (30 to 90 cm) high, depending on the species, and 18 to 24 inches (45 to 60 cm) in spread. USDA Plant Hardiness Zones 3 to 9.

Thalictrum
Meadow rue

PLANT PROFILE

THALICTRUM

thuh-LICK-trum

Bloom Color:
Lilac, pink, purple, and white

Bloom Time:
Varies by species; see
individual listings

Length of Bloom:
Varies by species; see
individual listings

Height:
Varies by species; see
individual listings

Spread:
Varies by species; see
individual listings

Garden Uses:
Cut flower garden, edging,
groundcover, mass planting,
mixed border, rock garden,
specimen plant, wildflower
meadow, woodland garden

Light Preference:
Full sun to shade

Soil Preference:
Humus-rich, moist, well-
drained soil

Best Way to Propagate:
Divide in spring

USDA Plant Hardiness Zones:
Varies by species; see
individual listings

To my mind, the nicest thing about meadow rues is that they have such great foliage. The lacy, pinnate leaves, beautifully cut and variously described as looking like columbine, maidenhair fern, or ginkgo leaves, usually have a distinct bluish cast and ensure that the plant looks great right through the growing season. Of course, the curious, fuzzy flowers are the main reason people choose meadow rues, but flowers don't last forever—and, especially in a shady corner, it's the subtle beauty of the foliage that most gardeners come to appreciate. So grow them for their flowers if you will, but don't forget to place them where you'll be able to see the beautiful leaves!

GROWING TIPS

First, it has to be said that not all meadow rues are truly shade-tolerant. And in a genus of some 130 species, such differences are to be expected. Some, especially the taller species like *Thalictrum delavayi* and *T. rochebruneanum*, are best in full sun or only partial shade, as they become floppy and need staking when the shade is too dense. The ones described here, however, all do splendidly in partial shade and beyond.

Rich, well-drained soils are best. In summer, they do prefer some moisture, although they can be quite drought-resistant once established. The shadier the spot, the less moisture they require.

Many shade-tolerant meadow rues are true species and therefore come true from seed. Fresh seed is best and should be sown outdoors when it matures, in late summer or fall. Expect it to germinate the following spring.

Cultivars are best multiplied by division. Go about it *delicately*, early in spring, while the plants are still dormant.

PROBLEMS AND SOLUTIONS

Leaf diseases are possible; remove damaged leaves. Leaf diseases tend to be more problematic where air circulation is poor and the soil is excessively moist.

TOP PERFORMER

Thalictrum aquilegifolium (columbine meadow rue): This is the classic meadow rue, the one your grandmother probably grew, and an all-around champion for ease of culture. That it has been such a successful garden plant for so many generations speaks for itself. Whether you live in the North or the South, this plant does about equally well. It is also particularly easy to grow from seed: Even packaged seed germinates readily. The fuzzy, pomponlike flowers appear in early summer and last several weeks where temperatures are cool. The attractive blue-green leaves are what give the plant its common name, columbine meadow rue—they truly do look like columbine leaves. Fortunately the insects that so love columbine leaves don't see the resemblance, so meadow rue leaves remain in perfect shape until fall. The typical flower color is lilac, but mixed seed will also yield various shades of white, pink, and purple. Cultivars grown from divisions, like 'Album' (white), and 'Purpureum' (purple), as well as the larger-flowered 'Thundercloud' (deep purple) and 'Sparkler' (white), are also available, at least from specialist nurseries. Most plants sold in the commerce are no-names, though, and their exact flower color is unpredictable. Height: 3 to 5 feet (90 to 150 cm). Spread: 2 to 3 feet (60 to 90 cm). USDA Plant Hardiness Zones 3 to 8.

MORE RECOMMENDED MEADOW RUES

Thalictrum kiusianum (Kyushu meadow rue): This tiny little charmer is so much smaller than the others one would hardly guess it is a meadow rue, yet a closer look reveals the blue-green maidenhair fern–like leaflets and the powder-puff flowers in pink, purplish pink, or white. The upright midsummer blooms are small but produced in huge numbers once the plant is well established. This species produces stolons, so it spreads quite willingly, creating a ground-hugging deciduous carpet; it is used, obviously, mostly as a groundcover. Many sources give a hardiness zone of only 6 or even 8, but my experience is that it is a solid Zone 5 and easy to grow with some protection even into Zone 3. Height: 4 to 6 inches (10 to 15 cm). Spread: Indefinite. USDA Plant Hardiness Zones 5 to 10.

Columbine meadow rue
(*Thalictrum aquilegifolium*)

LARRY'S GARDEN NOTES

The fuzzy-looking flowers of meadow rues are quite unique in appearance, and even more unique when you get a close look at them. First, unlike most other flowers, they are totally lacking in petals. Instead the sepals—the outer parts of the calyx, which are green in most plants—have come to look like petals and can be pink, purple, or other shades. However, most species go one step further: The main color comes from the numerous stamens (male sex organs) and pistils (female sex organs) that form a puffball in the center of the flower.

Tiarella

Foamflower

PLANT PROFILE

TIARELLA

tee-uh-REL-uh

Bloom Color:
White and pink

Bloom Time:
Late spring to midsummer

Length of Bloom:
4 to 6 weeks

Height:
6 to 12 inches (15 to 30 cm)

Spread:
12 inches (30 cm)

Garden Uses:
Edging, groundcover, mass planting, mixed border, rock garden, woodland garden

Light Preference:
Partial shade to shade

Soil Preference:
Rich, moist, well-drained, acid soil

Best Way to Propagate:
Divide in early spring

USDA Plant Hardiness Zones:
3 to 9

Once a minor player in landscaped woodland gardens, the handsome foamflower is beginning to create quite a reputation for itself as a stalwart and attractive plant with a long season of interest, thanks to evergreen leaves that take on beautiful reddish tints from fall through winter and a long blooming season from late spring to midsummer. This popularity is due to the influx of a profusion of new cultivars. The once-staid foamflower, with its plain green maple-shaped leaves and its fuzzy white flowerspikes, now comes in a range of foliage shapes and colors to rival its close relative, *Heuchera*, including deeply lobed, starlike leaves often heavily marked with deep purple. The flower range now stretches well into pink. All this on a plant that is tough as nails.

GROWING TIPS

Foamflowers of different species are found in forested areas throughout North America (one species is native to Asia), so they do have a handle on shade. Partial shade to shade is fine with them in all climates. And they cope perfectly with root competition as well, as long as the soil remains somewhat moist. Even though they like moist soil in summer, foamflowers are not good choices for truly wet spots.

In the wild they seem to prefer deep leaf litter and soil that is distinctly on the acid side. In culture, a good mulch can replace the leaf litter, and they tolerate more alkaline soils as well.

Some species and hybrids of foamflower are runners, spreading through underground stems to create a perfect carpet. They're not really invasive and can be stopped by root barriers, but they still bear a bit of watching, especially as the years go by. Others simply form clumps that slowly increase in size over time. This conveniently gives you the choice between cultivars better used as groundcovers (the spreaders) and those more interesting for more formal garden uses.

Multiplication of hybrid foamflowers is by division, as they do not come true from seed. That's especially easy to do in the case of the ones spreading by underground stems, as each separate plant is clearly defined, but nonrunners also provide plenty of material for multiplication through the division of their clumps.

PROBLEMS AND SOLUTIONS

Slugs and snails may damage young leaves but seem to dislike mature foliage. Foamflowers produce such a profusion of leaves that the damage is rarely evident.

TOP PERFORMER

Tiarella Hybrids (foamflower): There are now so many hybrids of foamflower that the original species are being pushed into the background. Some spread through underground stems, others are clump-forming. The following are just a few samples: There are dozens more where they came from! 'Black Velvet' has velvety, deeply cut leaves with a deep purple center and pink-tinged white flowers. 'Eco Running Tapestry' is a spreader, with medium green maple-shaped leaves with darker veins and white flowers. 'Jeepers Creepers' is in between a running variety and a clumper, spreading more densely than the true runners; it has well-marked maple-shaped leaves and cream-colored flowers. 'Neon Lights' has cut leaves with abundant deep purple coloration; its flowers are white and it is a clumper. 'Pink Skyrocket', a clumper, has deeply cut, well-marked foliage and myriad spikes of pink flowers. All are hardy to Zone 4 and do fine in Zone 3 under heavy snow. Height: 12 to 18 inches (30 to 45 cm). Spread: 16 to 20 inches (40 to 50 cm). USDA Plant Hardiness Zones 4 to 9.

MORE RECOMMENDED FOAMFLOWERS

Tiarella cordifolia (Allegheny foamflower): Not so long ago, this was the most popular of the foamflowers. The velvety maple-shaped leaves are usually green in summer, reddish in fall and winter, while the flower spikes are white or faintly tinged pink. *T. cordifolia* var. *collina*, a.k.a. *T. wherryi* (Wherry's foamflower) is a natural form that doesn't produce creeping stems and often has purple markings along the veins. Flowers may be white or pinkish. There are several cultivars, including the intriguing 'Heronswood Mist' with leaves mottled cream, pink, and green. Height: 6 to 12 inches (15 to 30 cm). Spread: 16 to 20 inches (40 to 50 cm). USDA Plant Hardiness Zones 3 to 9.

Allegheny foamflower
(*Tiarella cordifolia*)

KISSING COUSINS

The foliage colors of *Heuchera* now mingle with the great groundcover performance of *Tiarella*, thanks to some spectacular hybridizing. Foamy bells (× *Heucherella*) combine the best traits of both genera. 'Silver Streak' has deep purple leaves with silver mottling and white flowers tinged lavender. 'Sunspot' has bright chartreuse-yellow leaves with a red star in the center and pink blooms. There are dozens of others. Height: 6 to 12 inches (15 to 30 cm). Spread: 16 to 20 inches (40 to 50 cm). USDA Plant Hardiness Zones 3 to 9.

Tricyrtis
Toad lily

What a name to give to such a beautiful flower! The six-tepaled (three petals, three sepals) upward-facing flowers are almost orchidlike in appearance with a waxy texture, beautiful spotting, and striking passiflora-like anthers. In spite of their name, toad lilies are catching on in a big way with gardeners who appreciate their lilylike foliage (often mottled like the flowers) on upright or arching stems, and curiously beautiful flowers. They're often very late to bloom, which is a nice surprise in long-summer areas and frustrating in short ones, as you bite your nails annually, wondering which will win out: the toad lilies or the frost? For shade gardeners, they're a real treat: All are fine in partial shade, and many bloom up a storm in deep shade as well.

GROWING TIPS

Toad lilies are native to the moist woodlands of Asia. So they're going to love leaf litter (or mulch), rich soils, and even moisture. In hot-summer areas, they prefer shade; in cool-summer ones, they tolerate sun; in both, they just love partial shade.

Toad lilies are pretty much evenly divided between clump-forming species and those with creeping rhizomes. The first group, obviously, stays conveniently put; the latter tend to wander widely. Even so, the wanderer's open, non-threatening-to-other-plants habit and capacity to bloom up a storm when there is nothing else going mean that many gardeners forgive this sin and let them wander at will. If you're into formal beds, though, stick with the clumpers!

Mulching toad lilies is always wise: It keeps them cooler in summer in hot areas and protects from deep freezing in the colder ones. Most species would not be nearly as hardy as is claimed (only about Zone 7) if they were truly exposed to winter cold, but under a deep layer of mulch, they easily take Zone 5 (and I'm having no trouble with them in Zone 3). Multiplication is generally through division in early spring, while they are still dormant.

PROBLEMS AND SOLUTIONS

Slugs and snails have a penchant for the young spring leaves. See page 85 for suggestions on controlling them.

TOP PERFORMER

Tricyrtis Hybrids (hybrid toad lily): Like so many plants these days, species toad lilies are losing favor to hybrid varieties combining the best traits of all their varied parents. There are many complex hybrids with upward-facing flowers. 'Tojen' ('Togen'), a clumper, has lavender flowers that fade to white at the base, a yellow throat, and particularly broad leaves. It blooms over a long period from late summer until midfall. Although sturdy enough at first, it bends over under the weight of the blooms and should be planted where it can lean on neighboring plants. 'Sinonome', a spreader, produces white flowers with purple speckling. 'Empress' has huge flowers that are pale lavender heavily mottled with purple and look very much like orchids; it blooms late summer to early fall. 'Lightning Strike' is but one of many variegated toad lilies. The flowers are lavender, and the leaves are abundantly striped yellow. Height: 2 to 3 feet (60 to 90 cm). Spread: 2 feet (60 cm). USDA Plant Hardiness Zones 5 to 9.

Hybrid toad lily (*Tricyrtis* 'Tojen')

MORE RECOMMENDED TOAD LILIES

Tricyrtis hirta (common toad lily, hairy toad lily): This is indeed the most common species, with arching stems and abundant flowers that are white to pale purple with lots of purple spots that appear, contrary to the previous species, mostly at leaf axils. 'White Towers' has pure white flowers, and 'Miyazaki Gold' shows purple-spotted pink to white flowers and gold-edged leaves. Height: 2 to 3 feet (60 to 90 cm). Spread: 2 feet (60 cm). USDA Plant Hardiness Zones 4 to 9.

T. latifolia (broadleaf toad lily): This is the best choice for short-season climates, as it blooms in midsummer (early summer where summers are longer), far earlier than the other species, and therefore has time to complete its full 6-week flowering period before there is any danger of frost. The leaves are very broad, almost heart-shaped, and mottled when young, carried on strongly upright stems. The flowers, borne in terminal clusters, are yellow with deep purple spots. Height: 24 to 32 inches (60 to 80 cm). Spread: 24 inches (60 cm). USDA Plant Hardiness Zones 5 to 9.

LARRY'S GARDEN NOTES

How in the world did such a pretty plant get such an ugly name as "toad lily"? The truth is, no one knows, although theories abound. Some say the crushed flowers were used to kill toads, others say that the brown spots on the leaves make them look toadlike. Of course, the spots on the flowers may also look like warts. Horticulturist Alan Armitage has learned that the Tasaday tribe of the Philippines used to rub the juices from the flowers and leaves of one species on their hands before setting out to catch frogs. Frogs? Toads? It could be the link!

Trollius
Globeflower

PLANT PROFILE

TROLLIUS

TROH-lee-us

Bloom Color:
Yellow, orange, and cream

Bloom Time:
Late spring to early summer

Length of Bloom:
3 to 4 weeks

Height:
20 to 36 inches (50 to 90 cm)

Spread:
12 to 30 inches (30 to 75 cm)

Garden Uses:
Container planting, cut flower garden, edging, mixed border, rock garden, specimen plant, wildflower meadow, woodland garden; in wet areas

Light Preference:
Full sun to partial shade

Soil Preference:
Rich, moist, even soggy soil

Best Way to Propagate:
Divide in spring or early fall

USDA Plant Hardiness Zones:
3 to 9

Globeflowers are like giant civilized buttercups. Instead of spreading like wildfire through your lawn and garden bearing wiry, branching flower stalks of little golden cups, like the meadow buttercup (*Ranunculus acris*) is wont to do, globeflowers form dense clumps of dark green, deeply cut foliage and sturdily upright stems bearing huge (comparatively), distinctly rounded buttercup flowers, usually in golden yellow, but some orange or cream. There are over 30 different species, but not even botanists have an easy time telling them apart. All are easy to grow and early to bloom: a nice, bright way to get your spring garden up and right.

GROWING TIPS

In the wilds, globeflowers inhabit swamps and wet meadows, so they will be particularly happy in those damp corners where the soil is heavy and the drainage poor—areas that most other garden plants abhor. Such spots also tend to be cool, another thing they like. In northern gardens, where cooler summers mean less evaporation, they'll be fine in ordinary garden soil as long as they are mulched or at least watered during periods of drought and will even take full sun. In the South, they're really only happy in damp to boggy soil and partial shade: places where they are kept cool and wet, in other words. Bog gardens and edges of water gardens would be perfect.

Globeflowers stressed by heat or drought tend to go to pot by midsummer, with yellowing leaves that seem to say, "Please cut us back!" Do so: It won't hurt the plant (it's used to going semidormant in summer). In cooler climates or under boggy conditions, the foliage hangs on in fine shape for the rest of summer and is, in fact, quite attractive.

Divide globeflowers in spring or fall. Since they don't really like being disturbed and can take several years to settle in and begin blooming once they've been divided, put it off as long as possible. Only when the centers start to thin out, a sign the original clump has gotten far too crowded, should you consider digging, separating, and replanting.

PROBLEMS AND SOLUTIONS

Powdery mildew is a common problem when plants are kept too dry. Keep them moist and cool as a preventative measure. If it's too late for that, remove infested leaves.

TOP PERFORMER

Trollius × *cultorum* (hybrid globeflower): This hybrid species, resulting from crosses between *T. europaeus, T. chinensis,* and others, is by far the most commonly available species: In fact, just about all the cultivars on the market belong here. Among them are plants with yellow, orange, or cream flowers, all with the typical globe-shaped flowers. 'Earliest of All' has golden yellow flowers. Whether it is truly the earliest globeflower of all is debatable, but it is an early bloomer, in flower by mid-spring. 'Orange Princess' has golden orange flowers; 'Lemon Queen' has lemon yellow ones. 'Alabaster' is unusual in its pale cream-colored flowers in mid- and late spring; 'Cheddar' is perhaps a bit darker (creamy yellow) but blooms a bit later. There are many other cultivars, mostly in shades of yellow and yellowy orange. Height: 24 to 36 inches (60 to 90 cm). Spread: 18 to 36 inches (45 to 90 cm). USDA Plant Hardiness Zones 3 to 9.

Hybrid globeflower
(*Trollius* × *cultorum* 'Byrne's Giant')

MORE RECOMMENDED GLOBEFLOWERS

Trollius chinensis, syn. *T. ledebourii* (Chinese globeflower): There's little to differentiate between this plant and hybrid globeflower, but it is usually a bit later-blooming (starting in early summer), and the orange to yellow flowers are more open: bowl-shaped rather than truly globular. 'Golden Queen' is the classic cultivar and very widely available, with deep orange-yellow flowers. Height: 24 to 36 inches (60 to 90 cm). Spread: 18 to 36 inches (45 to 90 cm). USDA Plant Hardiness Zones 3 to 9.

T. pumilus (dwarf globeflower): This alpine species looks more like a buttercup than the others, thanks to its diminutive height and its smaller orange-yellow flowers, only 1 inch (2.5 cm) in diameter, that are wide open and not at all globular. It is summer-blooming. Height: 9 to 12 inches (23 to 30 cm). Spread: 12 inches (30 cm). USDA Plant Hardiness Zones 3 to 9.

KISSING COUSINS

If bright golden flowers are your thing, why not try growing buttercups? My favorite is the delightful miniature with the heart-shaped leaves: lesser celandine (*Ranunculus ficaria*), Zone 5, only 2 to 8 inches (5 to 20 cm) tall. It's a spring ephemeral, popping up from nowhere in midspring to bloom abundantly, then retreating underground in summer. Look for the noninvasive types, like the absolutely stunning 'Brazen Hussy', with bright yellow single blooms over shiny chocolate brown leaves. It is absolutely to die for!

Uvularia
Merrybells, bellwort

Native plants just don't get the respect they deserve, and that's certainly true of this delightful genus, absolutely shade-tolerant and absolutely easy to grow, yet hardly ever available outside of native plant nurseries. Merrybells form dense patches of upright stems that arch downward at the tip, with narrow strap-like leaves. At blooming time, large yellow flowers with twisted petals dangle from the stem tips, like a lily bowing its head. The attractive leaves persist through the rest of summer.

GROWING TIPS

Merrybells are native to the deep forests of the northeastern United States and Canada. They especially appreciate deciduous forests, as they are up early in spring to capture enough intense, unfiltered sun to carry them through summer. To keep them happy in the garden, just replicate their natural growing conditions: shade to partial shade throughout the growing season, and a good mulch. They adapt perfectly to most soils, but a rich, organic, loose one is heaven to them. Add a soaker hose to keep them moist in summer.

Merrybells spread by rhizomes—but don't panic, they don't take over a garden overnight. Instead, young plants first develop a dense clump, then they spread outward and slowly fill in empty spots in the garden. I like to establish them in pockets of deep soil among tree roots: Once they get going, they seem oblivious to root competition and slowly fill in spots where digging would have been impossible. If colonies get too big for their britches, just dig the extras out.

Division is the most obvious means of multiplying merrybells. Since they are up so early in spring when the ground is usually too cold and soggy to work with, it's best to wait until fall to divide them. Division is needed only to multiply them: You can plant merrybells permanently in the garden and they'll bloom abundantly year after year, never declining over time as some perennials do when they become overcrowded.

About the only thing complicated about growing merrybells is multiplying them from seed. Packaged seed, as received by mail, will be deeply dormant and can take 2, 3, or even 4 years to even germinate! Indoors it takes a series of alternating cold and warm treatments to get them going. Outdoors . . . well, just sow them in some out-of-the-way spot and wait. One of these days you'll discover the tiny grasslike plants of the new generation. It's much easier to grow them from fresh seed sown *immediately*, in late summer. There is then no dormant period—they'll sprout the following spring.

PROBLEMS AND SOLUTIONS

Merrybells seem to have few problems as long as they are growing in a cool forested setting with plenty of mulch.

TOP PERFORMER

Uvularia grandiflora (large-flowered bellwort, big merrybells): Tops in size and tops in performance! This plant is simply larger and showier than the others and so is now, and always has been, the only species *sometimes* available in regular nurseries. Its leaves are perfoliate, meaning that the stem grows right through them: an interesting fact you might want to point out to visitors, as it isn't obvious at first view. Large-flowered bellwort produces big, dense clumps and eventually colonies, flowering from mid-spring to early summer. The flowers are larger than those of other merrybells, with the same twisted petals. Height: 12 to 30 inches (30 to 75 cm). Spread: 12 to 18 inches (30 to 45 cm). USDA Plant Hardiness Zones 3 to 9.

MORE RECOMMENDED MERRYBELLS

Uvularia perfoliata (perfoliate bellwort, wood merrybells, strawbell): Think of this species as a smaller, paler version of large-flowered bellwort with the same unusual perfoliate leaves. It has pale yellow flowers, almost straw yellow, as suggested by the common name strawbell. It is ideal if you're looking for a more subtle shade of yellow. Height: 12 to 18 inches (30 to 45 cm). Spread: 12 to 18 inches (30 to 45 cm). USDA Plant Hardiness Zones 3 to 9.

Large-flowered bellwort
(*Uvularia grandiflora*)

LARRY'S GARDEN NOTES

As you may have guessed, the name *Uvularia* refers to the uvula, that dangling piece of flesh hanging from the soft palate behind your tongue. Botanists who first saw this plant saw a similarity between the uvula and pendant flowers of merrybells, but, well . . . I guess you had to have been there. It's not the world's most elegant comparison, but once you know it, you'll never forget the plant's botanical name again!

Vinca

Periwinkle, vinca

PLANT PROFILE

VINCA

VING-ka

Bloom Color:
Blue, purple, and white

Bloom Time:
Principally spring, but also summer and fall

Length of Bloom:
4 weeks or more

Height:
Varies by species; see individual listings

Spread:
Varies by species; see individual listings

Garden Uses:
Container planting, edging, groundcover, mass planting, rock garden, wall planting, woodland garden; along paths, on slopes

Light Preference:
Full sun to shade

Soil Preference:
Fertile, humus-rich, well-drained soil

Best Way to Propagate:
Replant rooted sections at any time

USDA Plant Hardiness Zones:
Varies by species; see individual listings

Periwinkles are possibly the most popular groundcovers in the world. Their long, creeping stems root at the nodes even in areas of serious root competition, and their shiny dark green or variegated evergreen leaves ensure beauty throughout the year. Their shade tolerance is legendary: Some places where periwinkles are seen thriving see no sun whatsoever and precious little reflected light. It would be a shame not to mention their beautiful star-shaped flowers that, although most abundant in spring, repeat at least lightly throughout summer and into fall.

GROWING TIPS

Periwinkles have an amazing capacity to adapt to almost all conditions, from full sun (as long as you keep their soil moist) to the deepest shade and in just about any well-drained soil. They prefer rich, humusy soil and even moisture, plus partial shade. In the deepest shade, they grow well and make a great carpet, but bloom only lightly if at all. A good organic mulch will help to get them started, keeping the young plants cool and moist.

Plant periwinkles relatively thickly, on about 1-foot (30-cm) centers. Cut back young plantings annually with a lawn mower for the first few years—pruning them back stimulates thick coverage. There are actually two kinds of stems: trailing or creeping ones that root as they grow, and more upright flowering stems that don't root. Pruning back the flowering stems encourages the plant to produce more creeping ones.

Multiply periwinkles by digging up and replanting rooted sections at any season. You can likewise take cuttings of non-blooming stems or layer the creeping branches by pressing a leaf node into the soil with a stone or a peg.

Think Twice: Be forewarned that periwinkles are hard to control. Root barriers certainly won't suffice: They spread above the ground, not below it. My suggestion? Plant them only in areas where you don't intend to have formal gardens—and even then, surround their planting area with surfaces they can't cross, like a terrace, a water garden, or a deck.

Think Twice: Don't confuse the true periwinkles (*Vinca* spp.)

with a garden annual commonly called vinca or Madagascar periwinkle (*Catharanthus roseus*) and formerly known as *Vinca roseus*. It has similar leaves but an upright growth habit, becoming spreading over time, and its much larger flowers are usually in shades of pink, white, or red. It is *not* a good shade plant, preferring full sun and hot, dry growing conditions.

PROBLEMS AND SOLUTIONS

Periwinkles are only rarely bothered by insects and diseases. Most infestations are minor and clear up all on their own.

TOP PERFORMER

Vinca minor (common periwinkle): This is the most widely grown of the two common periwinkles, largely because it is adapted to the widest range of climates: from very temperate to nearly tropical. It bears opposite oval to oblong, shiny dark green leaves. The violet-blue flowers are most abundant in spring.

The cultivars vary in both flower color and in foliage color, as there are many variegated cultivars. Among the green-leaved varieties are 'Atropurpurea' ('Purpurea' or 'Rubra'), with deep wine red flowers; 'Alba', with white flowers; and 'La Grave' ('Bowles' Variety'), with larger deep blue blooms. The variegated clones include 'Illumination'. Height: 4 to 10 inches (10 to 25 cm). Spread: Indefinite. USDA Plant Hardiness Zones 4 to 9.

MORE RECOMMENDED PERIWINKLES

Vinca major (greater periwinkle): As the name suggests, this is the taller of the two common species, and it has much larger leaves. The flowers too are slightly larger. This is the species most popular in the South: It doesn't need a winter rest and will grow well into the tropics. It sometimes succeeds into Zone 6 or even 5 . . . but a harsh winter will likely damage it or even eliminate it north of Zone 7. Bloom is heaviest in spring but can occur sporadically throughout summer and into fall. There are several cultivars, including 'Variegata' ('Elegantissima'), with leaves irregularly blotched creamy white. 'Wojo's Gem' has dark green leaves with a yellow stripe down the center. Height: 12 to 18 inches (30 to 45 cm). Spread: Indefinite. USDA Plant Hardiness Zones 7 to 11.

Common periwinkle (*Vinca minor*)

LARRY'S GARDEN NOTES

Don't forget that periwinkle trails beautifully from containers. In fact, many people prefer to use it that way. It may not necessarily be hardy enough to survive winter in a container in colder climates, as soil freezes more deeply in a pot than it does in the ground, so treat it as an annual when grown this way. If you already use periwinkle as a groundcover, however, you only have to harvest rooted sections each spring and plant them into a hanging basket or flowerbox for another summer of beauty.

Viola

Violet, pansy, viola

Even nongardeners recognize violets and pansies, at least by their names, although not all realize the two are so closely related. There are some 500 species from just about every climate, from tropical to subarctic, so you'll have plenty of choices. Here we'll look at some of the truly perennial species, usually those called violets; the ones generally used as annuals (i.e., garden pansies) are described on page 264. Violets are small-flowered, spring-blooming plants with well-separated petals arching outward like butterflies and heart-shaped to deeply cut leaves.

GROWING TIPS

Most species are denizens of cool, forested areas and will languish in the heat of the burning sun. They prefer partial shade to shade and rich, moist, well-drained soils with lots of organic matter. Mulching is always wise, especially in areas where summers are burning hot. Violets tend to be fairly long-lived, almost permanent plants.

It is not easy to be precise about multiplying violets. Some produce basal offsets that can be removed and replanted. Others have creeping stems and root as they grow, providing ample material for propagation. Others do neither and can be grown only from seed. Fortunately, many, in fact, self-sow, often very abundantly. Plant a few for an immediate effect and you'll soon have a forest full!

PROBLEMS AND SOLUTIONS

Leaf diseases and rot may be a problem. Cut back or remove infested plants: Usually there will be plenty of healthy self-sowers to fill in any bare spots.

TOP PERFORMER

Viola riviniana Purpurea Group (purpleleaf dog violet): This European species has been widely offered as *V. labradorica* or *V. labradorica* 'Purpurea' (Labrador violet), which is actually a different species and is not currently in culture. This explains a mystery that has long bothered me: the great adaptability of

Sweet violet (*Viola odorata*)

supposed "northern" plants to more temperate latitudes and even to the South, as
well as its total inability to thrive in
Zones 2 and 3 (one would, after all, expect a plant from Labrador to actually be
able to grow in Labrador!). No matter
what the name, though, this is probably
the best groundcover violet for temperate climates. It's a tiny plant with
purple flowers and pretty heart-shaped
leaves that are evergreen in warmer climates. It creeps readily,
rooting at the nodes, and also spreading through self-seeding.
Although it blooms most heavily in spring, it may bloom somewhat throughout summer. In warmer climates, it switches its
growing season to fall through spring, blooming all winter and
remaining more or less static in the heat of summer. The usual
clone is 'Purpurea', with purplish-flushed leaves during the
cooler parts of the year. Height: 1 to 4 inches (2.5 to 10 cm).
Spread: 12 inches (30 cm). USDA Plant Hardiness Zones 4 to 9.

MORE RECOMMENDED VIOLETS

Viola odorata (sweet violet): This is the sweet violet of
posies and poetry. The sweet scent makes it well worth lying
flat on the cold spring ground to take a whiff: heavenly! The
flowers are typical of violets, although larger then most. The
species has blue flowers, but there are innumerable cultivars
with both single or double flowers in a wide range of purples,
pinks, and whites. In makes an excellent cut flower, although,
with its short stems, it is suitable only for small arrangements.

Think Twice: Be forewarned that this beautiful species is
highly invasive, spreading both through stolons and flowers. Of
European origin, it is already well established in suitable climates throughout the world. You don't have to worry about re-
leasing a new invasive plant into your region's environment: It
is already there! Hardiness varies from one cultivar to another.
They bloom for a long time in early to late spring; some rebloom (lightly) in fall. Height: 2 to 10 inches (5 to 25 cm).
Spread: 6 to 16 inches (15 to 40 cm). USDA Plant Hardiness
Zones are variable, usually 5 to 9.

LARRY'S GARDEN NOTES

True violets (as opposed to pansies and violas) have a curious
habit. Many of them produce two
very different kinds of flowers.
Their spring flowers have petals
and are often scented, thus attracting insects as pollinators, but
during summer they often produce *cleistogamic* flowers: hidden
flowers, with no petals, generally
concealed among the leaves.
Cleistogamic flowers (from the
Latin word for "cloistered") never
open: They self-pollinate without
any insect help. The advantage
for a shade-loving garden is understandable—insects are fewer
in number in shady spots than
sunny ones to start with, and a
cool, rainy spring may mean that
many insects concentrate all their
pollinating efforts on plants in
sunnier quarters. With cleistoga-
mous flowers, violets can reproduce without needing insects:
They are able to await another
spring before cross-pollinating.

Waldsteinia

Barren strawberry

Just because a plant is little known to gardeners doesn't mean it doesn't have potential! Barren strawberries are beautiful woodland groundcovers with attractive, shiny leaves that produce beautiful and abundant five-petaled flowers in spring, then look good for the rest of the year—even through until the following spring, as they are evergreen in all but the coldest climates. They are closely related to strawberries (*Fragaria* spp.) and even produce similar but smaller fruit; however, the fruit is green and insignificant, which is why they are called barren strawberries. They also spread like strawberries, by runners—but their runners are shorter, producing new plantlets near the mother plant, so they spread more slowly and cover more densely than strawberries.

GROWING TIPS

Barren strawberries are easy-to-grow plants that cause few problems and require little maintenance. They are forest plants in the wild; in culture, they're likewise usually best in partial shade to shade, although they do wonderfully in full sun in cool-summer areas. They adapt to almost any soils that are moderately acid to neutral. Although they don't like soggy conditions, they also dislike drying out and may need supplementary watering during periods of drought.

Their habit of producing plantlets on short runners means they are extremely useful as groundcovers. They fill in perfectly, creating a solid carpet of greenery. They're a snap to keep under control: Just plant them within a root barrier, leaving a 1-inch (2.5-cm) lip aboveground, and they'll stay within bounds—essentially forever.

PROBLEMS AND SOLUTIONS

Slugs and snails could damage them if they have absolutely nothing else to eat, but that rarely happens.

TOP PERFORMER

Waldsteinia ternata (Siberian barren strawberry): All barren strawberries are equally beautiful, easy to grow, and garden-worthy. *Ternata* means "three" and refers to the leaf, which is distinctly divided into three leaflets. It's a nice compact plant with really dense growth—perhaps even a bit too dense, as the flowers are often partially hidden by the foliage. As the common name suggests, it is rock-hardy. It is, however, less happy in the South, except in mountainous areas where summers are cooler. 'Mozaik' is a very rare variegated form, with leaves irregularly mottled yellow. Height: 4 to 6 inches (10 to 15 cm). Spread: Indefinite. USDA Plant Hardiness Zones 3 to 9.

MORE RECOMMENDED BARREN STRAWBERRIES

Waldsteinia fragarioides (American barren strawberry): You can look at this plant as being an eastern North American version of Siberian barren strawberry. The two, in fact, can scarcely be told apart. The native species has very similar three-foliate leaves, flowers that are apparently identical, and, in fact, I suspect even barren strawberry experts couldn't tell the two apart unless they were growing side by side. Then you'll notice that American barren strawberry has a slightly more open habit than its Siberian cousin, largely due to its longer petioles (leaf stems). This is the choice for naturalizing in a wooded setting: Why introduce a foreign species when a native one would do? Height: 4 to 6 inches (10 to 15 cm). Spread: Indefinite. USDA Plant Hardiness Zones 3 to 9.

W. geoides (European barren strawberry): This is the only barren strawberry that is easy to tell from the others. *Geoides* means "like the earth," therefore rounded, and the leaves are entire and not trifoliate like the others. Their form is, however, variable, so some are more heart-shaped, although never cut right to the base as in the other species. Other than leaf shape, European barren strawberry is much like the others in both flower, appearance, and use, although more tolerant of hot summers than the previous species. Height: 4 to 6 inches (10 to 15 cm). Spread: Indefinite. USDA Plant Hardiness Zones 4 to 9.

American barren strawberry (*Waldsteinia fragarioides*)

KISSING COUSINS

There is another mock strawberry: *Duchesnea indica*, a.k.a. Indian strawberry. Botanically it is actually much closer to the true strawberry (*Fragaria* spp.), but it shares with *Waldsteinia* flowers in a very unstrawberrylike bright yellow. The berries look just like small rough-textured strawberries and are edible but bland, and both flowers and fruits are produced throughout the growing season. Like the strawberry, the genus *Duchesnea* was recently transferred to the genus *Potentilla*, so should really be referred to as *Potentilla indica*. It is amazingly adaptable, thriving in both cold and tropical climates. Height: 2 to 4 inches (5 to 10 cm). Spread: Indefinite. USDA Plant Hardiness Zones 3 to 11.

Yes, there are annuals for shady spots . . . and they can really
dazzle with their flower power and brilliant foliage.

Chapter 7

Annuals for Shade

I f I had to give a prize for the plants least likely to thrive in a shady location, it would have to go to annuals. After all, where light is at a premium, most plants take it easy, growing slowly but surely and not being at all in a hurry to flower. Yet annuals have no choice: They have to sprout, grow, bloom, and produce seed, all within one calendar year. Can it even be accomplished in shade? The answer to that is a resounding "Yes!" A few miraculous annuals do beat the obstacles—and are we gardeners ever thankful! They ensure something shade gardeners salivate over: constant bloom, from spring through fall. Where would we be without them?

FAST AND FURIOUS

Annuals are, in theory at least, plants that grow from seed to flower, produce seed themselves, and then die, all within just one calendar year. So they are called annuals, as in *annus,* Latin for year. Compare their life cycle to biennials, which complete their growth cycle in 2 years, and perennials that live 3 years or more.

Of course, many annuals don't even come close to living a full calendar year. In temperate climates where the growing season is short, they may only have a 5- to 6-month window of frost-free opportunity (and often even less) in which to bloom and produce seed. There is no second chance for annuals; if they don't succeed in producing viable seed within that time frame, they're dead meat. In fact, their entire race could become extinct. That's why they're in such a terrible hurry to get going.

That mad rush to bloom and produce seed is what makes them so beloved of gardeners. Why wait 2 or 3 years for a perennial to bloom? Or 8 or more for a tree? Annuals give nearly instant results! From an annual's point of view, producing just a few flowers or flowering over only a short period of time is a big risk: What if it rained and the pollinating insects stayed home? As a method of self-preservation (or propagation of the species, if you will), annuals have particularly numerous flowers and a particularly long flowering season because the more flowers they produce and the longer they bloom, the better they can be certain of being able to produce viable seed.

Cultivated annuals tend to bloom even more abundantly and over an even longer period than wild annuals. We've "improved" annuals by selecting varieties with longer blooming periods and more abundant blooms, to the point where the modern garden annual tends to flower right through summer until frost, while the original plant may have bloomed for only a month or so. Many annuals bloom nonstop as long as the weather allows: It takes frost or shortening days (less sunlight available in late fall and winter in most climates) to stop them from blooming.

The main flaw with shade-tolerant an-

WHEN ANNUALS AREN'T REALLY ANNUALS

SOME OF THE VERY BEST "SHADE ANNUALS," like garden impatiens (*Impatiens walleriana*), fuchsias, and begonias, aren't true annuals at all. They are, in fact, tropical perennials or even small shrubs! These "perannuals" (as some experts have started calling plants that are grown as annuals but are in fact tender perennials) are not as quick off the mark as true annuals. From seed, they *must* be started indoors (most true annuals can be sown outdoors and will still have time to bloom the first year), often 3 or 4 months early. Also, you can prolong their lives if you so choose. You can bring them indoors over winter and give them "tropical" growing conditions and they'll do fine: bright light (yes, even shade-tolerant plants need bright light indoors), warm temperatures, high humidity, and regular watering. A severe pruning when you bring them in, cutting them to about 1 inch (2.5 cm) from the ground, will rejuvenate them and help them better support the transition. Or bring in cuttings and root them indoors. Many "perannuals" will not only grow well indoors over winter, but they will bloom there as well. In spring, when all danger of frost has passed, acclimate them to outdoor conditions by exposing them to a few hours of outdoor light and temperatures the first day, then more on succeeding days, then plant them back outdoors for another season.

nuals is that they have to be replanted each year. That's not a major problem if your shade garden is a few flower boxes, but when you have vast flowerbeds to fill, it becomes an annoyance—and a major expense. Many gardeners who love annuals for their constant bloom but dislike the extra work their culture imposes compromise: They fill their beds with perennials and shrubs, but keep a few open patches for new annual plantings each year. That brings both the price and the work level down, yet lets you profit from their great performance outdoors.

Start Them from Seed . . .

Note that true annuals can be grown only from seed: By their very nature, they are temporary plants. They produce no offsets nor can they be grown from cuttings. Seed can be sown *in situ* in early spring (or fall for many varieties) and will come up when the growing conditions are appropriate. Gardeners like to give most annuals a head start, though, by sowing them indoors and bringing them to near-blooming size before planting them out. Given their rapid rate of growth, they rarely need more than 4 to 8 weeks' head start—more than that and they will grow too tall or begin to bloom too early. And an annual that is already in bloom indoors is not going to transplant well into the garden. How early to sow them will be indicated on the seed packet, usually as a number of weeks "before the last frost." As the last frost date varies from region to region, you'll have to check with your local county extension office or a garden center to find it. Then just get out a calendar and count backward. In a region where the last frost date is May 15, a seed pack that suggests a sowing date of 4 to 6 weeks before the last frost could be started indoors around the beginning to middle of April.

. . . or Buy Them Ready to Plant

Of course, you can also buy annuals already started in trays, flats, or cell packs. In fact, most gardeners do so: It saves time and indoor growing space. The downsides are more limited choices (you can order seeds by mail from anywhere in the world and thus obtain rare annuals very readily), and, of course, greater expense. For the cost of one tray, you can often obtain two or three packs of seed with hundreds of seeds per pack! However, the added convenience of ready-to-plant annuals is hard to beat—at least if your local nursery or garden center offers the ones you're looking for. Just pick off the buds and blooms (annuals don't transplant well when they are in bloom),

apply a pinch of mycorrhizal fungi, and plant as described on page 50. It couldn't be easier.

ANNUALS THAT SELF-SOW

In appropriate climates, most annuals will self-sow: Seeds fall to the ground in late summer or fall and new plants appear, as if by magic, in spring. Tropical perennials grown as annuals won't self-sow in colder climates, but many true annuals will; in fact, most true annuals will self-sow in any climate.

Knowing that annuals tend to self-sow, the question then becomes: Do you want them to? Few are true weeds, and if you like plants that self-sow, you're probably not the sort of person who worries much about plants that wander a bit. Just pull out the ones that are not wanted, or transplant them to more appropriate spots. You can prevent annuals from self-sowing, though, by using a thick mulch throughout your garden areas. Of course, the opposite may also be true: You'd like them to self-sow, but they can't germinate through a thick mulch. If you're a mulch user, leave unmulched spots here and there, where you want the annuals to self-sow, and they'll gladly oblige.

Saving Seed

Annuals are ideal subjects for saving seed. Just collect the seed capsules of annuals when they start to turn brown, crush the capsules to remove the seeds, store them in paper envelopes for winter, and plant them in spring. Do note, however, that an increasing number of annuals are of hybrid origin and won't come true from seed. These you'll have to buy fresh each spring, either in seed packs or as plants. Many popular annuals are still, however, "open pollinated" (nonhybrid), also sometimes labeled "heritage seed." Choose these if your goal is to save seed.

Begonia Semperflorens
Wax begonia, fibrous begonia, bedding begonia

This classic garden annual is not, of course, an annual at all: It's a tender perennial universally grown as an annual. It's not the easiest plant to grow from seed, but it's a snap to maintain when you buy it already started in trays or cell packs. In general the plants are compact, dense, and quite small, ideal for mass plantings. Their leaves have a waxy, shiny exterior, leading to their most common name: wax begonia. The flowers are often quite small, but they are so numerous they make up for any lack of individual impact.

GROWING TIPS

Ideal edging plants and superb in containers, wax begonias will grow almost anywhere. They're renowned for their ability to tolerate shade, yet many cultivars are very sun-tolerant, even in the Deep South. This is especially true of those with bronze foliage: It's as if the bronze coloration were a sort of inborn sunscreen. Still, they look far happier in a shady nook or in at least partial shade. They tend to be so dense as to appear artificial in full sun. They seem singularly indifferent to soil quality, although for particularly lush growth, make sure they get soil that is rich in humus. Their waxy leaves give them considerable drought tolerance—but don't push it. When truly dry, they wilt like lettuce and don't look nearly as nice. Mulching will help keep their roots cool and moist.

Buy plants in trays or cell packs—it's far easier than growing them from seed. And once you have a clone you like, you can multiply it by taking stem cuttings *ad infinitum.* The double-flowered ones usually are offered only as cutting-grown plants.

Don't plant wax begonias outdoors until evening temperatures remain above 50°F (10°C). They will tolerate lower temperatures, but a bout of cold air can set back their growth. Set them about 1 foot (30 cm) apart (half that if you're growing them in containers). Wax begonias will keep blooming right up until the first frost does them in. In tropical climates, in fact, they'll bloom almost nonstop for years; mow them down when they start to look uneven, and they'll quickly sprout again.

Before evenings even start to become crisp in fall months, it's time to take cuttings to bring indoors for winter. Or dig up a whole plant, pot it up, cut it back harshly, and bring it indoors. I always make a point to save special varieties, like double begonias and variegated ones, that are not so readily available in the average garden center.

PROBLEMS AND SOLUTIONS

Diseases of various sorts (such as stem rot and gray mold) are problems for begonias growing in cramped quarters or soggy soil. Slugs and snails can be an annoyance; see page 85 for solutions.

TOP PERFORMER

Begonia Semperflorens-Cultorum Hybrids (wax begonia): This is not a true species, but a group of similar hybrids of complex origin. All are fairly small plants with short but upright stems bearing ear-shaped leaves in green or bronze. Some are variegated. Single-flowered varieties are most common, as they can be raised from seed, but double-flowered forms, raised from cuttings, are also grown. There are literally hundreds of strains. Height: 6 to 12 inches (15 to 30 cm). Spread: 6 to 12 inches (15 to 30 cm).

MORE RECOMMENDED BEGONIAS

Begonia Dragon Wing Series (dragon wing begonia): This is a series of larger begonias resulting from crosses between *B.* Semperflorens-Cultorum and angel-wing begonias, a category usually used as houseplants. The large leaves are wing-shaped, and clusters of larger flowers appear at the stem tips throughout the growing season. As I write this, only pink- and red-flowered cultivars are available, both with dark green foliage, but that will undoubtedly change. Height: 14 to 16 inches (35 to 40 cm). Spread: 1 foot (30 cm).

LARRY'S GARDEN NOTES

Besides the traditional "bedding begonias" (*B.* Semperflorens-Cultorum and Tuberhybrida Hybrids, the latter a tuberous species described on page 279), there are literally hundreds of begonia species and hybrids presently grown mostly as houseplants or greenhouse plants that will succeed wonderfully outdoors when used as annuals. Just raid a plant store and take your pick! *B.* 'Richmondensis' and related hybrids are often grown outdoors, with arching stems bearing deep purple foliage and pink or white flowers, while rex begonias (*B.* Rex-Cultorum Hybrids) are generally creeping, rhizomatous plants with large, colorful leaves in all sorts of metallic shades on a background of red, green, purple, gray, pink, and bronze. They make great foliage plants for shady spots in the great outdoors.

Browallia
Browallia, bush violet

BROWALLIA

bro-AL-ee-uh

Bloom Color:
Purple, violet-blue, and white

Bloom Time:
Late spring to early fall

Length of Bloom:
12 weeks or more

Height:
8 to 24 inches (20 to 60 cm)

Spread:
Varies by species; see individual listings

Garden Uses:
Container planting, edging, hanging baskets, mass planting, mixed border, specimen plant, woodland garden

Light Preference:
Full sun to shade

Soil Preference:
Humus-rich, moist, well-drained soil

Best Way to Propagate:
Sow seed indoors in late winter

Hardiness:
Frost-sensitive perennial grown as a tender annual

It's a pity this beautiful annual isn't more widely available. It's a knock-out, with abundant trumpet flowers spreading out into a broad star at the tip and offered in an interesting range of purples, violets, and whites with a velvety texture that makes them truly stand out. The flowers are produced throughout the summer growing season toward the tips of the numerous branching stems, creating quite a show. I like to use this workhorse of a plant to replace impatiens, which is perhaps becoming a bit overdone in home shade gardens.

GROWING TIPS

Browallias are ideal choices in rich, evenly moist, well-drained spots in partial shade. They're fine in shade as well, especially in the South, although plants may grow a bit more straggly there without any direct sunlight at all. In cool-summer areas, they need more light, so consider partial shade to full sun.

Mulching is always wise, as it helps keeps the roots cool and moist. Browallias are not very drought-tolerant and quickly wilt in hot weather when no more moisture is available.

Browallia is one of those plants that I'd love to be able to purchase in ready-to-plant cell-packs and trays but usually can't. The plant remains little known to bedding plant producers and, since I can't trust local suppliers, I always start my own plants.

Gardeners in the South can sow browallias directly outside in early spring, but they have a very long growing season. Most other gardeners will be more satisfied with the results if they start their browallias indoors, about 8 to 10 weeks before the last frost. Don't cover the seeds with soil—they need light to germinate. Press them into the surface of a premoistened mix, and place the tray in a warm spot, about 65° to 75°F (18° to 24°C), that receives moderate light, not full sun. When the seeds germinate, in about 6 to 15 days, move the trays to a spot with some direct sunlight. Pinch the plants when they have about four to six leaves to stimulate better branching.

Browallias are frost-tender and shouldn't be planted out too soon. Set the plants about 1 foot (30 cm) apart to create a carpetlike effect.

PROBLEMS AND SOLUTIONS

Watch out for whiteflies, which seem to have a distinct affinity for browallias. Insecticidal soap is probably the most practical way of controlling them. Aphids may also occur: Blast them into oblivion with a sharp spray of water. Controlling insect populations will also be useful in preventing virus diseases. Avoid planting browallia in spots where tomatoes, eggplants, peppers, or other Solanum family members were grown in the previous 3 years, as they share similar enemies.

TOP PERFORMER

Browallia speciosa (browallia, bush violet, sapphire flower): This is by far the most common species, perhaps because it has the largest flowers: up to 2 inches (5 cm) in diameter. Their depressed veins give them an attractive textured appearance. The species is rather lanky in appearance and rarely grown, but there are several cultivars or series with a more compact habit and better branching that are ideal as garden plants. Some have somewhat arching branches and are useful as basket plants; most are more upright and look better in the garden. This species comes in a wide range of shades of purple, from deep violet to pale lavender, always with a contrasting paler or white eye, and there are also white varieties with no noticeable eye. Height: 10 to 24 inches (25 to 60 cm). Spread: 12 inches (30 cm).

MORE RECOMMENDED BROWALLIAS

Browallia americana, syn. *B. elata* (amethyst flower, Jamaican forget-me-not): This species has numerous flowers that are closer to a true blue than *B. speciosa*, with or without a white eye. The petals are clearly notched, giving them a heart-shaped appearance. There are also white and violet cultivars. The stems and leaves are slightly sticky. Height: 2 feet (60 cm). Spread: 2 feet (60 cm).

LARRY'S GARDEN NOTES

Although I first started growing *Browallia viscosa* (sapphire flower) strictly as an ornamental, I quickly found out it had a secondary use: as a sort of vegetable fly-paper! I regularly find fungus gnats and whiteflies sticking to the sticky new growth and, tragically, they perish there, unable to free themselves. I can't say that this helped me wipe out any infestations, but my thought is a fungus gnat or whitefly can lay dozens of eggs, so each one caught means many fewer pests in the future. I'd love to see hybridizers work on even stickier browallias: I could definitely use one that can catch groundhogs!

Browallia (*Browallia speciosa* 'Heavenly Bells')

Clarkia

Clarkia, farewell-to-spring

This old-fashioned garden annual is beautiful, easy to grow in cool conditions, and very adaptable, plus it makes a superb cut flower. There are several species, all with very complex flowers bearing frilly or deeply cut, crepelike petals. They are upright-growing plants with frail-looking stems that bear flowers along the leaf axils. Clarkias always look best when grown in close proximity to their neighbors because, individually, they look a bit thin. Group them together, though, and you create quite an impact: a dense mass of clarkias is not a sight you forget readily!

GROWING TIPS

Clarkias actually prefer sun, but in most gardens, they'll do best in partial shade because they don't like hot summers. Most gardeners will find they best succeed with clarkias by sowing them in partial shade with a cooling mulch to keep them from overheating. They actually grow best in soil that is of no more than average fertility. Rich soil causes rapidly elongating stems and floppiness.

This is a cool-climate annual, best in the Pacific Northwest, the upper New England states, and throughout Canada. Elsewhere it tends to bloom mostly in spring, while it is still cool, and then peter out in summer. In Zones 9 and 10, however, consider it a winter bloomer: Sow the seeds outdoors in late fall and watch it bloom its pretty little head off throughout winter.

Clarkias are true annuals, dying after they bloom. Ideally, sow the seed outdoors directly where it is to bloom, although you can get a heard start on the season by sowing them in peat pots indoors (you'll need to use peat pots because clarkias dislike transplantation). Don't start them too early, though: 4 to 6 weeks' head start is all they need.

Sow the seeds without covering them—they need light to germinate. Outdoors, sow them early in spring or even the previous fall: They'll appreciate the cooler ground conditions and will even tolerate light frosts. Indoors, give the peat pots cooler temperatures if possible. They germinate best at around 55° to 65°F (13° to 18°C). After germination, give them full sun indoors and try to keep them on the cool side—about 50°F (10°C).

Thin clarkias to only 4 to 6 inches (10 to 15 cm) apart or plant them out at the same spacing. That way the branches can mingle together and help hold each other up. Or place a few twiggy branches here and there so they can have something to lean on.

All clarkias will self-sow where happy; leave a few spots free of mulch if you want them to do so.

When grown as winter annuals, clarkias will start to peter out as spring temperatures rise; pull them out and replace them with summer annuals.

PROBLEMS AND SOLUTIONS

Clarkias like cool conditions; anything that helps keep them cool, like a thick mulch and a bit of moisture at all times, will be appreciated. Heat-stressed plants are subject to various leaf diseases, including leaf spot and downy mildew (see page 86).

TOP PERFORMER

Clarkia unguiculata (clarkia, farewell-to-spring, garland flower): Also sold as *C. elegans.* This plant, so favored by our grandparents, remains a beauty to this day. The wild form with single flowers is too open in appearance to attract much attention; only double forms, with extremely dense, frilly, crepelike flowers are usually sold. The upright stems are pinkish or reddish and bear lance-shaped to elliptical leaves, looking much like fuchsias until they come into bloom. The blooms come in a wide range of pinks, reds, purples, plus yellow (or deep cream) and white. Height: 12 to 36 inches (30 to 90 cm). Spread: 8 to 12 inches (20 to 30 cm).

MORE RECOMMENDED CLARKIAS

Clarkia concinna (red ribbons): Also called *Eucharidium concinnum.* A curious and very pretty but smaller plant with deeply incised petals that look like red ribbons. Red is the original color, but pink and white forms are available. The plant called pink ribbons, *C. brewerii,* is very similar, with rose-pink blooms. Height: 12 inches (30 cm). Spread: 8 to 12 inches (20 to 30 cm).

Clarkia (*Clarkia unguiculata*)

LARRY'S GARDEN NOTES

Clarkia was named in honor of William Clark of the celebrated Lewis and Clark expedition that set off to discover the Northwest Passage in the early 1800s and instead revealed the natural wonders of western North America. Among the dozens of new plants they brought back were several species of a brand-new annual discovered in open coniferous forests along the Pacific coast.

Fuchsia
Fuchsia, lady's eardrops

PLANT PROFILE

FUCHSIA

FEW-sha

Bloom Color:
Blue-violet, pink, purple, salmon, red, and white

Bloom Time:
Late spring to early fall; much of the year indoors and in mild climates

Length of Bloom:
12 weeks or more

Height:
6 to 60 inches (15 to 150 cm)

Spread:
12 to 42 inches (30 to 105 cm)

Garden Uses:
Container planting, edging, annual hedge, hanging baskets, mass planting, meadow garden, mixed border, rock garden, woodland garden; attracts hummingbirds

Light Preference:
Full sun to partial shade

Soil Preference:
Humus-rich, evenly moist, well-drained soil

Best Way to Propagate:
Take stem cuttings at any season

Hardiness:
Frost-sensitive shrub grown as an annual

Not your typical annual, the beautiful fuchsia is in fact a shrub grown as an annual in climates where it is not hardy. Its dangling two-part, two-color flowers that dance in the slightest breeze always remind me of a ballerina in a tutu, even down to the legs, made up of an exerted stigma and anthers. Of course, the flower has a few too many legs for classical ballet, but that's a moot point. It is said there are over 8,000 hybrids, including singles and doubles, large flowers and small, and essentially in just about any color combination that pleases you. It's a striking plant for both garden and container use—who can pass in front of a basket of fuchsia without instantly wanting it!

GROWING TIPS

Pretty as it may be, the fuchsia is not the easiest plant to grow in all climates. It likes cool temperatures year-round, yet most cultivars can't take frost; most of North America has hot summers and frosty winters. Still, if you're careful in placing your fuchsia in the right spot, you should be able to grow it.

For most gardeners, fuchsias are container plants. There are trailing and hanging types for baskets and flowerboxes and more upright growers for patio containers.

In general, fuchsias are sold fully grown and in full bloom in containers. You buy it, bring it home, and hang it up. Be forewarned that these plants are often beautiful but terribly underpotted. You'll have to watch their watering like a hawk, soaking the basket whenever it even starts to dry out. And I do mean soak: The single best way of watering container fuchsias is to plunge the pot in a pail with enough tepid water to cover the root ball, then let it drink until no more air bubbles appear. Or repot the plant into larger quarters and thus reduce its watering needs by half or more.

As you water, feed your fuchsia with a soluble fertilizer, such as liquid seaweed, diluting to one-eighth the usual rate. That will ensure it always obtains a small amount of minerals throughout the growing season. With such a dilute solution, you'd be able to fertilize daily, every time you water (and yes, some fuchsias under some conditions may need daily watering!), without harming the plant's roots.

Watering is only part of the challenge. Even more important is keeping it cool. Fuchsias, in general, dislike hot temperatures. That's why they do so much better in partial shade than in the sun in most climates. Morning sun is perfect, but they won't ap-preciate hot midday or afternoon sun. In cool-summer climates (the North and the Northwest, for the most part), they will tolerate and even thrive in full sun.

Fuchsia (*Fuchsia* 'Pippa')

Fuchsias are expensive enough plants that you'll probably want to overwinter yours for next year. In cooler regions of Zones 10 and 11, you can simply plant them in the ground. Else-where, you'll have to bring them indoors. You have two choices: Either cut them back hard and store them, nearly dry, in a coldroom or a barely heated garage until March, or grow them as houseplants in bright light and cool temperatures, maintaining a regular watering schedule.

PROBLEMS AND SOLUTIONS

Whiteflies are the bane of any fuchsia lover's existence. Wash all of its leaves in a solution of insecticidal soap and water be-fore the plant comes indoors for the winter, using a sponge or a cloth to rub each leaf, top and bottom.

TOP PERFORMER

Fuchsia Hybrids (fuchsia, common fuchsia, hybrid fuchsia, lady's eardrops): Also called *F.* × *hybrida.* These complex hy-brids mix genes from three or more parents, giving a wide range of cultivars of highly different forms and colors. There are dwarf fuchsias with tiny leaves and flowers, tall ones with huge leaves and long, dangling blooms, and dozens of intermediate types with upright, trailing, or hanging stems. The leaves are usually green but can be reddish, chartreuse, or variegated; the flowers can be single, semidouble, or double.

LARRY'S GARDEN NOTES

Did you know that almost all of us pronounce "fuchsia" incorrectly? This mistake has cost many a young student a win in a spelling bee. You see, we pronounce fuchsia as if it were spelled "sch": "few-shuh"—but take a second look. That's not how it's spelled. It is spelled "chs", or "fuch-si-a". To get it right, remember the plant was named after Leonhart Fuchs, a German botanist. Fuchs is pro-nounced "fouks" (actually, it means "fox") and is not an uncommon surname. If you can remember the plant is named for Dr. Fuchs, you should be able to spell fuchsia it correctly—but only the most pedant of horticulturists ever pronounces the name in a way that would truly honor Dr. Fuchs: "FOUK-see-uh".

Impatiens
Impatiens

PLANT PROFILE

IMPATIENS

im-PAY-shens

Bloom Color:
Varies by species; see individual listings

Bloom Time:
Late spring to early fall; year-round in frost-free climates

Length of Bloom:
12 weeks or more

Height:
Varies by species; see individual listings

Spread:
Varies by species; see individual listings

Garden Uses:
Container planting, edging, groundcover, hanging basket, mass planting, mixed border, woodland garden; attracts hummingbirds

Light Preference:
Full sun to shade

Soil Preference:
Humus-rich, evenly moist, well-drained soil

Best Way to Propagate:
Sow seed indoors in late winter; take stem cuttings at any season

Hardiness:
Frost-sensitive perennial grown as a tender annual

Need I even describe the garden impatiens (or "busy Lizzie," as your grandparents may have called it)? It has become the most popular annual of all, surpassing even the ubiquitous petunia as a garden staple. You'll find it in containers, in the ground, indoors—it seems the whole world has opened up to the beauty of the impatiens. This popularity is certainly not surprising: In a world where mature gardens are the rule and shade is a fact of life, here is a plant that truly does bloom in the shade. Nonstop bloom even in deep shade from spring through fall, and even all winter in mild climates? Not surprising the impatiens is such a star!

GROWING TIPS

You can grow impatiens from seed if you prefer, but most people simply purchase trays of cell-packs with ready-to-plant impatiens. The plant is a snap to grow, even transplanting well when in full bloom! Keep the soil moist all summer and you'll have pretty much nonstop bloom. If ever they get straggly (and that can happen in hot summers or when growing in very deep shade), simply cut them back by one-third and they'll be back in bloom in no time.

Impatiens grow best in partial to full shade. Full sun is acceptable only in areas where summers are cool or always cloudy. Mulching will help keep them moist and will reduce watering needs.

Most impatiens are not true annuals but tropical perennials, so you can overwinter them indoors in a bright window. It really isn't worthwhile bringing aging plants back indoors; young ones are more floriferous, so just take cuttings in fall. I usually overwinter only those impatiens that don't come true from seed, such as variegated cultivars and some of the double forms. Impatiens is very tender and will overwinter outdoors only in Zones 10 and 11.

Other impatiens are true annuals, like *I. balsamina* and *I. glandulifera,* and these are a snap to grow from seed, indoors or out. Just sow them and up they come!

PROBLEMS AND SOLUTIONS

In dry climates, spider mites can run rampant: Spray the leaves regularly with insecticidal soap to control them. Indoors the spider mite problem is even worse; I take all my impatiens to the sink once a week and rinse the little buggers off.

TOP PERFORMER

Impatiens walleriana (garden impatiens, busy Lizzie, patience plant): This is the popular garden impatiens that everyone grows. It produces watery green to purplish stems with pointed green to bronze leaves, sometimes variegated, and broad flat flowers in a wide range of colors—every color, really, except true blue and yellow! Most have single flowers, but there are a few doubles, not all of which come true from seed. Height: 6 to 24 inches (15 to 60 cm). Spread: 6 to 24 inches (15 to 60 cm).

MORE RECOMMENDED IMPATIENS

Impatiens auricoma Hybrids (yellow impatiens): Yellow-flowered impatiens are a rather new introduction to the impatiens repertoire. They have bright green leaves and hooded flowers, rather orchidlike, in different shades of yellow and orange. They can be grown from seed or from cuttings. Height: 10 to 20 inches (25 to 50 cm). Spread: 12 inches (30 cm).

I. balsamina (garden balsam): This is a true annual, growing rapidly from seed to bloom and suitable for sowing directly outdoors in most climates, or indoors only 4 to 6 weeks before the last frost. It usually has a distinctly pyramidal habit, but some recent cultivars are more rounded. Double forms, looking much like mini-camellias, are the norm and they come true from seed; singles have hooded flowers rather like orchids. Height: 12 to 30 inches (30 to 75 cm). Spread: 12 to 18 inches (30 to 45 cm).

Think Twice: *I. glandulifera*, syn. *I. roylei* (Himalayan balsam, policeman's helmet): I don't recommend this easy-to-grow giant impatiens because it can be so invasive in northern North America. It's a biggie, from 3 to 10 feet tall (1 to 3 m), with a thick reddish stem and long leaves. The helmeted flowers are pink to purple, rarely white. Spread: 2 feet (60 cm).

Garden impatiens
(*Impatiens walleriana* 'Deco Mix')

KISSING COUSINS

Would you believe there is actually a perennial impatiens? In fact, there are several, but only one, Mt. Omei impatiens (*Impatiens omeiana*), which grows high on the mountain of the same name in China, seems to be at all available. It comes through deep winter frosts with no complaints. I've overwintered it in Zone 3, but it wasn't particularly happy about the experience. Zones 6 to 9 better meet its needs. Don't count on it for flowers, though: The yellow snapdragonlike blooms come late in the season and are not terribly striking. Instead, it is the foliage that counts. The long, narrow leaves with crenate (scalloped) margins have a beautiful velvety texture and a striking creamy white stripe down the middle. It spreads fairly slowly by stolons to form lovely colonies in moist shade, a bit like pachysandra. Height: 8 to 18 inches (20 to 45 cm). Spread: Indefinite.

Lobelia
Edging lobelia

PLANT PROFILE

LOBELIA

low-BEE-lee-uh

Bloom Color:
Blue, lilac, purple, wine red, pink, and white

Bloom Time:
Late spring to early fall

Length of Bloom:
8 weeks or more

Height:
4 to 9 inches (10 to 23 cm)

Spread:
4 to 12 inches (10 to 30 cm)

Garden Uses:
Container planting, edging, hanging basket, mass planting, mixed border, rock garden, wall planting

Light Preference:
Full sun to shade

Soil Preference:
Humus-rich, evenly moist soil

Best Way to Propagate:
Sow seed indoors in late winter

Hardiness:
Frost-sensitive perennial grown as a tender annual

We've already seen stalwart, upright lobelias with large leaves in the perennials section, but there is also an African branch to the family. It is a much smaller, wispier plant, with numerous stems and very fine leaves. The flowers are tiny but numerous, essentially tubular but opening into two lips: a small upper one with two lobes, and a much broader lower one with three. It is very floriferous, producing masses of flowers that, because of the fine foliage, sometimes seem to float on air. The colors tend to be very intense, mostly shades of purple and blue, but also reds and whites, most often with white or yellow in the throat.

GROWING TIPS

Unless you're really good at growing plants from seed, it's better to buy trays or cell-packs of edging lobelia from your local nursery. That's because they're delicate when young then seem to toughen up as they reach flowering size. So why not let someone else take the risks?

Once they're up and growing, edging lobelias aren't that difficult to grow, although they remain essentially cool-season annuals, not really adapted to hot, dry summer areas. In the cool North and along breezy coasts, they do wonderfully. In the South, they are often grown as winter annuals, planted in late fall for bloom throughout the cool season, then pulled out and replaced when temperatures soar again in spring. Although tolerant of full sun, they do best in partial shade because temperatures are cooler there. Even fairly deep shade is acceptable, especially where summers tend to be hot. Keeping the soil moist also helps cool them off.

Although edging lobelia can indeed be used in edging, and often is, it is far more popular in containers than in the ground. The wispy foliage and tiny, bright flowers look just great tumbling from a hanging basket or flowerbox. This is especially true of the cascade types: They have a floppy habit that is of little interest in the garden but looks wonderful in containers or planted on walls. The true edging types, not as popular as they used to be, are slightly more upright in habit.

The main flaw with edging lobelia is its tendency to decline rather quickly. If left on its own, it will bloom heavily in spring, then peter out in summer as temperatures rise. Simply trim the plant back by half when any sign of decline appears. This stimulates the plant to produce abundant new branches and then to bloom again, as heavily as before. Don't wait until the stems are turning brown—the plants won't respond.

When to plant lobelias out is a delicate question: They love the cool spring air but won't tolerate hard frost. In containers that's not a problem—you can put them outdoors very early in spring, when most other "annuals" are still safely indoors, then bring them indoors overnight if frost threatens. If you want to plant them in the garden, wait until all danger of frost has passed before planting them out.

PROBLEMS AND SOLUTIONS

Damping-off can occur shortly after germination, so always use fresh packages of soil for lobelias to help avoid the problem. Midsummer dieback is a far greater challenge and suggestions for preventing it are described above.

TOP PERFORMER

Lobelia erinus (edging lobelia, border lobelia): This South African species is the only popular lobelia in its category. It is actually a fairly tall, very wispy plant that is rarely grown. Instead, dense, compact forms rule the roost in gardens. These can be more or less upright in habit (a form sometimes called *L. erinus* var. *compacta*) or trailing (*L. erinus* var. *pendula*), the latter form being most popular in containers. The deeply toothed leaves are very fine and can be dark green or purplish. The numerous cultivars come in shades of blue, violet, purple, lilac, wine red, rose, and white.

KISSING COUSINS

If edging lobelia is a perennial grown as an annual, another lobelia is an annual grown as a perennial! Hybrid lobelia (*L.* × *speciosa*) is an upright lobelia with fairly broad leaves, thick stems, and large, brilliantly colored flowers. It often has deep purple foliage, as in the popular cultivar 'Queen Victoria', with scarlet flowers. It makes a superb, stunning annual, but an often disappointing perennial, as it is not fully hardy. Don't count on it surviving beyond Zone 8. Even in Zone 7 it survives winter only when conditions are exceptionally mild. Height: 20 to 60 inches (50 to 150 cm). Spread: 16 to 20 inches (40 to 50 cm). USDA Plant Hardiness Zones 8 to 10.

Edging lobelia (*Lobelia erinus* 'String of Pearls')

Mimulus
Monkey flower

PLANT PROFILE

MIMULUS

MIM-you-lus

Bloom Color:
  Yellow, orange, pink,
  burgundy-red, and cream

Bloom Time:
  Late spring to early fall

Length of Bloom:
  12 weeks or more

Height:
  6 to 36 inches (15 to 90 cm)

Spread:
  6 to 36 inches (15 to 90 cm)

Garden Uses:
  Container planting, edging,
  groundcover, hanging basket,
  mass planting, mixed border,
  rock garden, woodland
  garden; in wet areas; attracts
  hummingbirds

Light Preference:
  Full sun to partial shade

Soil Preference:
  Rich, moist to wet, slightly
  acid soil

Best Way to Propagate:
  Sow seed indoors or outdoors
  in spring

Hardiness:
  Frost-sensitive to hardy
  perennial grown as a tender
  annual

Some like it wet—distinctly wet and soggy—and one of those would be monkey flower, a brilliantly colored annual with lots of pizzazz. This is one of those "put on the sunglasses" flowers: reds, yellows, and oranges dominate its color palette. Just what you need to liven up a dark corner! The flowers are tubular, with a wide mouth that opens up into five broad lobes: Its habit is generally mounding, with fuzzy stems and toothed leaves. All in all, it is an astounding plant, although not yet very popular. If you live in a damp, rainy climate, this is certainly a plant you must discover.

GROWING TIPS

Keep monkey flower really damp at all times and you'll have one happy camper. In the wild (various species are native from Alaska right through to South America) it often grows in marshes or streambeds. It will even grow with its roots in running water—but make that *shallow* running water—it's not quite an aquatic plant. It will grow in regular garden soil, though, if you make a habit of watering it regularly. A good mulch will go a long way in keeping it moist.

Try it, too, as a container plant in a large container you can keep moist. Put a large saucer under the pot and keep it full of water, or grow it under an air conditioner that is always dripping water.

Monkey flower is ideal in partial shade, where it is easier to keep it moist. It won't bloom very heavily in true shade, though: Some sun, and especially morning sun, is wise. If you're up to the extra watering or have a water garden, you'll find it does fine in full sun as well.

Most monkey flowers are hybrids of species varying greatly in hardiness. You never really know if they're going to behave as annuals or come back for a year or two as short-lived perennials. I suggest treating them as if they were annuals. That way, if they don't come through winter, you won't be disappointed. And if they do, you'll be pleased!

This is not the easiest annual to grow from seed, so if you can find it in trays (and it is becoming quite widely available), that's the way to go.

PROBLEMS AND SOLUTIONS

Aphids are an occasional pest: Spray them off with water. Watch out, too, for spider mites and whiteflies: Control them with insecticidal soap. Drought is of course the monkey flower's worst enemy—and the combination of humid fall air and dry soil is sure to bring on powdery mildew.

Warning: Most monkey flowers will readily self-sow where they are happy, so mulch heavily if you don't want this to happen.

TOP PERFORMER

Mimulus × hybridus (hybrid monkey flower): Most modern monkey flowers are complex hybrids far removed from any of the species. They come in a wide range of colors, from pale pastels to intense reds, oranges, and yellows, and come in not only the traditional spotted forms but single colors as well. Height likewise varies widely accordingly: Some series barely reach 6 inches (15 cm); others reach up to 3 feet (90 cm) tall. Spread: 1 to 3 feet (30 to 90 cm).

MORE RECOMMENDED MONKEY FLOWERS

Mimulus cardinalis (scarlet monkey flower): The flowers, as can be expected, are brilliant cardinal red, either pure or with some yellow spotting in the throat. Height: 18 to 36 inches (45 to 90 cm). Spread: 12 to 24 inches (30 to 60 cm).

M. cupreus (copper monkey flower): This one has yellow flowers that turn coppery red. Height: 18 to 24 inches (45 to 60 cm). Spread: 12 inches (30 cm).

M. guttatus (common monkey flower): This is the plant that gave the monkey flower its name, as the flowers are often heavily mottled with secondary colors. It is a highly variable plant with flowers in all shades of yellow, red, and orange, usually spotted burgundy. Height: 15 to 24 inches (38 to 60 cm). Spread: 12 to 24 inches (30 to 60 cm).

M. luteus (yellow monkey flower): Like common monkey flower, but with yellow flowers spotted brown. Height: 18 to 36 inches (45 to 90 cm). Spread: 12 to 24 inches (30 to 60 cm).

Hybrid monkey flower (*Mimulus × hybridus*)

LARRY'S GARDEN NOTES

Monkey flower gets both its common and its botanical names (*mimulus* means mime or clown) from the heavily spotted flowers of some species, said to look like a monkey or clown face. Although they certainly are colorful, it's not necessarily easy to see anything facelike in them. I suppose it's like Rorschach tests: You see in the spots what you want!

Nemophila

Nemophila, baby-blue-eyes, five spot

Charming! That is definitely the word that applies to this dainty little annual, always a hit with anyone who sees it. The small cup-shaped flowers often bear intriguing patterns that are hard to resist. It's a fast-growing, easy-from-seed annual. In its native California it blooms from late winter through spring, one of the "spring ephemerals" that sprouts up, seemingly from nowhere, after the fall rains. It will do the same in your garden where the climate suits it, self-sowing faithfully (although lightly) to provide early color while many other annuals have yet to bloom.

GROWING TIPS

Get your growing season straight with this plant. In cool-summer areas, you can sow it directly outdoors in spring for summer bloom. Where summers are hot and dry, though, it's best to start it indoors and plant it out early to enjoy its flowers as the tulips bloom. In the South, try it as a winter annual, planting it out in late fall and replacing it with more heat-tolerant annuals in spring. In fact, in areas with cool summers and mild winters, you can actually sow it outdoors twice in the season: in late summer for fall through winter bloom, then in late winter for spring through summer flowers.

In most climates it does best in partial shade, although it will take full sun where growing conditions are cool. Other ways of making sure it stays cool and happy include making sure its soil stays evenly moist, and mulching it.

One downside of nemophilas is the apparent lack of interest in growing it in commercial nurseries. You'll have no trouble finding seed, but plants are another story. Why this is the case is a mystery, as it grows quickly from seed indoors and transplants readily to the garden.

Fortunately, if you do choose to grow nemophilas from seed, you'll find they are a snap to grow. In cooler climates, sow the seed outdoors, broadcasting it where you want to see it grow and raking it in very lightly. Water well, and it should be up within a week. Thin the seedlings to about 6 to 12 inches (15 to 30 cm) apart. Or start it indoors and plant it out after all danger of frost has passed. Barely cover the seed and keep it moist. It's best to provide cool conditions indoors, though: It struggles in hot, dry air. This is a good plant to start in a cool basement or unheated but frost-free room. Or try starting it in a coldframe where the cool night temperatures will be very much to its liking.

PROBLEMS AND SOLUTIONS

Watch out for powdery and downy mildew when the plant is exposed to high humidity and dry soil. Keeping the soil moist at all times will help prevent such problems.

TOP PERFORMER

Nemophila menziesii (baby-blue-eyes): This West Coast native, also called *N. insignis,* is a low-growing, spreading annual that produces bright blue flowers about 1½ inches (4 cm) wide with a pale blue to white center. It is commonly offered in packs of mixed wildflower seed for shade and is not without interest. Two special selections, *N. menziesii* 'Pennie Black' and *N. menziesii* var. *atromaria* 'Snowstorm', clearly outshine the species itself and are more likely to be available in individual seed packets. 'Pennie Black' has flowers of such a deep purple that they can pass for black. The white margin surrounding each petal only helps make the flowers seem even blacker. Great for Halloween! 'Snowstorm', on the contrary, is almost pure white—but with an abundant sprinkle of tiny black dots, a combination much more attractive than it sounds. You really have to see these two flowers to believe them! Height: 8 inches (20 cm). Spread: 12 inches (30 cm).

MORE RECOMMENDED NEMOPHILAS

Nemophila maculata (five spot): This is the second of two species of *Nemophila* currently grown and is also from California. Its common name speaks for itself: Each of the five pure white petals bears a prominent violet-blue spot. To add to its charm, violet-tinted veins are often present. The plant has a more mounding habit than its spreading cousin but requires the same care. Height: 6 to 10 inches (15 to 25 cm). Spread: 6 to 12 inches (15 to 30 cm).

Baby-blue-eyes (*Nemophila menziesii* 'Pennie Black')

LARRY'S GARDEN NOTES

If you understand enough botanical Latin, you'll know right away that this plant is made for shade. *Nemo* means woodland, and *philo* means to love. In its native California, it's usually found on the shady side of gullies and ravines or in open forests. That isn't truly deep shade, though, so some morning sun will be necessary to obtain good blooming, especially in northern gardens where sunlight is naturally less intense.

Nicotiana

Nicotiana, flowering tobacco

NICOTIANA

ni-koh-shee-AH-nuh

Bloom Color:
Pink, red, salmon, and white

Bloom Time:
Late spring to early fall

Length of Bloom:
12 weeks or more

Height:
Varies by species; see individual listings

Spread:
Varies by species; see individual listings

Garden Uses:
Container planting, cut flower garden, edging, mass planting, meadow garden, mixed border, seasonal hedge, woodland garden; attracts hummingbirds and sphinx moths

Light Preference:
Full sun to partial shade

Soil Preference:
Evenly moist, well-drained soil

Best Way to Propagate:
Sow seed indoors in late winter, outdoors in late spring

Hardiness:
Frost-sensitive perennial grown as a tender annual

Year after year, nicotiana is found on the list of the ten most popular annuals thanks to its ease of care and attractive, nonstop flowers. Most gardeners, though, place nicotianas where they plant almost all other annuals: in full sun. There's nothing wrong with that, but perhaps the plant would be even more popular if they knew it also did so very well in partial shade. A typical nicotiana produces a basal rosette of apple green leaves, often sticky to the touch, plus leafy, upright stalks of tubular five-petaled flowers. The flowers of some species open only at night, but today's hybrid nicotianas are generally open for show 24/7.

GROWING TIPS

Nicotianas are no more difficult to grow than their even more popular cousin, the petunia. Sun or partial shade, rich soil or poor, acid or alkaline—as long as the plant gets good drainage, it's very likely to thrive.

Nicotianas are also one of the easier shade-tolerant annuals to grow from seed indoors. In spite of their tiny size, the dust-like seeds give rise to tough seedlings that are a snap to grow. Sow the seed about 6 to 8 weeks before the last frost, on moist, sterile growing mix, pressing lightly. Don't cover the seed: It needs light to germinate. Supply temperatures of 65° to 85°F (18° to 30°C) for germination. Don't forget to thin the seedlings—nicotiana is one of those plants where it seems every single seed germinates, and trays quickly become overcrowded.

Of course, if you choose to buy nicotianas rather then grow them from seed, that's no problem. They're available everywhere and transplant readily.

PROBLEMS AND SOLUTIONS

Aphids can be an annoyance—blast them to oblivion with a spray of water. Tobacco mosaic virus is talked about far more often that it is actually seen, but do keep nicotianas away from other members of the tobacco family (Solanaceae), such as tomatoes, peppers, potatoes, and eggplants, just in case. And rotate cultures in the garden, never planting them in the same spot 2 years in a row. To prevent leaf diseases, such as mildew and stem rot, keep the soil moist and the leaves dry.

TOP PERFORMER

Nicotiana × *sanderae* (common nicotiana, flowering tobacco): Also called *N. alata* and *N. affinis.* This hybrid genus offers a wide variety of traits, but most modern hybrids are day-blooming plants of moderate to dwarf height. The color range is very good, with lots of reds, pinks, whites, salmons, bicolors, and even some lovely lime-greens. There are dozens of cultivars of this charming annual: Just take your pick! Height: 8 to 24 inches (20 to 60 cm). Spread: 8 to 10 inches (20 to 25 cm).

MORE RECOMMENDED NICOTIANAS

Nicotiana langsdorfii (flowering tobacco): Truly a curiosity, with apple green, bottle-shaped flowers dangling from upright, branching stems, like wine bottles suspended from a mobile. Although fairly available commercially, at least by seed, this species has no other common name than flowering tobacco. If I had a choice of names, though, I'd call it "drunkard's dream"! This species is scentless. Recent hybrids with *N.* × *sanderae* are resulting in plants looking like *N. langsdorfii* in form, but with flowers that have green tubes with colorful red or pink lobes. Height: 12 to 14 inches (30 to 35 cm). Spread: 8 to 10 inches (20 to 25 cm).

N. sylvestris (flowering tobacco): This tall species, *the* flowering tobacco in Victorian times, went out of style when more dwarf, more highly colorful hybrid nicotianas became available, but it's making a solid comeback these days—thanks to its incredible perfume and perhaps just a pinch of nostalgia. The white flowers have long, thin tubes opening to wide petals and are borne on tall, branching stems. They do half-close during the day and have little or no scent at that time, but they make up for that with their incredible performance after dark. Plant them near an open window so you can enjoy them all night long! Height: 3 to 6 feet (90 to 180 cm). Spread: 2 feet (60 cm).

Flowering tobacco
(*Nicotiana sylvestris*)

LARRY'S GARDEN NOTES

When Frenchman Jean Nicot first introduced the tobacco plant (*Nicotiana tabacum*) to Europe, it was to help mankind. The plant was considered medicinal (and in fact, still is in some quarters) and used to treat so many diseases that it was almost a cure-all. It wasn't until later that smoking the leaves became such a status symbol that anyone who could afford the new plant was trying it. So Nicot's life-saving plant now kills far more people than it saves! Don't try smoking flowering tobacco plants, though—most ornamental types have far more nicotine than *N. tabacum* and are quite poisonous!

Nierembergia

Nierembergia, cupflower

NIEREMBERGIA

near-em-BER-gee-uh

Bloom Color:
  Violet and white

Bloom Time:
  Late spring to early fall; fall to
  winter in mild climates

Length of Bloom:
  12 weeks or more

Height:
  Varies by species; see
  individual listings

Spread:
  Varies by species; see
  individual listings

Garden Uses:
  Container planting, edging,
  groundcover, hanging basket,
  mass planting, mixed border,
  rock garden, wall planting,
  woodland garden

Light Preference:
  Full sun to partial shade

Soil Preference:
  Rich, evenly moist, well-
  drained soil

Best Way to Propagate:
  Sow seed indoors in spring,
  outdoors in late spring

Hardiness:
  Frost-sensitive perennial
  grown as a half-hardy annual

The cup-shaped flowers of nierembergia are often so numerous that "literally covered in flowers," a phrase one often hears bandied about for other plants, is actually fairly accurate—the foliage manages to peek through only here and there. It is truly an attractive plant, usually forming a perfect mound of spreading, finely cut foliage and more flowers than such a small plant could usually be expected to bear. I regularly hear visitors asking whether it is real. Well, the answer is yes! If only all our annuals performed as wonderfully!

GROWING TIPS

This is a cool-summer annual that will do best in very different environments depending on the local climate. Where summers are naturally cool, it actually does best in sun, although it tolerates partial shade. Where summers are hot, though, try to find a spot where it will be in shade from noon through the afternoon—in other words, partial shade. And to help keep it cool, make sure the soil remains at least slightly moist at all times. A cooling mulch is also wise.

You can sow nierembergia outdoors where the growing season is long enough: at least 4 to 5 months. Elsewhere, start it indoors. An 8- to 10-week head start will give plants time to grow to just the right size for planting out and will quickly reach full bloom. Sow the seed, just barely covering it with soil. It is easy enough to grow, germinating readily at room temperatures—but be forewarned that it germinates very slowly, taking up to a month.

Like many shade-tolerant "annuals," nierembergia can be grown as a summer annual and also a winter one. Where frost is rare, sow it in fall for winter bloom, or buy trays of plants.

Nierembergia tends to bloom so heavily that it runs out of energy. Theoretically, you should regularly pinch off the faded flowers to prevent them from going to seed, but that requires quite a bit of kneeling. Instead, after each flush of flowering, trim the plants back by one-third with pruning shears.

Although grown as an annual, nierembergia is actually quite hardy, often surviving the winter into Zone 7 as a short-lived perennial, at least in well-drained soils. Or bring it indoors for the winter. In fact, nierembergia is also sometimes offered as a houseplant.

PROBLEMS AND SOLUTIONS

Rot is a possibility where soils are poorly drained. Snails and slugs may be a problem in rainy weather; see page 85 for help. In most cases, though, nierembergias are trouble-free.

TOP PERFORMER

Nierembergia caerulea (cupflower, nierembergia): This species is more often sold under its old name, *N. hippomanica.* It's an attractive plant even when not in flower (although that rarely happens!), with small, stiff, fine leaves forming a low, creeping mound. The flowers are cup-shaped, as the common name suggests, and about ¾ inch (2 cm) across. They come in shades of violet to violet-blue and white. Only two cultivars are at all available and both are spectacular. 'Purple Robe' has lavender-blue flowers with a yellow throat, and 'Mont Blanc' has pure white flowers. The two cultivars are considerably more heat-resistant than the species and are the best choices for hot-summer areas. Height: 8 inches (20 cm). Spread: 8 inches (20 cm).

MORE RECOMMENDED NIEREMBERGIAS

Nierembergia repens (white cup): Also called *N. rivularis.* This is a much rarer plant with a distinctly creeping habit forming a low carpet of spoon-shaped leaves. The foliage is so different that, if it weren't for the cup-shaped flowers, you'd scarcely guess it was related to its more common relative. The flowers are much larger, about 1 to 2 inches (2.5 to 5 cm) in diameter. White is the usual flower color, although there are purple-flowered cultivars. This plant does not do well in hot-summer areas. Where summers are cool and winters aren't too cold, though, it can be a long-lived and even invasive groundcover, spreading via underground stolons. That would include Zones 7 and up. Elsewhere it can be overwintered indoors. Height: 2 inches (5 cm). Spread: 24 inches (60 cm).

Cupflower (*Nierembergia caerulea* 'Mont Blanc')

LARRY'S GARDEN NOTES

The genus *Nierembergia* was best known back in the Victorian era, then nearly disappeared from view. It was suddenly thrust into the limelight once again when a new cultivar, 'Mont Blanc', won an All-America Selection award. Since then, the cultivar 'Purple Robe' has also had some success on the market (not surprisingly, since it is a magnificent plant). Still, nierembergia remains an underused genus worthy of much greater success.

Schizanthus
Butterfly flower, poor man's orchid, fringe flower

SCHIZANTHUS

skizz-AN-thus

Bloom Color:
Red, magenta, rose, pink, blue, purple, yellow, and white

Bloom Time:
Late spring to early fall; fall to winter in mild climates

Length of Bloom:
12 weeks or more

Height:
12 to 48 inches (30 to 120 cm)

Spread:
9 to 18 inches (23 to 45 cm)

Garden Uses:
Container planting, edging, hanging basket, mixed border, rock garden, wall planting, woodland garden

Light Preference:
Full sun to partial shade

Soil Preference:
Rich, moist, well-drained soil

Best Way to Propagate:
Sow seed indoors in late winter for summer bloom; in fall for winter/spring bloom

Hardiness:
Tender annual

Thanks to its small but spectacular flowers, butterfly flower is attractive both near and far. From afar, it's the mass of color that attracts the eye, but it's worthwhile looking at the flowers close up. Each one is incredibly intricate: a yellow throat surrounded by two smaller upper lobes and two broader lower ones, all deeply cut, with a projection in the center that resembles the labellum of an orchid. As an added feature, the upper lip is dotted with burgundy, showing pollinators which way to go to find the treasure—the flower's sweet nectar. Each one looks like a butterfly or like an orchid, the sources of the plant's common names.

GROWING TIPS

This cool-season annual does best in partial shade in most climates, although it can tolerate full sun in the North and elsewhere where summers are cool. Alternatively, you can grow it as a winter annual in mild climates, sowing it in fall for flowers from late fall through spring. In both situations, help keep it cooler by watering as needed and mulching well.

In some areas you can find trays of butterfly flowers in nurseries at the proper planting season. In most areas, though, *Schizanthus* is not a common annual and you'll have to grow them yourself, from seed.

Where the season is cool and long (4 to 5 months or more), sow butterfly flower directly outdoors, starting about 2 weeks before the last frost. Elsewhere, start it indoors about 8 to 10 weeks before the last frost. Press the tiny seeds into premoistened sowing mix, but without covering them. Unlike most annuals, butterfly flowers need darkness in order to germinate, so place the seed trays in a cupboard or inside a black plastic bag. Check them daily for germination, and move them to a brightly lit spot as soon as seedlings are visible. Grow them cool, if possible, or at least place them in a spot that is cool at night: about 55°F (12°C).

Left on their own, most cultivars of butterfly flower produce thin, upright stems and are little inclined to branch out. To encourage them to do so, pinch the plants once when they're about 3 inches (8 cm) tall, then again when they are about 6 inches (15 cm) tall. That will give more compact but abundantly branched, abundantly flowered plants.

PROBLEMS AND SOLUTIONS

Chase off aphids with a sharp spray of water. Watch out for whiteflies: Use a sticky trap to catch them before they settle in.

TOP PERFORMER

Schizanthus pinnatus (butterfly flower, poor man's orchid, fringe flower): This is the most common species of *Schizanthus*. It comes in a wide range of sizes, from dwarf varieties no more than 1 foot (30 cm) tall to full-size plants that can reach 4 feet (120 cm) if left unpinched. All bear abundant flowers in a wide range of colors, most with a yellow throat and burgundy marbling. The mid-green leaves are fernlike in appearance: When the plant is in full bloom, they are essentially hidden beneath a wall of blossoms. Spread: 1 to 2 feet (30 to 60 cm).

MORE RECOMMENDED BUTTERFLY FLOWERS

Schizanthus × *wisetonensis* (hybrid butterfly flower): This is a cross between the common butterfly flower, described above, and *S. retusus*, which is now rarely grown. In actual fact, the resulting crosses are so similar to *S. pinnatus* that the two can't be readily told apart and they are much confused in the trade. Of course, unless you're a stickler for exact labeling, butterfly flowers are gorgeous plants no matter what name they are grown under—so whether your plants are *S. pinnatus* or *S.* × *wisentonensis* doesn't really matter. Height: 12 to 14 inches (30 to 35 cm). Spread: 1 to 2 feet (30 to 60 cm).

Butterfly flower
(*Schizanthus pinnatus*)

LARRY'S GARDEN NOTES

Not only do the complex flowers have an orchidlike appearance, they even have orchidlike methods of ensuring cross-pollination. The anthers are fixed to the back of the flower but spring forward when an insect lands on the flower, depositing a dust of sticky pollen on the insect's head. Then a series of dots, like lights on a runway, direct the insect to the nectar inside the tube. The blooming is timed so that, when the pollen is fresh, the stigma is not yet ready to receive pollen, so there is no danger the flower could pollinate itself. Ingenious, n'est-ce pas?

Solenostemon

Coleus, painted nettle

This plant has certainly come a long way! Grandma's colorful-leaved but somewhat ungainly houseplant—all height with no lower leaves!—has morphed into one of the most beautiful of all shade plants. New dwarf cultivars not as quick to burst into unwanted bloom are now filling shady beds and borders around the world—and what a show! The foliage colors are so spectacular you can truly say, "With leaves this beautiful, who needs flowers?"—and mean it. In fact, the insignificant spikes of tiny lavender to white flowers are usually just pinched off: The leaves carry the entire show.

GROWING TIPS

Coleus like moist growing conditions and rich soil but adapt to almost anything except dry conditions. They're renowned for their ability to adjust to shade, but most will also take full sun.

Keeping them moist will be a far more important goal than finding the right light. Provide a thick mulch and water as needed to keep the soil slightly moist at all times. They'll let you know instantly when they are getting too dry: They wilt like lettuce when soil even starts to dry out.

Most modern coleus are self-branching, compact plants, although you may occasionally run up against one of the older varieties that grows straight up unless pinched. The more you clip, the more they branch. On all coleus, too, self-branching or not, pinch off the flowerstalks as you see them. They appear from the stem tips and look like little bishop's caps at first, then stretch to reveal the tiny blooms. Stems that bloom tend to tie back, but removing the flowers early will prevent this decline.

Coleus like it warm, so don't plant them out too early. In fact, they'll likely be among the last annuals you'll want to put out in summer. The slightest hint of frost will spell an end to their display, so if you want to overwinter them get them indoors early.

There are two options for getting started with coleus: Grow them by seed for lots of very inexpensive plants quickly, or choose cutting-grown varieties. The difference is quite striking, as seed-grown coleus tend to bloom young and often. They may save you a bundle, but the price is extra maintenance in summer: You'll find you have lots of pinching to do to get rid of the flowers. The best cutting-grown plants, on the other hand, are reluctant to bloom (a good thing!) but cost a lot more. They're generally sold in individual pots, and planting an entire bed of such coleus would be prohibitively expensive. My suggestion: Buy one or two coleus early, a month or so before the last frost, then take cuttings. They grow so quickly you'll often have time to take cuttings of the cuttings! In no time, your summer garden will be full of them.

To start coleus from seed, simply press the seed into moist mix, about 8 to 12 weeks before the last frost date. Don't cover the seed; it needs light to germinate. About 10 to 20 days later, the first seedlings appear.

Cuttings are as easy as seed; in fact, no plant roots more readily from cuttings than a coleus, usually in only 3 to 5 days. Simply stick a cutting in a pot of moistened soil and keep it humid. Cuttings will readily root in water as well.

It is definitely worthwhile overwintering cutting-grown coleus. Rather than bring the adult plant indoors (older plants get woody and less productive), take cuttings in late summer or early fall and keep them over winter as houseplants.

PROBLEMS AND SOLUTIONS

Outdoors, coleus are generally pest-free. Indoors, they are subject to several insects, including mealybugs, whiteflies, and scale insects; control them with insecticidal soap.

TOP PERFORMER

Solenostemon scutellarioides (coleus, painted nettle, flame nettle): This plant has undergone a recent name change: You'll still see it sold as *Coleus blumei*. It exists in hundreds of cultivars, from giant types with huge leaves to dwarf or even creeping varieties. Leaves can be all one color (and just about anything *but* green) or of multiple hues, either marbled irregularly with one or more other colors or with distinct patterns. The original leaf shape was broadly oval, but many coleus now have fringed, narrow, deeply cut, or even "duckfoot" leaves.

Coleus (Solenostemon scutellarioides 'Winsom')

SMART SUBSTITUTE

There are plenty of tropical plants that make good "summering out" plants for the garden, but only a few have foliage as spectacular as the coleus. One exception is Persian shield (*Strobilanthes dyerianus*). Its upright, branching stems bear long, dark green leaves that are liberally flushed with purple and topped with a silver overlay. It's so colorful you'd swear it was from another planet! It adapts to both sun and shade but, like the coleus, does like warm temperatures: Don't bring it outdoors too quickly in spring. And what a stupendous winter houseplant! Height: 4 feet (120 cm). Spread: 3 feet (90 cm).

Torenia

Wishbone flower, bluewings

PLANT PROFILE

TORENIA

tor-REE-nee-uh

Bloom Color:
Varies by species; see individual listings

Bloom Time:
Summer to early fall; much of the year in frost-free climates

Length of Bloom:
12 weeks or more

Height:
6 to 12 inches (15 to 30 cm)

Spread:
Varies by species; see individual listings

Garden Uses:
Container planting, edging, groundcover, hanging basket, mass planting, mixed border, rock garden, woodland garden; attracts butterflies and hummingbirds

Light Preference:
Partial shade to shade

Soil Preference:
Humus-rich, evenly moist, well-drained soil

Best Way to Propagate:
Sow seed of dwarf varieties indoors in spring; take stem cuttings of trailing varieties at any season

Hardiness:
Tender annual

Not your usual garden annual, wishbone flower has been grown in modest proportions for generations. Recently, though, new cultivars with a creeping habit that trail wonderfully from containers have changed the plant's outline and, from the minor leagues, it has started to become a major player (at least as a hanging plant). All species have rather open tubular flowers and shiny leaves, but little else in common other than the wishbonelike construction inside the blooms.

GROWING TIPS

You'll find seedling-grown wishbone flowers, usually in trays, at good prices, as well as cutting-grown varieties that are much more expensive. The former are usually compact plants for garden use. Buy them in cell packs, if possible, as they transplant best when their roots aren't disturbed. If they're sold in trays, look for young plants not yet in bloom: They still transplant without too much of a shock. Cutting-grown varieties, usually the trailing types, are sold in individual pots and are generally used for containers and hanging baskets, but they also look wonderful as summer groundcovers.

Plant out wishbone flowers after all danger of frost has passed and the soil is thoroughly warm. You'll quickly discover that anything you do to keep them cool will give you the best results. Partial shade with protection from afternoon sun, for example, is ideal, although they tolerate even more shade in hot-summer climates. Full sun isn't wise, even in cool summer areas: The leaves tend to discolor or burn on truly sunny days. Keeping the soil moist also helps keep the plants cool, so water them as needed and apply mulch.

Rich soil with plenty of compost gives the best growth and flowering. If that is impossible, make sure you fertilize regularly. In fact, a twice-monthly spray with foliar fertilizer containing a decent proportion of potassium (the last number on fertilizer labels) will give copious amounts of bloom. There is no need to deadhead this plant—seed production doesn't seem to reduce its capacity to bloom in any way.

Wishbone flower is not available just anywhere, so you may

have to grow it from seed. If so, you'll find it presents no special care. Sow the seed directly outdoors where summers are long; in most climates, you'll probably find it is worth starting them indoors about 6 to 8 weeks before the last frost date. Sow them into peat pots, pressing the seeds into the growing mix without covering them, as they need light to germinate. Germination takes about 1 to 3 weeks at warm temperatures, about 70° to 75°F (21° to 24°C). Afterward, move the plants to a cool spot, with night temperatures about 55°F (13°C). This will keep the plants compact without pinching.

PROBLEMS AND SOLUTIONS

High temperatures and drought stress can lead to leaf and stem diseases. Cool temperatures and even soil humidity will help to prevent them. When watering, avoid moistening the leaves.

TOP PERFORMER

Torenia fournieri (wishbone flower): Only a few years ago, this was the only *Torenia* available, but it is now being overtaken by trailing wishbone flower in popularity. I still prefer it because I like growing my own plants from seed. It's a small, bushy annual with pale green leaves and flowers opening into five petals. The species has violet flowers with darker lobes, but there are cultivars with pink/rose and white/lavender flowers as well as pure white blooms. They all have a yellow spot inside the throat. Height: 4 to 12 inches (10 to 30 cm). Spread: 6 to 9 inches (15 to 23 cm).

MORE RECOMMENDED WISHBONE FLOWERS

Torenia flava (yellow wishbone flower): A most unlikely wishbone flower, looking nothing like the others except for the "wishbone" inside the throat. The flowers are medium yellow with a beautifully contrasting maroon throat, and the wishbone itself is nearly black. This is a spreading or trailing plant, especially used in containers. Height: 8 to 12 inches (20 to 30 cm). Spread: 12 to 24 inches (30 to 60 cm).

Wishbone flower
(*Torenia fournieri* Clown Series)

LARRY'S GARDEN NOTES

Wishbone flowers get their name from the curious arrangement of the anthers in unpollinated flowers: two anthers growing out then inward, joining at the tip in a wishbone pattern. The anthers are like a spring: When a bee enters the flower, the anthers snap apart and thump down on its back, coating it in pollen. Then, when the bee enters a different flower, the stigma picks up the pollen, and the bee is coated in pollen yet again.

Viola

Pansy

PLANT PROFILE

VIOLA

vy-OH-luh

Bloom Color:
Purple, lavender, blue, red, orange, bronze, yellow, white, and green

Bloom Time:
Very early spring to summer; fall to winter in mild climates

Length of Bloom:
12 weeks or more

Height:
6 to 9 inches (15 to 23 cm)

Spread:
9 to 12 inches (23 to 30 cm)

Garden Uses:
Container planting, pressed flower, edging, groundcover, mass planting, meadow garden, mixed border, rock garden, woodland garden

Light Preference:
Full sun to shade

Soil Preference:
Humus-rich, evenly moist, well-drained soil

Best Way to Propagate:
Sow seed outdoors in fall, indoors in winter

Hardiness:
Tender perennial grown as a hardy annual

Even nongardeners recognize pansies! And how could you not recognize them, with their perky baby faces? The broad petals form a rounded "face" with darker spots acting as eyes and a mouth, making for a particularly charming flower that has been popular for generations. The common name comes from the French *pensée*, or thought, because the flowers were formerly used to mark book pages so you wouldn't forget where you were—in other words, so you could "retrace your thoughts."

GROWING TIPS

We've seen other *Viola* species on page 228: the ones grown as perennials, often under the name "violet." The pansy, however, even though it is in fact a perennial or biennial, is inevitably grown as an annual. It has been developed to flower rapidly from seed and to give its best show the first year, although many types will survive winter to flower the following year. Just how perennial any pansy is will depend on your conditions and its genetic background. Some clones barely last the summer; others hang on over winter to bloom another year.

Like many "shade annuals," pansies don't really require shade, and they bloom wonderfully in full sun where temperatures are cool enough. Since they are usually planted for summer bloom, and in most climates summers are hot, they'll need at least partial shade with protection from the afternoon sun. They'll also do well in shade, especially in more southern regions, where the sun is intense enough to reach the ground even through fairly dense foliage.

There are various ways of using pansies in the garden, depending on your local climate. In cool-summer areas, they are planted out in spring and bloom all summer and into fall, like any other annual. In climates that have cold winters but hot summers, they are often used to fill flowerbeds temporarily in very early spring (they are very frost-tolerant and can be planted out as soon as the ground thaws), until it is time to plant other frost-tender annuals as their summer replacements. In mild-winter areas, even as far north as Zone 6, they're grown for fall and winter bloom, planted out at the end of summer.

Six-packs and trays of pansies are available everywhere, in both spring and fall in many climates. Just plant them in appropriate conditions (that is, where they can be kept cool for at least the next few months) and you'll find they do wonderfully. Keeping the soil moist and well mulched—plus ensuring at least partial shade—will help provide the coolness they crave, especially if you're trying for summer bloom. Pansies planted for fall and winter flowering will often get cool weather no matter where they are grown.

You can also grow pansies from seed. The easiest way to do so in the home garden is to treat them as biennials: Sow them directly in the garden in midsummer so they have time to produce clumps of foliage by fall, mulching them well in cold-winter areas. Then, depending on the conditions, they'll bloom through fall and winter or wait until the ground thaws the following spring.

PROBLEMS AND SOLUTIONS

Remove snails and slugs if they cause problems. It's best to rotate pansies, not growing them in the same spot year after year, as leaf diseases may develop over time and contaminate the soil.

TOP PERFORMER

Viola × *wittrockiana* (pansy): The "common garden pansy" is nowhere common in the wild and, in fact, doesn't exist outside of gardens. It is the result of man crossing various species of *Viola,* including *V. cornuta,* (horned violet) and *V. tricolor* (Johnny-jump-ups), to create a plant with much larger flowers than any of the wild forms. It is all alone in its category because all of the increasingly complex hybrids are put in the hybrid species *V.* × *wittrockiana,* which simply grows in numbers from year to year: There are literally hundreds of varieties and probably many more to come. There are small- and large-flowered varieties, ones with undulating margins, and a whole range of colors, either monochrome or regularly mottled with other shades. USDA Plant Hardiness Zones 6 to 9.

KISSING COUSINS

Looking for an interesting, long-flowering hanging basket plant? Try trailing violet (*Viola hederacea*), a subtropical violet from Australia that produces plantlets on long stolons that trail over the ground in the wild, but down and over the sides of pots in culture. The small, kidney-shaped leaves make a lovely background for the lavender flowers, and they are produced all summer, even into winter in frost-free climates. This tender perennial (Zone 9) can also be grown as a houseplant and does well under the same conditions as the pansy.

Pansy (*Viola* × *wittrockiana*)

With their ability to grow in spots that get only seasonal sun, bulbs can be among the most spectacular flowers in the shade garden.

Chapter 8

Bulbs for Shade

Bulbs are not the first plants one thinks of when it comes to shade gardening. I know my own mind immediately pictures a sunny garden chock-full of tulips when I hear the word bulbs. But then secondary images filter through: a forest floor blue with Spanish bluebells (*Hyancinthoides hispanica*), native trilliums in the deepest shade in woods out by my uncle's farm, and many others. Yes, you can grow bulbs in the shade—as long as you know what kind of shade, and what kinds of bulbs to choose.

A SEASON FOR SUN, A SEASON FOR SHADE

Most bulbs grown in shady locations really aren't all that shade-tolerant. Instead, they belong to the category of plants known as spring ephemerals: plants that sprout quickly in spring, produce leaves, flower, then disappear by the time summer has finally taken hold. The whole point of such a rapid growth cycle is to grab as much sun as possible while it is at its most abundant—in early spring. That's when deciduous trees and shrubs are leafless, letting sun not just filter through but blaze directly down on the forest floor. Some spring-blooming bulbs are up so early that they are, in some climates, actually winter-bloomers: They have time to go through their entire cycle of growth, bloom, seed production, and dormancy before a single leaf appears on trees overhead. Most others are a bit later—some actually almost at the end of spring (with a proper choice of spring bulbs, you can add up to 3 months of bloom to your growing season!). Many, in fact, bloom even as the trees leaf out, in mid- to late spring, depending on the climate, and still cling to their leaves as the darkness grows above them. However, almost all of these bulbs are fully dormant by midsummer.

What I find so amazing about spring bulbs is that most have only two or three fairly small leaves, yet they manage to store up as much solar energy (during what may be only a 2-month period of growth) as summer-growing plants do over 5 months or more. But then, that's what bulbs are designed for: storage. They store light energy (in the forms of starches and sugars) as well as minerals and moisture for next season's blooming. They are so efficient at storage that, under greenhouse conditions, most can be forced into bloom without any soil or nutrients and still bloom beautifully—once, at least. Bulbs of spring ephemerals are the most self-sufficient plants of all: They already contain all they need for next season's show, so they'll almost always give spectacular results the first year even if you plant them under abysmal growing conditions. The leaves they produce in your garden are, in fact, for *next year's* bloom—even as they flower, they are already storing up for the following season.

HARDY OR TENDER?

Bulbous plants can be divided into two main categories: hardy bulbs and tender bulbs.

Hardy bulbs are the ones most commonly used in colder climates. They are planted outdoors in spring or fall, depending on the type, and can be expected to come back year after year. Their dormancy needs are absolute: They *do* have a down season in summer, and you have to plant them in such a way that other plants can cover for them while they are hiding underground. There are many hardy bulbs adapted to summer shade.

Hardy bulbs can be further subdivided into three categories, depending on their blooming season: spring-blooming, summer-blooming, and fall-blooming. Each group has its particular needs.

Spring-blooming bulbs: These are the spring ephemerals described above and are

WHAT IS A BULB?

DEFINITION TIME! TO BE BOTANICALLY EXACT, you have to divide bulbs into several categories: true bulbs, tubers, corms, rhizomes—and even a few more. True bulbs are sphere-shaped and made up of overlapping scales surrounding embryonic leaves and flowers with a flat plate below from which roots grow; tubers are fleshy underground stems or roots; corms are swollen stem bases; rhizomes are thickened creeping stems. However, for the purposes of this book, the more general definition of a bulb suffices: It is used in the sense of an underground storage organ, no matter what its precise origin.

by far the most popular bulbs for shade because they offer color when little else is in bloom. They are planted in fall for bloom the following spring. Narcissus, snowdrops (*Galanthus* spp.), hyacinths, and so on are typical spring-flowering bulbs with some adaptation to shade.

Summer-blooming bulbs: They sprout later than spring-blooming bulbs and usually remain in foliage throughout summer, even after their flowers have faded. Only the lily is described in this chapter, as the genus does have a few shade-tolerant species; most other summer-blooming bulbs are sun-lovers. They are usually planted in spring, but sometimes in fall.

Fall-blooming bulbs: This is a very odd category, for the most part made up of plants that produce their foliage in spring but their flowers in fall. They can essentially be seen as spring ephemerals, with foliage that sprouts in spring and disappears quickly, but with off-season bloom. They should be planted as soon as the bulbs become available, in late summer or early fall. This is a very small group: Among them, only colchicums and some cyclamens are well adapted to shady conditions.

Tender bulbs are of tropical or subtropical origin. They may be able to take light frost, enough to kill the foliage, but will die if their rootstock freezes. In mild climates, they can stay outdoors all year—most adopt a summer-through-fall growth habit, then go dormant during the colder months, not sprouting again until the following summer is well underway. For most gardeners, though, these bulbs will have to be brought indoors to a frost-free spot for winter, then planted out again in summer. In fact, many are started in pots indoors to hasten their blooming season or are simply grown in pots year-round, which makes bringing them indoors and out much easier. Most tender bulbs prefer full sun, though, including the most popular ones: gladiolus, dahlias, and cannas. Only a few are adapted to shady conditions, including caladiums and the ever-popular tuberous begonia.

BULBS FOR SHADE

Theoretically, most spring- and fall-blooming bulbs can be grown in the shade of deciduous trees and shrubs, as they are dormant in summer and don't need light. However, in practice, some (like tulips and crocuses) generally do best where the ground becomes hot and dry in summer, and that's rarely the case in shade. So the hardy bulbs presented here are ones that do adapt to the often moist, cool conditions of summer shade. As for the summer-bloomers, only those that grow and bloom well in shade or partial shade are presented in the following pages.

Achimenes

Achimenes, Cupid's bower, hot water plant, widow's tears

PLANT PROFILE

ACHIMENES

a-KIM-uh-neez

Bloom Color:
White, pink, red, yellow, salmon, purple, and blue

Bloom Time:
Early summer to early fall

Length of Bloom:
8 weeks or more

Height:
3 to 24 inches (8 to 60 cm)

Spread:
10 to 15 inches (25 to 38 cm)

Garden Uses:
Container planting, edging, groundcover, hanging baskets, houseplant, mass planting, rock garden, wall planting, woodland garden

Light Preference:
Partial shade to shade

Soil Preference:
Rich, moist, well-drained soil

Best Way to Propagate:
Divide rhizomes in spring

Hardiness:
Tender bulb

A stunning plant with often very large, showy flowers in a nearly unlimited array of colors, including many with contrasting veins, achimenes has caught on in a fairly big way in subtropical climates but is not nearly well enough known in temperate areas. From a distance it could be mistaken for an impatiens, but the flowers are actually quite different when seen close up: a narrow trumpet flaring widely at the tip into five overlapping lobes. The foliage is not unattractive: mid- to dark green, red on the underside, with a shiny surface, a toothed margin, and minute white hairs.

GROWING TIPS

Achimenes is generally grown in hanging baskets, and most modern hybrids have appropriately arching stems—although, with a bit of looking you can also find mounding and erect types that would look good in a flowerbed. Often people obtain it in full bloom in summer and toss it when it stops blooming in fall, not realizing it has underground rhizomes that will sprout again in spring if you give them proper care.

To follow its growth cycle from the beginning, though, let's assume you've obtained rhizomes in spring. It's best to start them indoors. Since the rhizomes are very small and individual plants are quite open, they need to be potted up quite densely, about four to a 4-inch (10-cm) pot. Lay the rhizomes on their sides, with the growing point, if one is present, pointing upward, and lightly cover with growing mix. In Zones 10 and 11, the rhizomes can be planted directly outdoors.

Once growth begins, keep the medium moist at all times: This is *not* a plant that tolerates drying out. When stems are about 4 inches (10 cm) high, pinch them to promote better branching. Older cultivars have a stringier growth habit and may need a second pinching a few weeks later. Partial shade is ideal, but achimenes does surprisingly well in shade, although too little light can cause weaker growth.

Achimenes goes naturally dormant at summer's end, sometimes as early as late August, so simply stop watering and bring it indoors. It's easiest to simply bring in container-grown plants pot and all—just let the growing mix dry out, and cut off the dead stems. Or dig up or unpot the rhizomes and store dry in vermiculite, perlite, or wood shavings. This plant prefers somewhat warmer winter temperatures than most tender bulbs—50° to 60°F (10° to 15°C)—and can even be stored at room temperature with no harm.

Multiplication is a cinch with achimenes. First, by the end of summer, most cultivars will have produced five or more rhizomes for each original one. These can also be broken up into individual scales, each of which will give a new plant. Many also produce mini-rhizomes, called propagules, at leaf axils, and they can be harvested and stored over winter just like full-grown rhizomes.

PROBLEMS AND SOLUTIONS

Achimenes rarely suffer from insects or disease. They can be severely damaged by drought, so keep them evenly moist.

TOP PERFORMER

Achimenes Hybrids (achimenes, Cupid's bower, hot water plant, widow's tears): Almost all achimenes sold are of hybrid origin. These are mostly large-flowered, long-blooming plants and come in the full range of possible colors, often with a contrasting throat. Most are single-flowered, although some are double. Two old-fashioned cultivars are still popular: 'Ambroise Verschaffelt', with white blooms beautifully veined in purple with a yellow throat; and 'Purple King', a heavy bloomer with large purple flowers and dark green leaves. Height: 3 to 24 inches (8 to 60 cm). Spread: 10 to 15 inches (25 to 38 cm).

MORE RECOMMENDED ACHIMENES

Achimenes longiflora (long-flowered achimenes): This species is one of the main parents of the modern hybrids, having contributed notably the large flower size so lauded in the genus. Its purple flowers are actually even larger than most hybrids. It is a distinctly upright-growing plant. Height: 2 feet (60 cm). Spread: 2 feet (60 cm).

Achimenes (*Achimenes* 'Ambroise Verschaffelt')

LARRY'S GARDEN NOTES

Achimenes has more than its fair share of common names, most dating back to Victorian times when it was a very popular plant: widow's tears, cupid's bower, and orchid pansy. The most curious name of all, though, has to be hot water plant. It got this name because, back in the days before central heating, to get this tropical plant to sprout on a cold windowsill, you had to water it with "hot" water . . . well, that would be more like tepid water these days. In modern, heated homes, where windowsills are quite toasty, ordinary tap-temperature water will do just fine!

Alocasia
Giant taro, upright elephant's ear

If you're looking for a tropical effect for your shade garden, you've found the right plant! The huge arrow-shaped leaves of giant taro, shiny dark green with paler veins and a somewhat undulating edge, can reach 3 feet (90 cm) long and 2 feet (60 cm) wide (twice that outdoors in the tropics)! The leaves often look like they were put on upside down: Most arrow-shaped leaves point downward, but these sometimes point straight up, borne on thick petioles. This is one of those plants that becomes even more impressive with time. As lower leaves are replaced by newer ones, a thick woody trunk with prominent leaf scars appears, and the plant takes on a palmlike look. Definitely *not* your grandma's daffodil!

GROWING TIPS

Although giant taro is sold as a bulb, the only time you're likely to see its huge tuber is just after you buy it. Once it has been potted up (and, unless you live in USDA hardiness Zone 9 or above, you *will* be growing this monster in a pot!), you never really need to expose its tuber to the light again.

Put the large tuber in a 10-inch (25-cm) or larger pot, covering only the bulbous section at the base. Given warmth and even soil moisture, new leaves appear very quickly, and the plant needs only a few to impress.

This is a plant of the deepest jungles in its native Southeast Asia and is fine in shade or partial shade. You can also acclimate it to a sunny spot as long as you keep it moist at all times. It adapts well to ordinary soil moisture but is actually a swamp plant and will grow beautifully with its roots constantly sitting in water. Don't put it outside in summer until warm temperatures are well established.

Unlike most bulbs, giant taro does not need to go through a dormant period. If you want to use it as a summer patio plant and a winter houseplant, simply bring it indoors in fall and keep watering it. If space is lacking indoors, stop watering it in fall, cut its leaves back, and it will go dormant, sprouting anew whenever you begin watering it again. When planted outdoors in Zone 9, it may get frosted and lose its leaves, but it should sprout anew when warm weather arrives.

The most likely way of reproducing giant taro is to wait until it produces offsets on its own.

Although capable of bloom, giant taro rarely does produce its large, greenish white Jack-in-the-pulpit-type flowers outside of the tropics. When it does bloom, it usually self-pollinates, producing corn cob–like red fruits that contain seeds. Sown fresh, they are another means of propagation.

Warning: Giant taro is poisonous, and even its sap can cause skin irritation, so wear gloves when pruning it.

PROBLEMS AND SOLUTIONS

Giant taro is little bothered by pests outdoors but subject to mealybugs indoors. For control, touch with a cotton swab dipped in rubbing alcohol.

TOP PERFORMER

Alocasia macrorrhizos, syn. *A. macrorrhiza* (giant taro, upright elephant's ear): This is the huge plant described above. Besides the species, with green leaves, there is a variety with yellow-mottled leaves, 'Lutea' (it sometimes skips a year, producing only green leaves); one with purple-tinged foliage, 'Violacea'; and one with spectacularly mottled ivory and gray-green leaves, 'Variegata'. Height: 3 to 17 feet (1 to 5.2 m). Spread: 3 to 8 feet (1 to 2.4 m).

MORE RECOMMENDED GIANT TAROS

Alocasia 'Hilo Beauty' ('Hilo Beauty' alocasia): There are dozens of species of *Alocasia,* many with spectacularly colored foliage, but most are too dependant on tropical temperatures to be of much use outdoors, even in summer (except in the Deep South). Among the few species that do adapt to such a transition is 'Hilo Beauty', a plant of mysterious origin that I actually suspect might be a *Colocasia* (see "Kissing Cousins") or even a *Caladium.* The dark purple stalks bear medium-green leaves beautifully mottled with chartreuse, as if they were wearing combat camouflage. Often sold as a semiaquatic plant, it is also fine as a terrestrial and can be allowed to go dormant in winter. Height: 2 to 3 feet (60 to 90 cm). Spread: 2 feet (60 cm).

Giant taro (*Alocasia macrorrhizos*)

KISSING COUSINS

Taro (*Colocasia esculenta,* syn. *C. antiquorum*), also know by dozens of other names, including elephant's ear, dasheen, eddo, and cocoyam, is a very close relative of *Alocasia,* although lacking a "trunk." It grows from spreading tubers and produces thinner leaves than giant taro, more heart-shaped than arrow-shaped. The normal leaf color is green with a whitish bloom. There are numerous cultivars developed for edible tubers (they are toxic until cooked) and others grown strictly for ornament, like 'Illustris', with purple markings on the leaves; and 'Black Magic', which may be the same plant as 'Jet Black Wonder', with dark purple leaves and black stems. It is usually grown as a summer aquatic but will grow in garden soil of ordinary humidity as well.

Anemone
Wood anemone

No other bulb quite does the "carpet of spring flowers" thing quite as well as the wood anemone. Over time, individual plants expand to cover the forest floor with a carpet of attractive, deeply cut, dark green foliage, each plant bearing just one exquisite flower from its single stem. Forget the invasive nature of this plant: Yes, it runs, but it is such an ephemeral that, by the time summer plants start to take over, it is already dormant; its short height and off-season show mean it doesn't harm the plants it grows among or through. Instead, plant it and let it spread to its full glory—you'll never regret it!

GROWING TIPS

Both the Latin and common names (*nemorosa* means "of the forest") insist on this plant's need for shade. In fact, it will grow in full sun but neither needs nor likes it. It grows in the deepest forests in the wild and looks and grows best under partial to full *seasonal* shade; that is, in spots that do get at least some sun in spring.

You can buy flowering plants in spring, usually from local nurseries; or dormant rhizomes in fall, usually by mail order. The latter are considerably less expensive and even easier to plant.

For ease of planting, why struggle digging into the heart of a deeply wooded area to try to create a planting hole? Where roots are numerous, plant wood anemone on the edge of the woods, where roots are fewer and digging easier. It will spread deep into the forest, trust me! The rhizomes themselves have no particular upside or downside: Just scrape a hole 3 to 4 inches (8 to 10 cm) deep and plop them in any which way.

The ideal spot is in partial to deep shade, in humus-rich soil (or under a nice, thick, organic mulch), with ample humidity at flowering time. This plant cares little how dry the spot may get in summer or fall, although it succeeds perfectly in woodlands that are moist all summer.

Once you have plants, the best way to multiply them (besides letting nature take its course!) is to dig up and replant rhizomes as the foliage begins to fade in early summer. Fall transplanting is theoretically possible as well, but just try to find

such tiny rhizomes without at least some foliage attached to it!

Warning: This Eurasian plant should never be planted in a natural woodland in North America, where it could compete with native plants. Instead, it is a plant for the woodland "garden": a man-made assembly of plants in a wooded spot in a yard separated from any natural woods by at least a footpath or lawn border.

Wood anemone
(*Anemone nemorosa*)

PROBLEMS AND SOLUTIONS

Wood anemone is rarely affected by insects and disease, although rot is possible in truly soggy soils.

TOP PERFORMER

Anemone nemorosa (wood anemone): There are a surprising number of horticultural selections. Indeed, the natural form, with tiny white single flowers, is fairly uncommon in culture. You'll more likely find one of the dozens of cultivars with either much larger blooms in shades of white, pink, violet, or even green, or some of the double types, mostly white ones with smaller but very beautiful blooms. 'Vestal' is the traditional double white that was planted so long ago it has become thoroughly naturalized in some parts of the continent. 'Robinsoniana' is probably the most popular "blue" form (actually, the flowers are violet), and 'Rosea' is the most available pink. If you find a specialist nursery, though, you'll have so many choices you'll have a hard time making up your mind! Height: 4 to 6 inches (10 to 15 cm). Spread: Indefinite. USDA Plant Hardiness Zones 4 to 9.

MORE RECOMMENDED WOOD ANEMONES

A. ranunculoides (yellow wood anemone): Just like the above, but with brilliant yellow flowers. If that color is too intense, *A.* × *lipsiensis,* also sold as *A. seemannii,* is a hybrid between *A. nemorosa* and *A. ranunculoides,* looking like the latter but with lemon yellow flowers. Height: 4 to 6 inches (10 to 15 cm). Spread: Indefinite. USDA Plant Hardiness Zones 4 to 9.

SMART SUBSTITUTES

There is another genus of plants with cup-shaped anemone-like flowers: *Oxalis*, or wood sorrel. There are more than 800 species found in all climates, from cold temperature to tropical, and many are forest plants. The two described here have trifoliate leaves that close up at night and are often mistaken for three-leaf clovers. Redwood sorrel (*Oxalis oregana*), a West Coast native, is an attractive groundcover or edging plant with broad, mid-green, shamrocklike leaves, sometimes with silver markings, and pink to white flowers. Height: 8 inches (20 cm). Spread: indefinite. USDA Plant Hardiness Zones 5 to 9. It is replaced in the East by American wood sorrel (*O. montana*), with pink-veined white flowers. Height: 2 to 4 inches (5 to 10 cm). Spread: indefinite. USDA Plant Hardiness Zones 3 to 9.

Arisaema
Jack-in-the-pulpit

Not so long ago there was only one Jack-in-the-pulpit available on the market: *Arisaema triphyllum,* the native species of Eastern North America, and even then, only in a very limited fashion. But if you're a plant collector, you know these curious plants are now considered to be among the most desirable of all shade plants. There are now dozens of species to choose from, but most share the same (curious) traits: a tuberous base; one or sometimes two leaves, often deeply lobed; and one of the most bizarre flowers in the Vegetable Kingdom: a hooded spathe, often striped purplish brown or green, surrounding a central column of flowers (the spadix). In the popular imagination, the spadix looks like a little man in a pulpit, whence the common name.

GROWING TIPS

Arisaema tubers are rarely offered in garden centers. Instead you're likely to be offered plants in full growth and possibly bloom in spring or early summer—at heady prices. Tubers *are* available for fall planting, though, via mail order, and cost much less.

The care of *Arisaema* is pretty straightforward: Plant the tubers or plants about 3 to 6 inches (8 to 15 cm) deep, depending on tuber size, in a shady or partially shady spot (in the North, full sun is acceptable) in rich, relatively moist soil. Good drainage is important for some species, although most don't mind soggy soils, at least in spring. Most species hold onto their leaves until mid- or even late summer (some tropical and subtropical species, indeed, are evergreen), so they are best planted in spots that don't get too dry in summer.

Since Jack-in-the-pulpits do best when allowed to grow undisturbed, they often succeed better naturalized in wooded areas than grown in flowerbeds. That doesn't mean you can't divide them to obtain more plants, though. Most reproduce slowly, producing a first offset, then another. You probably won't want to divide your plants more than once every 5 to 10 years.

PROBLEMS AND SOLUTIONS

Slugs can be a problem in spring: Hand-picking is one solution.

TOP PERFORMER

Arisaema sikokianum (Shikoku Jack-in-the-pulpit): The dark purple-brown spathe with paler veins and an upward-pointing projection rises above a white, light bulb-shaped spadix, an effect so striking I've heard visitors gasp when they saw it! There are two leaves on mature plants, usually an upper one with three lobes and a lower one with five. Some clones have leaves with silver markings, adding to their charm. The plant appears fairly early in spring in the South, where it can be subject to frost damage. In cooler climates, it is slower to appear and thus often avoids damage. Bloom time: Midspring to early summer, depending on climate. Height: 12 to 24 inches (30 to 60 cm). Spread: 18 inches (45 cm). USDA Plant Hardiness Zones 5 to 9.

MORE RECOMMENDED JACK-IN-THE-PULPITS

Arisaema candidissimum (white Jack-in-the-pulpit): This is certainly one of the most beautiful as well as one of the easiest-to-grow species. Each tuber produces a single, huge, trifoliate leaf with a mottled stem, appearing fairly late in spring or even early summer, at the same time as the flower or even after. The spathe is white with greenish stripes on the outside and pinkish purple shading inside. Late spring or early summer. Height: 12 to 20 inches (30 to 50 cm). Spread: 18 inches (45 cm). USDA Plant Hardiness Zones 6 to 9.

A. consanguineum (consanguineous Jack-in-the-pulpit): The umbrella-like leaves, taller than the flowers, are spectacular, with up to 20 narrow leaflets, mid-green, sometimes marbled with silver, radiating outward like the spokes of the wheel. The inflorescence is striped green and purple with a drooping tip and appears much later than most Jack-in-the-pulpits, in mid- or even late summer. There are several selections with distinctly silvery leaves, like 'The Perfect Wave'. Height: 2 to 4 feet (60 to 120 cm). Spread: 1 to 1½ feet (30 to 45 cm). USDA Plant Hardiness Zones 6 to 9.

LARRY'S GARDEN NOTES

Warning: Jack-in-the-pulpits are considered toxic (although perfectly ripe fruits are an exception), and even the sap can cause skin irritation on people with sensitive skin, so wear gloves when handling them. Curiously, their toxicity has never stopped native peoples from using them medicinally and even from eating the tubers as food—*after* cooking them thoroughly to destroy the toxins they contain.

White Jack-in-the-pulpit
(*Arisaema candidissimum*)

Begonia
Tuberous begonia

BEGONIA

bih-GOAN-yuh

Bloom Color:
  White, red, orange, yellow, pink, peach, and bicolor

Bloom Time:
  Summer to early fall

Length of Bloom:
  12 weeks or more

Height:
  8 to 24 inches (20 to 60 cm)

Spread:
  10 to 12 inches (25 to 30 cm)

Garden Uses:
  Container planting, edging, hanging baskets, mass planting, mixed border, specimen plant, woodland garden

Light Preference:
  Partial shade

Soil Preference:
  Humus-rich, evenly moist, well-drained soil

Best Way to Propagate:
  Take stem cuttings in spring

Hardiness:
  Frost-sensitive bulb grown as a tender annual

This is probably the best known and most widely planted of all the shade-tolerant bulbs and is certainly the most colorful and long-blooming. The flowers are often enormous and double or semidouble, some with fringed edges or bicolor flowers set off with contrasting margins. And the array of forms is just as fascinating: low and compact for borders, tall and upright for the middle of the border, or with trailing stems for hanging baskets. Even the leaves are attractive, either green or bronze and rather like wings in silhouette, with jagged edges. Plant them in masses, plant them by spots of color, or plant them in containers: However you use them, they literally sparkle in the landscape!

GROWING TIPS

The easiest way to grow tuberous begonias is simply to buy them already in full growth. The Multiflora types, such as the Pin-Up and Nonstop Series (with smaller but much more numerous blooms than the giant-flowered garden varieties), especially (although also some Pendula types for hanging baskets), are offered by the millions in garden centers by nurserymen who have both the space and the know-how to grow them to perfection.

The greatest choice in tuberous begonias, though, lies in those sold as tubers. You'll find you have hundreds of varieties to choose from, especially if you order by mail. Start the tubers indoors about 2 months before the last frost. Just barely cover the tubers with soil at first, covering up the stems to solidify them when you plant them out. Place the tubers on a window ledge in bright light with little full sun and keep their growing mix slightly moist at all times.

No matter what your initial choice, you'll find yourself with plants in full growth ready to plant outdoors. Wait until the weather warms up and there is no further danger of frost: Begonias are notoriously cold-sensitive. Some modern cultivars are said to be able to take full sun (and it may even be true if you garden in the North where the sun is naturally less intense!), but the kingdom of the tuberous begonia has always been partial shade. One reason is that, even if tuberous begonias can't take cold temperatures, neither do they like hot, humid weather. So a good mulch and partial shade will help create that cool environment they so love. Remember, too, that some of the taller types will need staking, as the stems of tuberous begonias, no matter how thick and sturdy they may look, are actually very fragile.

Tubers have to be overwintered indoors in all but the mildest climates. Even in Florida, many gardeners prefer to bring them in for winter or at least move potted begonias under an overhanging roof, as winter rains are likely to cause rot.

When tubers sprout in spring, they usually produce several stems, and you can remove and root any excess ones. You can also cut older tubers in half, between two growing points, and pot them up individually. I suggest leaving the cut surface exposed (you could always plant the tubers on an angle) until it heals over.

Tuberous begonia
(*Begonia* Tuberhybrida Hybrid)

PROBLEMS AND SOLUTIONS

Leaf diseases and rot may occur. Providing good air circulation and watering from below, keeping the soil moist but not soggy, will help prevent them.

TOP PERFORMER

Begonia Tuberhybrida Hybrids (tuberous begonia): This is by far the most popular of the tuberous-type begonias, with literally hundreds of cultivars and a wide variety of growth habits, flower colors, and flower types. Oddly, though, there is no plant even similar to it in the wild. The tuberous begonia as we know it is a complex, man-made species developed by crossing several summer-blooming, tuberous species from South America. Height: 8 to 24 inches (20 to 60 cm). Spread: 10 to 12 inches (25 to 30 cm).

MORE RECOMMENDED
TUBEROUS BEGONIAS

Begonia boliviensis (Bolivian tuberous begonia): This is a beauty, with hundreds of long, narrow, hanging flowers in bright scarlet-orange on arching stems. It blooms in summer. Height: 2 feet (60 cm). Spread: 2 feet (60 cm).

LARRY'S GARDEN NOTES

To save or not to save? That truly is the question with tuberous begonias. Not all are worthwhile saving over winter. Those bought individually as tubers certainly are: After all, they are unique clones developed over years of breeding and offer unique characteristics. Many of the seed-grown lines, however, were developed for use as annuals, and some of the Multiflora types, like the Pin-Up and Nonstop series, form only tiny tubers that are hard to overwinter. They'll be available the following spring in six-packs at very reasonable prices, and from seed at unbeatable ones. So don't feel guilty if you feel it is easier to let them freeze than to store them indoors: Most gardeners do the same!

Bletilla
Ground orchid

BLETILLA

ble-TILL-uh

Bloom Color:
  Magenta and white

Bloom Time:
  Early to midsummer

Length of Bloom:
  2 to 3 weeks

Height:
  10 to 16 inches (25 to 40 cm)

Spread:
  Indefinite

Garden Uses:
  Container planting, mass planting, mixed border, rock garden, woodland garden

Light Preference:
  Partial shade

Soil Preference:
  Humus-rich, moist, well-drained soil

Best Way to Propagate:
  Divide in early spring

USDA Plant Hardiness Zones:
  5 to 9

Orchids are the most desirable of all flowering plants. That's fine if you grow houseplants, as most orchids are tropical plants, but most hardy orchids are expensive, difficult to establish, and really just not good garden plants. Ground orchids are one major exception. Here you have an inexpensive garden plant that requires no special care and produces abundant, very attractive flowers—scented to boot! And its blooms, while not gigantic, are at least large enough to be recognizable as orchid flowers, so you garner extra brownie points from your neighbors as a true plantsperson!

GROWING TIPS

Ground orchids are surprisingly easy to grow. They prefer a soil rich in humus, moist yet well drained. They prefer to neither soak in water nor be exposed to drought. You can also grow ground orchids in containers, in ordinary potting soil (orchid mixes are not required), and bring them indoors for winter—something you might want to try if you live in a climate where winters are too cold to raise them outdoors.

Partial shade is ideal: Like many hardy bulbs, they love full sun in spring, when it is still cool, but can burn in full sun. An eastern exposure is much to their liking: Morning sun is fairly cool. In northern gardens, where the sunlight is less intense, you could try them in full sun.

Ground orchids grow from flat-sided "pseudobulbs" (bulb-like structures) and may be sold as dormant bulbs or, again, in pots in full growth. Usually they are planted very shallowly with the tip of the pseudobulb exposed, but I've been experimenting with deeper planting depths as a means of adapting them to my colder-than-average climate and find they grow just as well, at least in fairly light soil, when planted 8 to 10 inches (20 to 25 cm) deep.

The advantage of deeper planting in colder climates is that it protects the pseudobulbs from the cold; in warmer ones, it helps delay sprouting. That's an important point, as one of the main flaws of ground orchids is that they tend to come up too early in spring and are thus subject to damage from late frosts. Deeper planting can help slow the apparition of the leaves by 2 weeks or even more!

Mulching is always wise with ground orchids. They are not very drought-tolerant, and mulch helps to keep the soil distinctly moister. Mulch also adds a bit more frost protection.

Ground orchids gradually form colonies and don't tend to become overcrowded and need dividing, so they make great choices for naturalizing. However, that does not mean you can't divide them if you need more plants for a different site.

Chinese ground orchid
(*Bletilla striata*)

PROBLEMS AND SOLUTIONS

Other than frost damage, this orchid tends to have few problems.

TOP PERFORMER

Bletilla striata (Chinese ground orchid, hyacinth bletilla): This is the only commonly available species of the relatively small genus *Bletilla* (9 to 10 species) and is also probably the hardiest. It produces three or four grasslike, pleated, deciduous leaves per pseudobulb very early in spring, followed by the very attractive flowers. They have the typical orchid shape of five relatively similar petals and sepals, with one petal much more highly developed, called the labellum. The usual flower color is magenta or pink with a darker labellum, but there are white-flowered varieties as well, usually offered under the cultivar name 'Alba'. *B. striata* 'Albostriata' is a charming clone with the usual magenta-pink flowers, but its leaves are bordered with a thin white band, creating a very elegant appearance in the garden when the plant is not in bloom. In fact, if you can find this plant at a good price, you'll probably prefer this to the species: It actually makes quite an attractive groundcover! 'Aurea' is new to me, with white flowers but a yellow labellum marked with purple.

LARRY'S GARDEN NOTES

Warning: There are plenty of other terrestrial orchids that do well in partial shade to shade, many of them natives, like the spectacular lady's slippers (*Cypripedium* spp.), but I hesitate to recommend any of them. First, they are very expensive and also very capricious: Unless you plant them in just the right spot, they quickly peter out, so the level of "gardener satisfaction" is usually quite low. More importantly, though, there is a huge underground market for these plants and, although they are protected almost everywhere, many plants are still taken from the wild every year, to the point where many species are considered threatened. And I don't want to encourage such exploitation. If you insist on growing native orchids, don't buy them from anyone but a dealer specifically advertising he sells only nursery-grown plants.

Caladium

Caladium, elephant's ear, angel wings

PLANT PROFILE

CALADIUM

ka-LAY-dee-um

Foliage Color:
  White, pink, red, and green

Foliage Time:
  Late spring until frost

Height:
  8 to 24 inches (20 to 60 cm)

Spread:
  8 to 24 inches (20 to 60 cm)

Garden Uses:
  Container planting, houseplant, mass planting, mixed border, rock garden, specimen plant, woodland garden

Light Preference:
  Partial shade to shade

Soil Preference:
  Humus-rich, well-drained, evenly moist soil

Best Way to Propagate:
  Divide tubers in spring

Hardiness:
  Frost-sensitive plant grown as a tender bulb

Not many plants can beat the ever-popular coleus (page 260) when it comes to colorful foliage, but caladiums are certainly neck-and-neck, if not ahead by a nose. Indeed, how not to fall instantly in love with such gaudy colors? The arrow- to heart-shaped leaves are awash in translucent whites, pinks, and reds, some with barely any green at all—only a few veins or perhaps a green margin. With a bit of light behind them, the leaves literally glow like fluorescent lights.

GROWING TIPS

You'll find merchants selling potted caladiums in full growth, as gift plants, from late winter right through fall, usually at outrageous prices. Wise (or cash-strapped) gardeners, however, know they are easily grown from tubers for a fraction of the cost. The dormant tubers can actually be started in just about any season for use as houseplants, but assuming you want to use them in the outdoor garden, don't start watering them in February or the show will nearly be over before summer arrives!

If you live in an area with long, hot summers, you can plant the tubers directly outdoors, about 3 to 5 inches (8 to 12 cm) deep, after all danger of frost is well past. There's no use planting them out until the soil is warm and nights are above 65°F (15°C): They may rot if placed in cool soil. At any rate, they need warmth to sprout.

Most home gardeners, though, will find it advantageous to start them indoors about 6 to 8 weeks before the last frost. That way they'll be already well advanced and ready to color your garden when you plant them out. Start them in pots, covering the tubers with about 2 inches (5 cm) of growing mix. It's easy to tell which side goes upward: There are sprouts present at planting time. Moisten the potting mix lightly, then place the pots in a warm, well-lit spot, but not in full sun. Water them as needed to keep the mix evenly moist. Once both the air and the ground have warmed up thoroughly, you can acclimate the plants to outdoor conditions, then plant them out. Sink the tuber an inch or two (2.5 to 5 cm) deeper into the ground than it was in the pot.

The ideal spot for planting out caladiums is in shade or partial shade (although some newer cultivars, notably in the Florida Series, are quite sun-resistant), in a rich, well-drained soil with little root competition (or leave them in their pots so the roots surrounding can't get in and choke them). Avoid windy spots—the large leaves are fragile.

Cut off any greenish white Jack-in-the-pulpit-like flowers that appear: They add nothing to the plant's appearance and drain the tuber of the energy it would otherwise store up for next year's show. Keep the plants moist at all times. When they start to go downhill, withhold water until the leaves wither on their own.

In most climates, lift and clean the tubers in fall and store them dry indoors over winter. Unlike most tender bulbs, they don't need (and indeed dislike) extremely cool temperatures: room temperatures, about 55° to 75°F (13° to 24°C), are fine for storage. In Zones 10 and 11, test leaving them outdoors for winter. Some cultivars will even naturalize if conditions are to their liking.

Caladium (*Caladium bicolor* 'Red Flash')

PROBLEMS AND SOLUTIONS

Rot or leaf diseases can be a problem if dormant tubers are kept too cool: Wait until you can ensure warm temperatures (65°F/18°C) before starting them. Spider mites and aphids, sometimes a problem indoors, can be sprayed away with water.

TOP PERFORMER

Caladium bicolor, syn. *C.* × *hortulanum* (caladium, elephant's ears, angel wings): This is the only species widely distributed. There are theoretically over 1,000 cultivars, but you'd be lucky to find more than 4 or 5 in most garden centers. There are two main categories: Those with broad, heart-shaped or arrow-shaped leaves, called fancy-leaf caladiums, are the most widely available. The so-called lance-leaf or strap-leaf caladiums have very narrow leaves that are less obviously arrow-shaped than the fancy-leaf types, and are usually available only by mail order. You can likewise find dwarf varieties (less then 12 inches/30 cm tall) or standards (1 to 2 feet/30 to 60 cm tall). Height: 8 to 24 inches (20 to 60 cm). Spread: 8 to 24 inches (20 to 60 cm).

LARRY'S GARDEN NOTES

Planting caladium tubers right side up gives large leaves, but they are relatively few in number. If you prefer a profusion of smaller leaves for a denser appearance, plant the tubers upside down, with the sprouts pointing toward the ground. This also causes the tuber to divide more prolifically, resulting in several new offsets the following growing season. Oddly enough, the tuber will essentially right itself during the growing season, so if you want to maintain this "dwarf but dense" appearance from year to year, keep repotting the tubers upside down!

Chionodoxa
Glory-of-the-snow

PLANT PROFILE

CHIONODOXA

kee-on-oh-DOX-uh

Bloom Color:
  Blue, white, and pink

Bloom Time:
  Early spring

Length of Bloom:
  2 to 4 weeks

Height:
  3 to 8 inches (8 to 20 cm)

Spread:
  2 to 3 inches (5 to 8 cm)

Garden Uses:
  Container planting, edging, mass planting, meadow garden, mixed border, rock garden, woodland garden

Light Preference:
  Full sun to partial shade in spring; indifferent in other seasons

Soil Preference:
  Any well-drained soil; moist in spring, drier in summer

Best Way to Propagate:
  Divide as leaves yellow

USDA Plant Hardiness Zones:
  3 to 8

Spring brings many bulb flowers, and glory-of-the-snow is one of the most prolific. Although each bulb bears only two or three narrow, grasslike leaves; the plants are only inches high; and the starry flowers, usually blue with a white eye, are not that large; their very number creates much impact in the garden. Planted in large colonies (and this bulb is cheap enough that you can afford to plant clumps of 30 or more), it really stands out from year one. Then, as long as you leave the seed capsules intact, the display gets better and better, as the plants self-sow prolifically. Soon you have a carpet of blue to greet the spring!

GROWING TIPS

The is one of the many spring ephemerals, up early in spring and totally dormant by summer. Since it is indifferent to summer conditions (exception bog conditions), you can pretty much plant it wherever you want: As long as the bulbs get some sun in spring, they'll do fine, even under the dense foliage of deciduous trees and shrubs. And the bulbs seem indifferent to soil type as well—poor or rich, even fairly compact—nothing seems to bother them.

Plant the bulbs 3 to 4 inches (8 to 10 cm) deep in fall and water once. From then on, they'll take care of themselves. There is no need to remove faded flowers (unless you don't want them to spread, of course), and the narrow leaves disappear all on their own. Glories-of-the-snow look as wonderful in flowerbeds as they do naturalized in lawns or woodlands.

All glories-of-the-snow are dependent on cold winters in order to bloom: Without at least 2 months of cold, the bulb doesn't get the signal to bloom and remains dormant. In warmer parts of the country, you'll have to judge whether your winters are severe enough for good results.

Most gardeners don't bother multiplying glories-of-the-snow. First, they're cheap enough to sow by the bucketful; second, they self-sow so prolifically. However, if you want to do so, the fastest way is to simply dig up, divide, and replant the bulbs when the foliage yellows. Even fairly small bulbs will bloom the following spring. You can also divide them in fall—if you can remember where you planted them! The seed capsules are fairly large and crack open to reveal numerous seeds you can also harvest and sow in an out-of-the-way corner of the garden. Personally, I just pick them up and fling them about (notably into my neighbors' yard; the poor people just don't have enough flowers!) to help the colony expand faster and farther.

PROBLEMS AND SOLUTIONS

Glory-of-the-snow rarely seems to suffer from insects or disease.

TOP PERFORMER

Chionodoxa forbesii (Forbes' glory-of-the-snow): Confusion is total when it comes to identifying glories-of-the-snow. Most bulbs sold are labeled *C. luciliae,* but according to botanists, that species, described below, is fairly rare in culture. What you have probably bought under that name is *C. forbesii.* Which glory-of-the-snow is which? I suggest not worrying too much about it: *C. forbesii* and *C. luciliae* are fairly similar in appearance and essentially identical in color and results. If you insist on knowing, *C. forbesii* produces more flowers per stem than its cousin—from 4 to 12—and therefore creates a mass of bloom more quickly. The flowers are blue with a white eye. 'Blue Giant' and 'Pink Giant', with attractive pink flowers, are common cultivars. There is also a *C. forbesii* 'Alba', with pure white flowers. Height: 3 to 8 inches (8 to 20 cm). Spread: 2 to 3 inches (5 to 8 cm). USDA Plant Hardiness Zones 3 to 8.

MORE RECOMMENDED GLORIES-OF-THE-SNOW

Chionodoxa luciliae (Lucile's glory-of-the-snow): Inexorably confused with *C. forbesii* on the market, *C. luciliae* is a similar blue color, although with a smaller white center, and best distinguished by the number of blooms per stem: only two or three. The bulbs sold as *C. gigantea* are now classified as *C. luciliae* Gigantea Group. They have larger flowers and taller stems: up to 8 inches (20 cm) high. *C. luciliae* 'Alba', with sparkling white flowers, is the most common of the white glories-of-the-snow. Bloom time: Early spring. Height: 4 to 6 inches (10 to 15 cm). Spread: 2 to 3 inches (5 to 8 cm). USDA Plant Hardiness Zones 3 to 8.

Forbes' glory-of-the-snow
(*Chionodoxa forbesii*)

KISSING COUSINS

× *Chionoscilla allenii* is one of the very rare intergeneric crosses available to outdoor gardeners—that is, crosses between plants of two different genera, much as a horse can be crossed with a donkey to give a mule. In this case, it is a cross between a glory-of-the-snow (*Chionodoxa forbesii*) and a squill (*Scilla bifolia*) and is actually very much intermediate between the two. You mostly notice its bright blue flowers without a white throat are smaller than those of its glory-of-the-snow parent, but borne in denser clusters. It is sterile (produces no seed) and must be multiplied by division, which explains its exorbitant cost.

Colchicum
Colchicum, autumn crocus, meadow saffron

Colchicums are the best fall-blooming bulbs, bar none. Imagine! A big, cup-shaped flower on a very short stem arises from the ground in fall without a single leaf to hide it—and there are often so many flowers you can't even see the soil. Curiously, the leaves do appear the following spring. They are lance-shaped, dark green, and quite shiny: not at all unattractive until they start to go dormant, creating a yellowing mess.

GROWING TIPS

The main secret to growing colchicums as garden plants is getting the bulbs (actually large corms) into the ground early enough. Depending on the species and cultivar, they start to bloom anywhere from late August to mid-October. I've planted them one day and seen the first blooms 2 days later!

Place the bulbs in a planting hole about 6 inches (15 cm) deep in a spot that is sunny to partially shady in spring. The species and cultivars described here adapt well to average garden conditions: good, well-drained soil and at least moderate spring sun. As long as they aren't sitting in water all the time, they'll probably do just fine. Colchicums are indifferent to summer shade. They do require 2 months or so of cool to cold temperatures in winter, so they will do well only in the parts of Zones 8 and 9 that meet those conditions.

How to deal with the large spring leaves, especially when they go through their "ugly duckling" phase as they go dormant in early summer? Try planting them through a groundcover like pachysandra (page 200) or periwinkles (*Vinca* spp., page 226), or in a bed of perennials with arching leaves, like hostas or daylilies (*Hemerocallis* spp.). Or naturalize them in a flowering meadow to extend its season of interest into fall.

Among the some 45 species of *Colchicum*, some have a different cycle. You'll find a few that produce both flowers and leaves in fall—and even one (the only yellow-flowered species: *C. luteum*) that produces both flowers and leaves in spring. All are summer-dormant.

Colchicums are among the most perennial of all bulbs. Plant

them today and your great-great-grandkids will still be enjoying them when they retire. The corms multiply slowly but surely: They don't need division to keep on blooming, but you might want to dig them up and separate them to obtain more bulbs.

Warning: All parts of this plant are poisonous, especially the bulb.

Colchicum
(*Colchicum* 'Lilac Wonder')

PROBLEMS AND SOLUTIONS

Slugs can be a problem. For solutions, see page 85.

TOP PERFORMER

Colchicum Hybrids (hybrid colchicums): The hybrid varieties are by far the most popular on the market and, indeed, often all that is available, at least from local garden centers. They generally have huge flowers in various shades of pink or purplish pink. *C.* 'The Giant' is goblet-shaped, with lilac-pink flowers lightly checked white and a white base. 'Lilac Wonder' has deep lilac-pink flowers with rather narrow petals; 'Violet Queen' produces checkered, scented pinkish violet flowers with pointed petals. The most spectacular one is 'Waterlily', with fully double pinkish lilac flowers. They truly are the size and shape of waterlilies! However, the huge blooms are also heavier than most and tend to flop when it rains, turning into a bedraggled mess. Bloom time: Late summer and early fall. Height: 6 to 8 inches (15 to 20 cm). Spread: 6 to 16 inches (15 to 40 cm). USDA Plant Hardiness Zones 4 to 9.

MORE RECOMMENDED COLCHICUMS

Colchicum autumnale (autumn colchicum): Although the lavender-pink flowers aren't as large as many of the hybrid colchicums, it spreads more rapidly than most, creating a sizeable colony with plenty of impact. 'Album' has white flowers. Height: 4 to 6 inches (10 to 15 cm). Spread: 6 to 16 inches (15 to 40 cm). USDA Plant Hardiness Zones 4 to 9.

KISSING COUSINS

One bulb we simply don't see enough of in gardens is spring meadow saffron or, more simply, bulbocodium (*Bulbocodium vernum*). It is just like a colchicum, with the same purple-pink funnel-shaped flowers, although with petals a bit more strap-shaped, but the major difference is that it blooms first thing in spring, with the crocuses. And the glossy leaves appear only after the flowers have finished, allowing them to shine in all their glory without any greenery to hide them. It is also easy to grow, multiplies rapidly by division, and is extremely hardy. Personally, I wouldn't be at all surprised to see taxonomists put this plant in the genus *Colchicum* one day: The two genera are really very similar! Height: 4 to 5 inches (10 to 12 cm). Spread: 4 to 5 inches (10 to 12 cm). USDA Plant Hardiness Zones 2 to 8.

Cyclamen
Hardy cyclamen

PLANT PROFILE

CYCLAMEN

SICK-la-men, SYKE-la-men

Bloom Color:
Purple, pink, and white

Bloom Time:
Spring or fall, depending on species

Length of Bloom:
12 weeks or more

Height:
4 to 6 inches (10 to 15 cm)

Spread:
6 to 12 inches (15 to 30 cm)

Garden Uses:
Container planting, mass planting, mixed border, rock garden, woodland garden

Light Preference:
Partial shade to shade

Soil Preference:
Humus-rich, well-drained soil; moist in spring, drier to dry in summer

Best Way to Propagate:
Replant self-sown tubers elsewhere

USDA Plant Hardiness Zones:
5 to 9

Everyone knows the florists' cyclamen (*Cyclamen persicum*), with its often huge upside-down flowers, but it is grown strictly as a houseplant. Its smaller, hardier cousins are less well known: perfect miniature replicas of the florists' cyclamen that you can pepper about a woodland area or rock garden. Curiously, you'll find spring-, summer-, and fall-blooming species: Mix them together for bloom through much of the year.

GROWING TIPS

In their native Eurasia, hardy cyclamens are plants of the deep woods, thriving in forest litter in just about any kind of soil. In culture, they like similar conditions. They're not plants for the "flower border," but rather for naturalizing in forested areas or in rock gardens where they can self-sow to their heart's content.

Ideal conditions would include lots of humus, cool soil fall through spring, and excellent drainage yet even moisture throughout the growing season. Species that are summer-dormant, though, are very drought-tolerant at that season. Hardy cyclamens seem indifferent to poor light and variable soil pH.

Establishing hardy cyclamen tubers is an art in itself, and controversy reigns supreme on how to plant them. Some people insist they be planted very shallowly, with only a slight covering of leaf litter; others insist they need deep planting. Actually, both are correct. In areas with mild winters (usually Zones 7 to 9), you'll see faster results if you simply scrape away a bit of soil from the planting site, drop the tuber in, and just push the soil back into place. Cyclamen tubers have contractile roots and will pull themselves down to the proper depth, according to local conditions, over time. In colder climates, though, certainly Zone 6 and below, the tubers will freeze unless they are planted deeply. Dig down, way down, and plant them at least 12 inches (30 cm) deep.

The tubers generally available commercially are in very poor shape. They hate sitting on store shelves for weeks on end! The best way to establish cyclamens is to therefore buy them in pots; then you can transplant them to the garden with their roots undisturbed, and success is almost guaranteed. Or buy tubers from mail-order sources specializing in hardy cyclamens—they harvest the tubers just before shipping, meaning you can replant them within days.

Once established, hardy cyclamens resent disturbance and, indeed, their tubers sink down to incredible depths, making harvesting them nigh to impossible. Rather than dividing them, wait for self-sown seedlings to appear, then dig them up carefully, and move them while they are young. Or just let them sow themselves about as they see fit.

PROBLEMS AND SOLUTIONS

Squirrels and voles can be a real nuisance: Deep planting will discourage them. Spider mites, cyclamen mites, and vine weevils are possible predators; insecticidal soap will help control them.

TOP PERFORMER

Cyclamen hederifolium (ivyleaf cyclamen, baby cyclamen, hardy cyclamen): This is the most widely available species, with a fall flower display that can last for months. Leaves appear after the flowers and last through winter, disappearing by summer. It is a variable plant, with flowers usually in various shades of pink, although white flowers are not uncommon; the leaves can be heart-shaped or triangular, toothed or not, green or purple below, and green or highly silvery marbled above. Height: 4 inches (10 cm). Spread: 6 to 12 inches (15 to 30 cm). USDA Plant Hardiness Zones 5 to 9.

MORE RECOMMENDED HARDY CYCLAMENS

Cyclamen coum (roundleaf cyclamen, eastern cyclamen, hardy cyclamen): Almost as widely available as *C. hederifolium*, but with smaller leaves. It is considered a "winterbloomer" in mild climates, flowering from late fall through to late winter, but a spring-bloomer elsewhere. The flowers are pink or purple-pink, and leaves are of variable color. *C. purpurascens* is similar but blooms in summer. Height: 2 to 4 inches (5 to 10 cm). Spread: 6 to 12 inches (15 to 30 cm). USDA Plant Hardiness Zones 6 to 9.

LARRY'S GARDEN NOTES

Don't ignore your cyclamens simply because they have stopped blooming: Watching the antics of the flowerstalks after they bloom is fascinating. After the petals fade and the seed capsule starts to form, the stalk lengthens but also starts to curl up, evenly forming a dense spiral, pulling the seeds closer to the tuber and down toward the ground, eventually planting them in the leaf litter near the mother plant.

Roundleaf cyclamen
(*Cyclamen coum*)

Eranthis
Winter aconite

PLANT PROFILE

ERANTHIS
er-ANTH-is

Bloom Color:
 Yellow

Bloom Time:
 Late winter to early spring

Length of Bloom:
 1 to 4 weeks

Height:
 2 to 4 inches (5 to 10 cm)

Spread:
 2 to 4 inches (5 to 10 cm)

Garden Uses:
 Container planting, edging, groundcover, mass planting, meadow garden, mixed border, rock garden, woodland garden

Light Preference:
 Full sun to shade

Soil Preference:
 Humus-rich, well-drained, moist, alkaline to slightly acid soil

Best Way to Propagate:
 Separate tubers after flowering

USDA Plant Hardiness Zones:
 3 to 8

Winter aconite offers blooms so early that, in many areas, it is still officially winter. In fact, in Zone 8 (about the highest zone where it receives the winter cold it needs), it may bloom in January! The plant itself is minimalist in the extreme: underground tuber, a single stem, a collar of foliage consisting of only two deeply cut leaves and one single cup-shaped, upward-facing blossom. On the other hand, the flower is nearly as big as the plant: Only the tips of the leaves show when it is in bloom. The color is so vibrant—a true buttercup yellow—that this tiny gem is an immediate attention-grabber.

GROWING TIPS

Winter aconites are a snap to grow once you have them established. The problem is getting to that point. You see, the tubers dislike drying out completely, yet they are shipped dry by the thousands each fall, and they sit on garden center shelves for weeks. The longer you wait to plant them, the weaker the tubers become, and soon you'll find you have little or no sprouting the following spring.

My suggestion? Buy them early, as soon as they arrive in the store, and don't wait to plant them. If you order them by mail, they usually arrive more promptly, but once again, plant them without waiting.

When you do plant winter aconite tubers, take the time to give them a good 24-hour soak in water: This helps plump up the tubers and gives them a good head start. Theoretically the flattened part of the tuber should point upward and the rounded part downward, but the plant soon rights itself if you get that wrong. Set them about 2 inches (5 cm) deep (twice that in colder climates) in humus-rich, well-drained soil.

All winter aconites really need to be happy is cool to cold winters (like many spring bulbs, they won't bloom without at least a 2-month cold period), spring sun, and soil that remains at least moderately moist all year. Those sun-baked, dry-to-the-bone beds that tulips so love are not for them: They do best in fresh meadows and moist, open woodlands. They are superior plants for naturalizing: Once established, they self-sow prolifically, creating gorgeous carpets of brilliant yellow flowers. They do equally well naturalized in lawns and forested areas.

After winter aconites finish blooming, their stems almost double in height and the leaves increase in size, presumably to better catch the sunlight. The seed capsules form as soon as the sepals drop and mature rapidly, providing plenty of brown seeds you can either allow to spread naturally, or harvest and broadcast. You can also harvest them and sow them without delay in a nursery for tubers to plant out in 2 or 3 years. Or dig up and divide the tubers (you may have to break or cut them between growing points) as the leaves start to go yellow in mid- to late spring.

PROBLEMS AND SOLUTIONS

Slugs are usually more an annoyance than a true problem, but you may have to control them (see page 85) if they are very numerous. There are few other problems.

TOP PERFORMER

Eranthis hyemalis (winter aconite): This is the most widely available species and if it is the one offered locally, go for it. There is so little difference between the different winter aconites that it really doesn't matter which you choose. This species is said to have greener leaves (never coppery) and somewhat later blooms (like, by a day or two) than *E. cilicica.* In my garden, though, both bloom precisely at the same time. Height: 2 to 4 inches (5 to 10 cm). Spread: 2 to 4 inches (5 to 10 cm). USDA Plant Hardiness Zones 3 to 8.

MORE RECOMMENDED WINTER ACONITES

Eranthis cilicica (Sicilian winter aconite): Most botanists now consider *E. cilicica* to be a mere variant of *E. hyemalis* (*E. hyemalis* Cilicica Group). The leaves have more divisions than the previous species and have a distinct reddish tinge as they appear in very early spring. The flowers may appear a tad earlier in some climates. Height: 2 to 4 inches (5 to 10 cm). Spread: 2 to 4 inches (5 to 10 cm). USDA Plant Hardiness Zones 3 to 8.

Winter aconite (*Eranthis hyemalis*)

LARRY'S GARDEN NOTES

Believe it or not, winter aconites get a leg up on spring by actually melting the snow around them. The tubers give off a small amount of heat, enough sometimes to create a circle of green around the plant in an otherwise white landscape. This internal heating technique, called thermogenesis, is actually not all that unusual: The eastern skunk cabbage (*Symplocarpus foetidus*) does the same thing on an even greater scale. Its huge flower bud can push right through a thick layer of ice by producing temperatures up to 63°F (35°C) greater than the surrounding air.

Erythronium

Trout lily, fawn lily, dog's-tooth violet

PLANT PROFILE

ERYTHRONIUM

ai-rith-RONE-ee-um

Bloom Color:
 Yellow, pink, and white

Bloom Time:
 Early spring

Length of Bloom:
 2 to 3 weeks

Height:
 Varies by species; see
 individual listings

Spread:
 Varies by species; see
 individual listings

Garden Uses:
 Mass planting, mixed border,
 rock garden, woodland
 garden; along paths

Light Preference:
 Partial shade to shade

Soil Preference:
 Humus-rich, well-drained soil;
 moist in spring, drier in
 summer

Best Way to Propagate:
 Separate bulbs as leaves
 yellow in summer

USDA Plant Hardiness Zones:
 Varies by species; see
 individual listings

These diminutive spring flowers send up their leaves and flowers in early spring, while the sun can still filter through the branches above. Most of the 22 species produce only two oval leaves, often lying flat on the ground. They tend to be attractively mottled reddish brown and green, although they can also be entirely green. The pendant flowers, borne alone or in groups from an arching stem, have dangling anthers, six curving petals/sepals, and look very much like miniature Turk's cap lilies (*Lilium* spp.).

GROWING TIPS

The bulbs lack any kind of tunic or any other protective covering, so they are very susceptible to drying out if left in the open air for any length of time. If you're buying them locally, do so early and store them cool, in lightly moistened peat moss, wood shavings, vermiculite, or perlite if you can't plant them at once. Better yet, order them by mail and the nursery will keep them cool for you, then ship them right at planting time.

This plant thrives in spots that have spring sun, but does surprisingly well under the constant shade of conifers as well. Sun is acceptable in the North or anywhere the leaves aren't exposed to burning-hot sun. The bulbs are very tolerant of root competition.

Plant the bulbs 4 inches (10 cm) deep in humus-rich soil. It is especially important to add mycorrhizal fungi inoculant with this bulb: Some species, notably *E. americanum*, seem dependent on it in order to bloom well. Covering the bulbs with mulch when you finish makes good sense: They usually live where there is lots of leaf litter in the wild. Trout lilies prefer conditions where they are never completely dry.

They really should be planted in fairly large clumps: no fewer than 15 to 20 bulbs for the smaller types, and 10 or so for the larger ones. The species are perfect naturalizers and indeed tend to look better in a wild surrounding, whether in an open woodland or a clearing. The taller types are large enough to hold their own in a flowerbed.

All trout lilies multiply by producing secondary bulbs at their base, and most will spread quite readily, albeit slowly, by self-sown seed. Some types produce underground stolons.

PROBLEMS AND SOLUTIONS

Slugs can be a problem and may need to be controlled; see page 85 for suggestions. There are occasional minor leaf problems, but treatment is rarely required.

TOP PERFORMER

Erythronium Hybrids (hybrid fawn lily, hybrid dog's-tooth violet): These are the big, I-can't-believe-they-are-fawn-lily types, with larger leaves than most species and much larger flowers. They form clumps but don't spread well on their own: You'll have to divide and replant them if you want to create large carpets of bloom. 'Pagoda' has sulfur yellow flowers bearing a brownish ring at their base and large, glossy, only slightly mottled leaves. 'Kondo' produces scented sulfur yellow blooms lightly touched with green and a burgundy center ring. Its leaves are nicely mottled at first, but the mottling fades after the plants bloom. 'Citronella' has clearer yellow flowers than the others, with mid-green leaves mottled light purple. All three bear three or four large flowers, sometimes more, per stem. Height: 6 to 14 inches (15 to 35 cm). Spread: 4 inches (10 cm). USDA Plant Hardiness Zones 4 to 9.

MORE RECOMMENDED TROUT LILIES

Erythronium dens-canis (European dog's-tooth violet): This is a highly variable species, common throughout Europe and also much of Asia, with white, pink, purple, or lilac flowers usually showing a ring of purple at the base and anything from heavily mottled foliage to pure green leaves to leaves with a silvery sheen. The hanging blooms are borne one per stem. Cultivars abound, among them 'Lilac Wonder', with rich lilac flowers and a chocolate brown ring; 'Rose Queen', with pink flowers; 'Snowflake', with pure white flowers; and 'Frans Hals', with imperial purple flowers with a greenish bronze ring. Height: 4 to 6 inches (10 to 15 cm). Spread: 4 inches (10 cm). USDA Plant Hardiness Zones 3 to 9.

Hybrid fawn lily
(*Erythronium* 'Pagoda')

LARRY'S GARDEN NOTES

The curious common names for *Erythronium*, trout lily and fawn lily, both refer to the plant's foliage, which is mottled like a trout or a fawn. In fact, *erythros* means red and refers to this mottling. As for the curious name dog's tooth violet, you have to dig up a bulb to figure it out: It is creamy white and rounded at the base, arching to a pointed tip like a dog's canine tooth. On the other hand, if dogs had canines that soft, they'd have to eat baby food!

Galanthus
Snowdrop

For many people, this is the first flower of spring and is therefore an absolute must. The grasslike plants quickly form thick clumps of narrow, dark green leaves from among which rise thin stems. These each bear one dangling flower on a thin, narrow thread that dances in the slightest breeze. The blooms are made up of three inner petals forming a small crown, white marked with green. The three outer petals are pure white and hang out over the inner ones rather like a propeller. All told, a sweet little plant that has to be planted in masses if you want to get much of an effect.

GROWING TIPS

Snowdrops evolved in a fairly humid environment and don't need the baking heat that some sun-loving bulbs need to mature. That also means they dislike drying out for any length of time. As soon as they arrive in stores in fall is the time to plant them: Delaying will just decrease your chances of success.

Plant the small bulbs about 3 to 4 inches (8 to 10 cm) deep in just about any kind of soil, as long as good drainage can be assured. In nature, they are plants of grassy meadows and open forest: They do like at least dappled spring sunshine. They quickly go dormant, and you'll find they do perfectly well in deciduous woods or planted under trees and shrubs, especially since root competition is tolerated with great aplomb.

The flowers can last and last if the weather is cool enough: I have seen them still in bloom 6 weeks after the buds first opened when the spring was extremely cold. Frost, even severe, doesn't seem to bother them in the slightest and they come unscathed through late snowfalls. A hot spell, though, could end the show much, much sooner.

Common snowdrop bulbs are about as cheap as they come, and there's no excuse for moaning about their insignificant blooms if you plant only 10 to 12. These are bulbs to plant by the hundreds: You'll want them popping up everywhere in lawns, gardens, and forests, where they are superb naturalizers. Each bulb quickly forms a clump, so the display just keeps getting better and better for the first 10 years or so. After that, it remains about the same from year to year, but at least it doesn't decline, so you don't have to divide the clumps to keep them going. One occasionally hears about clumps that are 40 years old or more and are still blooming away.

Warning: The bulb, leaves, and flowers are all slightly poisonous, so keep them away from children and pets—especially the bulbs, which could be mistaken for tiny onions.

PROBLEMS AND SOLUTIONS

Narcissus fly may attack large bulbs, but that doesn't stop the smaller ones nearby from flowering. Other than that, there are few problems.

TOP PERFORMER

Galanthus nivalis (common snowdrop): Sure, this is the ordinary, everyday snowdrop that every gardener knows, but it has the advantage of being widely available and inexpensive, putting it ahead of its peers. Besides, there is nothing more like one snowdrop than another, so does it really matter which one you buy? The flowers are small but numerous, and its rock-solid performance is a definite plus. There are lots of cultivars, most at outrageous prices, including 'Lutescens', with the inner petals marked with yellow instead of green; and 'Viridapicis', with green marks on both the inner and outer petals; but they're really only for collectors. More reasonable in price and more widely available is 'Flore Pleno', with double flowers. The main interest is that the flowers look fuller: From above, the point of view from which most of us see snowdrops, you won't notice they are double. Height: 4 to 8 inches (10 to 20 cm). Spread: 4 inches (10 cm). USDA Plant Hardiness Zones 3 to 9.

MORE RECOMMENDED SNOWDROPS

Galanthus elwesii (giant snowdrop): Both flowers and leaves are larger than those of the common snowdrop. It blooms a tad later (a week or so). Height: 5 to 9 inches (12 to 23 cm). Spread: 4 inches (10 cm). USDA Plant Hardiness Zones 4 to 9.

Giant snowdrop (*Galanthus elwesii*)

LARRY'S GARDEN NOTES

Are snowdrops really the first spring bulbs to flower? That will probably depend on your growing conditions, but it is certain that they are at least in a neck-and-neck race with one other bulb: the winter aconite. One or the other can bloom as early as January in the right climate and are often in flower only a few days after snowmelt in others. Try both and see which wins in your yard!

Hyacinthoides
Bluebells

HYACINTHOIDES

hy-a-sinth-OY-dees

Bloom Color:
Blue, pink, and white

Bloom Time:
Late spring

Length of Bloom:
2 to 4 weeks

Height:
8 to 18 inches (20 to 45 cm)

Spread:
4 to 6 inches (10 to 15 cm)

Garden Uses:
Mass planting, meadow garden, mixed border, rock garden, woodland garden

Light Preference:
Sun to shade

Soil Preference:
Well-drained, evenly moist soil

Best Way to Propagate:
Divide as leaves go dormant in summer

USDA Plant Hardiness Zones:
4 to 9; frost-sensitive perennial grown as a tender annual

Bluebells are often seen in the thousands in open woods throughout Europe, where they form carpets of blue flowers as far as the eye can see. The flowers are bell-shaped, dangling from upright stems that arise from a cluster of grasslike leaves, and do look rather like open hyacinths, to which they are related, as their botanical name suggests. They're long-lived, floriferous, and bloom late in spring, filling the gap between when most spring bulbs stop blooming and the perennials start to dominate.

GROWING TIPS

Bluebells don't need or even appreciate a dry period during summer months. They like a bit of moisture at all times. Other than that, they are very simple to grow, adapting to most soil types and everything from full sun to deep summer shade (at least some spring sun is needed, however, for good bloom the following year). They're at their best in dappled shade, as they begin to bloom fairly late in the season when the trees have leafed out, and aren't terribly visible in deep shade. As for full sun, they tolerate it mostly in the North where the sun is less intense or, elsewhere, in spots where the soil really does remain a bit moist at all times.

Bulbs are sold in fall and should be planted fairly quickly. Plant them about 2 to 4 inches (5 to 10 cm) deep (4 to 5 inches/10 to 12 cm deep at the northern limits of their range) and about 4 to 6 inches (10 to 15 cm) apart. A bluebell on its own is a very wispy thing, so plant them in large numbers—at least 20 bulbs.

They are slower to establish than most bulbs: Sometimes they take 2 or 3 years to get going and really start blooming. Plus the bulbs multiply prolifically, and it is only once the baby bulbs begin bloom that you get truly good results. So plant them now for a true show—in 7 or 8 years!

Their slowness to establish means bluebells are not ideal choices for busy flowerbeds where they would be easily disturbed by hoeing and digging. They are at their best when naturalized in a forested area or in a partly shady meadow. Try to plant them so their foliage, which starts turning yellow in midsummer, won't be too visible at that season, such as among hostas or ferns.

Warning: Bluebells self-sow with abandon. In fact, they can even become weedy over time, so make sure you plant them in gardens, not in natural forests.

PROBLEMS AND SOLUTIONS

Bluebells are rarely affected by pests and diseases.

TOP PERFORMER

Hyacinthoides hispanica, syn. *Scilla hispanica, S. campanulata, Endymion hispanicus* (Spanish bluebells): These are the most showy and robust of the bluebells. They bear their bell-shaped flowers all around the stem rather than to just one side as with English bluebells. There are cultivars in shades of blue, pink, and white, with several cultivars per color. It really doesn't matter which ones you buy: They all perform well. 'Danube' (syn. 'Donau') is a deep blue; 'Excelsior' is a lighter blue with a dark stripe down each petal. 'Queen of the Pinks' and 'Rosabella' are two of the pinks; 'Alba' and 'White City' are popular whites. You many simply find bulbs labeled blue, white, or pink! Please note that many plants listed as *H. hispanica* are probably in fact hybrids between *H. hispanica* and *H. non-scripta* and should theoretically be listed as *H. × massartiana.* Height: 12 to 18 inches (30 to 45 cm). Spread: 4 to 6 inches (10 to 15 cm). USDA Plant Hardiness Zones 4 to 9.

MORE RECOMMENDED BLUEBELLS

Hyacinthoides non-scripta, syn. *Scilla non-scripta, S. nutans, Endymion non-scripta* (English bluebells): Many people, and especially those of British extraction, grow nostalgic over English bluebells, and this contributes more to its popularity than its performance in the garden. Actually, the Spanish bluebells usually give far more satisfying results: They're hardier, more robust, more floriferous, and more attractive. At any rate, it is very similar to Spanish bluebells anywhere, although a bit smaller and with a one-sided flowerstalk. Height: 8 to 16 inches (20 to 40 cm). Spread: 4 to 6 inches (10 to 15 cm). USDA Plant Hardiness Zones 5 to 9.

Spanish bluebells
(*Hyacinthoides hispanica*)

LARRY'S GARDEN NOTES

Where English bluebells (*Hyacinthoides non-scripta*) and Spanish bluebells (*H. hispanica*) are planted together, they readily intercross, producing offspring looking more like Spanish bluebells than English ones, and they have proved much more vigorous than either parent. As a result, hybrid bluebells (*H. × massartiana*) are spreading like wildfire in Britain, threatening the native species, and vast campaigns to eradicate the interloper have been undertaken.

Hyacinthus

Hyacinth

PLANT PROFILE

HYACINTHUS

hy-a-SIN-thus

Bloom Color:
White, blue, purple, pink, red, salmon, and yellow

Bloom Time:
Early spring

Length of Bloom:
2 weeks or more

Height:
8 to 12 inches (20 to 30 cm)

Spread:
3 to 6 inches (8 to 15 cm)

Garden Uses:
Container planting, edging, forcing, mass planting, meadow garden, mixed border, rock garden, specimen plant, wall planting, wildflower meadow, woodland garden

Light Preference:
Full sun to partial shade in spring

Soil Preference:
Humus-rich, well-drained soil; moist in spring

Best Way to Propagate:
Buy new bulbs

USDA Plant Hardiness Zones:
4 to 9

Hyacinths are among the most highly perfumed of all hardy plants and would probably be grown for their perfume alone—if it weren't for the fact that their flowers are just gorgeous, too! The star-shaped blooms come in a vast array of colors and are borne on dense, solid stems the first year. This creates a stiff, artificial appearance that looks perfect in formal gardens and in pots, but makes placement in a cottage-type garden a bit difficult. By the second year, though, the bulbs split and start producing multiple, arching stems and more open clusters: to my eyes, a great improvement.

GROWING TIPS

Hyacinth bulbs are large and quite expensive, so it is worth making sure they get the best possible conditions. First, pick out only healthy, thick, unblemished bulbs. For outdoor use, look for caliber 17/18. These are medium-size bulbs and will give good results in the garden. Smaller bulbs (and there are several calibers, down to 13/14) are less expensive but also less impressive in bloom; larger bulbs (calibers 18/19 and 19+) produce such huge flowerstalks that they may come crashing down in the slightest wind, so are best reserved for forcing in pots indoors.

Unlike most of the hardy bulbs described in this chapter, hyacinths are not good naturalizers. In fact, in most climates, they tend to be short-lived bulbs best used for high-impact, temporary displays. Expect no more than 2 or 3 years of bloom, then yank them out and replace them with new bulbs. That said, in areas where conditions are to their liking—that is, with cool, fairly moist summers—they can be quite permanent.

If you intend to grow hyacinths for just one season of bloom, it really doesn't matter what conditions you plant them under—as long as the soil drains well, they will do fine. You can even grow them in pure sand or gravel. For longer life in the garden, look for a rich, humusy, well-drained soil and a spot that is sunny to partly shady in spring; as with most ephemeral bulbs, hyacinths aren't bothered by summer shade. The bulbs tolerate drought while they are dormant— yet hyacinths perennialize well only where they profit from even summer moisture. A cool, shady, moist (but well-drained) spot will keep them going for a decade or more; hot, sunny, dry spots lead to decline in just 2 or 3 years.

Plant the bulbs about 6 inches (15 cm) deep (twice as much in Zone 4 and colder) in fall. Buy bulbs early and store them cool until planting time. Unlike many other bulbs described here, they *don't* have to be planted immediately upon arrival—any time up to November is fine in most climates.

Since hyacinths decline rather than increase in numbers in most gardens and they are complicated to grow from seed, multiplication is not really a possibility. If you want more, buy fresh bulbs!

Warning: Hyacinths are somewhat poisonous and should not be eaten. Professional bulb handlers sometimes break out in "hyacinth rash" simply from touching them, but this rarely occurs if you handle only a few dozen bulbs a year. If in doubt, though, wear gloves when you plant them.

Hyacinth (*Hyacinthus orientalis* 'Kronos')

PROBLEMS AND SOLUTIONS

Rot is possible in poorly drained soil.

TOP PERFORMER

Hyacinthus orientalis (hyacinth, Dutch hyacinth): There is only one species of hyacinth commonly grown, but it offers a huge range of cultivars: single or double forms, and an almost unlimited range of colors. The varieties with dense, cylindrical flowerheads, called Dutch hyacinths for the country where they were developed, dominate the market and are usually the only varieties available. There are also Multiflora hyacinths, with several stems per bulb and looser flowerheads, but they are hard to find. A sampling of cultivars would include 'Carnegie' (pure white), 'Ostara' (deep lavender-blue), 'Gipsy Queen' (salmon-pink), and 'Hollyhock' (double red), but there are hundreds of others.

LARRY'S GARDEN NOTES

Hyacinths are forcing bulbs *par excellence*. They even make a good class project for the kindergarten set! Pot them up tightly, cramming as many bulbs as you can into the pot for best effect, leaving the bulb tips barely exposed, then water well and store in a cool (about 40°F/4°C) area for about 12 to 14 weeks, then bring them into the light. The flowers are stupendous, and the perfume will knock your socks off!

Leucojum
Snowflake

LEUCOJUM
loo-KOH-jum

Bloom Color:
White

Bloom Time:
Varies by species; see
individual listings

Length of Bloom:
2 weeks

Height:
Varies by species; see
individual listings

Spread:
Varies by species; see
individual listings

Garden Uses:
Container planting, cut flower
garden, mass planting,
meadow garden, mixed
border, rock garden,
woodland garden

Light Preference:
Full sun to partial shade

Soil Preference:
Humus-rich, well-drained,
evenly moist soil

Best Way to Propagate:
Separate bulbs as leaves turn
yellow

USDA Plant Hardiness Zones:
Varies by species; see
individual listings

You can think of these white-flowered bulbs as season extenders for snowdrops (*Galanthus* spp., page 294) which they resemble closely. Indeed, spring snowflake replaces snowdrops as they fade, then is replaced in turn by summer snowflake—and there is even an autumn snowflake for fall blooming. The pendulous flowers are bell-shaped and white in color, usually with green tips. The straplike leaves of snowflakes are upright and look a lot like narcissus leaves.

GROWING TIPS

Snowflakes do differ from snowdrops in their cultural needs. For one thing, their blooming isn't tied to cold winters, so they'll do much better in warmer parts of the country. In fact, in California and other places with a Mediterranean climate, they'll switch over to blooming during winter months, when rain is more available, going dormant in spring rather than following the spring bloom/summer dormancy habit of most other bulbs. Also, the two main species prefer distinctly moister growing conditions and will even grow in bogs and on pond edges. Even so, they adapt perfectly well to average garden soils as long as they don't dry out completely.

They need quite a bit of light while they are in foliage—even full sun—but their leafing out corresponds to the period when the trees above are dormant, so they are fine in seasonal shade. Plant the bulbs in fall about 3 to 4 inches (8 to 10 cm) deep. They look great in flowerbeds but are probably best used for naturalizing in fields and open woodlands.

Snowflakes reproduce readily in culture, each bulb soon forming a clump that can be divided after 3 or 4 years, as the leaves start to yellow. Or grow them from seed, which will take 3 or 4 years to reach blooming size.

PROBLEMS AND SOLUTIONS

Snowflakes are rarely bothered by insects or diseases, but slugs (page 85) and narcissus fly can be problems. The latter seem to attack only larger bulbs and leave smaller ones alone.

TOP PERFORMER

Leucojum aestivum (summer snowflake): In spite of the common name, summer snowflake is a midspring bloomer. It got its name in comparison to spring snowflake, which does bloom much earlier. This is the showiest of the snowflakes—its greater height and larger white, green-tipped flowers, usually two to eight per stem, make it much more visible than its smaller cousins. The species reaches 18 to 24 inches (45 to 60 cm) tall, but the more widely available 'Gravetye Giant' cultivar reaches 30 to 36 inches (75 to 90 cm) tall. Spread: 8 to 10 inches (20 to 25 cm). USDA Plant Hardiness Zones 4 to 9.

MORE RECOMMENDED SNOWFLAKES

Leucojum autumnale (autumn snowflake): This is the odd man out in the genus *Leucojum.* Not only does it bloom at the opposite time of the year (late summer and early fall), but the narrow, thread-shaped, grasslike leaves, which appear in fall and remain through winter, go dormant in summer and look nothing like the straplike foliage of the others. Even their cultural needs differ: Autumn snowflake prefers dry conditions in summer and tolerates poorer soil. The flowers are similar, but smaller—white flushed pink or even red, two to four per stem. They lack the green tips of the other snowdrops but have the same inverted bell shape. Height: 4 to 6 inches (10 to 15 cm). Spread: 4 inches (10 cm). USDA Plant Hardiness Zones 5 to 9.

L. vernum (spring snowflake): This is a smaller plant with similar white, green-tipped flowers to the summer snowflake, but it blooms fairly early in spring, usually just as the snowdrops (*Galanthus* spp.) are coming to an end in the South; often several weeks later in the North. It is a hardier plant that seems to do equally well in Zone 3 as in Zone 9. Usually only the species is offered, but *L. vernum* var. *carpathicum,* with yellow-tipped flowers, is devastatingly charming and well worth looking for. There is usually only one flower per stem. Height: 8 to 12 inches (20 to 30 cm). Spread: 8 to 10 inches (20 to 25 cm). USDA Plant Hardiness Zones 3 to 9.

LARRY'S GARDEN NOTES

If you can't for the life of you tell snowdrops (*Galanthus* spp.) from snowflakes (*Leucojum* spp.), the easiest way is to look at the flowers. Both are pendulous and white with green tips, it's true, but snowdrop flowers have six petals of equal length, making them look like little bells. Snowflakes, on the other hand, have two pairs of petals: three short inner ones reunited in a crown and not too noticeable unless you look at them from below, and three longer, outer arching ones, which, to me, always make the flower look like a propeller.

Spring snowflake
(*Leucojum vernum*)

Lilium

Lily

PLANT PROFILE

LILIUM

LIL-ee-um

Bloom Color:
  Varies by species; see individual listings

Bloom Time:
  Varies by species; see individual listings

Length of Bloom:
  2 to 3 weeks

Height:
  Varies by species; see individual listings

Spread:
  Varies by species; see individual listings

Garden Uses:
  Background, container planting, cut flower garden, mass planting, meadow garden, mixed border, specimen plant, woodland garden

Light Preference:
  Full sun to shade

Soil Preference:
  Humus-rich, moist, well-drained soil

Best Way to Propagate:
  Divide in late fall or early spring

USDA Plant Hardiness Zones:
  Varies by species; see individual listings

Lilies are not usually thought of as shade plants, although most do quite well in partial shade. However, there are a few exceptions to the rule: lilies that evolved as woodland plants in their native lands. Shade lilies may surprise gardeners used to the huge trumpet flowers of so many sun-loving varieties. They tend to be fairly modest in size and are inevitably of the Turk's-cap type; that is, with hanging flowers whose petals curve upward at the tips, leaving the brown- to orange-tipped stems to dangle below. The resulting flowers look like multilegged ballerinas in tutus.

GROWING TIPS

Lilies are unlike most of the hardy bulbs described in this chapter. They behave more like perennials, with nonstop growth spring through fall, rather than a long period of summer dormancy, so they need even moisture throughout much of the year. Also, bulbs are usually available in spring rather than in fall (some mail-order growers do ship in fall, though).

Lily bulbs are soft and made up of scales. Lacking a tunic, they do not tolerate drying out. If possible, plant them as soon as they become available, even in pots, when they land in local markets unseasonably early (you can plant them out later when all danger of frost has passed). Or store the bulbs in peat moss, wood shavings, vermiculite, or perlite, in a cool spot such as a cold room or refrigerator, until you can plant them. Bulbs received in fall should be planted out immediately.

Lilies like humus-rich soil and even moisture, so mulch them well. The size of bulbs varies widely: The best rule for planting is to dig a hole three times the height of the bulb, whatever that may be.

The easiest way to multiply lilies is to divide established clumps. Do this first thing in spring or late in fall.

Only species lilies come true from seed: When the capsule splits open, remove and sow the seeds. Germination can take place quickly the following spring, or you may have to wait yet another year to see signs of growth.

PROBLEMS AND SOLUTIONS

Lilies have plenty of enemies: slugs, snails, deer, groundhogs, voles, rabbits, viruses, and gray mold, among others. See Chapter 4 for possible solutions. The worst pest is the lily beetle, described in "Larry's Garden Notes."

TOP PERFORMER

Lilium martagon (common Turk's-cap lily, martagon lily): This is a mid-spring–blooming lily producing well-spaced whorls of leaves. The flowers are numerous and very small for a lily: rarely more than 2 inches (5 cm) in diameter. They are pendant with very rolled-up petals and usually dull pink with darker spots, although the coloration can vary from white to purple. This is a very shade-tolerant lily—probably the best choice for those who really have no sun. It naturalizes wonderfully. Used in hybridization, it produces the Martagon Hybrids, notably a series called the Backhouse Hybrids, with orange, yellow, and buff cultivars that are just as tough as the species. Height: 3 to 8 feet (90 to 240 cm). Spread: 12 to 18 inches (30 to 45 cm). USDA Plant Hardiness Zones 3 to 9.

MORE RECOMMENDED LILIES

Lilium canadense (Canada lily): The holy grail of lily lovers, this beautiful lily, native to northeastern North America, is considered difficult but really only "vants to be left alone." It produces from a few to dozens of hanging yellow or orange trumpet-shaped flowers, often spotted, in a candelabra-like inflorescence far out of proportion to the rather thin foliage. It prefers partial to fairly deep shade. Cool, moist summers are perfect: It finds hot, dry ones torture. Unlike most lilies, its bulbs are annual structures, with new ones appearing to replace the old, on creeping underground stolons. As a result, it tends to move about the flowerbed, popping up in the most unlikely places. Digging in and around this "wanderer" is likely to do it in. Obviously, it will do better naturalized than in a meticulously maintained bed. Midsummer flowers. Height: 3 to 6 feet (90 to 180 cm). Spread: 12 to 18 inches (30 to 45 cm). USDA Plant Hardiness Zones 3 to 8.

Common Turk's-cap lily
(*Lilium martagon*)

LARRY'S GARDEN NOTES

Warning: The lily beetle (*Lilioceris lilii*), a beautiful orange beetle of Eurasian origin, is devastating lily beds in the Northeast and spreading rapidly. The adults eat holes in both buds and leaves and the voracious larvae eat leaves whole: Untreated plants are stripped of all leaves and buds. With no natural predators in the New World, it seems impossible to control other than by localized treatments. In my own garden, I've managed to keep damage to a minimum by seriously cutting back on my lily collection and spraying the remaining plants bimonthly with neem oil. The lily beetle seems to attack lilies growing in full sun first, so your shade-grown lilies may be safe . . . for a while!

Narcissus
Narcissus, daffodil, jonquil

Narcissi are perhaps the perfect spring flower. They come in a wide variety of sizes, colors, and forms; bloom from late winter through late spring (if you choose the right types); are usually very perennial; and have varieties to suit almost every climate. The flowers are botanically quite complex. The outer segments, called the perianth, form a halo around the center cup, called the crown (if it is short) or trumpet (it if is long). The perianth is white or yellow (rarely orange); the crown/trumpet can be white, yellow, orange, red, green, multicolor, or "pink" (actually salmon). The leaves are usually upright and strap-shaped, but can be tubular. As for size, anything goes: The smallest narcissi (or narcissuses, both are correct!) are barely 2½ inches (7 cm) tall, the tallest, over 20 inches (50 cm)!

GROWING TIPS

The narcissus is a typical spring ephemeral. Leaves and flowers appear in spring or even winter, then the plant goes dormant in summer (there are a few aberrant narcissi that bloom and leaf out in fall instead, but they're rarely grown). As a result, it will tolerate even deep shade if it gets spring sun, so it is well adapted to the seasonal shade found under deciduous trees and shrubs.

Most species and hybrids need excellent drainage and will not prosper in heavy clay soils, especially ones that remain wet throughout winter. Bulbs are available in fall and should be planted shortly after they arrive in stores or kept cool until planting time. They are tough bulbs, but delays in planting can hold up the first spring's flowering. Planting depth depends on bulb size—and narcissus bulbs can be as small as a pea or as large as a peach. Let the "rule of three" reign: Plant the bulb three times as deep as it is high.

Hardiness is variable. Most hybrids are derived from northern species and need a long, cold winter. Obviously they'll do best where local conditions concur. A few, though, don't even like cold and freeze in Zone 6 and below, but will do wonderfully even in parts of Zones 8 and 9 with very mild winters.

Most narcissi are very perennial and multiply abundantly by division. When a "plant" has clearly become a "clump," it can be divided and the individual bulbs and bulblets replanted. This is best done as the plant is going dormant in early summer but also in fall—if you can locate the bulbs without their foliage to guide you. Most narcissi are hybrids and do not come true from seed, plus seeds can take 7 years or more to reach blooming size, so seed production is rarely an option.

There is no need to deadhead narcissi, but do let the foliage turn yellow before cutting it back. Old-fashioned techniques like weaving leaves together or tying them together don't let the leaves absorb enough light and are just bad horticulture. Some types, though, have leaves that hang on inordinately long: If they're still there 6 weeks after the flower has faded, they have done their job and you can remove them.

PROBLEMS AND SOLUTIONS

There are several insects that attack narcissi. The best-known and most widely distributed pest is the narcissus fly, a large larva that hollows out bulbs and leaves them for dead. Dig out and destroy infected bulbs.

TOP PERFORMER

Narcissus Hybrids (narcissus): There are over 50 species of narcissi, but most are rarely grown. Instead, the market is flooded with hundreds of cultivars in all sizes, shapes, and colors. Just take your pick! Specialists divide narcissi into 12 different divisions, but these mostly describe the flower's shape (trumpet narcissi, double narcissi, and so on) and are of little help in helping to choose a narcissus particularly adapted to your conditions. In general, though, the Tazetta Hybrids are the best choices for southern gardens; the others do best anywhere but in the Deep South! As for flower color, blooming period, height, and so on: Let the label or the catalog be your guide!

Narcissus (mixed *Narcissus* Hybrids)

LARRY'S GARDEN NOTES

Daffodil, jonquil, or narcissus: Which is the proper term? Actually, they all are. Daffodil is an old word of English origin used for any *Narcissus* species. Narcissus refers, of course, to the Greek legend about a youth named Narcissus who fell in love with his own reflection in a pond and died of chagrin. He was changed by the gods into a flower that continues to face downward, looking for its reflection. As for jonquil, it's from French for little rush—*jonc* (rush) plus *ille* (a diminutive), thus *jonquille*—and referred originally to a specific species, *Narcissus jonquilla*, with leaves like rushes.

Puschkinia
Striped squill

PLANT PROFILE

PUSCHKINIA

push-KIN-ee-uh

Bloom Color:
  Pale blue and white

Bloom Time:
  Early spring

Length of Bloom:
  2 to 3 weeks

Height:
  2 to 6 inches (5 to 15 cm)

Spread:
  3 inches (8 cm)

Garden Uses:
  Edging, mass planting,
  meadow garden, mixed
  border, rock garden,
  woodland garden; along
  paths

Light Preference:
  Full sun to shade

Soil Preference:
  Well-drained soil, rich or
  poor; moist in spring, drier in
  summer

Best Way to Propagate:
  Separate bulbs as leaves turn
  yellow

USDA Plant Hardiness Zones:
  4 to 9

If you just like lots of flowers without any effort, this may well be the bulb for you. This little bulb naturalizes just about everywhere where winters are reasonably cold and really doesn't need any kind of helping hand: Just plant it, water it once, and watch it grow and spread. It's a tiny little plant with two or three insignificant grasslike leaves (ideal for naturalizing in a lawn, for example) and a flowerstalk bearing a dense cluster of three to eight bell-shaped, semi-upright flowers. They are pale blue to white and faintly scented. On its own, it really has very little impact, but plant it in groups of 20 or more and it will really stand out.

GROWING TIPS

Tiny striped squill bulbs are widely available locally in fall and "keep" fairly well, even under store conditions. Plant them out before the ground freezes, about 3 to 4 inches (8 to 10 cm) deep, in well-drained soil. They seem to grow equally well in sand and gravel as in rich soil, in soil that is acid or alkaline, so there is no need to make any major changes to accommodate them. They need full sun or at least fairly good light while they are in leaf, but are quite at ease in spots under deciduous trees that become shady in summer. They do require about 2 months of cool (although not necessarily freezing) temperatures in winter, so in the warmer end of their potential range, Zones 8 and 9, they'll do well only where that condition can be met.

Striped squills are considered snow-melt plants and really need moisture only during winter months and in early spring, as their roots form and their leaves and flowers appear. In summer, they don't mind the even moisture one finds in most flowerbeds thanks to mulching and irrigation, but are also fine in areas that become bone-dry. And as with most spring bulbs, they are very tolerant of root competition.

Striped squills multiply spontaneously both through division and self-sowing. Dig up clumps after a few years and separate and replant the bulbs, or just let them do their thing: They naturalize readily into both lawns and open forests. Seedlings may already start to bloom when only 2 years old—quite fast for a bulb. There is really no need to collect and sow seed yourself.

PROBLEMS AND SOLUTIONS

Striped squill rarely seems to suffer from insects or disease, and squirrels won't touch it.

TOP PERFORMER

Puschkinia scilloides subsp. *libanotica*, syn. *P. libanotica* (striped squill): For reasons unknown, the species itself, with blue flowers marked by a darker midvein, is rarely sold. Indeed, plants labeled *P. scilloides* inevitably turn out to be the subspecies, *P. scilloides* subsp. *libanotica*. It has white or very pale blue flowers with an attractive mid-blue stripe up the center of each petal: From a distance, it inevitably looks pale blue. There is also a pure white selection, 'Alba', that is just as attractive and comes true from seed. Since there is only the one species in the genus *Puschkinia*, it is easy to build up a complete collection! This plant is very close to both *Chionodoxa* and *Scilla* in appearance (it differs from them only in minor details), and I wouldn't be surprised to see it repatriated to one or the other genus one day.

Striped squill (*Puschkinia scilloides* subsp. *libotanica*)

LARRY'S GARDEN NOTES

No, *Puschkinia* was not named after the Russian poet Aleksandr Sergeyevich Pushkin, but rather for Count Apollos Mussin-Puschkin, the eighteenth-century plant collector who first discovered the genus. As for *scilloides*, it means "like a *Scilla*" or squill, which is certainly true. *Libanotica*, as you may have guessed, refers to Lebanon, where the subspecies was discovered.

Sanguinaria
Bloodroot, puccoon

PLANT PROFILE

SANGUINARIA

sang-gwi-NAHR-ee-uh

Bloom Color:
White and pink

Bloom Time:
Early spring

Length of Bloom:
2 to 4 weeks

Height:
6 to 8 inches (15 to 20 cm)

Spread:
12 inches (30 cm)

Garden Uses:
Edging, groundcover, mass planting, meadow garden, mixed border, rock garden, woodland garden; along paths, on slopes

Light Preference:
Partial shade to shade

Soil Preference:
Humus-rich, moist, well-drained soil

Best Way to Propagate:
Divide after flowering

USDA Plant Hardiness Zones:
3 to 9

This charming woodland flower is found wild throughout eastern North America, from Mexico to northern Canada. Its starry flowers are a pristine white, and dirt and mud never seem to stick to them. The blooms are very short-lived, rarely more than 8 to 10 days, but established clumps produce flowers here and there for up to a month. After the flowers fade, the leaves expand and they're almost as nice as the flowers, bluish gray and deeply incised.

GROWING TIPS

This forest dweller seems to be totally oblivious of shade: You find it in the wild in spots so dark that you almost need a flashlight to find your way around in broad daylight! Of course, that would be *summer* shade. It does like getting its share of spring sun as it filters its way through the still-naked branches of the deciduous trees above. And it is remarkably resistant to root competition.

Bloodroot is a plant of rich forests, so why disappoint it in culture? Add lots of organic matter at planting time, supply a good mulch to replace the leaf litter it would have in the wild, or naturalize it in a wooded area and let it go wild!

In local nurseries, you'll most likely see bloodroot for sale in pots, in bloom or in leaf, in spring or early summer: The rhizomes don't appreciate being exposed to the air for any length of time, which rules out mass-marketing of dried rhizomes. Plant it in a shady nook without disturbing its roots, and off it grows! You can often obtain dormant rhizomes for fall planting via mail-order sources for considerably less money. Plant them about 4 inches (10 cm) deep.

Bloodroot needs even moisture from winter through spring and prefers it to continue through summer, if possible. If it becomes too dry, it goes into dormancy early; where it is kept moist, the lovely leaves often hang on right through most of summer. It makes a stupendous groundcover if you can forgive the possible disappearance of the leaves by midsummer.

Ideally, everyone would have the budget to plant bloodroot in groups of at least 10 to 15 plants, but it is not inexpensive, and most people choose the cheap but slow method: Plant it and let it spread on its own. It spreads slowly at first, but as the number of rhizomes increases it picks up speed. Still, it can take 10 to 15 years to create a nice groundcover from a single plant.

Multiplication is inevitably by division, especially for double types, which produce no seed. Dig up established plants after they flower, even though they are still in leaf; cut the rhizomes into sections with at least one leaf or bud; and replant without delay. Or let the plants self-sow. Seed is difficult to germinate indoors, needing alternating periods of warmth and cold.

PROBLEMS AND SOLUTIONS

Bloodroot rarely seems subject to insects and diseases.

TOP PERFORMER

Sanguinaria canadensis (bloodroot, puccoon): This is the only species in the genus *Sanguinaria*. Most plants are pure white; cultivars with pinkish flowers are sometimes seen, but at outrageous prices! Certainly one of the most desirable of all bulb flowers is the double form—and bloodroot has two. 'Multiplex' ('Pleno') is the more symmetrical of the two; 'Flore Pleno' is a bit less formal looking. Both produce a spectacular double flower with up to 50 petals: With its pure white blooms, it looks like an Indian lotus! The flowers last twice as long as the single ones. A stunning plant every gardener wants to own, but oh so expensive for such a small plant!

Bloodroot (*Sanguinaria canadensis*)

LARRY'S GARDEN NOTES

Make sure you ask where the plants come from before you buy when purchasing a bloodroot. It is subject to overharvesting throughout much of its range, not only for sale to gardeners but also because its blood-red sap, although known to be somewhat toxic, is considered beneficial by folk healers. You'll want to be sure your plants were nursery-grown. The double and pink forms are available only through nurseries, so you can buy those without asking.

Scilla

Squill

SCILLA

SKILL-uh

Bloom Color:
Blue, white, and pink

Bloom Time:
Early to midspring; fall for some species

Length of Bloom:
2 to 3 weeks

Height:
Varies by species; see individual listings

Spread:
Varies by species; see individual listings

Garden Uses:
Container planting, edging, mass planting, meadow garden, mixed border, rock garden, woodland garden; along paths, on slopes

Light Preference:
Full sun to shade

Soil Preference:
Humus-rich, moist, well-drained soil

Best Way to Propagate:
Lift and divide as leaves turn yellow

USDA Plant Hardiness Zones:
Varies by species; see individual listings

This is actually a fairly large genus of nearly 90 species, although only a few are currently grown. The common ones are inevitably small plants with only a few grasslike leaves that bloom in early or midspring, depending on the species. The flowers are small in size but big in impact, as they multiply abundantly. Indeed, a carpet of Siberian squill turning a lawn blue is one of the great joys of spring. All can also readily be forced in containers and, indeed, one (*Scilla peruviana*) is usually grown that way.

GROWING TIPS

With one exception, the bulbs described here are small, spring-blooming types and need about the same care. Plant the small bulbs about 3 inches (8 cm) deep in most climates (4 inches/10 cm in Zone 3). Good-draining, humus-rich soil is best, but squills are tough plants and can even set up shop in heavy clay soils (usually the last place you think of planting bulbs) and still thrive. Like other spring ephemerals, they need some spring sun but are indifferent to summer shade, so they can be readily established in deciduous forests and under shrubs. Bulbs are inevitably inexpensive, so plant them in quantity: 50 bulbs is not too much!

Essentially no care is needed. Plant the bulbs, and let 'em rip. They naturalize beautifully, never needing division no matter how many bulbs appear at their parents' base over the years (and there will be hundreds eventually!), and self-sow with abandon. You'll find you'll obtain the "carpet of flowers" in very little time. If you so desire, you can dig up established clumps and divide them, but most gardeners just let their squills do their own thing.

PROBLEMS AND SOLUTIONS

Rarely suffers from insects or diseases.

TOP PERFORMER

Scilla siberica (Siberian squill, blue squill): In most climates, this is the best bulb for naturalizing. It creates perfect carpets of blue both in sun and summer shade. There is nothing in the vegetable kingdom to compare with a lawn that is blue with Siberian squills, and the plants conveniently die back just as the time comes for the first mowing. It's a small plant with down-facing, star-shaped, deep blue flowers, one to five per stem. It is the latest of the spring squills, although still considered early. 'Spring Beauty' has larger, deeper blue flowers; 'Alba' has pure white blooms. Height: 4 to 6 inches (10 to 15 cm). Spread: 2 inches (5 cm). USDA Plant Hardiness Zones 2 to 8.

MORE RECOMMENDED SQUILLS

Scilla biflora (two-leaf squill): As the Tubergen squill (see below) reaches its climax and before the Siberian squill is quite open, this dainty little squill fills in, with deep mauve-blue flowers. The blooms are half the size of those of other squills, yet more numerous (usually six to eight per stem), so they are just as effective. Besides, the star-shapes face upward, revealing attractively fuzzy stamens. There are several cultivars in various other colors. 'Rosea', indeed, is more widely available than the species, yet its pale pink flowers aren't nearly as showy. Height: 4 to 6 inches (10 to 15 cm). Spread: 2 inches (5 cm). USDA Plant Hardiness Zones 4 to 8.

    S. mischtschenkoana 'Zwanenburg', syn. *S. tubergeniana* (Tubergen squill): The species, *S. mischtschenkoana*, with blue flowers, is rarely grown. Instead, plants so labeled inevitably have white flowers, and therefore belong to the cultivar 'Zwanenburg'. Actually, the flowers do have a very faint blue midrib, but it is scarcely noticeable. Unlike Siberian squill, the flowers are semi-upright, and each bulb produces several flowerstalks, so the impact the first year is greater. This is the earliest-blooming spring squill—as early as February in some climates. Height: 4 to 6 inches (10 to 15 cm). Spread: 2 inches (5 cm). USDA Plant Hardiness Zones 4 to 8.

Siberian squill (*Scilla siberica*)

KISSING COUSINS

Cuban lily (*S. peruviana*) is a taller plant than the other squills and essentially subtropical, and it remains in leaf year-round. Its more numerous, broader leaves form a rosette around a dome-shaped inflorescence bearing up to 100 star-shaped, upward-facing, indigo-blue flowers at a time, in late spring to early summer. It is grown outdoors only in Zones 8 and up (7 with winter protection) but makes a great houseplant elsewhere. Keep it moist at all times. Height: 6 to 18 inches (15 to 45 cm). Spread: 8 to 18 inches (20 to 45 cm). USDA Plant Hardiness Zones 8 to 11.

Trillium

Trillium

TRILLIUM

TRIL-yum

Bloom Color:
  White, yellow, red, and pink

Bloom Time:
  Mid- to late spring

Length of Bloom:
  3 to 5 weeks

Height:
  Varies by species; see
  individual listings

Spread:
  Varies by species; see
  individual listings

Garden Uses:
  Mass planting, rock garden,
  woodland garden

Light Preference:
  Full sun to shade

Soil Preference:
  Humus-rich, moist, well-
  drained soil

Best Way to Propagate:
  Divide after foliage dies back

USDA Plant Hardiness Zones:
  Varies by species; see
  individual listings

If you've ever taken a spring walk in a forested area almost any-where in North America, you certainly know trilliums. They are *the* native spring bulb par excellence, North America's answer to Asia's tulip and Europe's narcissus. Almost every region has at least one species: In many areas, the woodlands are blanketed with them. They are easily recognized, even by rank beginners: one stem, three green leaves, three green sepals, three colored petals. Depending on the species, the flowers can be upright or hanging, but they are always charming.

GROWING TIPS

Trilliums and forest go together. That's where they're found in the wild and where they do best in culture, as well. They're best grown naturalized in woodlands or, in more formal plantings, allowed to poke up through groundcovers.

In cool-summer areas, trilliums can be grown in full sun. However, they are at their best in seasonal shade: a spot that gets reasonably plentiful spring sun, but partial to full shade for the rest of the season. Unlike many spring bulbs, the leaves don't fade away as the trees leaf out, but stay on through much or even all of summer.

Rich, humusy soil is ideal for trilliums, although they'll put up with most soil types as long as you add plenty of organic matter to get them started. They are champions at surviving and even thriving in spite of the worst possible root competition.

The best way to grow trilliums is to purchase plants in pots while they are in bloom. First of all, this gives you the satisfaction of seeing them instantly bloom in your garden, but most importantly, since trilliums grown from seed can take 7 years or longer to bloom, starting off with flowering plants is a good way to ensure that you have mature ones. Once they have begun blooming, trilliums will bloom year after year, and even their offsets will usually bloom their very first spring.

Trilliums multiply naturally, albeit slowly, forming clumps or spreading bit by bit and self-sowing where happy, especially when naturalized in a deciduous woodland. To speed up the process, divide them after several years (these are certainly not "mile-a-minute" plants!). When you see the foliage turn yellow, *carefully* dig well down into the soil, lift, separate, and replant. You can also divide the rhizomes (each bump can give a plant).

Warning: Purchase only nursery-grown trilliums. In spite of laws in most areas designed to protect wild trilliums, illegal harvesting is still being practiced on a massive scale.

Great white trillium
(*Trillium grandiflorum*)

PROBLEMS AND SOLUTIONS

Trilliums are fairly pest- and disease-free. Where they have nothing else to eat, though, deer will devour them.

TOP PERFORMER

Trillium grandiflorum (great white trillium, showy wakerobin, large-flowered trillium): This is a truly striking plant with very showy three-petaled flowers with yellow anthers that open creamy white, quickly turning purest white, then, after several weeks of bloom, fade to pink. 'Flore Pleno' and 'Snowbunting' have gorgeous double white flowers, looking for all the world like huge gardenias. Unfortunately, they are so pricey that most gardeners shy away. Height: 8 to 18 inches (20 to 45 cm). Spread: 12 inches (30 cm). USDA Plant Hardiness Zones 2 to 9.

MORE RECOMMENDED TRILLIUMS

Trillium erectum (red trillium, stinking Benjamin): This is a smaller plant with dark red flowers. Although the name 'stinking Benjamin' suggests it is very malodorous, the musky scent of this eastern North American native is not that intense. It has given rise to several nonstinky varieties, including *T. erectum* var. *albiflorum*, with white flowers; and the much rarer *T. erectum* var. *luteum*, with yellow flowers. Height: 1 foot (30 cm). Spread: 10 inches (25 cm). USDA Plant Hardiness Zones 2 to 9.

LARRY'S GARDEN NOTES

"Leaves of three, let it be" was designed to discourage people from touching poison ivy, that plant whose oil provokes such terrible skin reactions in most people, but it can be useful in preventing nonexperts from harvesting trilliums. These beautiful flowers look so pickable that many end up in vases every spring. Tragically, to harvest the flower you also have to harvest the plant's leaves, which strips it of any hope of storing up any solar energy for the season. At best, the plant is set back years; in most cases, though, it dies. Think of trilliums as pretty woodland flowers—that should stay in the woodlands. Never use them as cut flowers!

Zantedeschia

Calla, calla lily, arum lily

PLANT PROFILE

ZANTEDESCHIA

zan-te-DESH-ee-uh

Bloom Color:
  White, yellow, pink, red, purple, and green

Bloom Time:
  Summer

Length of Bloom:
  2 months or more

Height:
  24 to 30 inches (60 to 75 cm)

Spread:
  Varies by species; see individual listings

Garden Uses:
  Background, container planting, cut flower garden, mass planting, meadow garden, mixed border, specimen plant, woodland garden; in wet areas

Light Preference:
  Full sun to shade

Soil Preference:
  Humus-rich, moist soil

Best Way to Propagate:
  Divide corms as foliage turns yellow

Hardiness: Frost-sensitive plant grown as a tender bulb

There is something about the calla's flower that really creates an impression. It consists of a variously colored, funnel-shaped bract called a spathe surrounding a column, or spadix, of tiny flowers. That sounds fairly simple, but the flower is so large and majestic it inevitably turns heads. There are several different species with foliage that is either lance-shaped or arrow-shaped, green or green-spotted white, all used as permanent garden plants in the South but tender bulbs in the North, either for summer bloom or as a year-long houseplant.

GROWING TIPS

In Zone 8 and above (and in protected spots of Zone 7), you can grow this spectacular plant as if it were a perennial: Plop the thick rhizome into rich, moist soil in spring and let it go through its cycle. A planting depth of 4 to 6 inches (10 to 15 cm) is fine. For gardeners in temperate climates, pot up the tuberous rhizomes about 4 to 6 weeks before the last frost, just barely covering the corm, and keep the mix slightly moist at first, then evenly moist as growth appears. A good-size clump (and the rhizome produces numerous offsets over time) may bloom throughout much of summer or, indeed, right through the year.

Partial shade gives the best results, especially a good dose of morning sun with protection from the heat of the midday blast furnace. In the North, where the sun is weaker and summers cooler, full sun is fine. And *Z. aethiopica,* our "top performer," is very well adapted to shade. All species need bright light with as much direct sun as possible, though, when grown indoors over winter.

With callas, dormancy is optional. If you want them to grow year-round (in climates where frost is rare, for example), keep them moist at all times. If you want a winter break or to protect it from the frost (they are hardier when dormant than when in full growth), stop watering them and let them go dormant. In cold climates, dig up the rhizomes in fall and let them dry out before storing them for winter in wood shavings or peat moss. Potted plants can be allowed to remain dormant in their pots.

For more plants, divide the rhizomes. This is usually done just before bringing callas out of dormancy but can be carried out while the plant is in full growth. Seeds germinate fairly well and give flowering plants in 2 or 3 years, but hybrids will not, of course, come true from seed.

PROBLEMS AND SOLUTIONS

Good drainage helps prevent rhizome rot. Hand-pick Japanese beetles.

TOP PERFORMER

Zantedeschia aethiopica (white calla): This is the queen of the callas, with huge blossoms of thick texture in pure white surrounding a creamy spadix. The large leaves are arrow-shaped. It can be grown as a container plant, a garden plant, or even as a semi-aquatic: You get to choose! The popular 'Green Goddess' has a green spathe that is white only at the base. 'Crowborough' is a typical white calla in appearance but hardy enough to grow outdoors in Zone 7. Height: 24 to 30 inches (60 to 75 cm). Spread: 24 inches (60 cm). USDA Plant Hardiness Zones 8 to 10.

MORE RECOMMENDED CALLAS

Zantedeschia Hybrids (hybrid calla lily): Hybrid callas have essentially replaced the other *Zantedeschia* species on the market. They usually have green lance-shaped leaves, sometimes with white spots. The narrow funnel-shaped flowers come in a broad range of colors, including white, pink, red, purple, yellow, and orange. Some are nearly black! No particular cultivar stands out from the (increasingly large) crowd: Pick and choose according to availability. Height: 24 to 30 inches (60 to 75 cm). Spread: 12 to 20 inches (30 to 50 cm). USDA Plant Hardiness Zones 9 to 10.

White calla
(*Zantedeschia aethiopica*)

LARRY'S GARDEN NOTES

In North America, the white calla was long used as a funeral flower because it blooms year-round in greenhouses. Although that tradition died out in the 1940s, some people feel uneasy about growing callas in their gardens. Remember this is entirely a cultural phenomenon. In France, it is the chrysanthemum (*Chrysanthemum × morifolium*) that is rarely used outside of funeral arrangements, while callas are often used in bridal bouquets!

The feathery fronds of ferns help lighten up the coarse foliage
of hostas, heucheras, and foamflowers.

Chapter 9

Ferns for Shade

But of course! Probably no other type of plant is as well known for its shade tolerance as the fern. It is always the plant gardeners seem to turn to when they feel they have so much shade they can't grow anything else. And indeed, shade suits ferns like a hand fits a glove. Most thrive in the darkest corners of the landscape, even in spots under huge conifers or on the north side of 53-story buildings that have never seen a ray of direct sun. Ferns will, in fact, grow in caves—well, at least just inside the *mouth* of caves, and that's about as dark as any plant can take. So if all else fails (and it probably won't if you follow the advice in the other chapters of this book), you can always resort to ferns.

MORE THAN JUST A FANCY FROND

Of course, in case you're so new to gardening that you don't already know this, ferns don't bloom—ever! They're considered primitive plants, having evolved back with the first land animals, and are only a few notches above mosses on the evolutionary scale. Plants were still experimenting with growing on land at the time and had yet to discover colorful flowers attracting buzzing insects as a means of reproduction. Instead, ferns produce spores, usually on the backs of their fronds, and they are rarely of more than minor visual interest. So ferns are, necessarily, foliage plants.

The error many gardeners make is to turn up their nose at anything that doesn't have big, bodacious blooms. After all, flowers aren't everything in the garden, and in the shade garden, where even shade-tolerant plants bloom more modestly or the flowers they produce are less visible due to the reduced light, they're even less vital. Most gardeners come eventually to appreciate how attractive foliage can be—and ferns have some of the nicest leaves around.

Fern leaves are called fronds, although if you call them leaves, the only person it might upset is a botany professor. For the vast majority, they are composed of a petiole (fern fanciers prefer to call it a rachis) that attaches to a ground-hugging stem. The leaf blade can be simple but is far more often compound, usually pinnate (arranged like the plumes on a feather), although it can be palm-shaped or come in other patterns. The leaflets borne by compound fronds are called pinnae, and they can in turn be divided (bipinnate) or, if they are divided yet once again, tripinnate.

It's the deeply cut, feathery nature of the fronds that adds so much grace to the fern's appearance. Most ferns have a vaguely feather-duster appearance that helps lighten heavy landscaping and adds a touch of softness to harsh angles. And the fronds have universal appeal: They look good with flowers, wood, stone, and metal; on their own; and, in fact, with just about everything. I particularly like to combine light-as-a-feather ferns with the heavy, coarse leaves of hostas, another denizen of shady gardens.

Fern fronds are, for the vast majority, green, although the petiole is often black or brownish and can be covered with plush. But don't think that the predominance of green results in a lack of color. In fact, there are all sorts of shades of green, from reddish green new fronds to dark green mature ones; from fronds that are bluish green to others that are distinctly yellow-green; and some fronds have an attractive silvery overlay. Their texture is partly dependant on how deeply cut the foliage is but also on the surface of the pinnae, which can be anything from dull to shiny, even waxy or mirrorlike.

PRIMITIVE OR SUCCESSFUL?

IT ALWAYS BOTHERS ME TO HAVE TO DESCRIBE FERNS AS PRIMITIVE PLANTS, even though it is true in an evolutionary sense, because "primitive" has such a negative connotation. It seems to suggest outdated, old-fashioned, an evolutionary failure. Yet ferns are none of that. If they were evolutionary failures, would they still be around 400 million years after they first evolved, back in the Devonian era? On the contrary, ferns are survivors—true botanical success stories. They outlived the giant amphibians, they outlived the dinosaurs, they outlived the mastodons, and they'll probably still be on this planet long after the human race is long gone! Tough as nails, that's what they are, and more than able to keep up with the most evolved "higher" plants.

Most temperate ferns have a distinct crown: The fronds all part from one growing point (or at least seem to). There are also ferns with running rhizomes, in which case individual fronds are spaced well apart: They tend to be invasive and not too popular in gardens. Then there are a few climbing ferns, plus hosts of tree ferns, but most of them are of tropical or subtropical origin.

And all the possibilities we've just discussed are multiplied when you consider the fern's size (you can have tiny ferns and gigantic ones), the color of the sori (the fruiting bodies of spores), the habit (upright, arching, or creeping), ferns that change color in fall, and ferns that have evergreen fronds. There is therefore no end to the interest of ferns, nor is there a limit to the variety they offer. You could indeed have a garden entirely composed of ferns and still have a very interesting landscape.

FERNS FOR EVERY CLIMATE

No plant group except mosses has as wide a distribution as ferns. From well above the Arctic Circle right through the Tropics; from deserts to swamps, you'll find ferns. Indeed, there are aquatic ferns and even ferns that are epiphytes (grow on other plants). That means there are plenty of ferns to choose from, no matter where you live. In this chapter, I've concentrated mostly on hardy ferns for outdoor growing in temperate climates, but there is an even greater choice of tropical ferns. Not only will the latter thrive in the warmer Zones (9 and above), but many make great houseplants. Who doesn't have an image of a giant Boston fern (*Nephrolepis exaltata* 'Bostoniensis') standing on a pedestal in a shady alcove in a grandparent's home or a schoolroom? Well, indoor ferns can become outdoor ferns in summer, moving out to shady patios or somber corners. I like to experiment with tree ferns in my backyard. These are ferns that produce a trunk and look like particularly lacy palms. Most are tropical or subtropical. They sulk during winter in the drier, stagnant air indoors but pick right up when outside in the buoyant air in summer. They actually like quite a bit of light—even sun—once they are acclimated, and they certainly give the backyard that tropical look!

All temperate ferns necessarily go dormant in winter, and most lose their fronds. If so, make sure you mark their location; it is easy to damage ferns by digging into them while they are leafless, as many leave no visible trace of their dormant presence. Some, though, like the Christmas fern (*Polystichum acrostichoides*) and the Western sword fern (*P. munitum*), are evergreen and add a lovely touch of color to the winter landscape.

Adiantum
Maidenhair fern

No one confuses maidenhair ferns with any other fern. First, the leaflets are quite distinct: fan-shaped and clearly recalling the maidenhair tree (*Ginkgo biloba*). Clearer yet are the thin but wiry-looking, black or deep purple stems that are distinctly hair-like in appearance. For the most part, the some 200 species of maidenhair ferns are tropical in origin, but there are a few hardy species suited to temperate gardens. They are charming ferns with multibranched, arching stems.

GROWING TIPS

Maidenhair ferns are among the relatively few ferns native to neutral to alkaline soils, so they are especially useful where soils tend in that direction, notably in much of western North America. That said, they seem quite indifferent to acid soils as well and certainly thrive in my distinctly acid garden.

As with most ferns, maidenhairs prefer partial to deep shade, although they can tolerate considerable sun in the North and where soils remain moist most of the time. Once established, they are fairly drought-tolerant, but they look better and develop more rapidly where irrigation and mulch are used to ensure things don't dry out too much. This is not a fern for areas with dry air: In arid climates, grow them near a source of water.

Maidenhairs spread by short, thin, underground rhizomes you'll never really notice unless you wash off the soil. As a result, they produce no clear crown but a thick clump of fronds that expands slowly outward as they grow. Occasional offsets are the most likely source of material for multiplication: Cut one free and plant it somewhere else. Usually, though, if you want more plants you'll have to dig up and separate a mature clump when the plant is dormant, in early spring or fall. Growing from spores is always possible, although very slow.

Besides the hardier maidenhairs described here, there are many evergreen tropical species used as houseplants or grown outdoors in Zone 9 and above.

PROBLEMS AND SOLUTIONS

Few and far between in the garden.

TOP PERFORMER

Adiantum pedatum (American maidenhair fern, Northern maidenhair): This is the common wild maidenhair throughout eastern and central North America, with, curiously, a disjunct population in Eastern Asia. Its leaflets are bluish green against black stems, making a charming combination. It is best distinguished from the more tropical maidenhairs by the "pedate" structure of the fronds: The stem divides, then arches backward in a pattern that always reminds me of bicycle handlebars. Easy to grow, but it has been subject to overcollecting in the wild, so make sure the plants you buy are nursery-grown! Height: 12 to 24 inches (30 to 60 cm). Spread: 12 to 24 inches (30 to 60 cm). USDA Plant Hardiness Zones 3 to 8.

MORE RECOMMENDED MAIDENHAIR FERNS

Adiantum aleuticum (Aleutian maidenhair fern): This fern, native to western North America, is still listed as *A. pedatum* subsp. *aleuticum* by many nurseries. The two are very similar in appearance, but Aleutian maidenhair has more deeply incised leaflets. There are several subspecies and cultivars, including 'Miss Marples', with golden green leaflets; and dwarf maidenhair (*A. aleuticum* subsp. *subpumilum*), rarely more than 6 inches (15 cm) tall. Height: 18 to 30 inches (45 to 75 cm). Spread: 18 to 30 inches (45 to 75 cm). USDA Plant Hardiness Zones 3 to 8.

A. venustum (Himalayan maidenhair fern): Superficially like the previous species in appearance, its fronds arch straight outward with no "bicycle handlebar." It is semi-evergreen, losing its fronds in winter in the North. New fronds are a pleasing pink in spring. Height: 6 to 12 inches (15 to 30 cm). Spread: 12 to 18 inches (30 to 45 cm). USDA Plant Hardiness Zones 5 to 9.

LARRY'S GARDEN NOTES

Adiantum comes from the Greek *adiantos*, meaning "can't be moistened," a statement that begs testing, don't you think? Get out a spray bottle and sprinkle the fronds with water. Darn if the Greeks weren't absolutely right: Water beads up on the blades' surface but won't sink in, much like the well-known perennial lady's mantle (*Alchemilla mollis*). The water droplets lining the pinnae, like rows of minimagnifying lenses, make a most charming sight on dewy mornings or after a rainfall.

American maidenhair fern (*Adiantum pedatum*)

Asplenium
Spleenwort

PLANT PROFILE

ASPLENIUM

a-SPLEN-ee-um

Foliage Color:
Green

Length of Foliage Season:
Evergreen

Height:
Varies by species; see
individual listings

Spread:
Varies by species; see
individual listings

Garden Uses:
Container planting,
groundcover, houseplant,
mass planting, rock garden,
wall planting, woodland
garden; along paths, on
slopes

Light Preference:
Partial shade to shade

Soil Preference:
Humus-rich, evenly moist,
well-drained soil

Best Way to Propagate:
Divide in spring or fall

USDA Plant Hardiness Zones:
Varies by species; see
individual listings

The best way to describe spleenworts is that . . . they have almost nothing in common! This huge genus of some 700 species covers the gamut of fern habits, from the deeply cut fronds one expects to straplike, undivided ones; from distinct crowns to creeping rhizomes; and from a terrestrial to epiphytic habitat! Most are tropical plants, but the genus also includes some truly hardy species—in fact, some live well above the Arctic Circle. Indeed, there are spleenworts found on all continents except Antarctica! Good news: Even the hardy species tend to be evergreen—or at least semi-evergreen—losing their fronds only after the coldest winters, thus ensuring year-round interest in many gardens.

GROWING TIPS

In spite of their diverse origins, spleenworts require much the same care. They prefer partial shade or shade and well-drained, rich, evenly moist soil. The hardy species tend to be found in alkaline soil in the wild, but they adapt without complaint to the slightly acid soils of most gardens.

Multiply spleenworts by division in spring or fall. The hardy species either have distinct crowns or grow in tufts, so it is fairly easy to see where one fern ends and the other begins. You can also multiply them by spores, although the cultivars will come true to type only when divided.

Other than the hardy forms described here that are grown outdoors year-round, there are numerous tropical spleenworts that are sold as houseplants and that can be used outdoors in summer. The best-known is the spectacular bird's-nest fern (*Asplenium nidus*), with apple green lance-shaped fronds forming a "nest" with a fuzzy brown base, among which sit unfurled, rounded crosiers that serve as eggs. It is hardy only in tropical areas Zone 10 and above.

PROBLEMS AND SOLUTIONS

Scale insects are a problem indoors. There are few problems outdoors.

TOP PERFORMER

Asplenium scolopendrium (hart's-tongue fern): This plant is quite unlike any other hardy fern, for its fronds are not cut but entire. Hart's-tongue is quite appropriate: The fronds do indeed look like an animal's tongue. It was formerly placed in its own genus as *Phyllitis scolopendrium* and is often still sold under that name. This fern is native to both eastern North America and Europe. The much commoner European form (it differs from the American form by its heart-shaped base) is widely available in culture, both in its tongue-shaped natural form and also as a multitude of horticultural selections with variously twisted, cut, and crested fronds. 'Crispum' is one of the most popular, with extremely undulated margins, rather like vegetable lasagna. 'Undulatum' is similar, but with margins that are more wavy than undulate. 'Cristatum' produces fronds that are normal at the base, then split into curious cock's comb–like extensions at the tip. 'Kaye's Lacerated' has fronds with curiously shredded edges ... and the list of horticultural oddities goes on and on! These mutated forms frequently develop new growth types, thus leading to even more varieties. And self-sown plants from spores (some cultivars are sterile, though) may do the same. Thus there is practically no end to the potential for weird plants with hart's-tongue fern! Height: 8 to 28 inches (20 to 70 cm). Spread: 24 inches (60 cm). USDA Plant Hardiness Zones 5 to 8.

Hart's-tongue fern
(*Asplenium scolopendrium* 'Angusto-Undulatum')

MORE RECOMMENDED SPLEENWORTS

Asplenium trichomanes (maidenhair spleenwort): The spleenwort that wants to be a maidenhair fern! This cosmopolitan fern, found in temperate climates throughout the world, has the same nearly black stalks as *Adiantum*, but with mid-green pinnae that are longer and rounded at the tips, not fan-shaped. This is a tough smaller fern and, being evergreen in many climates, makes a great groundcover. Height: 3 to 16 inches (8 to 40 cm). Spread: 12 to 18 inches (30 to 45 cm). USDA Plant Hardiness Zones 2 to 8.

LARRY'S GARDEN NOTES

The curious and not terribly attractive name spleenwort, used for many of the species, comes from the former medicinal use of the species in treating insufficiencies of the spleen. The botanical name also makes the same reference: *A* is Greek for without; *splen* means spleen. Don't chew on your spleenworts in order to fix your spleen disorders, though—it hasn't been used that way since ancient times!

Athyrium
Lady fern

PLANT PROFILE

ATHYRIUM

ath-EE-ree-um

Foliage Color:
Green

Length of Foliage Season:
Spring to fall

Height:
2 to 4 feet (60 to 120 cm)

Spread: 2 feet (60 cm)

Garden Uses:
Background, container planting, groundcover, mass planting, mixed border, woodland garden; along paths, on slopes

Light Preference:
Partial shade to shade

Soil Preference:
Humus-rich, evenly moist, well-drained soil

Best Way to Propagate:
Divide in spring or fall

USDA Plant Hardiness Zones:
Varies by species; see individual listings

If you like ferns that look like ferns yet have a tough constitution, the lady fern is for you. This is one of those cosmopolitan ferns that seem to get around so readily by spores: You'll find lady fern throughout the Northern Hemisphere and even in South America. It's a fairly large fern of graceful appearance, with deeply cut, light green fronds growing upright at first, then arching outward. Some *Athyrium* species have silver-marked fronds; these are described on pages 326–327. Since the fronds rise up around a central crown, the whole plant takes on a shuttlecock appearance when grown in isolation. It rarely grows in isolation, though, as lady fern offsets readily and soon creates its own little fern colony.

GROWING TIPS

Typical fern conditions are ideal: shade to partial shade in moist, humus-rich soil, although lady fern is tolerant of less-than-perfect soil and even grows well in heavy clay. This plant is also fairly drought-resistant once established, although it tends to turn yellow or go dormant if it dries out completely. It's better to ply lady fern with mulch and water as needed: A happy lady is a pretty lady. Likewise, this fern is more tolerant of full sun than many people give it credit for being, but it is likely to suffer frond discoloration if grown that way in the South.

Lady fern fronds are sometimes broken by strong winds, so plant it in a forested area or other protected site. On the other hand, any damage done is usually quickly corrected, as lady fern produces fresh new fronds throughout the growing season.

Since lady fern soon forms offsets all around the mother plant, multiplication is a breeze. Just dig up and move the offsets in early spring or after the fronds drop off in fall. If you're patient, you can multiply the species by collected spores. Of course, where lady fern is happy, she often self-sows all on her own. The cultivars must be multiplied by division: They don't come true from spores.

PROBLEMS AND SOLUTIONS

Rarely suffers from insects or diseases—and deer dislike lady ferns.

TOP PERFORMER

Athyrium filix-femina (lady fern): This one species has given rise, through natural selection or mutation, to some 300 varieties. Some of those with very intricate, lacy leaves are not good garden plants: Their frilly fronds catch every drop of rain and soon come crashing down. The following varieties are more interesting for the average home garden.

Northern lady fern (*A. filix-femina* var. *angustum*) is the typical form for northern North America, with narrower fronds and considerably greater hardiness than the species (Zone 2). This fern has a Dixie sidekick, the southern lady fern (*A. filix-femina* var. *asplenioides*) from the southern United States that is a good choice for hot-summer climates. Height: 2 to 4 feet (60 to 120 cm). Spread: 2 feet (60 cm). USDA Plant Hardiness Zones 4 to 9.

Crested lady fern (*A. filix-femina* 'Vernonia Cristatum') is one of many cultivars with ruffled foliage, in this case ending in a fluffy, lacy tassel. Quite the contrary to her crested sister, the tatting fern (*A. filix-femina* 'Frizelliae') is a minimalist, with leaflets so reduced (mere circles on either side of the stalk) that she has a very necklace-like appearance. Height: 2 to 4 feet (60 to 120 cm). Spread: 2 feet (60 to 120 cm). USDA Plant Hardiness Zones 4 to 9.

MORE RECOMMENDED LADY FERNS

Athyrium alpestre (alpine lady fern): There are some 180 species of *Athyrium* ferns, but, other than the lady fern and the silver-flushed *Athyrium* ferns described on page 326, not many of them are cultivated. The alpine lady fern, found in mountainous areas in North America and Eurasia, is sometimes available and is an interesting choice for colder climates, looking much like a smaller version of her lowland cousin. Not a good choice for hot-summer areas. Height: 1 to 2 feet (30 to 60 cm). Spread: 1 to 2 feet (30 to 60 cm). USDA Plant Hardiness Zones 3 to 6.

Lady fern (*Athyrium filix-femina* 'Hollandae')

LARRY'S GARDEN NOTES

If there is a lady fern (and guess what *filix-femina* means?), there must be a male fern, right? Well, there is: *Dryopteris filix-mas; mas* of course means male. Yet they belong to two different genera, so they can never intermarry. The reason behind the incongruous names is that, in Europe during the Middle Ages, no one yet knew about spores, and the reproduction of ferns was a mystery. Yet two ferns often grew side by side: one very dainty and ladylike, and one more robust and masculine. People took them to be a couple, and the names have remained ever since, even though we know they aren't compatible.

Athyrium
Painted fern

PLANT PROFILE

ATHYRIUM

ath-EE-ree-um

Foliage Color:
Silver and burgundy on a
green background

Length of Foliage Season:
Late spring to fall

Height:
12 to 18 inches (30 to 45 cm)

Spread:
12 to 24 inches (30 to 60 cm)

Garden Uses:
Container planting, edging,
groundcover, mass planting,
rock garden, woodland
garden

Light Preference:
Partial shade to shade

Soil Preference:
Humus-rich, evenly moist,
well-drained soil

Best Way to Propagate:
Divide in spring or fall

USDA Plant Hardiness Zones:
4 to 9

Who says ferns can't be colorful? This fern is one of the few that goes beyond green foliage and interesting texture to add color to your landscape. In fact, the fronds, as deeply and as intricately cut as any other fern, are almost anything *but* green—at least on top! There are some *Athyrium* species with green fronds; these are described on pages 324 and 325. The rachis (as the leaf stem is called on a fern) is a beautiful deep burgundy-red, a color that extends outward into the leaflets. The latter are, however, otherwise silvery. The result always reminds me of a silvery feather with a wine-red center. This unusual coloration has made this fern the most popular of all the *Athyrium* and also led it to be become, in 2004, the first fern ever to be chosen a Perennial Plant of the Year by the Perennial Plant Association.

GROWING TIPS

This is a tidy, easy-to-grow fern that prefers rich, humid, well-drained soil, but which seems to adapt to just about everything but truly dry conditions. Mulching, of course, is *de rigueur,* and it will likely need some watering during periods of drought.

Of course, like many ferns, painted fern is truly a plant of shade and partial shade. Only at the northernmost limits of its range should you consider growing this fern in full sun—even with a good mulch, it will tend to burn elsewhere.

Plant it and leave it is the best advice I can give for this plant. It is a slow-growing plant of modest size and can grow for decades without any intervention. Of course, you *can* divide it if you need new plants. The best season to do so is in fall in most climates, although in Zones 3 and 4, where winter damage to freshly planted ferns could be a problem, it would be best to wait until new growth appears in spring before proceeding.

In appropriate climates, painted fern will self-sow through the spores it produces under its leaves. The variation in coloration is quite surprising, with some being quite silvery and others distinctly redder than the usual species.

This fern is reliably hardy to Zone 4, but will thrive in Zone 3 where snow cover is trustworthy. Otherwise a fall mulch of chopped leaves will also help it through winter.

PROBLEMS AND SOLUTIONS

This fern is not terribly subject to insects or diseases.

Japanese painted fern (*Athyrium niponicum* var. *metallicum*)

TOP PERFORMER

Athyrium niponicum var. *metallicum* syn. *A. niponicum* var. *pictum* (Japanese painted fern): The species form, called simply *A. niponicum* or Japanese lady fern, is attractive enough but rarely grown, with all-green fronds. The painted fern so popular these days is *A. niponicum* var. *metallicum,* described here. For many years, it was the only colored form available, but over the last few years a number of special selections have been released, all offering "improvement" over the normal form. First to arrive on the scene was 'Ursula's Red', with much more red coloration, but there are now dozens with either better coloration or, more recently, crested or doubled segments. Whether their coloration or forms can truly be seen as improvements or just variants will largely depend on your taste in ferns. Among the many varieties are 'Silver Falls', with more silver on distinctly arching plants; 'Burgundy Lace', with crested fronds; and 'Pewter Lace', with grayer fronds. Most are slightly larger than the species. Height: 12 to 18 inches (30 to 45 cm). Spread: 12 to 24 inches (30 to 60 cm). USDA Plant Hardiness Zones: 4 to 9.

MORE RECOMMENDED PAINTED FERNS

Athyrium otophorum (silver lady fern): The green lady ferns (*Athyrium* spp.) are discussed on page 324, but there is another colorful lady fern: silver lady fern. It's a taller fern with deeply cut fronds that are distinctly silvery in coloration. On the better clones, the petiole is also distinctly reddish. This fern is certainly not as colorful as the Japanese painted fern, but it is a very nice and equally easy-to-grow plant where you're looking for something a bit taller. Height: 24 to 30 inches (60 to 75 cm). Spread: 24 inches (60 cm). USDA Plant Hardiness Zones 4 to 9.

LARRY'S GARDEN NOTES

One important thing to remember about Japanese painted fern is that it is *very* slow to sprout in spring, and until it does sprout, it is entirely undetectable—not leaving, as with many ferns, any visible aboveground structures. It is therefore very important to make sure you clearly mark its spot: It is so easy, when arriving home in spring with a trunkload of new plants, to see any open space as a good spot to plant—and that could quickly eliminate the painted fern, still dormant when almost every other plant is up, from your garden. I use unobtrusive black plastic markers to indicate where I've put plants like this and thus manage to keep them going in spite of my tendency to "fill in any holes" without hesitation.

Dryopteris

Wood fern, male fern, shield fern, buckler fern

DRYOPTERIS

dree-OP-ter-is

Foliage Color:
Green

Length of Foliage Season:
Spring to fall; some species evergreen

Height:
Varies by species; see individual listings

Spread:
Varies by species; see individual listings

Garden Uses:
Background, groundcover, mass planting, mixed border, rock garden, woodland garden; along paths, on slopes

Light Preference:
Partial shade to shade

Soil Preference:
Humus-rich, evenly moist, well-drained soil

Best Way to Propagate:
Divide in spring or fall

USDA Plant Hardiness Zones:
Varies by species; see individual listings

The name "wood fern" pretty much reveals this fern's favorite habitat, doesn't it? Well, it certainly gives me a good handle on what it likes! There are some 200 species of *Dryopteris*, mostly found in temperate areas around the world. Most of the cultivated species, at least, are semi-evergreen ferns of medium to large size with solid stems and upright, arching, deeply cut fronds with a generally swordlike silhouette. The plants of the cultivated species tend to have that typical shuttlecock shape we so love in ferns.

GROWING TIPS

Wood ferns are tough, no-nonsense ferns: Just plant them and walk away. They do best in rich, humusy soils that have good drainage yet remain evenly moist, but they tolerate most soils and even put up with a bit of drought. Mulching is always wise and, when naturalized, they'll love spots with deep leaf litter. Most normally grow in acid soils, but they will tolerate some lime. Partial shade to shade is best, although morning sun is even better. Many will tolerate full sun when kept moist.

Growing wood ferns from spores is an option for only the very patient. Besides, the most desirable cultivars are mutations and don't come true from spores. So divide established plants in early spring or late fall if you need more.

Warning: Wood ferns are toxic, especially if consumed in great quantities—although I haven't the foggiest idea why you'd want to do that!

PROBLEMS AND SOLUTIONS

Leaf diseases are possible but rare, and insects, slugs, and deer avoid them.

TOP PERFORMER

Dryopteris filix-mas (male fern): This species is a big 'un, sometimes 5 feet (1.5 m) high. It is found throughout almost all of the Northern Hemisphere, including all 50 states, although it may have been introduced to Hawaii. The species has robust, upright, arching, dark green fronds, deeply cut. The fronds are semi-evergreen, surviving through winter in all but the coldest climates. Male fern has given rise to dozens of cultivars, most considerably shorter than the species, including 'Cristata', with crested segments all along the frond; and 'Linearis Polydactyla', with crested fronds so fine they look like Venetian lace. Collectors will find many more in fern nurseries. Height: 2 to 5 feet (60 to 150 cm). Spread: 2 feet (60 cm). USDA Plant Hardiness Zones 2 to 9.

MORE RECOMMENDED WOOD FERNS

Dryopteris affinis (golden-scaled male fern): This fern is very similar to male fern and, in fact, was long considered just a variant of the better-known species. It has leathery fronds and stalks that are covered in golden scales, especially visible as the fronds unroll in spring. Like this plant's brother, it offers a wide variety of cultivars, including 'Crispa Gracilis', with crested, ruffled fronds; and 'Pinderi', with very fine fronds. Height: 2 to 5 feet (60 to 150 cm). Spread: 2 feet (60 cm). USDA Plant Hardiness Zones 4 to 9.

D. erythrosora (autumn fern): This is one of the most colorful fern species. The new fronds are coppery red at first, then turn dark green. The spore cases under the fronds turn brilliant red in fall. Since the fronds persist through winter (in fact, they are evergreen), the fall show continues until new growth covers it up in spring. This is, though, one of the least-hardy wood ferns. Height: 1 to 2 feet (30 to 60 cm). Spread: 2 feet (60 cm). USDA Plant Hardiness Zones 5 to 9.

D. marginalis (marginal wood fern): This eastern North American native is among the most evergreen of the hardy wood ferns and so makes a good choice in fairly cold climates where the fronds often stand up all winter through the snow. A bad winter will kill them back, but new ones appear in spring. This is a very thick-textured, leathery fern, dark green with a bluish tinge. Height: 18 to 24 inches (45 to 60 cm). Spread: 18 to 24 inches (45 to 60 cm). USDA Plant Hardiness Zones 3 to 9.

Male fern (*Dryopteris filix-mas*)

KISSING COUSINS

Woodsia ferns (*Woodsia* spp.) certainly *sound* like they belong in the same environment as wood ferns, but actually their name has nothing to do with forests. Instead, it honors the English botanist James Woods. As luck would have it, though, they do indeed like woody areas and look like dwarf versions of wood ferns. Give these ferns excellent drainage, as they often grow on rocks in the wild. Blunt-lobed woodsia (*Woodsia obtusa*), the most widely grown species, is actually fairly large for its genus. It is native to eastern North America. Height: 16 inches (40 cm). Spread: 10 to 16 inches (25 to 40 cm). USDA Plant Hardiness Zones 3 to 7.

Matteuccia

Ostrich fern, ostrich feather, shuttlecock fern, fiddlehead fern

MATTEUCCIA

ma-TOO-chee-uh

Foliage Color:
Green

Length of Foliage Season:
Spring to fall

Height:
4 to 6 feet (120 to 180 cm)

Spread: 3 feet (90 cm)

Garden Uses:
Background, mass planting, meadow garden, mixed border, specimen plant, vegetable garden, woodland garden; along paths, on slopes, at the back of beds and borders, in wet areas

Light Preference:
Partial shade to shade

Soil Preference:
Humus-rich, evenly moist, well-drained, acid soil

Best Way to Propagate:
Divide in spring or fall

USDA Plant Hardiness Zones:
2 to 8

Possibly the most majestic of all the temperate ferns, ostrich feather is certainly the most widely planted, at least in North America. It's a big fern, as tall as most people who plant it, with the perfect shuttlecock shape we so like in ferns: arching upward and outward from a compact base. The fronds are tall and deeply cut, with, as the common name suggests, a distinctly featherlike appearance. And at that size, it's definitely an ostrich feather, as suggested by the Latin species epithet as well: *struthio* (ostrich) and *pteris* (fern). Also fairly unusual, in mid- to late summer it produces fertile fronds quite different from the sterile fronds that appear in spring. They are shorter, grow straight up, and quickly turn brown without ever fully expanding, making for an interesting contrast with the foliage. They also persist through winter, unlike the sterile fronds.

GROWING TIPS

This plant grows in a wide band right across the Northern Hemisphere, from Alaska through almost all of Canada, dipping down into New England, then right across northern Europe and Asia. Right from the bat, then, you know it is going to be hardy. However, it does surprisingly well in milder climates too, even in mountain areas of Zone 8.

In the wild this plant grows in both full sun and deep shade; on dry land and in soggy swamps. However, it will take full sun only where it can be assured of constant, even moisture. For most gardeners, it's best to consider ostrich fern a plant for shade to partial shade. Established plants take drought in stride, though they may enter into summer dormancy, in which case their beautiful fronds die back pitifully. Rather than see them in such a sorry state, either grow them where they can profit from abundant leaf litter, or mulch them well and water during times of drought.

This is not a good fern for alkaline soils. In fact, it prefers soils that are "moderately acid," with a pH of about 5 to 5.5. It's therefore perfect with rhododendrons and other acid-lovers, but nonetheless adapts perfectly to a more "normal" garden soil pH closer to 6.5.

Ostrich fern produces offsets on stolons a foot or so (about 30 cm) from the mother plant, usually at a rate of about one or two per year. As a result, it fills in fairly quickly when planted as a groundcover or naturalized into a wooded area or a swamp. This also gives plentiful material for propagation: Dig out and move the offsets in spring or fall. Ostrich fern can also be grown from spores.

Warning: Ostrich fern is not a threatened species on the whole, although it can be locally rare. Even so, it is unfortunate to see plants being harvested indiscriminately for sale to gardeners, as digging ostrich ferns out of an otherwise pristine environment can harm the entire forest ecosystem. Always make sure you buy nursery-grown plants.

PROBLEMS AND SOLUTIONS

This is pretty much a no-problem plant.

TOP PERFORMER

Matteuccia struthiopteris var. *pensylvanica* (ostrich fern, ostrich feather, shuttlecock fern, fiddlehead fern): This is the North American variant of this international species, differing from the original Eurasian species, *M. struthiopteris,* by its taller size and somewhat darker fronds. It produces deeply cut, mid-green, broadly lance-shaped fronds of variable height, growing tallest in cool, moist, rich soils and considerably shorter in hot, dry, poor ones. Its rhizomes are thick and erect, looking like tree fern stumps when bare of fronds in winter. Surprisingly for a fern so widely planted, there are no common cultivars. Europeans are sold *M. struthiopteris,* about 1 foot (30 cm) shorter. Height: 4 to 6 feet (120 to 180 cm). Spread: 3 feet (90 cm). USDA Plant Hardiness Zones 2 to 9.

LARRY'S GARDEN NOTES

This is the fern that gives the edible fiddlehead so beloved of eastern Canadians and New Englanders. In fact, it is Vermont's state vegetable! The unrolled crosiers of mature plants are harvested as soon as they appear in spring, but never more than three per plant so as not to harm it. They have to be boiled before eating, as they are somewhat toxic when eaten raw.

Ostrich fern (*Matteuccia struthiopteris* var. *pensylvanica*)

Onoclea
Sensitive fern, bead fern

ONOCLEA

o-NOH-clay-uh

Foliage Color:
  Green

Length of Foliage Season:
  Spring to early fall

Height:
  12 to 24 inches (30 to 60 cm)

Spread:
  Indefinite

Garden Uses:
  Dried flower, edging, groundcover, mass planting, mixed border, woodland garden; along paths, on slopes, in wet areas

Light Preference:
  Sun to shade

Soil Preference:
  Humus-rich, moist to wet soil

Best Way to Propagate:
  Divide in spring or fall

USDA Plant Hardiness Zones:
  2 to 9

Sensitive fern is the only common fern that is generally sold in the groundcover section of garden centers. Not that the several others couldn't do the job, but they're slow to fill in—not this one. Sensitive fern is a creeper: Its stolons march off in all directions, branching abundantly and producing fronds as it wanders. If given a spot of its own, it will fill it completely; if planted among other plants, it will wander among them, filling in gaps. In other words, it does just what a groundcover is supposed to do: cover ground! Just plant it where it will encounter only plants its own height or taller—it's aggressive enough to smother smaller plants.

GROWING TIPS

This is certainly a low-care fern. Just plant it, water it, and walk away. Indeed, in areas where it is native (eastern and midwest North America, from Mexico to Canada, and also East Asia), it often shows up on its own, meaning no effort at all is required on your part.

Of course, all of that is true only if you plant it in the right conditions. Intense, hot sun is not to its liking, except in areas where soil humidity is abundant, such as in a swamp or alongside a water garden. Instead, think of it as groundcover for shade or partial shade. Sensitive fern *prefers* humus-rich, moist, acid soil but will put up with much, much less. In fact, just about any soil will do, from sand to clay, as long as it doesn't dry out too deeply. Likewise, it may *prefer* moderately acid soils (a pH of about 5.5 would be just right), but it grows without complaint even in neutral soils.

Sensitive fern adapts surprisingly well to extremes, both Siberian winters and impossibly humid summers. It does not, however, tolerate dry air, so it is not a good choice for arid climates.

The ideal place to plant sensitive fern is in a forested area, bog, or anywhere it can simply be allowed to go wild. It naturalizes extremely well and quickly becomes a permanent element of the local ecosystem. In formal gardens, make sure you prevent it from creeping outside of its allotted area by inserting barriers into the ground around the planting. Because the rhizomes are very shallow, even a simple plastic lawn border will do. Do not plant this fern in a rock garden: It readily takes over and, once it has rooted into the rocks, is nigh to impossible to extricate.

Multiply it by digging up sections, preferably when the fern goes dormant in fall or is just starting to come out of dormancy in spring. There is little need to multiply such a prolific offsetter by spores.

PROBLEMS AND SOLUTIONS

Rarely suffers from pests and diseases. Deer ignore it!

TOP PERFORMER

Onoclea sensibilis (sensitive fern, bead fern): This is actually not the most fernlike of all ferns, as the fronds are less feathery than most. They appear individually along the creeping rhizomes, sterile ones first, in spring. They are coppery to start, maturing to pale green, borne on an upright stem that arches over at the top so the blades are essentially horizontal. They are triangular in outline, coarsely cut down to near the stalk, with a wing of green between each lobe and its neighbor: a helpful key to identification, as few garden ferns have such wings. Erect fertile fronds—shorter, brown, and with beadlike segments— appear in summer. They dry well and can be used in arrangements. Their beadlike appearance gives this fern one of its common names: bead fern. There is only one species of sensitive fern and no cultivars, although some individuals have distinctly more spring color and it would be interesting to choose those for the garden.

Sensitive fern (*Onoclea sensibilis*)

LARRY'S GARDEN NOTES

Sensitive fern is said to have gotten its name from how quickly the fronds die back in fall. Just a touch of frost is all it takes to send this fern into winter dormancy. And it *will* go dormant; even in frost-free winters it loses its leaves and disappears from sight during the shortest days of the year.

Osmunda

Flowering fern, osmunda

OSMUNDA

ahz-MUN-dah

Foliage Color:
  Green

Length of Foliage Season:
  Spring to fall

Height:
  Varies by species; see individual listings

Spread:
  Varies by species; see individual listings

Garden Uses:
  Background, groundcover, mass planting, meadow garden, mixed border, seasonal hedge, specimen plant, woodland garden; at the back of beds and borders, in wet areas

Light Preference:
  Partial shade to shade

Soil Preference:
  Humus-rich, evenly moist, well-drained soil

Best Way to Propagate:
  Divide in early spring or fall

USDA Plant Hardiness Zones:
  Varies by species; see individual listings

Flowering ferns are big, spreading, luxuriant plants that need lots of space to look their best: Don't cram them in, or you'll cramp their style. Because of their size, they tend to have an almost tropical appearance, one that will best be appreciated in northern areas. Flowering ferns produce tall, bright green fronds that darken to deeper green in summer. The most curious feature of this genus, though, are the fertile fronds: Upright, thick, and usually a rich brown in color, they look for all the world like a drying flowerstalk, giving them the curious name of flowering fern!

GROWING TIPS

In the wild, flowering ferns are mostly found in swampy areas and may even be completely inundated for weeks in spring or sit with their roots soaking in water all summer. In spite of that, they do very well in typical garden conditions, although they start to wilt and lose their leaflets during a true drought. Mulching and irrigation will keep them happy where summers tend to be dry. They are at their best, often reaching huge sizes, in wet spots, such as near a water garden.

Flowering ferns range in the wild from the cold North to the hot, humid South and are equally adapted to varying conditions in culture, although they tend to be smaller under hot conditions. They are all deciduous, although they may hang onto their fronds well into winter in mild climates.

It is easy enough to divide fairly young flowering ferns in spring or fall and move them to the desired spot. Older plants, though, develop thick, woody bases, and dividing them may require a chain saw!

PROBLEMS AND SOLUTIONS

There really aren't any significant problems with these ferns.

TOP PERFORMER

Osmunda regalis (royal fern, flowering fern): This cosmopolitan fern, found almost everywhere but Australasia, is the largest and least fernlike of the flowering ferns. Indeed, with its brown stalks imitating branches and its small, well-spaced leaflets on branching fronds, you'd be forgiven for mistaking it for a shrub. The shrublike effect is compounded when the heretofore sterile fronds produce a brownish upright fertile section at their tip in mid-summer: You could then almost mistake the shrub for a false spirea (*Sorbaria* sp.) going to seed! Under ideal conditions, the royal fern can reach 10 feet (3 m) tall, but 4 to 6 feet (1.2 to 1.8 m) is more likely under garden conditions. In subtropical climates, try to locate plants selected locally—such natives do better in mild winters than those of northern origin. Indeed, sometimes they are nearly evergreen! 'Purpurascens' is one of the few cultivars: Its new fronds are quite purplish and the stalks retain that color all summer. Spread: 4 feet (1.2 m). USDA Plant Hardiness Zones 3 to 10.

Royal fern (*Osmunda regalis*)

MORE RECOMMENDED FLOWERING FERNS

Osmunda cinnamomea (cinnamon fern): Like *O. regalis,* cinnamon fern is quite cosmopolitan, found on most continents in the wild. It is a delightful, large fern, with a distinctly more fernlike appearance than its royal cousin. Indeed, with its stately shuttlecock silhouette, you'd be forgiven for mistaking it for an ostrich fern. The most obvious difference, though, is the beautiful cinnamon-colored fertile fronds that rise from the center of the rosette. They, plus the cinnamon-colored young crosiers, helped give the plant its common and botanical names. Older plants have massive, dark brown, knobby rhizomes, sometimes up to 1 foot (30 cm) tall, creating the appearance of a trunk at the base—about as close as you can come to a hardy tree fern. By the way, the spring crosiers are edible, much like those of the better-known ostrich fern (*Matteuccia struthiopteris,* page 331). Height: 3 to 5 feet (90 to 150 cm). Spread: 3 feet (90 cm). USDA Plant Hardiness Zones 3 to 10.

LARRY'S GARDEN NOTES

The massive, woody rhizomes of the cinnamon fern (*O. cinnamomea*) are harvested and sold as a soil amendment under the name osmunda, notably used in orchid culture. However, the huge structures take decades or even centuries to reach a harvestable size, and the supply of usable flowering ferns is now much smaller than before. These days tree fern trunks, which grow much more quickly, are used for the same purpose. Curiously, perhaps out of habit, the product is still often called osmunda, although the tree ferns now used are not in the genus *Osmunda* at all.

Polystichum

Hollyfern, sword fern, Christmas fern

PLANT PROFILE

POLYSTICHUM

pah-LIH-stih-kum

Foliage Color:
  Green

Length of Foliage Season:
  Evergreen

Height:
  Varies by species; see
  individual listings

Spread:
  Varies by species; see
  individual listings

Garden Uses:
  Container planting, cut
  foliage, edging, groundcover,
  mass planting, mixed border,
  rock garden, specimen plant,
  wall planting, woodland
  garden; on slopes

Light Preference:
  Partial shade to shade

Soil Preference:
  Humus-rich, well-drained soil

Best Way to Propagate:
  Divide in spring

USDA Plant Hardiness Zones:
  Varies by species; see
  individual listings

The genus *Polystichum* offers some 200 species of small to medium ferns, often with very different characteristics. However, they share one important trait: tough, wiry, evergreen foliage you almost could scrub a pot with! They can put up with strong winds, ice storms, wandering deer, and cross-country skiers—and still manage to look good year-round. They are thus invaluable in landscaping: essentially the mini-conifers of shade borders and woodland gardens, giving that stamp of permanence to beds that the hopelessly seasonal annuals and perennials simply can't come close to matching.

GROWING TIPS

Aesop could have been writing about the *Polystichum* fern when he wrote, "Slow but steady wins the race." They're slow-growing but ever so trustworthy, super ferns for beginning shade gardeners, and they are so hard to kill. They do prefer cool, moist growing conditions, so mulching is always wise and watering may be needed the first year. Once established, though, they become very drought-resistant. These are not ferns for soggy bottomlands: They prefer good drainage at all times and so are ideal on slopes. Rich loam soils and shade to partial shade are best, but they adapt to almost anything—even full sun if the ground remains fairly moist. Although evergreen, fronds don't live forever: Those of *Polystichum* are slow to disappear on their own, and you may feel the need to cut them off when they turn brown. Some gardeners simply cut the whole plant back in spring to make room for new fronds.

Polystichum spp. form tight rosettes and offset quite readily (albeit slowly), giving you a good source of material for propagation.

PROBLEMS AND SOLUTIONS

Polystichum are generally disease- and insect-free.

TOP PERFORMER

Polystichum acrostichoides (Christmas fern): Every region of North America has its own local hollyfern, if not several. This is the most widely distributed species in eastern North America and is also readily available in nurseries. It forms a symmetrical rosette of dark green, sword-shaped fronds with small leaflets. This species offsets very infrequently, so buy several plants to create an interesting effect. Height: 12 to 18 inches (30 to 45 cm). Spread: 12 inches (30 cm). USDA Plant Hardiness Zones 3 to 9.

MORE RECOMMENDED HOLLYFERNS

Polystichum munitum (western sword fern, giant hollyfern): This is western North America's version of the Christmas fern, similar in appearance, although much bigger and also more upright. Height: 3 feet (90 cm). Spread: 5 feet (150 cm). USDA Plant Hardiness Zones 4 to 9.

P. setiferum (soft shield fern, hedge fern): This larger species is the most common European hollyfern, widely grown around the world as an ornamental. It is one of the few *Polystichum* species that is *not* evergreen: They die back in winter in cold climates. The fronds are soft to the touch (hence "soft" shield fern) rather than rough like the others. This species has produced a bewildering array of cultivars with variously crested, twisted, and otherwise mutated fronds. Among them are 'Congestum Cristatum', a dwarf with dense leaflets on a frond forked at the tip; 'Divisilobium', whose frond is highly divided and therefore very lacy in appearance; and the list goes on and on! Height: 12 to 30 inches (30 to 75 cm). Spread: 18 to 36 inches (45 to 90 cm). USDA Plant Hardiness Zones 5 to 9.

P. tsus-simense (Korean rock fern, dwarf hollyfern): This is a tiny replica of the soft shield fern, ideal for rock gardens and also, indoors, for terrariums. It forms neat, compact clumps of triangular dark green fronds, sometimes with a purple tinge as they emerge. The stems are nearly black. Height: 6 to 12 inches (15 to 30 cm). Spread: 12 inches (30 cm). USDA Plant Hardiness Zones 6 to 9.

Christmas fern
(*Polystichum acrostichoides*)

KISSING COUSINS

There is another holly fern: the genus *Cyrtomium*. The two genera have little in common other than fronds that are thick and waxy, like holly leaves. Instead of the tiny leaflets of *Polystichum* species, *Cyrtomium* species bear large, broad, sickle-shaped leaflets. The most widely available is the Japanese holly fern (*C. falcatum*): It is commonly used as a houseplant where it won't survive winter outdoors. Height: 2 feet (60 cm). Spread: 3½ feet (105 cm). USDA Plant Hardiness Zones 7 to 10.

Ornamental grasses and grasslike plants are among the hottest items in the modern shade garden—
and when they look this good, no wonder!

Chapter   10

Grasses   for   Shade

Grasses seem particularly likely choices for a shade garden. After all, when you think of a grass, either a lawn comes to mind, or a vast prairie of tall grasses, or perhaps grasses holding back the elements on a sand dune . . . all in full sun. But that would be underestimating the power of grasses. The grass family (Poaceae) is one of the largest families of flowering plants, with over 500 genera and 8,000 species. And among those thousands of species, there are actually hundreds adapted to shade and partial shade—and many of those offer great ornamental value as well.

WHAT IS A GRASS?

Definition time! A true grass is a member of the wide-ranging grass family (Poaceae, formerly Graminae). It shares such characteristics as narrow leaves with parallel veins that wrap around the plant's stem at their base, and stems that are generally cylindrical and hollow (or become hollow at maturity), with swellings (nodes) at spots where leaves are or were once attached.

That said, gardeners also tend to lump other plants in with grasses: the sedge family (Cyperaceae), rush family (Juncaceae), and cattail family (Typhaceae) are just a few of the plants you may be familiar with that look like grasses and are often called grasses, but are not. None of those belong to the family Poaceae, so they can't be grasses; however, in a garden setting, they look like grasses and are used like grasses. As a result, they are usually lumped in with grasses, at least in gardening books.

Then again, there are grasses that don't much look like grasses. Bamboos immediately come into mind on that account: Their stems are woody and often thick, plus they build on their previous season's growth, thus growing taller from year to year (other grasses start fresh from ground level every year). They also have branches much like a shrub, yet they have the same narrow, pointed leaves and hollow, rounded stems—complete with nodes—that grasses have. Bamboos can perhaps be thought of as shrubby grasses, but they are grasses nonetheless.

Clumpers and Runners

Gardeners who have some experience with ornamental grasses always ask the same question when presented with a new grass. Does it run, or does it clump? That's because most have had at least one bad experience with a running grass and prefer to be forewarned!

Running grasses produce creeping underground rhizomes (runners or stolons) that often pop up quite a distance from the parent plant. As a result, they can easily become invasive. In fact, one of the best-known weeds worldwide is quackgrass, a (*Agropyron repens*), noxious grass that is so efficient at producing plantlets at a distance that it is nearly impossible to eradicate. Left on their own, running grasses will create a carpeting effect and therefore make good groundcovers, although you may want to avoid introducing them to a formal border where their habit of popping up where unwanted is rarely appreciated.

The term "clumping grass" is a bit of a misnomer, leading you to believe it simply forms a clump and stays that size. Actually, all perennial grasses expand outward, but clumpers do it much more sedately. Instead of sprouting well away from the parent plant, clumping grasses produce offsets at the base of the original plant, then these produce equally tightly spaced offsets in their turn. So they do spread, but very slowly, in a fairly symmetrical outward direction centered on the original plant. As a result, they naturally take on the appearance of a clump or tussock.

Of course, there are also grasses of intermediate habits. For example, certain clumpers occasionally produce an offset a certain distance from the parent plant that starts a new, independent clump. And other grasses usually considered clumpers, like northern sea oats (*Chasmanthium latifolium*), actually form a fairly loose clump and will definitely spread over time, so are sort of a "running clumper."

Obviously, this growth habit affects the way you deal with grasses. Clumping grasses can be planted and ignored—for years if necessary. When the clump gets too large, usually not before 10 years later or so, just divide it to keep it in its place. Running grasses spread rapidly—some send out runners up to 5 feet (1.5 m) long—and need some control in most garden settings. The easiest thing to do is to plant them within a root barrier (see page 54): The runners will have nowhere to go, so they accumulate within the barrier, soon forming a dense mass of vegetation that looks just like, well, a clumping grass! In fact, there are actually commercial barriers designed specifically to control bamboos—many of which are runners, and some of which produce runners thicker than a carrot. Bamboo barriers are generally about 2 feet (60 cm) high and are made of thick

40-mil plastic. Sink one of those into the ground and just dare your bamboo to try and escape!

Culture

Grasses come from a wide variety of climates and conditions (sun/shade, arctic/tropical, wet/arid, etc.), so you'll have to read the individual descriptions to get a handle on their needs. In general, annual grasses need to be treated like any other annuals (see Chapter 7, beginning on page 233). Since few annual grasses are included in this book (most annual grasses are sun-lovers), the cultural techniques described here apply mostly to perennial grasses.

Perennial grasses are very similar to other herbaceous perennials as far as cultural needs are concerned. If you've grown perennials, you can grow grasses: It's as simple as that. However, it is helpful to know whether you're growing cool-season or warm-season grasses in order to grow them with more success.

Cool-Season and Warm-Season Grasses

Grass experts like to divide grasses into two groups: cool-season grasses, and warm-season grasses. I must admit that I don't to-tally agree with that classification (lots of grasses are exceptions to one or more of the criteria), but it can be a handy point from which to start.

Cool-season grasses sprout early in spring and come quickly into bloom. They don't do much of anything in summer (indeed, some go summer-dormant in arid climates) but start growing again with the return of cooler weather in fall. In mild climates, some grow right through winter. Most are evergreen, or at least "winter-green"—they may turn brown in summer. Since cool-season grasses grow vigorously both early and late in the season, they can be planted or divided in either spring or fall. The majority of the truly shade-tolerant grasses are cool-season ones.

Warm-season grasses are slow off the mark in spring: They wait until the ground warms up before sprouting, then grow all summer, usually flowering in late summer or fall. They go fully dormant in winter, and often their foliage dies but still stands tall, turning attractive shades of beige or brown. Since warm-season grasses are slow to root, they're best planted and divided in spring. This allows them a full season to settle in before having to deal with winter. Most warm-season grasses require full sun; only a few of those that also tolerate partial shade are described here.

Arrhenatherum

Bulbous oat grass, onion couch grass

ARRHENATHERUM

a-ren-A-the-rum

Foliage Color:
Green-and-white

Length of Foliage Season:
Spring to fall

Bloom Color:
Silver-green

Bloom Time:
Summer

Category:
Cool-season grass

Height (foliage):
6 to 12 inches (15 to 30 cm)

Height (flower):
18 to 24 inches (45 to 60 cm)

Spread:
12 inches (30 cm)

Garden Uses:
Container planting, edging, groundcover, mass planting, mixed border, rock garden, woodland garden

Light Preference:
Full sun to partial shade

Soil Preference:
Poor to rich, moist, well-drained soil

Best Way to Propagate:
Divide in spring or fall

USDA Plant Hardiness Zones:
4 to 9

There's nothing new about this deciduous ornamental grass! It's an old-fashioned charmer, handed down from gardener to gardener over the generations. It's a nice, mounding, cool-season grass, up bright and early in spring, making a small but thick clump of upright gray-green leaves with a broad white margin. As a result, the entire plant seems almost white and, in fact, this is probably the whitest of all the ornamental grasses. The flower stem is likewise upright, with oatlike spikelets colored silvery green at first, but fading to white: quite charming!

GROWING TIPS

Bulbous oat grass is an easy-to-grow ornamental grass for places where you need something small and colorful, such as edging or rock gardens. It also makes a great groundcover: Space plants 8 inches (20 cm) apart so they touch at the edges, and you'll soon have a nice, rolling carpet of greenish white. Although popular in rock gardens, be forewarned that it does tend to spread a bit through its bulbous stem bases being displaced accidentally. I once saw it sprouting in a bird's nest, obviously having been carried there by a mother bird who figured the stem would be an ideal building material!

This grass is very tolerant of a wide range of soils, although it does best in moderately rich soils that remain evenly moist. It is, however, quite drought-resistant when well established. It burns out very quickly in hot-summer areas when grown in full sun, so it's considered uniquely a partial shade plant there. In the North or in areas where summers are cooler, either partial shade or full sun is fine.

Bulbous oat grass tends to choke itself out after 4 or 5 years through overproduction of offsets at its base. If yours starts to look weak or bare in the middle, just divide it, cutting out the barren parts; replant it; and it will fully recover in just a few weeks. As you divide, remove all green sections, if any.

If the plant seems to decline in appearance in late summer (sometimes a problem in hot areas, in blazing sun, or if it is diseased), cut it back harshly and it will sprout again, looking just as perky the second time around as the first one.

You can't grow this one from seed. The only cultivar available, 'Variegatum', is self-sterile and produces fertile seed only when near wild plants of the same species—and even then, the plants produced are not variegated. You can, however, grow it from "bulbs" taken from the plant's base and planted elsewhere.

PROBLEMS AND SOLUTIONS

Rust can be a problem toward the middle of summer. The easiest solution is to cut the plant back, forcing it to grow a whole new wardrobe.

TOP PERFORMER

Arrhenatherum elatius subsp. *bulbosum* 'Variegatum' (variegated bulbous oat grass, variegated onion couch grass): The botanical name is very nearly as long as the plant is large! There is no problem choosing here: It is the only *Arrhenatherum,* a genus of meadow grasses, grown as an ornamental. The original form comes from Europe, but both tall oat grass (*A. elatius*) and its bulbous-based subspecies, bulbous oat grass (*A. elatius* subsp. *bulbosum*), are now well established in pastures and fields throughout the temperate world. 'Variegatum' is the ornamental selection of the latter.

This is the most easily recognizable of the variegated grasses—if you're willing to bend over and give it a feel or pull off a stem. The base of the stem is covered with a short series of onion-shaped "bulbs" set one after the other like beads on a string; no other grass has such structure. The "bulbs" are not too visible, though: They're well hidden by the foliage throughout the growing season, thus the need to feel the stem or yank off a piece.

LARRY'S GARDEN NOTES

Make sure you plant grasses at the same depth as they were originally. Many, especially when small, are subject to rot if planted too deeply. As with most plants, keep them fairly moist for the first growing season. And a mulch is always welcome.

Variegated bulbous oat grass (*Arrhenatherum elatius* subsp. *bulbosum* 'Variegatum')

Carex

Sedge

The genus *Carex* is a huge one, with over 2,000 species and undoubtedly many more as yet undescribed. It is fully cosmopolitan, found everywhere in the world except Antarctica, and so variable it contains all sorts of species: tropical and arctic, drought-resistant and swamp-dwelling, tall and tiny, persnickety and easy-to-grow. However, there is a specific group especially grown in shade gardens, commonly called "woodland sedges," and they *do* share a few traits: They are small grasslike plants with usually insignificant flowers and usually evergreen foliage, often variegated in horticultural selections. They are sedges and not true grasses. The best way of telling them apart is that "sedges have wedges"— sedge stems are wedge-shaped (triangular) in cross-section.

GROWING TIPS

Woodland sedges are plants of moist forests and thus do best in partial to full shade, although they're fine in full sun in cool-summer areas. They prefer even soil moisture, but not, unlike their swamp-dwelling cousins, soggy soil. They'll even adapt to periodic drought, although you'll find they do better if you keep them mulched and watered during dry summers. They're quite adaptable to soil type, although (like almost every plant) they do like lots of humus.

None of the plants described here has very visible flowers, but neither are the flowers unattractive, so you can simply ignore them. The deciduous species lose their leaves in fall so they essentially take care of themselves, but evergreen ones, by far the majority, can get a bit messy over time if allowed to grow on and on. It is worthwhile cutting them back annually in early spring—you may even be able to mow them if they are accessible with a lawn mower.

Woodland sedges are best known as groundcovers, creating perfect carpets of green or green-and-white in even the deepest shade, but they also make handsome container plants and are stunning in shady rock gardens as well.

Division in spring or fall is the ideal means of multiplication; some will self-sow where they're happy.

PROBLEMS AND SOLUTIONS

If rust or other leaf diseases strike, cut the plants back harshly and they'll produce fresh, symptom-free foliage.

TOP PERFORMER

Carex siderosticha (broadleaf sedge): This is a rather unusual sedge, actually, for it has broad rather than narrow leaves and is deciduous in all but the mildest climates—in a genus where 95 percent of the species are evergreen! It is also a stunner—the broad, dark green leaves arch out sideways, forming a thick, rounded clump that expands slowly outward, rather like a creeping hosta. The species itself is rarely grown, but variegated forms abound, starting with the appropriately named 'Variegata', with broad white margins and some central white striping, pinkish in spring. 'Shima Nishiki' (sold as 'Island Brocade') has creamy yellow striping rather than white; the leaves of 'Lemon Zest' are entirely golden. Flowers are insignificant. This plant is much hardier than previously supposed—it's absolutely stunning in my Zone 3 garden under snow! Height (foliage): 8 to 12 inches (20 to 30 cm). Height (flower): 8 to 12 inches (20 to 30 cm). Spread: Indefinite. USDA Plant Hardiness Zones 4 to 9.

MORE RECOMMENDED SEDGES

Carex morrowii (Japanese sedge): A much more typical sedge than the previous one, with leaves both narrow and evergreen. It is the classic sedge of Japanese gardens, forming a perfect rounded mound of arching leaves that just gets thicker and thicker over time. The species itself, with green leaves, is rarely grown, but variegated cultivars abound, starting with 'Variegata', the best-known cultivar, with leaves margined in white. 'Goldband' is its yellow-margined counterpart—and there are plenty more where they came from! Height (foliage): 12 to 18 inches (30 to 45 cm). Height (flower): 12 to 18 inches (30 to 45 cm). Spread: 6 to 12 inches (15 to 30 cm). USDA Plant Hardiness Zones 5 to 9.

Broadleaf sedge
(*Carex siderosticha* 'Variegata')

LARRY'S GARDEN NOTES

The main description covers only two of 2,000 sedges, so you can imagine the other possibilities! In choosing, though, why look abroad when there are so many beautiful native woodland sedges? There are hundreds of them (and I'm not exaggerating!). That dense, carpet-forming, grasslike plant in a forest near you is probably a sedge, and it would likely look just great in your own woodland garden. Commercially available natives include palm sedge (*Carex muskingumensis*), plantainleaf sedge (*C. plantaginea*), and Gray's sedge (*C. grayi*), all hardy in Zones 3 through 8.

Chasmanthium

Northern sea oats, spangle grass, Indian wood oats

PLANT PROFILE

CHASMANTHIUM

kaz-MAN-thee-um

Foliage Color:
Green

Length of Foliage Season:
Spring to fall

Bloom Color:
Green to brown

Bloom Time:
Late summer to early fall

Category:
Warm-season grass

Height (foliage):
3 to 4 feet (90 to 120 cm)

Height (flower):
4 to 5 feet (120 to 150 cm)

Spread:
2 feet (60 cm)

Garden Uses:
Background, container planting, cut flower garden, dried flower, mass planting, meadow garden, mixed border, seasonal hedge, woodland garden

Light Preference:
Full sun to shade

Soil Preference:
Humus-rich, moist, well-drained soil

Best Way to Propagate:
Move self-sown seedlings in spring

USDA Plant Hardiness Zones:
2 to 9

Most shade grasses are smaller plants best suited for edging or groundcover use, but here's a sturdily upright grower that can help bring the look of the taller prairie grasses to shadier parts of your lot. It forms an open clump of upright stems with lance-shaped, fairly broad, arching leaves and has rather a bamboolike appearance. Foliage color varies during the growing season, from pale green in sun to dark green in shade, but changes to copper in late fall and brown in winter. The flowers are definitely part of this grass's charm: First upright, then dangling, the flattened, spike-edged blossoms go from green as they form in late summer to brown in winter. And they look great in both fresh and dried arrangements.

GROWING TIPS

Northern sea oats is native to a large area through eastern and midwestern North America, from Texas to southern Canada, and lives in a wide variety of habitats, from dense woodlands to open prairies to river edges, which gives you an idea of its great adaptability. In fact, just about any garden condition will suit it, from poor soil to rich soil, constant moisture to severe drought, and full sun to shade. For really good-looking plants, though, ensure at least fairly good soil and even moisture. Partial shade to shade is best, as the leaf tips tend to burn in full sun, especially when exposed to severe drought.

Here's one grass you can grow from seed. There are, as yet at least, no cultivars that require vegetative propagation and the plants will bloom, albeit lightly, the first year from seed. In nurseries, too, it is usually grown from seed. In the garden it self-sows readily, so you'll probably find the best way of multiplying it is simply moving self-sown seedlings to where you want to see them grow. Of course, you can also grow this grass from divisions taken in spring.

Warning: Northern sea oats can be a bit invasive, mostly due to self-seeding (it also spreads by clump expansion, but less aggressively). For modest control (it *will* self-sow, but only very lightly), simply mulch well—that will prevent the majority of seeds from sprouting. For total control, harvest the flowerheads for flower arrangements before the seed matures in late fall. Most gardeners don't find it too weedy, though, and certainly young plants are easy enough to pull out.

PROBLEMS AND SOLUTIONS

Northern sea oats seem essentially immune to insects and diseases.

TOP PERFORMER

Chasmanthium latifolium (northern sea oats, spangle grass, Indian wood oats): There are six species of *Chasmanthium*, but only this one is grown as an ornamental. With its upright stems and well-spaced leaves it looks quite bamboolike, at least until its flowers appear in late summer. Both the arching leaves and the flattened flowerheads dance in the slightest breeze, creating an appealing rustling sound. Northern sea oats is an attractive plant throughout the entire summer and fall and well into winter, although it is perhaps at its most attractive against the white background of the first snows. The foliage and flowers don't always hold through the entire winter, though: They generally collapse before spring, so cut the plant back at winter's end to leave room for the coming season's growth. Surround northern sea oats with spring bulbs—they fill in during the grass's downtime, then the grass takes over the stage as the bulbs fade. A perfect partnership!

Northern sea oats
(*Chasmanthium latifolium*)

LARRY'S GARDEN NOTES

Oh what a tangled web we weave . . . when we try to make any sense of common names. Why is *Chasmanthium latifolium* called northern sea oats, I wondered, when it is a forest grass, not a seaside one? After mucho research, I discovered that our plant had once been known as *Uniola latifolia* and was thus thought related to a grass called sea oats (*Uniola paniculata*), so named because it does grow near the ocean and has a vaguely oatlike flower. I assume calling *Chasmanthium latifolium* "inland sea oats" sounded too weird and so didn't catch on, but the incongruous "northern sea oats" did.

Dactylis

Variegated orchard grass, variegated cock's-foot grass

Variegated orchard grass looks much like a larger version of bulbous oat grass (page 342). Like its distant relative, it produces dense clumps of narrow, white-striped dark green leaves and is essentially grown for its foliage alone (since it flowers only irregularly). Some find it unfortunate that the flowers are so rare—they are quite attractive, fluffy, light green turning whitish, and almost bristly looking, much denser than those of most shade grasses, and borne on one-sided flowerstalks. Those who use this plant as a groundcover, on the other hand, prefer the regularity of the foliage's dense coverage and snip the flowers off when they appear.

GROWING TIPS

This is not a true shade grass but a grass for partial shade or sun. It looks best in partial shade, where the white-striped leaves add lots of luminosity to the garden, but it is fine, if not quite so striking, in sun as well. It readily adapts to most soils except the heaviest clays, although it grows much more densely and quickly when the soil is rich and evenly moist. It is very drought-tolerant and will go fully summer-dormant during periods of prolonged drought, only to spring to life as if nothing had happened with the return of fall rains.

As with many cool-season grasses, variegated orchard grass produces two spurts of growth: in early spring, and again in late summer or fall. If it starts looking ratty before the end of summer, cut it back to about 3 inches (8 cm) from the ground; that will encourage it to renew itself earlier than usual. In many gardens the foliage is evergreen, although it may be killed back by cold weather in northern climates. Even that is variable: Under reasonable snow cover, it often retains its leaves. In either case, it is worth "tidying" the plant up a bit in late winter or early spring by cutting it back to 3 inches (8 cm) from the ground to give the new leaves room to grow and fill in.

This thick grass is at its best as a groundcover in partial shade. As to habit, it is one of the "in-between" grasses: Although essentially clump-forming, it also produces rhizomes, so over time it develops into a series of individual clumps that usually meet at the edges, meaning it creates a very nice carpet all on its own. It is also fairly fast-spreading: Planted on 10-inch (25-cm) centers, small plants will often fill in completely the first year.

The most important factor in this plant's maintenance is to remove any all-green sprouts. It produces them regularly. See "Larry's Garden Notes" for more details.

Variegated orchard grass
(*Dactylis glomerata* 'Variegata')

PROBLEMS AND SOLUTIONS

Insect and disease problems are rare.

TOP PERFORMER

Dactylis glomerata 'Variegata' (variegated orchard grass, variegated cock's-foot grass): The species, *Dactylis glomerata,* the only one in the genus *Dactylis,* is never grown as an ornamental but is a fodder and pasture grass of minor importance. Imported from Europe generations ago, it has since gone thoroughly native and is now found in all 50 states and also in inhabited parts of Canada as a wild grass, especially in orchards. It is considerably taller than its ornamental offspring, with flowerstalks up to 5 feet (1.5 m) high. Apparently the variegation of variegated orchard grass, with the reduced chorophyll that results from the white striping on the leaf, means the plant absorbs less energy than the species and thus stays smaller and fails to bloom regularly. In spite of that, 'Variegata' shows no lack of vigor in the garden and can even be a bit invasive. There are no other cultivars of *Dactylis glomerata.*

LARRY'S GARDEN NOTES

Variegation, the abnormal coloration of plant tissues (normally green leaves with stripes or splotches of other colors), is a common mutation in plants and one highly prized by gardeners. However, variegated plants tend to "revert"—produce branches or sections of the original all-green form—variegated orchard grass more so than many others. Reversions should be removed, as they have more chlorophyll than the variegate and thus more energy, and therefore tend to outgrow it. Soon the green sections have taken over entirely, and your beautiful variegate has been lost!

Deschampsia

Hair grass

Hair grasses are renowned for their gigantic but ever-so-light inflorescences, arching up and out above the dense clumps of narrow, dark green foliage below. The result is a billowing, see-through mass of light green (or purplish or golden, depending on the cultivar and the season) hovering over the flowerbed—and a show that lasts from spring right through winter if the stalks are not harvested. True enough, bits do break off from late summer on, and the display becomes thinner as winter advances, although it is still very attractive. The sight is so ethereal yet so beautiful that it can lighten up even the heaviest landscape. This is one grass you really must try!

GROWING TIPS

Hair grasses adapt well to most garden conditions, but to reach their peak performance and fullest size (and who wants a runty hair grass? Doing "ethereal" requires some height!), they need rich, evenly moist soils and cool conditions. In most areas, they'll do best in partial shade to shade but bloom well only in full shade in the South. Full sun, on the other hand, is fine in the North. Hair grasses can be said to be "drought-tolerant" but not "drought-happy": Mulch them, water them, but do keep them at least slightly moist. They can look terribly ratty in areas of high summer heat, although they survive it. They really are not good choices for hot climates.

It's probably best to categorize hair grasses as "evergreen wannabes." Although the flowerstalks change color with the season, from green to purplish in spring and early summer to various golden shades by fall, the leaves stubbornly hold onto their green summer color until heavy frost hits. In the North, they're killed back to the ground; in the South (generally, Zones 8 and 9), they do remain evergreen, although they take on a yellowish tinge; and elsewhere the bases remain green and rest of the leaf turns golden brown. By spring, they're in need of a good haircut to leave room for fresh growth. But don't delay—trimming them back too late can damage the flowerstalks, which start to form surprisingly early. Flowerstalks should be harvested in fall anyway (they look stupendous in dried arrangements!) if you want to keep the plants from self-seeding.

Although hair grasses readily self-sow, all those offered commercially are cultivars and none comes true from seed, leaving division, which can be carried out in spring or fall, as the only logical means of multiplication.

PROBLEMS AND SOLUTIONS

Rarely subject to insects and diseases, and deer avoid it.

TOP PERFORMER

Deschampsia cespitosa (tufted hair grass): This is the most common species in culture and is likely very common in the wild, found throughout the temperate to cold zones of the entire Northern Hemisphere. There are dozens of cultivars, including 'Goldgehänge' ('Golden Shower'), with golden yellow panicles; 'Bronzeschleier' ('Bronze Veil'), with brassier blooms; and 'Northern Lights', smaller than most, with cream-variegated foliage. In hot-summer climates, consider heat-tolerant *D. cespitosa* subsp. *holciformis,* now considered a separate species: *D. holciformis.* Height (foliage): 16 to 24 inches (40 to 60 cm). Height (flower): 24 to 48 inches (60 to 120 cm). Spread: 16 to 36 inches (40 to 90 cm). USDA Plant Hardiness Zones 3 to 9.

MORE RECOMMENDED HAIR GRASSES

Deschampsia flexuosa (wavy hair grass, crinkled hair grass): Another Northern Hemisphere native, this one tends to dwell on mountaintops; tufted hair grass is a valley girl. As the name suggests, the flowerstalks are wavy rather than straight but create the same hazy effect as *D. cespitosa*—of which it can be considered a dwarf, drought-resistant version. 'Tatra Gold' ('Aurea') is an even more dwarf form (flower height: 8 inches/20 cm) with lime green foliage. Height (foliage): 6 to 8 inches (15 to 20 cm). Height (flower): 12 inches (30 cm). Spread: 12 inches (30 cm). USDA Plant Hardiness Zones 2 to 9.

Tufted hair grass (*Deschampsia cespitosa* 'Goldstaub')

KISSING COUSINS

Of course, mention must be made of the most amusing of all the hair grasses: *D. cespitosa* var. *vivipara.* Sold as 'Fairy's Joke', this unusual grass looks just like any other tufted hair grass at first, but instead of producing seed, tiny plantlets develop on the flowers at the end of summer. Soon the flowerstalks arch farther and farther down until they touch the ground—then the plantlets root and take over your garden! Fun to try, but don't let it get out of hand!

Hakonechloa

Japanese forest grass, Hakone grass

PLANT PROFILE

HAKONECHLOA

ha-cone-ey-KLO-uh

Foliage Color:
Green, green-striped yellow, and white

Length of Foliage Season:
Mid-spring to fall

Category:
Cool-season grass

Height (foliage):
12 to 18 inches (30 to 45 cm)

Spread:
18 inches (45 cm)

Garden Uses:
Container planting, edging, groundcover, mass planting, mixed border, rock garden, specimen plant, wall planting, woodland garden

Light Preference:
Full sun to shade

Soil Preference:
Humus-rich, moist, well-drained soil

Best Way to Propagate:
Divide in spring or fall

USDA Plant Hardiness Zones:
5 to 9

The dense, arching stems of this grass form a beautiful mound, creating an appearance quite unlike that of any other true grass, although a look at its thin, narrow leaves does reveal its true affinities. It is the variegated forms that are the most popular: They shine like a beacon in shady areas and never fail to attract attention. The result is that this grass, scarcely known to gardeners as recently as the late 1990s, is quickly becoming a staple plant for the shady garden. Don't count on it for flowers, though: The flowerspikes are thin and wispy, so insignificant that many gardeners don't even notice their Japanese forest grass is in bloom. This is one species where the foliage definitely carries the show!

GROWING TIPS

This is quite an adaptable plant, growing in most well-drained soils without difficulty, although it does prefer rich, evenly moist conditions, as is witnessed by its much faster establishment there. Mulching and the occasional watering will be useful to keep it more humid, especially in drier spots. It is likewise adaptable when it comes to light needs, growing well from full sun (especially in the North) to very shady spots. However, for best results (and certainly quicker fill), partial shade is ideal.

One flaw with this plant is that it can take several years to fill in and create that dense, mounding look for which it is reputed. And a very young plant is very wispy and insignificant indeed! I suggest biting the bullet and buying a fairly large, well-established plant rather than thin specimens in 4-inch (10-cm) pots. This is especially important if your growing space is closer to full shade than to partial shade, as truly shaded plants are even slower-growing than the average. Of course, if you need large quantities, for example if you'll be using this grass as a groundcover (a use for which it is imminently suitable, by the way), you can save a bundle by buying "liners" (small plants usually sold for potting up). If so, just be patient: Your Japanese forest grass *will* fill in!

Limited hardiness is an issue with this species. You'll often see it listed as Zone 6, but I have a simple trick for ensuring it will be fully hardy in Zone 5: Don't cut it back until spring! The stems and leaves of the previous year are dense enough to make a perfect protective mulch. In fact, if you can leave well enough alone (I know; some gardeners just can't bring themselves not to "tidy up" in fall!), you'll probably have good success even in Zone 4. Personally, I grow it without problem in Zone 3, but under heavy snow cover.

Cut back the foliage in spring to leave room for new growth. In snowy climates, there really is no need to clean up at all: The weight of the snow will have flattened the stems to the ground by spring and will no longer prevent the new stems from "doing their thing."

Division is the only way to multiply the variegated cultivars of Japanese forest grass: Seed is not true to type. You can easily divide this clumping grass in spring or fall.

PROBLEMS AND SOLUTIONS

This species is not particularly subject to insects or disease.

TOP PERFORMER

Hakonechloa macra (Japanese forest grass, Hakone grass): This is the only species available. 'Aureola' was the original form and is still the most popular. It is bright yellow in color, with thin green lines running through it, and creates the impression of a mound of gold in the garden. 'Albovariegata', also sold as 'Albostriata', is the most common white-striped variety. It is just as attractive as 'Aureola' in the garden, although it is more likely to burn in full sun. 'Alboaurea' combines the traits of both 'Aureola' and 'Albovariegata': Its leaves are striped green, yellow, *and* white! 'All Gold' is a more recent introduction. It has more upright leaves than the others and, in fact, a rather spiky appearance instead of the mounding shape one usually associates with Japanese forest grass. There are also several other cultivars, although none as popular as the four described above. Oddly, the species, *H. macra,* with all-green leaves, is rarely available.

LARRY'S GARDEN NOTES

One very attractive way to use Japanese forest grass is as a "grass cascade." Plant a series of them in a meandering pattern leading down a slope, ideally intermingling them with attractive, water-worn rocks. The arching leaves tend to bend mostly toward the bottom of the slope, creating a cascading appearance that draws the eye the full length of the planting, just as if water was cascading over rocks. Any of the variegated forms would work particularly well with this style.

Japanese forest grass
(*Hakonechloa macra* 'Aureola')

Luzula
Woodrush

Woodrushes are not well known to gardeners, and that's a great shame: They are easy to grow, attractive year-round, and surprisingly shade-tolerant. Most are small, evergreen, grasslike plants forming relatively low, ground-hugging rosettes. Some have striking flowers; others are mostly foliage plants. They really shine in winter and early spring when everything else is dull and gray—and there they are, dressed in their best green, acting as if winter had never happened! There are over 80 species found worldwide in temperate climates, but only 1 or 2 are available occasionally in the trade: You're probably more likely to spot wild woodrushes in a forest near you than in a garden center!

GROWING TIPS

Woodrushes are made for the shade. Almost without exception, they're native to dense deciduous forests with fairly abundant, even soil moisture. Plant woodrushes in full or partial shade in almost any soil—although, like so many other plants, if they had their druthers they'd prefer rich, humusy soil. Spring sun is fine, but most will burn in summer sun unless truly humid conditions are provided. In spite of their origin in almost swampy soils, they are surprisingly tolerant of dry soils, at least once well established. Their capacity to tolerate root competition is legendary: Entire carpets of evergreen woodrushes will develop over time beneath even the most shallow-rooted trees. They can also tolerate being under water for short periods in late winter.

Although they do have other uses, woodrushes are an especially obvious choice as groundcovers under trees and shrubs. You can even create a woodrush lawn: Mow them once, early in spring, to clean up the tangle of soon-to-fade leaves from the previous year to leave room for the new generation. They even tolerate some foot traffic, but don't try playing soccer on them!

Exposed plants sometimes suffer winter damage: Cut off the frosted leaves and new ones will take their place.

Woodrushes are mostly clump-forming but also spread

through creeping rhizomes, thus creating their own carpets over time. Multiplication is best accomplished by digging up and replanting such offsets. Seed is rarely produced in culture, as their flowers tend to be self-sterile and a different clone of the same species is needed for pollination.

PROBLEMS AND SOLUTIONS

Woodrushes seem immune to insects. Leaf disease problems are possible but easily solved: Cut back infected plants to stimulate a fresh set of leaves.

TOP PERFORMER

Luzula nivea (snowy woodrush): A European species that is truly remarkable in all seasons. The plant produces broad rosettes of gray-green foliage edged with soft, downy white hairs and is attractive enough without flowers. It also produces absolutely charming umbels of fluffy white blooms in late spring or early summer: Quite a show for such a small plant! Height (foliage): 8 inches (20 cm). Height (flower): 16 inches (40 cm). Spread: 12 inches (30 cm). USDA Plant Hardiness Zones 4 to 9.

Snowy woodrush (*Luzula nivea*)

MORE RECOMMENDED WOODRUSHES

Luzula sylvatica (greater woodrush): This species has a flatter rosette and broader leaves surrounding a depressed "eye." In fact, its form always reminds me of a bromeliad, not a silhouette you often see in hardy plants! It is essentially a foliage plant: The stalks of yellowish green spring flowers turning brownish later are not unattractive (but they don't inspire states of rapture, either). There are several superb cultivars, including 'Marginata', the "classic" cultivar, with yellow-margined leaves; 'Aurea', with brilliant chartreuse leaves from fall to late spring, lime green in summer; and 'Hohe Tatra', with larger leaves that form a more upright rosette. Height (foliage): 8 to 12 inches (20 to 30 cm). Height (flower): 20 to 28 inches (50 to 70 cm). Spread: 12 to 18 inches (30 to 45 cm). USDA Plant Hardiness Zones 4 to 9.

LARRY'S GARDEN NOTES

The genus *Luzula* indirectly gets its botanical name from the soft, downy hairs that line the leaves or, in some cases, cover them. They catch the early morning dew and, in the right light, sparkle like diamonds—or, if you want to get the allusion, like fireflies. The Italian name for firefly is *lucciola* which, adapted to botanical Latin, is *Luzula* . . . well, you had to be there!

Milium
Wood millet

PLANT PROFILE

MILIUM

MI-lee-um

Foliage Color:
Yellow

Length of Foliage Season:
Year-round

Bloom Color:
Yellow

Bloom Time:
Late spring to early summer

Category:
Cool-season grass

Height (foliage):
6 to 18 inches (15 to 45 cm)

Height (flower):
18 to 36 inches (45 to 90 cm)

Spread:
8 inches (20 cm)

Garden Uses:
Container planting, mass
planting, mixed border,
specimen plant, woodland
garden

Light Preference:
Partial shade to shade

Soil Preference:
Humus-rich, moist, well-
drained soil

Best Way to Propagate:
Move self-sown seedlings

USDA Plant Hardiness Zones:
6 to 9

Golden wood millet is an upright, open, clumping grass with narrow "golden yellow" (read "lemon yellow": no plant truly has golden leaves!) leaves in spring, darkening to lime green in summer and persisting that way right through winter until the following spring. The delicate feathery flowers are the same so-called golden yellow. Plop this grass in a somber part of the garden, either in deep shade or near dark green foliage, and watch the whole landscape light up!

GROWING TIPS

As the name wood millet suggests, *Milium effusum* is a plant of the forest. In its native Europe, it grows in open woodlands and on shady riverbanks. In the garden, it prefers partial shade or even shade. Even more than the species, the golden form, *Milium effusum* 'Aureum', is very subject to sunburn and to excessive heat so really should not be exposed to direct sun except early in spring and in the early morning. Although preferring humus-rich, evenly moist soils, it will do fine in most garden soils as long as they remain somewhat moist most of the time. It will tolerate light drought but not much more; mulch it well and water it occasionally during dry weather if you want to keep it happy.

Although a perennial, wood millet is often treated as an annual, notably in container gardens for shady spots. That it comes true from seed and reaches a decent size the first year makes it invaluable for adding golden notes to temporary arrangements.

This is not the hardiest of grasses, so you may have to take the claim it is evergreen (more appropriately, "everyellow") with a grain of salt; in many climates, the foliage does die back in cold weather. If so, just clip it off in early spring.

Golden wood millet's capacity to come true from seed (a rather unusual trait, in passing: most plants with "golden" foliage can be propagated only vegetatively) means it can also be used well beyond its theoretical hardiness zone. Though often thriving farther north, it really isn't solid in climates colder than Zone 6. However, if you do try it beyond its limit and it dies, remember it offers a safety blanket: Its much-hardier seeds live on, so it will reappear the following spring as self-sown seedlings. It does this even in my Zone 3 garden.

You could divide wood millet in spring or fall, but almost no one ever does. Instead, it reproduces on its own through seedlings that pop up here and there, and these can be dug up and transplanted elsewhere. Excess seedlings, with their lemon yellow color, are easy to spot and dispose of.

PROBLEMS AND SOLUTIONS

Golden wood millet is rarely subject to insects and disease.

TOP PERFORMER

Milium effusum 'Aureum' (golden wood millet, Bowles' golden grass): The species, *M. effusum,* with pale green leaves, is never grown as an ornamental, but its cultivar, *M. effusum* 'Aureum', has a long history of culture. It produces a rather open clump of soft, limp, arching lemon yellow leaves in early spring, quickly followed by very light and airy flowerstalks of the same color. As summer arrives it does become greener, but lime green is still a color that packs a punch out in the shade! A new cultivar, 'Yaffle', is green with a broad yellow band down the center of each leaf. Unfortunately, it does not come true from seed. Height (foliage): 6 to 18 inches (15 to 45 cm). Height (flower): 18 to 36 inches (45 to 90 cm). Spread: 8 inches (20 cm). USDA Plant Hardiness Zones: 6 to 9.

MORE RECOMMENDED WOOD MILLETS

Milium effusum subsp. *esthonicum* (Estonian wood millet): This is a taller subspecies of wood millet (*Milium effusum*), with light green leaves that give off a delicious new-mown hay scent when the leaves are crushed. Height (foliage): 3 to 4 feet (90 to 120 cm). Height (flower): 5 feet (150 cm). Spread: 12 inches (30 cm). USDA Plant Hardiness Zones 6 to 9.

Golden wood millet
(*Milium effusum* 'Aureum')

LARRY'S GARDEN NOTES

You may have noticed that *Milium effusum* 'Aureum' is often called Bowles' golden grass. The name comes from celebrated British plantsman E. A. Bowles (1865 to 1954). He was the first European to grow many plants that later become classics. He was also very generous with his plants but not the greatest record-keeper: He shared plants with friends without bothering to give their cultivar name. Over time, therefore, people came to call the plants after the man who gave them to him. So there was a Bowles' golden grass, *Vinca minor* 'Bowles' Variety', *Cyclamen* 'Bowles' Apollo', and so on.

Molinia
Purple moor grass

Purple moor grasses are clumping grasses *par excellence.* They form extremely dense clumps (the word "tussock" is truly appropriate here) that no weed could possibly work its way into. The narrow leaves are rather stiffly upright, arching only slightly outward, mid-green in general but purplish at the base, turning bright yellow in fall. The yellow-tinged flowerstalks are likewise very stiff and upright, opening into narrow panicles of purplish spikelets at the tip. The see-through appearance of the stalks is purple moor grass's main claim to fame: Plant them according to the height of the foliage, not the flowers, and they'll create a hazy foreground to the taller plants behind.

GROWING TIPS

Although these Eurasian grasses are native to soggy, acid moors (as the common name moor grass suggests), they actually adapt well to a wide range of soils. They do not do well in dry soils, so a good mulch and regular watering are *de rigueur.* All do well in full sun; only purple moor grass (*Molinia caerulea* subsp. *caerulea*) adapts to shadier conditions, so be careful when you're choosing plants.

One very ungrasslike habit is that purple moor grasses are slow off the mark: Small plants may not even begin to bloom for 2 or 3 years, and dividing them will likewise set them back considerably. For fast results, impatient gardeners should buy new plants—big, well-established ones at that. It's harder on the pocketbook, but if you just can't wait . . .

You won't find you need to divide purple moor grass very often. In fact, in most cases, just plant them and leave them alone: They'll still look great decades later. Division becomes necessary only if you want more plants. It can be carried out in early spring, or in fall when the leaves drop. Purple moor grass is very slow from seed, and the varieties currently sold are all cultivars, none coming true from seed, so sowing it is really only interesting if you're out to develop new varieties.

PROBLEMS AND SOLUTIONS

Problems are infrequent.

TOP PERFORMER

Molinia caerulea subsp. *caerulea* (purple moor grass): This is the only species recommended for shady conditions and indeed, only partial shade at that. It is much smaller than *M. caerulea* subsp. *arundinacea* (described below), although of very variable height. There are several popular cultivars, including:

'Variegata': The most popular of all, with green-and-white striped leaves. Absolutely charming! Height (foliage): 12 inches (30 cm). Height (flower): 18 inches (45 cm). Spread: 12 inches (30 cm). USDA Plant Hardiness Zones 4 to 9.

'Heidebraut': Short leaves, unbelievably tall flowers: *the* choice for that hazy appearance! Height (foliage): 20 inches (50 cm). Height (flower): 48 inches (120 cm). Spread: 12 inches (30 cm). USDA Plant Hardiness Zones 4 to 9.

'Moorhexe': Very deep purple flowers. Height (foliage): 8 inches (20 cm). Height (flower): 12 inches (30 cm). Spread: 10 inches (25 cm). USDA Plant Hardiness Zones 4 to 9.

'Overdam': A true mini with mid-purple blooms. Height (foliage): 6 inches (15 cm). Height (flower): 10 inches (25 cm). Spread: 8 inches (20 cm). USDA Plant Hardiness Zones 4 to 9.

'Strahlenquelle': More arching than the species. Great specimen plant. Height (foliage): 12 inches (30 cm). Height (flower): 24 inches (60 cm). Spread: 16 inches (40 cm). USDA Plant Hardiness Zones 4 to 9.

MORE RECOMMENDED PURPLE MOOR GRASSES

Molinia caerulea subsp. *arundinacea* (tall purple moor grass): This much taller plant is not a good choice for shady spots and deserves a mention in a shade book essentially as a warning: When you buy purple moor grasses for the shady border, look for shorter varieties! This species offers lots of cultivars as well: 'Skyracer' is especially choice. Height (foliage): 2 feet (60 cm). Height (flower): 6 to 8 feet (180 to 240 cm). Spread: 4 feet (120 cm). USDA Plant Hardiness Zones 4 to 9.

Variegated purple moor grass (*Molinia caerulea* subsp. *caerulea* 'Variegata')

LARRY'S GARDEN NOTES

Moor grasses have a very ungrasslike habit: They are self-cleaning. Almost any other grass you can think of holds on to its leaves over winter, whether they are alive (as in evergreen grasses) or dead (as in deciduous ones), and thus require a bit of spring cleaning. This is one deciduous grass that is truly deciduous: Both leaves and flowers drop off on their own in late fall. In protected spots in mild climates, they may hang on through much of winter, but normally this grass is one of the few with no winter interest.

Phalaris

Gardener's garters, ribbon grass

PHALARIS
fa-LAH-ris

Foliage Color:
Green-and-white, pink, and yellow

Length of Foliage Season:
Year-round

Bloom Color:
Whitish green

Bloom Time:
Summer

Category:
Warm-season grass

Height (foliage):
2 feet (60 cm)

Height (flower):
3 feet (90 cm)

Spread:
Indefinite

Garden Uses:
Container planting, groundcover, mass planting, meadow garden, mixed border, woodland garden

Light Preference:
Full sun to shade

Soil Preference:
Poor to rich, moderately moist to wet soil

Best Way to Propagate:
Divide in spring or early summer

USDA Plant Hardiness Zones:
3 to 9

This probably was the first grass to be used as an ornamental. Imagine: It has been known since at least the seventeenth century—and the same clone is still being traded among gardeners to this day! It is a running grass that quickly produces carpets of narrow green-and-white striped leaves on rather weak stems. They're its main drawing card, as the small, dense, greenish white, early-summer flowers are not too spectacular. This plant is a choice if somewhat irregular groundcover: A carpet of gardener's garters is a stunning sight, especially in shade, where it truly lights up the landscape.

GROWING TIPS

Warning: The first rule with gardener's garters is: Control it! It practically defines "running grass": Let a single plant loose in a mixed bed, and you'll probably never get it under control again. It's lesson many gardeners have learned—after the fact. Don't be one of them. Plant it within a root barrier (page 54).

That said, you can still let it wander if you plant it in a spot where its invasive nature is not a problem. Just unleash it far from any established or future flowerbeds and let it go to town. It looks best when allowed to create vast carpets or when mingling freely with taller plants (it will shade out lower or weaker ones). It is also stupendous in containers—and it can't escape from one of those.

This is one grass that *doesn't* prefer rich soil. In fact, it tends to collapse in midsummer if given too much nitrogen (if it does flop, simply mow it down and it will spring back again immediately), so avoid applying compost or organic matter to the soil at planting and don't bother fertilizing. Poorer growing conditions also help it fill in more densely: The individual plants can be spaced too far apart in rich soil.

It tolerates both sun and shade, although partial shade is best. It may not bloom in shady spots, but then its flowers are not a major attraction anyway. This is not a good choice for dry soils: The lower leaves will turn brown, detracting from its appearance. Average soil humidity is fine, with irrigation in times of drought, and it will tolerate wet soils or even growing with its roots under an inch or two (2.5 to 5 cm) of water.

In theory, this is an evergreen grass, although its winter appearance is not terribly impressive. In colder parts of its range, freezing temperatures kill back the leaves. It is probably best to mow it once in early spring so fresh new growth can take over.

Propagate this plant only by division: It does not come true from seed.

Gardener's garters
(*Phalaris arundinacea* var. *picta*)

PROBLEMS AND SOLUTIONS

It has no serious insects or diseases. Watch for its highly invasive habit.

TOP PERFORMER

Phalaris arundinacea var. *picta* (gardener's garters, ribbon grass): The species, a taller plant with entirely green leaves, is never grown as an ornamental—very cosmopolitan, it probably thrives in a field or woodland near you. *Phalaris arundinacea* var. *picta* is the common selection, an heirloom ornamental grass with green-and-white striped leaves. It is very subject to flopping and has been surpassed by other cultivars. Unless you're creating a heritage garden, you'll probably prefer *P. arundinacea* var. *picta* 'Feesey' (syn. 'Feesey's Variety', 'Strawberries and Cream'), which is sturdier and has a pinkish tinge in spring. *P. arundinacea* var. *picta* 'Dwarf Garters' is, as the name suggests, a dwarf form only about 1 foot (30 cm) high, with green-and-white leaves. It grows more densely and fills in better, too, so it makes a better groundcover. 'Luteopicta' has green-and-yellow leaves but is otherwise identical to *P. arundincea* var. *picta*. It tends to revert, so remove any green plants. There are several other choices, all variegated.

KISSING COUSINS

There is one other *Phalaris* you're likely to run into: canary grass (*P. canariensis*), a medium-height to tall annual cereal grass also called canary seed because its shiny, rounded seeds are excellent as bird food, including food for canaries. It readily sprouts under bird feeders and has thus become a nearly cosmopolitan weed, although it is easily controlled by mowing or hand-pulling. It has essentially no ornamental value but does attract birds to the garden in fall!

Sasa
Dwarf bamboo, kuma bamboo

PLANT PROFILE

SASA

SA-sa

Foliage Color:
Green; beige-edged in fall

Length of Foliage Season:
Year-round

Category:
Bamboo

Height:
Varies by species; see individual listings

Spread:
Indefinite

Garden Uses:
Container planting, groundcover, mass planting, seasonal hedge, specimen plant, woodland garden

Light Preference:
Full sun to shade

Soil Preference:
Humus-rich, evenly moist, well-drained soil

Best Way to Propagate:
Divide in early spring

USDA Plant Hardiness Zones:
6 to 11

There are some 60 *Sasa* species, all small to medium-size bamboos native to Asia. Only two are currently grown, both with large, broad, dark evergreen leaves much bigger than those of what most of us would consider "typical" bamboos. The leaf edges of one, *Sasa veitchii,* die back and turn beige in fall, persisting that way through winter, giving the plant a variegated appearance that is its principal attraction. These are running bamboos, ideally used as groundcovers on vast spaces, although very attractive in containers as well. Well-controlled, they make superb hedges.

GROWING TIPS

Warning: Do not even think of letting dwarf bamboos loose in your garden without controlling them. They have thick rhizomes that can run for several yards (meters) under obstacles, such as a driveway, popping out on the other side—or growing right through the asphalt. Consider using a commercial bamboo barrier (see page 340).

So much for garden use: You *can* let them loose in areas where you never intend to do any formal gardening, such as in a wooded area or an abandoned field, where they will create a nonstop, weed-free, evergreen carpet that might be exactly what you're looking for. *Never* release them into a natural forest, though, as they can take over and prevent regeneration.

For such prolific, spreading plants, bamboos start out very sedately. Experts say, "First they sleep, then they creep, then they leap." If you want to create a groundcover with any speed, pull out your pocketbook (these are not cheap plants!) and buy enough in gallon (4-liter) pots to space them about 2 to 3 feet (60 to 90 cm) apart over the area you want covered.

The species described here tolerate almost any condition except severe cold. They grow best in moist, rich soils, but will grow in hard clay, pure sand, or gravel and tolerate full sun or deep shade; once established, they'll survive considerable drought. In fact, they are especially nice in areas of dry shade (usually caused by severe root competition). They'll be slow to take off and may need a bit of babying for the first few years, but then just watch them: They'll thrive even under Norway maples (*Acer platanoides*).

Winter hardiness is hard to define for these bamboos. With no protection, they'll survive in Zone 6 but may die to the ground during severe winters, yet in far colder climates (I grow them in Zone 3), they suffer no damage because they bend down under the weight of falling snow and remain covered all winter. In Zone 7 and above they should remain evergreen.

Bamboos dislike being disturbed, but division is essentially the only means of multiplying them in a home environment, especially since seed is essentially never available. Do this in early spring, as soon as the soil can be worked. With a sharp shovel and an ax, hack out a large clump and replant it.

Kuma bamboo (*Sasa veitchii*)

PROBLEMS AND SOLUTIONS

Slugs may attack young shoots in spring; hand-pick to control them.

TOP PERFORMER

Sasa veitchii (kuma bamboo, dwarf bamboo): This is the most widely distributed *Sasa* and one of the most attractive. The culms (stems) are purplish to green with a glaucous covering. The evergreen leaves, up to 10 inches (25 cm) long, bear a large beige margin in winter. Height varies according to conditions: 2 to 3 feet (60 to 90 cm) in full sun, 4 to 6 feet (120 to 180 cm) in the deepest shade. Spread: Unlimited. USDA Plant Hardiness Zones 6 to 11.

MORE RECOMMENDED DWARF BAMBOOS

Sasa palmata (broadleaf bamboo): Much like the previous species, but taller and with its larger leaves borne in clusters at the culm tips, giving them an attractive palmlike appearance. The leaf edges remain green all winter. Height: 5 to 7 feet (1.5 to 2 m). Spread: Unlimited. USDA Plant Hardiness Zones 6 to 11.

LARRY'S GARDEN NOTES

Entire books have been written about bamboos, and there is obviously room to give them only a brief mention here, but they are fascinating plants well worth discovering. Think of them as "shrubby grasses," as their stems, although sometimes pliable, persist from year to year. Foliage is generally evergreen. Most are tropical or subtropical and only a minority are hardy enough for general use in temperate climates, but even those remain little-known and underused in colder climates. Like other grasses, bamboos can be clumpers or runners. Most grow for decades without blooming, so flower appearance is rarely a factor in choosing them. Many of the tall species with the thick stems ("culms") that we associate with bamboos are more likely to create shade than to tolerate it. Look to the dwarf varieties for shade-tolerant plants.

Sesleria

Moor grass

SESLERIA

ses-LAIR-ee-uh

Foliage Color:
Green

Length of Foliage Season:
Year-round

Bloom Color:
Whitish green

Bloom Time:
Varies by species; see individual listings

Category:
Cool-season grass

Height (foliage):
Varies by species; see individual listings

Height (flower):
Varies by species; see individual listings

Spread:
Varies by species; see individual listings

Garden Uses:
Edging, groundcover, mass planting, meadow garden, mixed border, rock garden, woodland garden; along paths

Light Preference:
Full sun to shade

Soil Preference:
Humus-rich, evenly moist, well-drained soil

Best Way to Propagate:
Divide in spring or fall

USDA Plant Hardiness Zones:
4 to 9

Moor grasses (not to be confused with purple moor grasses, page 358) are fairly modest, small, not terribly well-known grasses with much potential for the home landscape, but their noninvasive, clumping habit; disease and insect resistance; and general ease of care make them plants more gardeners really should get to know. Their flowers are fairly insignificant, so they are grown mostly for their interestingly colored evergreen foliage. They are super choices for groundcover use and for mass plantings (especially under trees and shrubs), look great in rock gardens, and are wonderful filler material in and among perennials and bulbs where their "always-ready-to-serve" trustworthiness allows them to cover for their neighbors' down periods.

GROWING TIPS

These are easy-to-grow grasses adapted to most garden conditions, from rich to poor and even alkaline soils, full sun to considerable shade, and moist to fairly dry conditions. They tolerate drought well once established, at least if it is occasional: In areas where summers are often dry, though, they'll probably need irrigation. Avoid full sun in hot-summer areas: They'll need more deep shade than in northern gardens. Partial shade, though, is a sure bet in any climate.

Moor grasses are generally multiplied by division in early spring or fall. Curiously, there seem to be few cultivars of any of the moor grasses, which means they will come true from seed, so growing from seed is also an option. Sow seed in spring or fall; 1-year-old plants will be ready for planting in the garden.

PROBLEMS AND SOLUTIONS

Not terribly susceptible to pests and diseases.

TOP PERFORMER

Sesleria caerulea (blue moor grass): Probably the most widely available moor grass and, like the others, a fairly small grass forming dense clumps. The narrow leaves are powder blue below and green above but twist as they grow, revealing both sides and giving the whole plant a blue-green appearance. The button-shaped flowers, purplish at first, then golden brown, appear quite early in spring and last until summer. It would seem to me that this plant could use a hybridizer's touch: There is plenty of potential here for a magnificent blue shade grass! Height (foliage): 8 inches (20 cm). Height (flower): 12 inches (30 cm). Spread: 10 inches (25 cm). USDA Plant Hardiness Zones 4 to 9.

MORE RECOMMENDED MOOR GRASSES

Sesleria autumnalis (autumn moor grass): This species is a bit larger and blooms much later, usually in fall, though as early as May in mild climates. Its leaves are yellowish green (nearly chartreuse), so they stand out wonderfully in shady spots or near dark foliage. The rather modest purplish flowerspikes are soon covered with white filaments: What color that makes them depends on your mood the day you see them! Height (foliage): 12 inches (30 cm). Height (flower): 18 inches (45 cm). Spread: 16 inches (40 cm). USDA Plant Hardiness Zones 4 to 9.

S. heufleriana (Balkan moor grass): This one is rather like blue moor grass, with leaves powder blue below and green above, but instead of twisting to reveal the blue below they grow nearly straight upright, so both sides are visible. Even so, it is not quite as bluish in color as blue moor grass. The deep purple to black flowers scarcely peek above the foliage, so are of only moderate impact. They last from early spring until summer. Height (foliage): 12 inches (30 cm). Height (flower): 16 inches (40 cm). Spread: 12 inches (30 cm). USDA Plant Hardiness Zones 4 to 9.

S. nitida (gray moor grass, nest moor grass): After *S. caerulea*, this is the most available of the moor grasses. It's an evergreen, mounding grass with gray-green to gray-blue leaves bearing whitish green cigar-shaped flowers from late spring into summer. From seed, you often get some excellent silvery gray plants: It would be worthwhile selecting for that feature. Height (foliage): 20 inches (50 cm). Height (flower): 24 inches (60 cm). Spread: 20 inches (50 cm). USDA Plant Hardiness Zones 4 to 9.

Gray moor grass (*Sesleria nitida*)

KISSING COUSINS

If you're looking for an even smaller mounding grass, perhaps for a shady rock garden, why not check out the fescues (*Festuca* spp.)? Unlike the better-known blue fescues (*F. glauca* and others) that need full sun, bearskin fescue (*F. gautieri*, formerly *F. scoparia*) actually prefers shade to partial shade. It is a neat little grass with stiff green leaves, prickly at the tips, forming a perfect mound at first, then creating a carpet as it begins to offset over time. The fine, narrow flowerspikes start out green and are scarcely noticeable until they turn gold. It needs about the same conditions as the moor grasses. There are also more dwarf selections, like 'Pic Carlit', a mere 2 to 3 inches (5 to 8 cm) tall and ideal for containers! Height (foliage): 4 to 6 inches (10 to 15 cm). Height (flower): 4 to 6 inches (10 to 15 cm). Spread: 12 inches (30 cm). USDA Plant Hardiness Zones 4 to 9.

Climbers, like this star jasmine (*Trachelospermum jasminoides*), add both height and color to the garden. Just give them something to climb on and watch them strut their stuff!

Chapter 11

Climbing Plants
for Shade

Climbing plants (also known as vines, climbers, lianas, and so on; the words are pretty much interchangeable) are curious plants. Almost all other land-dwelling plants use their own internal structure (mostly a cell component called lignin) to hoist themselves upward on their own through solid, tough stems, branches, and trunks. Even annuals and perennials use lignin to solidify their stems, but woody plants are masters of the art. Wood is full of lignin and that is why trees are able to grow so tall. Without lignin, they'd flop over like rubber. However, building a strong structure out of lignin is a slow process requiring a great deal of energy, and often the tallest plants of the forest are the slowest-growing ones.

Climbing plants, though, have little use for huge quantities of lignin: They've found a way around that constraint. They hook or wrap themselves around host plants that *do* produce abundant lignin and use their host's hard-won structure to reach for the sky. So climbing plants are essentially profiteers, almost parasites, taking advantage of other plants and giving them little if anything in return.

We ought to find the actions of climbing plants reprehensible; instead, we very much take advantage of their sneaky ways. Climbers, you see, are the ideal plants for "filling in" open spaces. They hoist themselves up walls and fences as readily as they do trees, and our gardens usually have lots of such barren spots to cover. So we plant them to cover up unwanted views and to add interest to otherwise dull structures: You can use them to cover up an old stump or even bring a dead tree back to life by letting vines cover it. In fact, we purposely add structures just for climbing plants to grow on:

trelles, arbors, and pergolas. After all, what are they if not fast-and-easy supports for climbers?

As climbers reach ever upward, they don't take up a lot of space on the ground. Perennials and annuals need large flowerbeds, shrubs and conifers have spreading branches that just eat up space, and trees, with their thick trunks and massive root systems, are true space hogs. Climbers need only a small space—a single planting hole—to reach out in all directions . . . but uniquely vertically. If fact, you can usually cover an entire fence or wall with just one climber, using little horizontal space indeed. Where gardening space is rare, such as in small urban gardens, climbing plants allow you to have abundant greenery without losing virtually any usable space. So with climbers, you can have the patio, the swing set, the sandbox, and the pool . . . and still garden!

BORN TO CLIMB

Botanists believe climbers evolved from nonclimbing ancestors that "learned" a faster way to reach the sun. They began as tall but weak-stemmed plants that started to lean on their neighbors rather than put too much of their own energy into building a solid structure. Over time, they became so good at leaning they abandoned all other means of vertical growth. As generations passed, different climbers evolved different and often more effective means of taking advantage of their host. Here are the main ones.

Scandent climbers: These are also called clamberers; they are the least specialized climbers. They still essentially lean on their neighbors, but as their stems reach upward they manage to mingle with the branches of their host and thus gain extra support. They have no special structures to aid them in climbing, nor do they twist around their host. Where they find no host nearby to lean on, they usually contain enough lignin to grow as arching shrubs. In the garden, you'll have to either attach scandent climbers to their support or wind them through lattice or nearby branches to get them off the ground. Winter jasmine (*Jasminum nudiflorum*) is a well-known scandent shrub.

Hook climbers: They're also fairly primitive and are also called clamberers. They don't twist or stick to their host, only lean and mingle like scandent climbers, but they have the added advantage of thorny stems that can hook onto their hosts. In the garden, they too usually have to be attached to their supports; otherwise they'll grow as tall, arching shrubs. The best-known clamberer is the climbing rose.

Weavers: Just a step up from scandent climbers, weavers mostly lean on their host but also undulate as they grow and thus manage to work themselves in and out among the branches they grow through. In the garden, they may still need some help from the gardener in getting started (you may have to attach them to their supports initially) but will usually weave their way in and out of a trellis or chain fence on their own once they get going. Without a support, they simply flop, not having enough lignin to hold themselves upright. Confederate jasmine (*Trachelospermum jasminoides*) is a weaver.

Twining climbers: Also called twiners, they don't just undulate, they twist around their host, with stems that grow in a spiral. Depending on the species, they may grow clockwise or counterclockwise. They are very efficient climbers—if you don't supply a support, they'll creep along the ground until they find one. They don't make good groundcovers, though, as they keep reaching up in search of a support, so they appear irregular. Often several branches will twist around each other and attempt to grow upright, usually flopping back down again, as they don't contain enough lignin to go very far. Morning glories (*Ipomoea* spp.) and wisterias are well-known twiners.

Root climbers: These are called rooters for short. Actually, they are officially called "adventitious root climbers," but "rooters" is so much easier to say. They produce specialized roots called holdfasts on the underside of the stem; these cling to bark, wood, brick, stone, and so on. Unlike other twiners, they are able to climb flat surfaces like stone walls without a trellis or grid. On the other hand, they won't climb up open fences (such as chain link): They seem to need broad surfaces on which to take root. Rooters usually make good groundcovers,

TOUCHY-FEELY PLANTS

EVERYONE REALIZES PLANTS REACT TO LIGHT, but did you know they also have a sense of touch? Twining vines twist about at random until they make contact with a vertical support, then they wrap themselves tightly around it. Their "sense of touch" tells them whether they need to draw tight circles, such as around a cord or thin branch, or much larger ones, as around a thicker support. If they make contact with a horizontal branch, though, they don't tighten at all but continue to twist openly. It's as if they examine the object they touch and then decide whether it is worth wrapping around or not.

Rooting climbers likewise show their touchy-feely side: They produce no roots unless the stem is pressed against an object—and even then they produce their roots only on the side touching the object.

This response of plants to touch is called thigmatropism, in case you just had to know.

as they hug the ground when they can find no support. The best-known rooter is English ivy (*Hedera helix*).

Clinging climbers: Also called clingers, these climbers have specialized appendages that attach them solidly to their host. The best known are tendrils, such as seen on grape vines: They are special growths that twist as they grow, wrapping around their support. Sometimes it is the leaf petiole that twists around objects, or the leaf tips. In general, tendrils can wrap around only fairly thin objects: They'll grow around string, wire, or thin branches but may need to be attached to heavier supports, such as thicker lattices and trellises.

The most specialized of the clingers are Virginia creeper and its relatives (*Parthenocissus* spp.). They bear adhesive disks at the tips of their tendrils: They'll wrap themselves around thin objects like other clingers but can also climb flat surfaces, like walls and trunks. Many clingers make good groundcovers where there are no nearby objects to cling.

Nature, of course, hates man's attempt to neatly package its species into convenient groupings, so not all plants stay in their assigned categories. Many climbers are not climbers all their lives, for example. English ivy and its relatives (*Hedera* spp.), for instance, are typically climbing plants in their youth but change into shrubs at maturity. That is, when an ivy has grown high enough up into the tree canopy to get the light it needs, it suddenly starts producing woody branches complete with larger, rounder leaves instead of climbing stems. It is only the woody form that flowers and fruits. Oddly, once an ivy matures, it will never again produce climbing stems, and even cuttings taken from mature growth will grow as shrubs, never as climbers.

Climbing hydrangea (*Hydrangea anomala* subsp. *petiolaris*) does just the opposite: It starts off as a shrub with solid woody branches and may grow that way for years. Then suddenly, for reasons unknown, it decides it is time to climb and sends out stems that stick to nearby surfaces. Still other climbers, winter jasmine for one, will start producing woodier branches if pruned regularly and will then happily live the rest of their life as a shrub. And who hasn't seen a wisteria changed, by harsh pruning, into a small tree?

Don't be stunned if your climber starts behaving in a very unvinelike fashion: Climbers are full of surprises!

HERBACEOUS OR WOODY?

Climbers can be either herbaceous or woody. Herbaceous climbers, like herbaceous perennials and annuals, die to the ground at the end of the season. Some die entirely (there are many annual climbers!); others resprout from underground roots the following season. Practically by definition, herbaceous climbers tend to be comparatively short: There is a limit to how much growth they can put on in a single season. Even so, some reach 20 feet (6 m) or more in just one season and are among the fastest-growing plants known.

Woody climbers have perennial stems that become tough and fibrous. Because they don't die to the ground each year, they can build on the previous year's growth and thus grow taller and taller over time. Some reach well above 50 feet (15 m) in height over the years. In general, woody climbers are slower-growing than herbaceous ones and may take years to reach their maximum height. Note that "woody" is used in the sense of permanent: Not all "woody climbers" produce stems covered with bark that look woody to the eye.

Of course, herbaceous and woody are terms most appropriate to temperate climates. Many tropical vines that grow as annuals in the North are actually long-lived tropical vines in their native land, with stems that grow taller from year to year. Some morning glories (*Ipomoea* spp. and *Convolvulus* spp.), for example, are true annuals, but others are tropical climbers grown as annuals. And in extremely cold climates, many woody climbers will die to the ground most winters and sprout anew in spring, as if they were herbaceous.

For the most part, shade-tolerant vines are woody: In adapting to poor light, they found it simpler to grow slowly upward over time, putting on a bit more height each year. Starting from scratch each season takes lots of energy! In this chapter you'll find mostly woody climbers. For sun-loving, fast-growing herbaceous vines that create shade rather than grow in it, see page 28.

SHADE AND CLIMBERS

Many of the climbers described in this chapter are equally well adapted to both sun and shade . . . and that's because of their unique growth cycle. They're adapted to germinating in deep shade where the competition for space is less intense. From there, they either slowly build up energy or ramble about, looking for a host to climb on. Even when they find support, they are still in shade, but climbers persevere, reaching up and up through the host's dense foliage until they finally begin to pierce its crown. In general, it is only when climbers reach full sun that they begin to bloom.

Most of the "shade-tolerant" climbers described here are therefore actually sun lovers who are just biding their time. They can grow for decades in very deep shade . . . as foliage plants. But many of them rarely bloom there. You'll notice that most of the plants described here are grown for their attractive growth habit and beautiful leaves rather than for their flowers.

Actinidia

Kiwi vine

PLANT PROFILE

ACTINIDIA
ac-ti-NID-ee-uh

Bloom Color:
White

Bloom Time:
Varies by species; see individual listings

Length of Bloom:
2 to 3 weeks

Height:
Varies by species; see individual listings

Spread:
17 to 20 feet (5 to 6 m)

Garden Uses:
Arbors and trellises, background, container planting, specimen plant, woodland garden; edible fruits

Light Preference:
Full sun to shade

Soil Preference:
Humus-rich, evenly moist, well-drained soil

Best Way to Propagate:
Take cuttings in midsummer

USDA Plant Hardiness Zones:
3 to 8

The kiwis described here are not the subtropical ones that supply the large fuzzy fruits that are seen in supermarkets, but hardier species grown mostly for ornamental use. Most are vigorous woody vines that climb by twining about a support: If none is as available, they'll grow as large, arching shrubs. The spring flowers are often numerous and usually creamy white and highly scented, although inevitably partially hidden by the foliage. Their main claim to fame is their beautifully variegated foliage. Small, sweet, grape-size fruits are produced on female plants in fall on mature specimens: They are not fuzzy like their large-fruited cousin and can be popped into the mouth and eaten as is.

GROWING TIPS

Kiwis prefer full sun for best blooming and fruiting, but are very ornamental in partial shade and grow well in shade, although often losing their leaf variegation. Any well-drained soil will do.

If you want to enjoy their fruit, make sure you plant both male and female plants (one male will pollinate eight or more females). Although plants may flower fairly young, it often takes 7 or 8 years before they manage to produce their first fruit.

Prune in early spring for better foliage; for fruit production, prune after flowers drop. These are vigorous, shrubby vines taking up considerable space in their youth until they begin to climb, and so are not for small gardens.

Warning: Be forewarned that cats adore *Actinidia kolomikta* and *A. polygama*, reacting to them as if they were catnip, and may not always content themselves with just rubbing against them: They'll often chew young *A. polygama* plants to death. Surround them with chicken-wire fencing for the first few years until they've grown enough that they are largely out of kitty's reach!

PROBLEMS AND SOLUTIONS

Cats chew stems and leaves. Few serious pests and diseases.

TOP PERFORMER

Actinidia kolomikta (variegated kiwi vine): A very dense-growing vine, especially appreciated for the coloration of its leaves. They are purple-tinged at first, then the lower half turns silvery pink in spring and eventually silvery white in summer. Not all the leaves are variegated, and the coloration is highly variable: Cooler growing conditions and sun to partial shade help bring out the color. Several cultivars with more highly variegated foliage, such as 'Arctic Beauty', are available, though many of those grown mostly for their fruit are not very colorful. Blooms early, in late spring. Sweet yellow-green fruits are produced in fall. Height: 15 to 35 feet (4.5 to 10 m). Spread: 17 to 20 feet (5 to 6 m). USDA Plant Hardiness Zones 2 to 9.

MORE RECOMMENDED KIWI VINES

Actinidia arguta (hardy kiwi): This summer-blooming species has entirely green leaves and is grown more for its small but abundant fruit than as an ornamental, although its dense cover, dark green bristle-edged leaves, and scented white flowers make it very useful for decorative purposes as well. 'Issai' is a self-fruitful variety (it produces both male and female flowers on the same plant), ideal for smaller spaces. It is not a particularly prolific cultivar, though: There are dozens of better fruit producers. Height: 20 to 30 feet (6 to 9 m). Spread: 20 to 30 feet (6 to 9 m). USDA Plant Hardiness Zones 3 to 9.

A. polygama (silver vine): This summer-blooming species is a decidedly less vigorous grower than the others and can easily be accommodated in a small space. It is grown especially for its green leaves with silvery white tips, although the small yellow-green fruits are edible. Beware: This species is especially subject to cat damage. Height: 5 to 15 feet (1.5 to 4.5 m). Spread: 8 feet (2.4 m). USDA Plant Hardiness Zones 4 to 9.

Variegated kiwi vine
(*Actinidia kolomikta*)

KISSING COUSINS

Kiwi vines (sometimes known as gooseberry vine and Chinese gooseberry) became known as "kiwifruit" through an incredibly successful mass-marketing campaign by New Zealand growers who renamed the fruit (New Zealanders are often called "Kiwis") and made it their own. The species most often grown is *Actinidia deliciosa*, which produces fruit well only in mild climates (Zones 9 and 10), although it is hardy to Zone 7. Elsewhere it can be grown as a potted plant for large sunrooms. Make sure you have a male and a female—and invite some bumblebees indoors during the blooming season. Height: 20 to 35 feet (6 to 10 m). Spread: 10 to 20 feet (3 to 6 m). USDA Plant Hardiness Zones 7 to 9.

Akebia

Chocolate vine, akebia

PLANT PROFILE

AKEBIA
ah-KEE-bee-uh

Bloom Color:
  Purple

Bloom Time:
  Early spring

Length of Bloom:
  2 to 3 weeks

Height:
  20 to 40 feet (6 to 12 m)

Spread:
  20 to 40 feet (6 to 12 m)

Garden Uses:
  Arbors and trellises,
  groundcover, woodland
  garden; on slopes

Light Preference:
  Full sun to shade

Soil Preference:
  Humus-rich, moist, well-
  drained soil

Best Way to Propagate:
  Take cuttings in early to
  midsummer

USDA Plant Hardiness Zones:
  4 to 10

This is a vigorous, dense, semi-evergreen, twining vine: Grown on a fence, it will create a perfect wall of green, and as a ground-cover it makes a smooth carpet. The palmate leaves are curiously notched at the tips, as if a tiny bird had taken a bite out if each one. They attempt to be evergreen, turning purplish in fall and clinging to the plant until early winter, but are eventually frosted off below Zones 7 or 8. The hanging, cup-shaped flowers are deep purple, sometimes even nearly chocolate-colored (whence "chocolate vine") but have little impact in the garden: You have to be right up close to notice them. Curious sausage-like fleshy purple fruits are produced and are edible, but insipid. Hanging on until winter, they are much more visible than the flowers but rarely produced.

GROWING TIPS

Here is a nice "grow-anywhere" vine, adapting equally well from sun to shade (although partial shade to shade is preferable in hot-summer climates) and almost any soil except ones that are extremely dry or extremely wet. Its growth is rampant: Plant it at the base of its future support so it can grow straight up, or it will go wandering all over your yard looking for a host. It makes a superior groundcover about 6 to 12 inches (15 to 30 cm) tall for spots where there is nothing for it to climb on. As a ground-cover it is often best established among tall trees—it climbs by twining and can't manage thick trunks.

Pruning is well accepted; indeed, it will die to the ground in colder climates and still reach a good 20 feet (6 m) the following spring. Many gardeners prefer to cut it back each year to prevent it from getting out of bounds: After all, if left alone it will readily leave its original fence or trellis and invade neighboring trees, especially in mild-winter areas. Major pruning is usually done in early spring (late fall in the North). Wayward or invasive branches can be cut off at any season.

The male and female flowers are borne together in clusters on the same plant. (Hint: The female flowers are larger and darker and borne at the base of the clump; males are smaller

and found at the tip.) Where fruits are produced, fall-sown seed germinates readily the following spring, but usually chocolate vine is multiplied by softwood or semiripe cuttings.

PROBLEMS AND SOLUTIONS

Chocolate vine seems virtually immune to insects and disease but may die back severely in cold winters.

TOP PERFORMER

Chocolate vine (*Akebia quinata*)

Akebia quinata (chocolate vine, fiveleaf akebia): This is by far the most common species, with very attractive, schefflera-like leaves with five leaflets. They are dark green above, bluish green below. This species has scented flowers, said to smell of vanilla or cinnamon. There are a few cultivars, among which is the outstanding 'Variegata', with pale pink flowers and leaves marbled white. Height: 20 to 40 feet (6 to 12 m). Spread: 20 to 40 feet (6 to 12 m). USDA Plant Hardiness Zones 4 to 10.

MORE RECOMMENDED CHOCOLATE VINES

Akebia × *pentaphylla* (hybrid chocolate vine): This is a cross between *A. quinata* and *A. trifoliata*, looking much the same as *A. quinata*, with four or five leaflets (occasionally six or seven), but the leaves are paler green and the flowers likewise not as dark purple, with a much fainter scent. Height: 20 to 40 feet (6 to 12 m). Spread: 20 to 40 feet (6 to 12 m). USDA Plant Hardiness Zones 4 to 10.

   A. trifoliata (threeleaf akebia): As the name suggests, it's easy to tell this akebia from the other species by its leaflets, borne only three per leaf. They are also different in color: emerald green. The distinctly paler purple flowers are scentless but produce the same purple sausage-shaped fruit as the other chocolate vines. This species is deciduous in all climates and, although no hardier in actual survival rate than the others (Zone 4), its branches are more cold-hardy so it makes a better choice for garden use in Zones 4 to 6 than the others. Height: 20 to 40 feet (6 to 12 m). Spread: 20 to 40 feet (6 to 12 m). USDA Plant Hardiness Zones 4 to 10.

LARRY'S GARDEN NOTES

Although chocolate vines produce both male and female flowers on the same plant, they are self-sterile: Two clones are needed to insure pollination. Since most nurseries produce their plants from cuttings, all plants in the same nursery are likely clones, so even buying two plants doesn't ensure you'll obtain fruit. For guaranteed success in producing fruit, grow plants from seed or plant a different species: All species make fully compatible parents. In Zones 6 and above, it is perhaps best *not* to plant two clones together, as chocolate vine has been known to escape from culture there.

Ampelopsis

Porcelain berry, ampelopsis

The genus *Ampelopsis* is made up of about 25 species of climbing plants very much like grape plants, although with smaller berries. They climb vigorously by tendrils and readily ascend fairly thin supports like small branches and chain-link fence. The foliage varies in shape, but is usually deeply lobed and maplelike. The leaves are deciduous on most species but usually make up for that by turning brilliant fall colors. Although they are perhaps best seen as foliage plants (certainly their clusters of greenish flowers lack impact), their berries are also very attractive, changing color as they mature and often showing several colors in the same cluster.

GROWING TIPS

Like many woody climbers, porcelain berry usually starts off its life in shade and works its way upward into sun; thus it is readily adapted to almost any light condition, although it will bloom and fruit heavily only in partial shade or sun. It is likewise adapted to most soil conditions except soggy soil. Irrigation during times of drought is certainly appreciated.

Opposite each leaf is a tendril that readily twists around objects of modest size, allowing the plant to grow to great heights over time. The tendrils are not very efficient at wrapping around thick objects, though: Even latticework is a bit much for them. You'll often find you have to attach this plant to its support or weave its stems through fencing or trelliswork to allow it to climb. The stems also look quite elegant when allowed to cascade down from a support, such as from the roof of a pergola. Where no support is available, it makes a wonderful groundcover, spreading indefinitely because the branches self-layer wherever they touch the soil.

Pruning is mostly done to control wayward stems and can be done at any time of the year.

The most obvious way to multiply ampelopsis is by layering: Most produce dangling branches that can easily be fixed to the ground. Cuttings also work well, and seed-grown plants come fairly true to type.

PROBLEMS AND SOLUTIONS

Leaf diseases are frequent but rarely serious enough to need treating. Flea beetles and Japanese beetles are major annoyances: Spray with insecticidal soap to treat the former; handpick or spray the latter.

TOP PERFORMER

Ampelopsis brevipedunculata (porcelain berry, porcelain vine): A charming and elegant climber with dark green three- to five-lobed leaves that look much like maple leaves. The fruits are the most attractive element of this plant, changing color from green to turquoise-blue to purple as they mature, often with all three colors visible at the same time. They are shaded with a crackled effect much like porcelain (whence the common name). Height: 10 to 30 feet (3 to 9 m). Spread: 10 to 30 feet (3 to 9 m). USDA Plant Hardiness Zones 4 to 9.

MORE RECOMMENDED PORCELAIN BERRIES

Ampelopsis aconitifolia (monkshood vine): There are dozens of interesting species of *Ampelopsis*. This one has leaves much like those of monkshoods (*Aconitum* spp.): very deeply and elegantly lobed and dark, glossy green. They turn beautiful shades of orange, yellow, and red in fall. The small yellow-orange fruits are also attractive in fall. 'Chinese Lace' is a new cultivar with very lacy foliage. Height: 10 to 40 feet (3 to 12 m). Spread: 10 to 30 feet (3 to 9 m). USDA Plant Hardiness Zones 4 to 9.

A. brevipedunculata var. *maximowiczii* 'Elegans' (variegated porcelain berry): This gorgeous cultivar has deeply cut leaves that are highly mottled white and pink, and bright pink new shoots. It has often been used as a houseplant. It bears the same green, turquoise, and blue berries as the species. Height: 3 to 10 feet (1 to 3 m). Spread: 3 to 10 feet (1 to 3 m). USDA Plant Hardiness Zones 6 to 9.

Porcelain berry
(*Ampelopsis brevipedunculata*)

LARRY'S GARDEN NOTES

Ampelopsis looks so much like its cousins, grapes (*Vitis* spp.) and Boston ivy and Virginia creeper (*Parthenocissus* spp.) that you can be forgiven for confusing them. They are best told apart from *Vitis* by their smooth bark (grape stems become rough at maturity) and white pith (the interior of grape stems is brown). As for *Parthenocissus* species, they all have adhesive disks at the tip of their tendrils, while *Ampelopsis* species have only tendrils.

Euonymus
Wintercreeper

PLANT PROFILE

EUONYMUS
yew-ON-i-mus

Bloom Color:
Greenish white; insignificant

Bloom Time:
Summer

Length of Bloom:
3 or more weeks

Height:
4 inches to 70 feet
(10 cm to 21 m)

Spread:
Indefinite

Garden Uses:
Arbors and trellises, container planting, edging, groundcover, hedge, mass planting, mixed border, rock garden, wall covering

Light Preference:
Full sun to shade

Soil Preference:
Humus-rich, evenly moist, well-drained soil

Best Way to Propagate:
Take cuttings in summer

USDA Plant Hardiness Zones:
4 or 5 to 10

Wintercreeper is truly a triple-purpose plant: It is abundantly used as a groundcover, makes a great small shrub, and will also climb beautifully. It's a beautiful foliage plant, with glossy, dark green, oval leaves, usually with a serrated edge, with paler veins and purplish in winter. Most cultivars commonly available are highly variegated in shades of white and yellow. The leaves are fully evergreen, making this plant attractive in all seasons and one of the hardiest evergreen climbers. The flowers are insignificant, but the fruits, which open whitish to reveal a bright orange-red interior, are very attractive.

GROWING TIPS

Wintercreeper is most adaptable when grown as an evergreen groundcover. It adapts to both full sun and deep shade, rich soils and poor ones—all it really needs to be sure of is evenly moist soil (it will need irrigation during periods of drought) and good drainage at all times.

Some wintercreeper cultivars are quite shrubby, but most will grow up walls or tree trunks if given a chance to do so. They climb via holdfast roots: Plant them where you want them to climb and let them make their own moves. Wintercreeper will not find trellises, latticework, or thin fences at all attractive for climbing. It prefers much broader surfaces, such as posts, trunks, and walls, where its roots will find something solid to sink their tips into.

Although hardy to Zone 5 (some cultivars to Zone 4), it will not climb well when exposed to harsh, cold winds, so it can be trusted to climb to any great height only in Zone 7 and above. In a well-protected spot, though, it will climb modestly, reaching up to 15 feet (4.5 m) or so even at the northern limits of its range. In mild climates it can reach up to 70 feet (21 m).

For groundcover use, plant smaller plants about 1 foot (30 cm) apart; up to 3 feet (90 cm) for well-developed plants in large containers. Wintercreeper is a fairly slow grower, so mulch well to prevent weeds from taking over while it spreads.

This is one climber not known for its exuberant growth! Not

that it is weak—it simply grows slowly and densely, sticking tight to its host, without the long "whips" common to other vines. Pruning is therefore mostly a question of cutting out any winter damage, trimming back leading stems when they reach the limits of the plant's desired territory, and removing any reversions (some of the variegated types are not very stable). Prunings can be used to make cuttings: Those taken from lateral branches will climb more readily

Wintercreeper (*Euonymus fortunei* 'Emerald 'n Gold')

than those taken from vertical ones. When used as a ground-cover, wintercreeper readily self-layers and the resulting "rooted cuttings" can be dug up and moved to other spots.

Warning: Wintercreeper berries are poisonous, though so rarely produced they aren't a major threat.

PROBLEMS AND SOLUTIONS

Mildew and fungal problems can be treated on a case-by-case basis. More serious are scale insects: Carefully inspect all wintercreepers before buying them, as this pest doesn't get around well on its own. Control it with horticultural oil.

TOP PERFORMER

Euonymus fortunei (wintercreeper): This is the only common wintercreeper that climbs (the others are shrubs or small trees) and also one of the rare evergreen species, so it really is in a class of its own. There are dozens of cultivars, including *E. fortunei* var. *radicans*, the most commonly available running/climbing variety, with dark green leaves. It is extra-hardy (to Zone 4). Most of the variegated types have an upright habit at first but will produce lateral branches that, if planted near a wall or trunk, will soon begin to climb. Examples are 'Emerald Gaiety' (white-margined green leaves with a pinkish tinge in winter) and 'Emerald 'n Gold' (similar but with yellow-margined leaves).

LARRY'S GARDEN NOTES

So where are the berries? No one really misses the greenish white flowers of wintercreeper, but the berries that follow are very attractive. However, like ivies (*Hedera* spp.), wintercreeper has two forms: a juvenile one that creeps and crawls and sends up short upright growth but never bears flowers or fruits, and a mature one with thicker, leathery, more rounded leaves that both blooms and produces berries. The downside is that it usually doesn't reach its mature form until it is 20 feet (6 m) or more up in a tree! Occasionally a shrubby wintergreen will bear a fruit or two; otherwise you usually have to wait a decade or so until your plant reaches maturity.

Hedera

Ivy

PLANT PROFILE

HEDERA
HEAD-er-uh

Foliage Color:
Green and variegated

Foliage Time:
Year-round

Length of Foliage Interest:
Year-round

Height:
50 feet (15 m)

Spread:
Indefinite

Garden Uses:
Container planting, edging, erosion control, groundcover, rock garden, wall covering, woodland garden

Light Preference:
Full sun to shade

Soil Preference:
Humus-rich, moist, well-drained soil

Best Way to Propagate:
Divide rooted sections in any season; take cuttings in spring or fall

USDA Plant Hardiness Zones:
7 to 9
(some cultivars to Zone 5)

A true triple-purpose plant, ivy can be used as an evergreen climber, a creeping groundcover, or a trailing container plant. In all cases, though, the dark, leathery leaves are evergreen, making the plant attractive year-round. Few plants are as variable as ivy, with literally hundreds of cultivars, most with star-shaped or maple leaf–shaped foliage, but there are also curly, fringed, or lacy leaves. Many ivies have white to yellow variegation, another plus.

GROWING TIPS

Ivies are tough, no-nonsense plants. They don't need any care, really—except pruning to keep them in check. They will tolerate almost any conditions except constant drought. Their degree of shade tolerance is legendary: Ivies will often grow in spots so dark they're otherwise totally devoid of vegetation. Not that they can't tolerate sun (they can, especially in cooler climates), but they do prefer shade or partial shade.

Warning: Ivy leaves and berries may be somewhat poisonous to humans. While the foliage is not terribly attractive to children, the black berries can and should be pruned off.

In colder climates, ivy can be grown outdoors only as a groundcover. Surrounding a bed of groundcover ivy with a footpath is enough to keep it within bounds; ivy won't stand much foot traffic.

If you want an ivy to climb, choose a species that is sufficiently hardy for your region, then plant it near a wall or tree trunk and let it grow. It will start to grow upward all on its own, hoisting itself thanks to numerous adhesive roots that will cling to almost any surface.

PROBLEMS AND SOLUTIONS

Ivies are not immune to insects and disease problems, including aphids, mealybugs, caterpillars, leaf spot, and powdery mildew, but they rarely seem to cause major problems.

TOP PERFORMER

Hedera pastuchovii (Russian ivy): This ivy grows over the widest range of any ivy, so almost any reader of this book can grow it. A cold-hardy ivy, it will make a good groundcover nearly everywhere and will climb even in Zone 5 (and warmer parts of Zone 4). The leaves are more rounded than English ivy, even heart-shaped, with paler veins, and they turn burgundy-red in winter. Height: 40 feet (12 m) or more. Spread: Indefinite. USDA Plant Hardiness Zones 3 to 9 (as a groundcover); 5 to 9 (as a climber).

MORE RECOMMENDED IVIES

Hedera canariensis (Canary Island ivy, Algerian ivy, Madeira ivy): This is a very large-leaved ivy grown as a groundcover or climber in Zones 8 to 10. The heart-shaped leaves with three to seven lobes are very shiny and measure up to 6 inches (15 cm) in diameter. 'Gloire de Marengo' (also sold as 'Variegata'), with leaves edged silvery white, is the most common cultivar. Height: 40 feet (12 m) or more. Spread: Indefinite.

H. helix (English ivy): This is by far the most popular true ivy in culture and is offered in a bewildering choice of cultivars—some all green but many variegated white or yellow. Hardiness varies enormously from one cultivar to the next, with most not fully hardy beyond Zone 6, and some only to Zone 8. 'Baltica', 'Wilson,' and 'Thorndale,' though, are hardy enough to be used as groundcovers in Zone 5 and as climbers in warmer parts of Zone 6. They have dark green leaves. Irish ivy (*H. hibernica* 'Hibernica', often sold as *H. helix* 'Hibernica') is very similar but not as hardy (Zones 8 to 10). Irish ivy can be invasive and is banned in some areas. Height: 40 feet (12 m) or more. Spread: Indefinite.

English ivy
(*Hedera helix* 'Goldheart')

LARRY'S GARDEN NOTES

The ivies usually grown are juvenile forms. Young ivies are creepers or climbers; when they reach maturity, usually once they're old enough (many ivies can take decades to reach full maturity!) and have been exposed to enough light, they undergo a radical transformation to a mature plant. The latter are not climbers or creepers but have an upright, rounded habit with sturdy branches and leaves that are usually much larger and thicker and also more rounded than the juvenile leaves. Only the adults form flowers, bearing rounded balls of creamy white flowers followed by black berries. Many gardeners prune off the adult sections to prevent the plants from spreading, as birds love the berries and carry them (and the seeds they contain) far and wide.

Hydrangea
Climbing hydrangea

PLANT PROFILE

HYDRANGEA
hy-DRAIN-gee-uh

Bloom Color:
White

Bloom Time:
Early summer

Length of Bloom:
2 to 3 weeks

Height:
Varies by species; see
individual listings

Spread:
Varies by species; see
individual listings

Garden Uses:
Arbors and trellises,
groundcover, specimen plant,
wall covering, woodland
garden; along paths, on
slopes

Light Preference:
Full sun to shade

Soil Preference:
Humus-rich, evenly moist,
well-drained soil

Best Way to Propagate:
Sow ripe seed

USDA Plant Hardiness Zones:
Varies by species; see
individual listings

This is a most unusual and attractive deciduous climber, both in and out of bloom. It produces huge domed flowerheads, up to 10 inches (25 cm) in diameter, composed of a cluster of fairly modest, highly scented, whitish fertile flowers surrounded by a ring of much larger pure white sterile ones. They dry to a nice beige and last much of summer, adding to the plant's interest. The glossy dark green leaves are charming as well and turn a nice golden color in some climates (elsewhere they fall green). In winter the naked branches show off their bark: thick, flaky, and a rich cinnamon brown. It produces two types of shoots: climbing ones that cling to vertical surfaces, but also outward-growing ones. Thus, unlike most climbing plants whose leaves cling to their host like shingles, climbing hydrangea fills up plenty of aerial space. It's quite the show plant!

GROWING TIPS

Like so many woody vines, climbing hydrangea is adapted to a wide range of conditions, from deep shade to full sun (at least in cooler climates) and to most types of soil. For best results, though, give it a good, rich soil with even moisture and good drainage. It is only moderately drought-resistant, so it will appreciate a good mulch and occasional watering. In colder climates, plant it on the north or east side of a house or large tree for protection from the harsh winter sun.

This is the slowest of the vines described in this chapter. Plants grow like shrubs for the first few years and you begin to wonder whether someone hasn't sold you the wrong thing. After 3 to 5 years, though, it starts showing its true colors and sends out climbing shoots. Growth is ever so slow: It easily takes a decade for this plant to start to look good, and two or more for it to be at its best!

Warning: Don't try to force climbing by tying its woody branches to a support: They're not flexible like most other vines, and you're likely to damage them. Just let it do its own thing and it will climb when the time comes.

This is not a plant that needs a lot of pruning. Remove

branches that are heading in unwanted directions whenever you notice them. If you want to cut an overgrown one back, do so over a period of several years, pruning as the blooms fade.

Although climbing hydrangea is easy to grow, it is also very difficult to multiply. Cuttings of semigreen wood are possible, but the failure rate is high. It may self-layer eventually and you could remove the resulting plants, but in general, either grow it from seed (if you're incredibly patient!) or buy new plants.

PROBLEMS AND SOLUTIONS

It's not usually subject to insects or diseases.

TOP PERFORMER

Hydrangea anomala subsp. *petiolaris* (climbing hybrangea): This is the usual form sold in nurseries, with beautiful heart-shaped leaves. You may find it sold under the name *H. petiolaris*. It differs most notably from the true species, *H. anomala*, because its leaves are heart-shaped while the latter has pointed leaves. *H. anomala* is just as attractive as *H. anomala* subsp. *petiolaris* but rarely available. Height: 9 to 50 feet (3 to 15 m). Spread: 9 to 35 feet (3 to 10 m). USDA Plant Hardiness Zones 3 to 9.

MORE RECOMMENDED CLIMBING HYDRANGEAS

Hydrangea seemannii (evergreen climbing hydrangea): This is a much rarer species and is only for those who have mild winters. It has similar blooms to *H. anomala* subsp. *petiolaris,* although smaller, and long, dark, glossy evergreen leaves. Similar, but with larger flower clusters lacking sterile blooms, is *H. serratifolia.* Both grow in shade but need some sun to bloom. Height: 10 to 50 feet (3 to 15 m). Spread: 7 to 17 feet (2 to 5 m). USDA Plant Hardiness Zones 8 to 10.

KISSING COUSINS

Schizophragma hydrangeoides (Japanese hydrangea vine): Just by looking at this plant, you can see it is a very close relative to the climbing hydrangea. The leaves are fairly similar in shape although not indented at the base, and the flowerhead is also composed of fertile flowers surrounded by sterile white blooms. It differs, though, because it has a drooping form and produces only one large, pointed sepal, unlike the four rounded ones of the hydrangeas. Plus, this plant grows flat against its host, without any outward-arching branches. 'Moonlight' has typical white flowers but silvery blue-green leaves with green veins; 'Rosea' has rose-flushed bracts. Culture is as per *H. anomala* subsp. *petiolaris.* Height: 9 to 40 feet (3 to 12 m). Spread: 9 to 35 feet (3 to 10 m). USDA Plant Hardiness Zones 5 to 9.

Climbing hydrangea (*Hydrangea anomala* subsp. *petiolaris*)

Menispermum

Moonseed

MENISPERMUM
men-ih-SPUR-mum

Foliage Color:
  Green

Foliage Time:
  Spring to fall

Length of Foliage Interest:
  3 months or more

Height:
  15 feet (4.5 m)

Spread:
  Indefinite

Garden Uses:
  Climbing plant, groundcover, hanging basket, woodland garden

Light Preference:
  Full sun to shade

Soil Preference:
  Humus-rich, moist, well-drained soil

Best Way to Propagate:
  Divide offsets at any time

USDA Plant Hardiness Zones:
  3 to 9

I'm always surprised that moonseed is not better known. True enough, its small greenish flowers are not showy, but the leaves are very beguiling—large and oval to heart-shaped, often with intriguing lobes—and they totally cover the plant, meaning it can completely hide even the most annoying view. The only explanation for this plant's surprising lack of popularity is that it is a native plant, and unfortunately we tend to look down on our native varieties and praise importees instead. I suggest doing an about-face and taking a second look at this unusual home-grown beauty. You won't regret it.

GROWING TIPS

As with many climbing plants, moonseed can be used as either a groundcover or a vine. As it climbs by entwining, it will need a support it can wrap itself around, such as a thin trunk, a post, a wire, or a trellis. Otherwise it will run across the ground and form a carpet of greenery.

It is native to the eastern third of North America, from Québec and Manitoba down to the Deep South, so it is widely adapted to a nearly complete range of climates. It does best in rich, well-drained soils and is fairly drought-tolerant once established, though it thrives if mulched and watered regularly. In the wild it grows about equally well in sun and fairly dense shade and will do the same in your garden.

Like many vines, actually growing moonseed is a snap—it requires just about nothing from you to remain in top shape—but what it may well need is a bit of selective pruning. Given the chance, it will gladly leap from the trellis you choose for it to a nearby shrub or tree (or even telephone pole), then take that over, too. It also spreads by offsets produced by underground rhizomes, so be ready to cut it back whenever its stems outstep their bounds. As for the invasive roots, ideally you should always plant this vine within a root barrier (see page 54) so it can never escape and cause any problems. Otherwise you *will* find it popping up here and there, such as in your lawn.

Multiplication is usually done by digging up offsets appearing in the ground near the mother plant (if you used a root barrier) or anywhere within 10 feet (3 m) if you didn't. This can be done at any time the plant is not dormant. Fresh seed is rarely available unless you have wild moonseeds growing in your area. If so, harvest the seed when the grapelike berries are ripe (in early fall), remove the pulp, and plant the seed without delay. Germination will then take place the following spring, after the seeds have been exposed to winter's coolness. Stored seed, such as that offered in seed packs, often goes into prolonged dormancy and may need more than one period of cold in order to germinate. Seed-grown moonseed plants put on only modest growth the first year or so but, after that, quickly do their duty as a carpeting groundcover or object-concealing vine.

PROBLEMS AND SOLUTIONS

Moonseed is reputed to be essentially insect- and disease-free.

TOP PERFORMER

Menispermum canadense (moonseed, Canada moonseed): This is the only species with much of a commercial distribution and even then, it is quite rare in nurseries. Since there is a considerable amount of variety in the shape and size of the leaves, it's a shame that special cultivars are not available. Height: 15 feet (4.5 m). Spread: Indefinite. USDA Plant Hardiness Zones 3 to 9.

MORE RECOMMENDED MOONSEEDS

Menispermum dauricum (Asian moonseed): Much rarer in culture, Asian moonseed is very similar to its North American cousin, varying mostly in the number of flower clusters found at each axil (two instead of the single cluster found on *M. canadensis*). Since the flowers are insignificant anyway, there is no reason to prefer one species over the other: Choose whichever is the most readily available in your area. Height: 15 feet (4.5 m). Spread: Indefinite. USDA Plant Hardiness Zones 5 to 9.

Moonseed
(*Menispermum canadense*)

LARRY'S GARDEN NOTES

The clustered berries of moonseed, grapelike in shape and black in color, are not unattractive even though they are often at least partly hidden by the foliage. On the other hand, they are also toxic. Rather than having to suppress them when you have children over, you can practice a form of horticultural birth control by asking, when you purchase the plant, for a male specimen. Moonseed, unlike most other plants, has flowers of different sexes on different plants, so if you choose a male plant, it will produce flowers that bear pollen but never fruit.

Parthenocissus

Parthenocissus, Virginia creeper, Boston ivy

PLANT PROFILE

PARTHENOCISSUS
par-then-oh-SIS-us

Bloom Color:
Greenish white

Bloom Time:
Early summer

Length of Bloom:
2 to 3 weeks

Height:
Varies by species; see individual listings

Spread:
Varies by species; see individual listings

Garden Uses:
Arbors and trellises, background, container planting, groundcover, mass planting, wall covering, woodland garden; on slopes

Light Preference:
Full sun to shade

Soil Preference:
Humus-rich, evenly moist, well-drained soil

Best Way to Propagate:
Take cuttings from spring to fall

USDA Plant Hardiness Zones:
Varies by species; see individual listings

Parthenocissus will grow on almost anything. Trellises, fences, stumps, rusting cars: It does it all. In nature, it is famous for scrambling up the tallest trees, then leaping from one to the next, leaving dangling woody stems that would leave Tarzan's lianas in the dust. In the garden, people love the way it climbs vertical walls then drips down, creating a dancing green curtain. Don't look for attractive flowers: They're greenish and hidden by the leaves, but the deeply cut foliage is stupendous with its brilliant display of fall colors. When the leaves drop, they reveal blue or black berries that draw hordes of hungry birds in winter. No wonder parthenocissus is the queen of the hardy vines!

GROWING TIPS

These vines are among the most adaptable of all, seemingly immune to sun or shade, and any type of well-drained soil will do. They'll even grow in cracks in pavement!

Perhaps the nicest thing about parthenocissus is that they grow so quickly. Most woody vines take a few years to get going, but these babies are already well up your wall within a few months. Their tendrils are equipped with holdfasts that allow them to climb walls, tree trunks, or any vertical surface, yet the tendrils still twist so they can also mount trellises, latticework, fences, and the like.

Fast growth has a price, though, and that's likely to mean some pruning. Cutting back stems that try to work their way into the gutter or cover the window is likely to become an annual tradition if you grow them on a house. They can overwhelm an arbor or pergola in just a few short years—and did you really want them to *completely* cover that tree? It's best to learn to cut them back every few years, or even annually: They resprout quickly from the base and can easily grow back 20 feet (6 m) in a single summer.

Don't neglect parthenocissus as a groundcover either—most species create a superb green carpet in shade or in sun.

If you need more plants, just take cuttings: Both green, semigreen, and woody cuttings root readily. Plus, they self-layer where their stems touch the ground. You can also extract seeds from the fruit in fall: Sown outdoors, they'll sprout in spring. Of course, cultivars will not come true to type.

PROBLEMS AND SOLUTIONS

Mildew has an annoying habit of showing up in late summer but does little real damage, nor do other diseases. Leaf-eating insects are another story: Grape flea beetle, Japanese beetle, and leaf skeletonizer may require a few sprays with insecticidal soap.

TOP PERFORMER

Parthenocissus quinquefolia (Virginia creeper, woodbine): This ubiquitous climber is native to middle and eastern North America, from Mexico to Canada, but is now grown around the world, from the tropics almost to the Arctic Circle. Its compound leaves with five leaflets are reddish in spring, dull dark green in summer, and brilliant red in fall. The bluish black berries are evident only in fall and winter. 'Star Showers', with leaves green-and-white in summer then pink-and-red in fall, is a weaker grower, ideal for spots you don't want to see overwhelmed. Engelmann ivy (*P. virginiana* var. *engelmannii*), with smaller leaves, is commonly grown; *P. henryana* (Zones 7 to 9) has similar leaves but with a spectacular silver overlay. Height: 40 to 50 feet (12 to 15 m). Spread: 30 feet (9 m). USDA Plant Hardiness Zones 2 to 10.

MORE RECOMMENDED PARTHENOCISSUS

Parthenocissus tricuspidata (Boston ivy): A shiny-leaved version of the previous, with variable leaves, mostly maple-shaped but sometimes trifoliate. It conveniently dies to the ground each winter in cold climates, saving you a lot of pruning! There are several cultivars, including 'Veitchii', with smaller leaves and purple fall color instead of scarlet; and 'Fenway', with golden leaves. Height: 50 to 70 feet (15 to 21 m). Spread: 20 feet (6 m). USDA Plant Hardiness Zones 4 to 10.

Virginia creeper
(*Parthenocissus quinquefolia*)

LARRY'S GARDEN NOTES

Virginia creeper covers nearly all the bases. First, it bears tendrils on its stems that wrap around branches and other fairly thin objects. If there are none around, the tendrils are tipped with adhesive disks, so it can climb up thick trunks and walls. As its "trunk" (and the stem certainly comes to look like a trunk!) gets heavier, it also starts to produce holdfast roots, like an ivy. But what if there are is nothing nearby with a trunk to grasp? Good news! Its stems also twine and weave as they grow, allowing it to grow through brush as well. About the only means of climbing it *doesn't* use are thorns—but give it a few more million years and it will probably evolve those, too!

Trachelospermum

Confederate jasmine, star jasmine

PLANT PROFILE

TRACHELOSPERMUM
tra-key-lo-SPUR-mum

Bloom Color:
White

Bloom Time:
Mid-spring to early summer

Length of Bloom:
6 weeks or more

Height:
Varies by species; see individual listings

Spread:
Varies by species; see individual listings

Garden Uses:
Arbors and trellises, container planting, groundcover, hanging baskets, houseplant, mass planting, wall covering, woodland garden; on slopes

Light Preference:
Full sun to shade

Soil Preference:
Humus-rich, evenly moist, well-drained, acid soil

Best Way to Propagate:
Take cuttings in spring or summer

USDA Plant Hardiness Zones:
9 to 10; frost-sensitive perennial grown as a tender annual

This vine gets its common name, Confederate jasmine, not from its home country, Asia, but from its great popularity in the southeastern United States. It is now just as popular in Southern California as well. It's a twining vine with shiny, dark green, oval leaves, tinted purple in winter, that are attractive in their own right. This plant's best attribute, though, are its beautifully creamy white flowers, with five petals slightly twisted to one side like a pinwheel. They are so highly scented, especially at night, it is most likely you'll smell it before you see it. This plant can reach considerable heights—or it can be grown as an evergreen groundcover or even as a houseplant. You choose!

GROWING TIPS

Confederate jasmine can be grown outdoors year-round only where temperatures don't drop much below 23°F (–15°C). It prefers a rich, moist, acid soil and is not very drought-tolerant; keep it well watered in times of drought. Although full sun is fine when it's summering outside in the North, elsewhere it does best in shade or partial shade: The starry flowers truly brighten up the darkest corners. Indoors, grow in a medium-size pot on a small trellis, or train it to run around a hoop made from a wire coat hanger. Outdoors it will grow up arbors and pergolas, cover stumps, and even climb into trees.

For use as a groundcover, space the plants about 2 to 3 feet (60 to 90 cm) apart under tree or shrub cover or to the North of walls or buildings. It grows quite quickly, forming a dark green carpet about 10 to 16 inches (25 to 40 cm) tall.

Although Confederate jasmine is a fairly strong climber, it does have trouble getting started, so it is permissible to fix it to its support to start. With time, its twining, weaving stems will manage to work themselves in among the crossbars of a trellis or through latticework. Don't be afraid to prune back the excessively long shoots it sometimes produces. Otherwise, prune to shape it after it finishes blooming.

This plant roots readily from stem cuttings taken spring through fall outdoors, or year-round indoors. The cuttings exude a sticky white sap called latex: Plunge their tips into water to cause the sap to congeal before inserting them in moist growing mix.

PROBLEMS AND SOLUTIONS

Insects and disease are infrequent.

TOP PERFORMER

Trachelospermum jasminoides (Confederate jasmine, star jasmine): This is the most common species, with snow white flowers. Although very popular, it is not the hardiest species: Where it is borderline hardy outdoors, consider *T. asiaticum,* described below. 'Variegatum' has leaves beautifully marbled white with a pinkish tinge in winter. 'Madison' is a hardier selection, said to do well in protected spots of Zone 7. Height: 3 to 30 feet (1 to 9 m). Spread: 10 to 17 feet (3 to 5 m). USDA Plant Hardiness Zones 9 to 10.

MORE RECOMMENDED STAR JASMINES

Trachelospermum asiaticum (Japanese star jasmine): This is a hardier plant than the previous one and worth trying where Confederate jasmine is suffering. It has smaller leaves and similar but dangling flowers, creamy white at first, more yellow after a few days. Height: 3 to 20 feet (1 to 6 m). Spread: 10 to 17 feet (3 to 5 m). USDA Plant Hardiness Zones 8 to 10.

Confederate jasmine
(*Trachelospermum jasminoides*)

SMART SUBSTITUTES

Gardeners from colder climates who want to try a true jasmine outdoors should probably go with winter jasmine (*Jasminum nudiflorum*), the hardiest plant of its genus. It flowers up a storm very early in the year—in late winter, when nothing else is in bloom, it has hundreds of bright yellow flowers on whiplike green stems. The dark green leaves appear only once the flowers have faded. Unfortunately, if you're looking for perfume you're out of luck: This is one jasmine with no scent! Winter jasmine is more a clamberer than a true climber and must lean on other plants to gain any elevation. You could train it onto a fence or trellis, or prune it into an arching shrub. Height: 10 feet (3 m). Spread: 10 feet (3 m). USDA Plant Hardiness Zones 6 to 9.

RESOURCES

Would but that we all had the world's most complete plant nursery within wheelbarrow distance of our gardens. Unfortunately, that just is not the case. I therefore would like to recommend the following mail-order sources of plants that will be of help to you in locating those plants in the book that have inspired you but are just not available locally.

UNITED STATES

André Viette Farm & Nursery
P.O. Box 1109, State Route 608
Fishersville, VA 22939
Phone: (800) 575-5538
Fax: (540) 943-0782
E-mail: info@inthegardenradio.com
www.inthegardenradio.com

Bluestone Perennials
7211 Middle Ridge Road
Madison, OH 44057-3096
Phone: (800) 852-5243
Fax: (216) 428-7198
E-mail: bluestone@bluestoneperennials.com
www.bluestoneperennials.com

W. Atlee Burpee & Co.
300 Park Avenue
Warminster, PA 18974
Phone: (800) 888-1447
www.burpee.com

Busse Gardens
17160 245th Avenue
Big Lake, MN 55309
Phone: (800) 544-3192
Fax: (763) 263-1473
www.bussegardens.com

Heronswood Nursery Ltd.
7530 NE 288th Street
Kingston, WA 98346
Phone: (360) 297-4172
Fax: (360) 297-8321
E-mail: info@heronswood.com
orders@heronswood.com
www.heronswood.com

Louisiana Nursery
5853 Highway 182
Opelousas, LA 70570
Phone: (337) 948-3696
E-mail: dedurio@yahoo.com
www.durionursery.com

Niche Gardens
1111 Dawson Road
Chapel Hill, NC 27516
Phone: (919) 967-0078
E-mail: mail@nichegardens.com
www.nichegardens.com

Park Seed Company
1 Parkton Avenue
Greenwood, SC 29647
Phone: (800) 213-0076
E-mail: info@parkscs.com
www.parkseed.com

Plant Delights Nursery
9241 Sauls Road
Raleigh, NC 27603
Phone: (919) 772-4794
E-mail: office@plantdelights.com
www.plantdelights.com

Plants of the Southwest
3095 Agua Frai Street
Santa Fe, NM 87507
Phone: (800) 788-7333
E-mail: contact@plantsofthesouthwest.com
www.plantsofthesouthwest.com

Singing Springs Nursery
8802 Wilkerson Road
Cedar Grove, NC 27231
Fax: (919) 732-6336
E-mail: plants@singingspringsnursery.com
www.SingingSpringsNursery.com

Siskiyou Rare Plant Nursery
2825 Cummings Road
Medford, OR 97501
Phone: (541) 772-6846
E-mail: customerservice@srpn.net
www.srpn.net

Song Sparrow Perennial Farm
13101 East Rye Road
Avalon, WI 53505
Phone: (800) 553-3715
E-mail: info@songsparrow.com
www.songsparrow.com

Spring Hill Nurseries
P.O. Box 330
Harrison, OH 45030-0330
Phone: (513) 354-1509
www.springhillnursery.com

Thompson & Morgan Inc.
Box 1308
Jackson, NJ 08527-0308
Phone: (800) 274-7333
Fax: (888) 466-4769
E-mail: tminc@thompson-morgan.com
www.seeds.thompson-morgan.com/us/en

Wayside Gardens
1 Garden Lane
Hodges, SC 29695-0001
Phone: (800) 213-0379
E-mail: info@waysidecs.com
www.waysidegardens.com

White Flower Farm
P.O. Box 50, Route 63
Litchfield, CT 06759-0050
Phone: (800) 503-9624
www.whiteflowerfarm.com

CANADA

Fraser's Thimble Farms
175 Arbutus Road
Salt Spring Island, British Columbia V8K 1A3
Phone/fax: (250) 537-5788
E-mail: thimble@saltspring.com
www.thimblefarms.com

Gardens North
5984 Third Line Road North
North Gower, Ontario K0A 2T0
Phone: (613) 489-0065
Fax: (613) 489-1208
E-mail: seed@gardensnorth.com
www.gardensnorth.com

Mason Hogue Gardens
3520 Durham Road 1, RR 4
Uxbridge, Ontario L9P 1R4
Phone: (905) 649-3532
www.masonhogue.com

RECOMMENDED READING

Armitage, Allan M. *Armitage's Manual of Annuals, Biennials, and Half-Hardy Perennials.* Portland, OR: Timber Press, 2001.

———. *Herbaceous Perennial Plants.* Champaign, IL: Stipes Publishing, 1997.

Brickell, Christopher, and Judith D. Zuk, eds. *The American Horticultural A–Z Encyclopedia of Garden Plants.* New York: DK Publishing, 1995.

Bryan, John E. *Bulbs.* Portland, OR: Timber Press, 2002.

Burras, J. K., ed. *The New Royal Horticultural Society Dictionary, Manual of Climbers and Wall Plants.* Portland, OR: Timber Press, 1994.

Christopher, Thomas, and Michael A. Ruggiero. *Annuals with Style: Design Ideas from Classic to Cutting Edge.* Newtown, CT: Taunton Press, 2002.

Cole, Trevor. *New Illustrated Guide to Gardening in Canada.* Montreal, Canada: Reader's Digest Association (Canada) Ltd., 2000.

Coombes, Allen J. *The Collinbridge Dictionary of Plant Names.* Portland, OR: Timber Press, 1986.

Cravens, Richard H. *The Time-Life Encyclopedia of Gardening: Vines.* Alexandria, VA: Time-Life Books, 1979.

Davis Cutler, Karan, ed. *A Harrowsmith Gardener's Guide: Vines.* Charlotte, VT: Camden House Publishing, 1992.

Dewolf, Gordon P., et al. *Taylor's Guide to Ground Covers, Vines & Grasses.* Boston: Houghton Mifflin Company, 2002.

———. *Taylor's Guide to Perennials.* Boston: Houghton Mifflin Company, 2001.

Greenlee, John. *The Encyclopedia of Ornamental Grasses.* Emmaus, PA: Rodale Inc., 1992.

Grounds, Roger. *The Plantfinder's Guide to Ornamental Grasses.* Portland, OR: Timber Press, 2003.

Heath, Brent, and Becky Heath. *Narcissus for North American Gardens.* Albany, TX: Bright Sky Press, 2001.

Hodgson, Larry. *Annuals for Every Purpose.* Emmaus, PA: Rodale Inc., 2002.

———. *Les Bulbes Rustiques.* Saint-Constant, Québec, Canada: Broquet, 2004.

———. *Perennials for Every Purpose.* Emmaus, PA: Rodale Inc., 2000.

MacKenzie, David S. *Perennial Ground Covers.* Portland, OR: Timber Press, 2002.

Pleasant, Barbara. *The Gardener's Bug Book.* Pownal, VT: Storey Communications, 1995.

———. *The Gardener's Guide to Plant Diseases.* Pownal, VT: Storey Communications, 1994.

Schmid, W. George. *An Encyclopedia of Shade Perennials.* Portland, OR: Timber Press, 2002.

Sinnes, A. Cort, and Larry Hodgson. *All about Perennials.* Des Moines, IA: Meredith Books, 1996.

Taylor, Jane. *Kew Gardening Guides: Climbing Plants.* Portland, OR: Timber Press, 1992.

Valleau, John. *Perennial Gardening Guide.* Abbotsford, British Columbia, Canada: Valleybrook International Ventures Inc., 2003.

PHOTO CREDITS

Em Ahart *87 (left center), 349*

Brian Carter/Alamy Images 95 (top)

Nigel Cattlin/Alamy Images 86 (left)

Andrea Jones/Alamy Images 60

Steven Wooster/Alamy Images 77

Gregg Anderson 137

Mark Bolton 16

Karen Bussolini 88, 89

Rob Cardillo 119, 123, 129, 149, 232

Walter Chandoha 1, 2, 11, 63, 94 (top), 95 (center), 98 (bottom), 125, 127, 157, 187, 189, 191, 199, 201, 309, 338, 343

Eric Crichton/Corbis 70, 114

Grace Davies 26, 80

Richard Day 66

John Beedle/Garden Picture Library 293

Mark Bolton/Garden Picture Library 259, 361

Brian Carter/Garden Picture Library 249

Eric Crichton/Garden Picture Library 289, 297, 325

Francois De Heel/Garden Picture Library 355

Christopher Fairweather/Garden Picture Library 357

John Glover/Garden Picture Library 253, 311

Sunhiva Hark/Garden Picture Library 205

Mayer/LeScanff/Garden Picture Library 313

Graham Rice/GardenPhotos.com 59, 87 (left)

Howard Rice/Garden Picture Library 181, 263, 295, 307

J. S. Sira/Garden Picture Library 299

Jonathan Weaver/Garden Picture Library 18

Didier Willery/Garden Picture Library 277, 329, 363

Steven Wooster/Garden Picture Library 331

judywhite/GardenPhotos.com 85 (left), 85 (left center), 255

Alison Miksch/Getty Images 57

Bill Johnson 87 (right), 155, 365, 377, 385

Dency Kane 121, 133, 141, 159, 165, 169, 195, 203, 219, 229, 239, 287, 347, 379

Andrew Lawson 139, 147, 179, 185, 213, 221, 241, 243, 261, 275, 283 323

John Neubauer 36

Clive Nicholas 153, 173, 225, 227, 245, 285, 291, 301, 303, 353, 373, 381, 389

Jerry Pavia 131, 135, 145, 167, 171, 197, 207, 209, 211, 215, 217, 251, 257, 279, 281, 315, 321, 337, 345, 351, 359, 366, 375

Richard Pomerantz 56, 84 (left), 91

Patricia J. Bruno/Positive Images 73

Gay Bumgarner/Positive Images 82, 98 (top)

Lee Lockwood/Positive Images 10

Pam Spaulding/Positive Images 93, 95 (bottom), 316

Daniel Proctor 49

Paul Rezendes 8, 151

Cheryl R. Richter 19, 83, 247

Mae Scanlan 90

Richard Shiell 39, 40, 85 (right center), 273

Neil Soderstrom 97, 383

Betsy Strauch 193, 327

Joseph G. Strauch Jr. 84 (right), 85 (right), 86 (center), 86 (left), 87 (right center), 143, 161, 163, 175, 223, 231, 265, 271, 305, 335

Graeme Teague 14

Mark Turner 7, 69, 75, 76, 78, 92, 94 (bottom), 100, 112, 177, 183, 266, 333, 387

Kimberly Burnham/Unicorn Stock Photos 84 (center)

INDEX

Boldface page references indicate photographs and illustrations.
<u>Underscored</u> references indicate boxed text and tables or charts.

USDA PLANT HARDINESS ZONE MAP

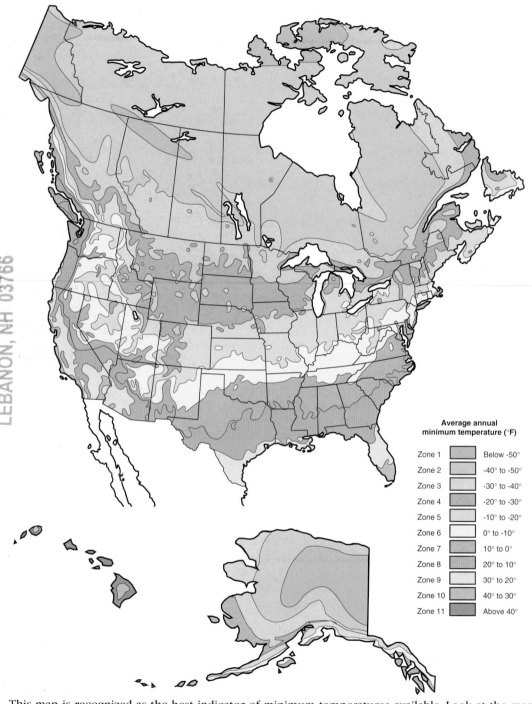

**Average annual
minimum temperature (°F)**

Zone 1		Below -50°
Zone 2		-40° to -50°
Zone 3		-30° to -40°
Zone 4		-20° to -30°
Zone 5		-10° to -20°
Zone 6		0° to -10°
Zone 7		10° to 0°
Zone 8		20° to 10°
Zone 9		30° to 20°
Zone 10		40° to 30°
Zone 11		Above 40°

This map is recognized as the best indicator of minimum temperatures available. Look at the map to find your area, then match its pattern to the key below. When you've found your color, the key will tell you what hardiness zone you live in. Remember that the map is a general guide; your particular conditions may vary.